光 明 城
LUMINOCITY

看 见 我 们 的 未 来

To Illuminate the Future

改变：
阿科米星的
建筑思考

庄慎 华霞虹 著

Change is More:
Architectural Thinking
by Atelier Archmixing

ZHUANG Shen   HUA Xiahong

同济大学出版社
Tongji University Press
中国·上海

阿科米星：
当代中国富有探索精神的
建筑师工作室

　　我大概是最熟悉阿科米星建筑设计工作室的一名教师，因为我曾经是阿科米星主创建筑师庄慎的硕士研究生导师，也曾经和他共同设计了海宁的钱君匋艺术研究馆和嘉兴市行政中心大楼，庄慎的设计创造力在这两件作品中得到了充分的展示。学生时代的庄慎对知识的探求十分广泛，爱好文学和艺术。毕业后他成为体制内的建筑师，在同济大学建筑设计研究院工作，打下了坚实的技术基础。2001 年与柳亦春和陈屹峰创办大舍建筑设计工作室，2009 年与任皓、唐煜、朱捷合伙成立阿科米星工作室。自 2009 年至今的 10 年间，阿科米星已经发展成为当代中国最具创造力的建筑师工作室之一。

　　尽管独立建筑师事务所在我国已经有将近 30 年的历史，但要生存并发展却绝非易事，这取决于建筑师的学识、理念、技术和处事能力，也受益于今天的城市日益重视文化，重视有创造精神的建筑。在崇尚大叙事的同时，也激励探索精神。阿科米星工作室作品秉承现代建筑重技务实，革故鼎新的理性精神，体现了同济学派的特点，建筑师既是设计师，也是建筑理论家，不仅设计作品，也不断探索设计方法，从设计中寻求改变和突破，10 年间有 60 多件优秀的作品问世。诚如老子所言："处无为之事，行不言之教，万物作焉而不辞，生而不有，为而不恃，功成而弗居。"

　　纵观阿科米星的作品不仅跨越了建筑与艺术这两个领域，同时也跨越了设计与研究。庄慎从来就没有脱离同济大学，从来没有离开学术，他和夫人华霞虹教授共同探讨建筑理论和设计的方法论，作品从而表现出浓烈的匠心，正如美国艺术评论家、策展人、设计师和建筑师阿龙·别茨基提出的观点："建筑不是艺术，艺术也不是建筑，尽管两者似乎正在相互趋近。我会认为这并非时尚或不可避免的趋势，这只是两个领域对传统任务的一种回应。完全有可能形成第三种综合的领域，对此我们还没有找到合适的名称，它也有可能试图重塑现实。"

　　这是一部有深度的理论文献集，有王骏阳教授的综述和葛明教授、鲁安东教授的对谈，将阿科米星评价为不追求时尚，不想成为明星和网红建筑师，而是以"另一种建筑／建筑学"作品寻求人文主义的表现，寻求多元的价值。期待阿科米星建筑设计工作室有更多作品和文章问世。

郑时龄

2019 年 12 月 8 日

Atelier Archmixing: An Exploring Architectural Studio in Contemporary China

Probably, I am the professor who knows Atelier Archmixing best, because I was the master thesis advisor for Zhuang Shen, the cofounder partner and principal architect of Atelier Archmixing. We have worked together on Qian Juntao Arts Research Center in Haining and Administrative Center of Jiaxing, both in Zhejiang Province more than twenty years ago. Zhuang Shen's creativity has fully displayed in these two projects. When he was at university, his search for knowledge was extensive, showcasing his passion for literature and arts. After graduation, he joined Architectural Design and Research Institute of Tongji University and built up solid technological foundation. In 2001, together with Liu Yichun and Chen Yifeng, Zhuang Shen co-founded Atelier Deshaus. In 2009, he partnered with Ren Hao, Tang Yu, Zhu Jie, to create Atelier Archmixing. After 10 years' growth, Archmixing has now become one of the most creative architectural studios in contemporary China.

Although independent architectural studios have seen almost 30 years' history in China, it would never become more accessible for them to survive and develop. Their success is not only rooted in the leading architects' knowledge, ideas, techniques and interpersonal skills, but also benefited from the macro environment of highlighting the urban culture and architectural creativity. We admire grand narration, also encourage exploration. Atelier Archmixing's design practice has continued the spirit of Modern Architecture in emphasizing technology, pragmatism, pursuing for innovation rooted in traditional transformation. As the representative of Tongji School, the principal architects are both designers and theorists. They not only design, but also explore design methods to seek change and breakthrough. Within a decade, Atelier Archmixing has completed more than 60 excellent works. This is a perfect example of Lao Tzu's philosophy: "let things take their course, don't preach; then everything will commit instead of shunning duty; create but not declare ownership; achieve but not dwell on the achievements."

Archmixing's work has covered the fields of architecture and arts, bridged the gap between design and research. Zhuang Shen has never really left Tongji University or from academics. His discussions on architectural theories and design methodologies with his wife, Professor Hua Xiahong have led to ingenious works. Their endeavor is an embodiment of what the art critic, curator, designer and architect Aaron Betsky once said, "architecture and art are distinctive fields, though some overlaps between them are emerging. I don't think this is some fads or unavoidable trends, but a response to the traditional tasks in these two fields. A third field encompassing these two is very likely to emerge, for which we haven't found a proper name and which might as well reshape our reality."

This book is an in-depth theoretical work, including commentary by Professor Wang Junyang and interviews with Professor Ge Ming and Professor Lu Andong. They praised Atelier Archmixing for seeking humanity and diversity by pursuing "an another architecture", never contenting in a fad of internet celebrities. We are expecting more design works and theoretical thinking from Atelier Archmixing.

Zheng Shiling

ZHENG Shiling
Dec. 08, 2019

改 变 是 一 个 常 识

Change is a Common Sense

目录
Contents

综述
Review

阿科米星十年：
寻找另一种建筑／建筑学
A Decade for Atelier Archmixing:
In Search of
an Another Architecture

王骏阳
WANG Jun-Yang

2009 年，中国建筑界发生了一件不大不小的"大事"：作为"大舍建筑设计工作室"主持建筑师之一的庄慎从大舍独立出来，与新的合伙人成立阿科米星建筑设计工作室。彼时，随着中国社会数十年的改革开放进程，建筑师从原有设计单位（无论是大型国有设计院或者商业设计机构，还是小型设计事务所）独立出来自己单干的情况时有发生，人们对之也习以为常——事实上，大舍本身也是在柳亦春、庄慎、陈屹峰三位主持建筑师从工作多年的同济设计院独立出来之后成立的。而且在这样的氛围中，分后又合的情况也不罕见。比如，正如大舍在访谈中说到的，在其设计的上海青浦私企协会大楼项目中，与他们配合的结构事务所原本由从华东院出来的合伙人组成，不过私企协会项目还没做完，他们又回华东院了。[1]

然而，大舍并非这些分分合合的设计公司中的任何一家。从 2001 年成立到 2009 年，大舍已经是当代中国成就斐然且最具盛名的"独立建筑设计工作室"（相对于大型国有设计院和大型私营设计公司而言）之一。特别是 2005 年后，随着夏雨幼儿园 [图1] 和青浦私营企业协会办公楼 [图2] 等项目的完成，大舍以非同凡响的设计理念和

建造完成度享誉业界，成为当代中国建筑一张耀眼的名片，出现在数量众多的国内外建筑展和建筑出版物之中，令世人瞩目。

对于一名从业建筑师而言，这种来之不易的品牌效应无疑至关重要。然而，庄慎还是决定另起炉灶。可以肯定，这绝不是一般意义上的"分家"，公司运营常有的因为项目的名和利发生纠纷而导致的分道扬镳甚至反目成仇在这里都不适用。与此同时，即便有设计理念和建筑诉求不尽相同的情况，合伙人建筑设计事务所／工作室采取的项目负责人制完全可以实现一个共同品牌下的"和而不同"。且不说大型设计院已经趋向分解为诸多小型工作室进行运作，与大舍同属"独立建筑设计事务所／工作室"的"都市实践"就是在一个共同品牌下成功合作（甚至是深圳—北京异地合作）的著名案例。尽管"都市实践"之后也曾经历朱锫的"独立"，但是这个变化在坊间的影响似乎远不及庄慎离开大舍引发轰动的程度——至少，我本人听到这个消息之时是有相当震惊之感的。

我相信，离开大舍另起炉灶是庄慎相当艰难但也深思熟虑的一个决定。庄慎当时究竟怎样想的我没有问过，但

In 2009, something of a "bombshell" was dropped in the domain of architecture in China: Zhuang Shen, one of the principals of Atelier Deshaus broke away to start Atelier Archmixing with new partners. Certainly, decades after the open-up policy and market economy reform in China, it was not the new phenomenon that an architect got decoupled from former workplace, normally large state-owned design institutes, to form his or her own. So was the case of Deshaus, co-founded by Liu Yichun, Zhuang Shen, and Chen Yifeng who, after years of work at the Architectural Design and Research Institute of Tongji University, decided to carve out their own practice. Under such circumstances, it was not unusual to see remerge either. For example, as mentioned by Deshaus in an interview, the structural engineers cooperating with Deshaus for the Headquarters of Qingpu Private Enterprise Association, turned out to be the former employees of East China Architectural Design and Research Institute, the largest state-run institution of architectural design in East China, but went back to ECADRI even before the Headquarters project got completed.

Meanwhile, since its founding in 2001 and up to 2009, Deshaus had become one of the most renowned "small and independent architecture firms", a phenomenon that becomes remarkable in contemporary China only in relation to the dominance of state-run as well as privately-owned design giants in the market. In particular, after projects like Xiayu

Kindergarten [fig.1] and the Office Building of Qingpu Enterprise Association [fig.2] both completed in 2005, Deshaus got renowned for its extraordinary design concepts and excellent architectural completion. Its projects were included in various domestic and international architectural exhibitions and published widely in China and abroad. Indeed, by the year of 2009, Deshaus had been widely recognized as a shining name card for contemporary Chinese architecture.

For a professional architect, such a hard-won brand effect is vital. Yet Zhuang Shen decided to start anew. Why not maintaining an already successful firm while looking for diversities within it? A good example that comes to mind in this latter connection is URBANUS, another well-known "small and independent architectural design firm", that consists of not only different partners, but also is based in two different cities, Shenzhen and Beijing. That said, URBANUS itself had gone through a breakaway of Zhu Pei, one of its founding partners, but this seemed to occur in much more silent fashion than the stir caused by Zhuang Shen's leaving. At least, the news came as a great shock for me personally.

To Zhuang Shen, I believe, the decision was a rather tough one. I am not sure about what exactly was in his mind back then, but looking at the first ten years of Archmixing, one may tell that he would not have done so much differently had he remained under one and the same roof of Deshaus. For

是回顾阿科米星十年来的历程，有些事情确实不是继续在同一个品牌"屋檐"下能够做到的。比如，2015 年建成的大舍西岸工作室 [图3] 无疑是一个极具大舍精神气质和专业诉求的建筑，建成之后也确实成为大舍的一个品牌窗口。与此同时，阿科米星却几度搬家，"栖身"位于老式居民区旧房改造的办公空间之中。当然，这种"栖身"并非不得已的"流落"，而是一种主动选择——用阿科米星的话来说，"比起正规漂亮、充满设计感的写字楼来，我们更习惯这个轻松而有点随意的办公室。相安无事中，我们也成为这个社区进进出出的一分子，日常社区生活的旁观者。在这里，某种程度上，我们对于城市建筑的认知从抽象状态变得更加具体了，工作室最初确立的概念化的混合设计理念慢慢发展为对日常城市的改变、调整、有效建造等的观察和认知，我们的设计实践同时寻找着结合与检验这些认知的方式。"2

　　五年后，由于房屋业主对建筑另做他用，阿科米星的第一个办公室走到尽头。有趣的是，在获得另一个相对永久的办公地点之前，一个过渡用房的经历让阿科米星发现"城市在不断转手或空置出来各种有意思的地方"，进而对

1　大舍建筑：夏雨幼儿园
　　Atelier Deshaus: Xiayu Kindergarten

2　大舍建筑：青浦私营企业协会办公楼
　　Atelier Deshaus: Office Building of Qingpu
　　Private Enterprise Association

one thing, as Atelier Deshaus completed its own firm office on the West Bund in 2015 [fig.3], a front showcase of the firm ever since, Archmixing was moving around inhabiting in office buildings located in different old renovated neighborhoods. To quote Archmixing's own words about such a vagabond action, "compared with neat, pretty, and trendy buildings, we prefer this office area, relaxing and even a bit casual. We become part of this community in and out, the observer of what happens here every day. By living here, our cognition of urban architecture has to some extent turned more concrete from an abstract status. The mixed design concepts initially established gradually develop into observation and perception of changes, adaptations, effective constructions to the daily city, for which our design practice is seeking ways to combine and test." I

　　Five years later, Archmixing's first office tenancy came to an end. Interestingly, before finding another relatively long term leasing, Archmixing got a transitional location that made them realize the city is full of "fun spaces from continuous renting or vacancy," and think over "whether to have a location used for a decade or ten locations each for a year". II For Archmixing, what got involved in this process was not only a matter of running the firm differently, but also the reflections on "internal spaces in the building and the city". III Apparently for practical reasons though, Archmixing finally decided to go for the former option. Today, one finds Atelier Archmixing

3　大舍西岸工作室
　　Atelier Deshaus: Office on West Bund

4 阿科米星桂林路小白楼工作室（2018–）
Little White House, Atelier Archmixing's Office on Guilin Road

5 勒·柯布西耶：《走向一种建筑》法文版封面
Le Corbusier: *Vers une architecture*

6 富勒：代马克松住宅
Fuller: Dymaxion House

"选择一个十年的办公空间还是十个一年的办公空间"的问题产生思考。这些思考不仅涉及办公方式的改变，更对"建筑的内部空间和城市的内在空间"的建筑学反思带来影响。[3] 当然，也许出于实际的考虑，阿科米星最终选择了前者。今天的阿科米星建筑设计工作室 [图4] 位于桂林路园区一个不起眼的彩钢板建筑之中，内部布置透露着放松和随意，而不是大舍那样的秩序井然和形式感。可以认为，这些差异并不能以一般意义上的同一个工作室／事务所内部在设计理念和建筑诉求上的不同予以理解。

再比如，随着西岸龙美术馆和艺仓美术馆的建成与运行，大舍自觉不自觉地参与到各种时尚文化和艺术界的活动之中。应该说，在崇尚时尚文化的今日，建筑师作为时尚文化艺术的参与者甚至是引领者，不失为让建筑融入社会，某种意义上也是话语权争夺的一种有效途径。相比之下，阿科米星的建成作品毫无这种潜力，难以成为时尚文化艺术的一部分。尽管在建筑实践之外，阿科米星也运行着自己的"那行"，其中既有阿科米星组织的学术活动，也不乏对外出租的商业经营，但是处于都市深处且毫无惊人之处的"那行"对时尚文化圈毫无吸引力，实际上也与

in a humble color plate building located in a former industrial district on Guilin Road [fig.4]. Its casual interior forms a stunning contrast to the neat formality of Deshaus.

What is more, since the completion of the Long Museum West Bund and the Yicang Art Gallery, both celebrated domestically and internationally, Atelier Deshaus is increasingly becoming involved in trendy circle and vogue culture. Admittedly, this might well be a way to merge architecture into society, and to get the voice of the profession heard, which is very much needed under today's circumstances in China. However, this has not been the case of Archmixing, even though in addition to architectural practice, it is also running a small workshop called NEXTMIXING organizing exhibitions and academic activities or renting out to other uses. What Archmixing is aiming at, I believe, is to get architecture merged with the society in a different manner. All in all, be it the choice of office locations or the way of operating NEXTMIXING, or, whether in terms of professional practice or theoretical writing, I would like to say that Archmixing is committed to go its own way that ultimately means an "another architecture", or *"une architecture autre"*, to borrow the word once used by Reyner Banham.

Another Architecture—from Le Corbusier to Reyner Banham

The issue of an "another architecture" had been raised

之无关。阿科米星寻求的是以不同的方式在不同的层面上让建筑融入社会。也许我们还可以说，无论是事务所搬家还是那行的建立，也无论专业实践还是理论写作，阿科米星都一直在摸索中朝着自己的方向迈进——寻求另一种建筑/建筑学，如果在此我们可以通过建筑/建筑学的并置表明 architecture 在中文语境中具有的双重含义，同时凸显阿科米星的建筑（实践）中包含的建筑学思考的话。

另一种建筑/建筑学：从勒·柯布西耶到班纳姆

何谓另一种建筑/建筑学？这个问题的回答无疑需要一定的参照点，而这个参照点在不同时代又不尽相同，从而导致"另一种"自身含义的差异。1923 年，勒·柯布西耶的划时代著作 Vers une architecture [图5] 问世。之后，它以英国艺术家和建筑师弗雷德里克·艾切尔斯的英译本 Towards a New Architecture 在全世界广泛传播。也正由于艾切尔斯的英文版本，柯布的这部著作在中文建筑学语境中一直被译为《走向新建筑》，这在一定程度上导致对柯布这部著作甚至整个现代建筑的误解。关于这个问题，笔者曾经撰文对之进行讨论，[4] 在此不再重复。但是

有一点也许与这里的议题不无关系：与其像艾切尔斯那样出于"宣传家而非评论家"[5] 的目的称其为《走向新建筑》，不如将柯布这里的 une architecture 理解为"（另）一种建筑/建筑学"更为准确。这个"（另）一种建筑/建筑学"有别于当时占主流地位的巴黎美院建筑学，但却并非全新——事实上，它在很大程度上保留了传统建筑学的成分。英国建筑史学家约翰·萨默森甚至认为，作为 20 世纪最为重要的建筑论著，组成 Vers une architecture 的一系列批判性论文"与其说提出了绝对新的建筑原理，不如说是用现代的眼光将相当一部分已经被遗忘的内容重新展现出来，而且这一展现还是以极其矛盾的方式完成的"。[6]

对艾切尔斯的英文译名，史学家们似乎从一开始就有质疑，表现之一是他们常常宁愿在自己的英文著作中使用法文原文 Vers une architecture，而不是艾切尔斯的翻译。不过据我所知，第一个真正对这个问题进行明确讨论的是英国建筑史学家雷纳·班纳姆。他在自己的博士论文基础上修改完成并于 1960 年出版的《第一机械时代的理论与设计》中指出，如果 Vers une architecture 的原标题只是"走向一种建筑"之意，那么将其译为 Towards a New Ar-

more than once before Banham, most notably Le Corbusier's *Vers une architecture* [fig.5] published in 1923. Thanks to the English translation by British artist and architects Frederick Etchells in 1927, the book has been almost unanimously known under the name of *Towards a New Architecture*, and so is the case with three different versions in Chinese too. Yet the new title is more or less unfortunate since it has in many ways led to the misunderstanding of both Le Corbusier's seminal work and modern architecture in general. Although it is not the right context to go into this, one point may well be relevant to the present topic: instead of naming the book *Towards a New Architecture*, it might be more accurate to comprehend Le Corbusier's "une architecture" as "another architecture". This is because, while opposing much of the mainstream represented by the French *Beaux-Art* architecture, it was not that brand-new as Etchells claimed. Rather, it was connected to traditional architecture in one way or another. To quote the British architectural historian John Summerson, as "the most consequential book written on architecture in 20th century", *Vers une architecture* was actually a work wherein "nothing absolutely new is proposed in the way of architectural principle, but a great deal that had been forgotten is brought into light of the present and exhibited with a quite uncommon flair of paradox." [IV]

It seems that right from the very beginning architectural historians have been skeptical about the English title coined by Etchells, for more often than not, they tend to use the origi-

nal title in French instead of Etchells'. As far as I know, however, the first one who clearly addressed this issue was the British architectural historian Reyner Banham. In *Theory and Design in the First Machine Age from 1960*, Banham observed: "whereas the original title *Vers une architecture*, simply says 'Towards an Architecture'", the title of the English translation "put an entirely different slant on the matter, though not one that is entirely unsupported by the text." [V] Meanwhile, Banham's insightful remarks also included a critique of Le Corbusier. In Banham's view, what underlined Le Corbusier's *Vers une architecture* was the "rediscovery of the old in the new" in which "the Beaux-Arts tradition has been laid under tribute for much of the detailing". [VI] What is more, Le Corbusier favored "machine aesthetic" rather than authentic machine, and this caused the architecture he advocated trapped in a conundrum of losing true technological momentum. Seen from Banham's perspective, this was also the conundrum that had largely haunted modern architecture from the outset.

Banham had long been unhappy with the course of modern architecture, particularly that in the U.K, and he adopted the phase *une architecture autre* in an article entitled"The New Brutalism" in the *Architectural Review*, 1955. At the first sight, one might suspect the expression was targeting at Le Corbusier, urging a transition from "une architecture" to "une architecture autre". But, as Banham himself told in the article, the concept was derived from *un art autre*, an issue raised

chitecture，不仅为整个问题赋予了完全不同的色彩，而且这一色彩不能在书中找到充分支持。[7] 当然，与对柯林·罗1947 年发表的《理想别墅的数学》的赞许立场不同，班纳姆的上述阐述同时包含着对柯布建筑主张的批评。在班纳姆看来，柯布与学院派看似势不两立，实则藕断丝连。他的建筑只是诉诸"机械美学"，而不是真正的机器，这导致其主张的现代建筑失去了基于技术发展的真正的历史动力，从而陷入困境。在班纳姆那里，这一困境也是现代建筑的普遍困境。

班纳姆自己早已不满现代建筑发展的现状，特别是现代建筑在英国的现状。1955 年，他在《建筑评论》杂志发表《新粗野主义》一文，首次提出"另一种建筑"（une architecture autre）。乍看起来，这个用法语表述的"另一种建筑"有针对柯布之意，似乎在呼吁从柯布的 une architecture 向 une architecture autre 转变。不过，正如班纳姆自己在文中阐明的，这个概念其实是法国艺术家、评论家米歇尔·塔皮耶 1952 年提出的 un art autre（另一种艺术）之说的变体。[8] 此外，鉴于这是一个在论述"新粗野主义"的文章中提出的概念，它也与"新粗野主义"有

着某种不可或缺的关系。尽管班纳姆没有阐明什么是"粗野主义"，也没有告知读者"新粗野主义"之"新"究竟体现在何处——对于班纳姆来说，一切似乎不言自明，无需再进行论述，但是纵观班纳姆全部理论生涯，这一点也许并非那么重要，因为"新粗野主义"只是班纳姆致力寻求的"另一种建筑／建筑学"的阶段性成果。之后的重要内容还包括《第一机械时代的理论与设计》对"未来主义"的重构，以及对作为"真正的机器"（而不是柯布和现代主义的"机械美学"）的富勒的代马克松住宅 [图6] 的推崇，以及他为 1960 年的《建筑评论》杂志主持的"盘点"系列涉及的"预设设计""全包式设计服务""夹式组件"，直至"更易碎的美学"、对"阿基格拉姆"小组的理论代言，等等。1969 年出版的《环境调控的建筑学》和移居美国后完成的《洛杉矶：四种生态的建筑学》[图7] 更是班纳姆"另一种建筑／建筑学"的另外两个高峰，前者将《第一机械时代的理论与设计》对富勒的肯定拓展为一种广义的"环境调控建筑学"，后者则通过洛杉矶这个非同一般的案例展现了"另一种建筑／建筑学"在城市"生态"（系统）方面的涵义。

some years earlier by the French artist and critic Michel Tapié. Besides, given the title of the article, it was largely dedicated to the "New Brutalism", a term first used in 1953 in a statement by Alison and Peter Smithson for their Soho House project, though Banham neither made effort to elucidate the definition of the "Brutalism", nor tried he to clarify what was new about it.

Put in the whole context of Banham's theoretical development, however, one might say that this matter did prove to be of minor significance, because he soon seemed to have dropped such a Smithsonian term and went his own way of searching for "une architecture autre". This included a reassessment of "Futurism" in *Theory and Design in the First Machine Age* that ended up with Buckminster Fuller and his Dymaxion House [fig.6], the Stocktaking series hosted for the *Architectural Review* in 1960 including "Anticipatory Design", "All-in Package Design Service", "Clip-on Components", "A More Crumbly Aesthetic", as well as the endorsement for the Archigram group. Later, Banham's lifelong searching for "une architecture autre" got highlighted by two seminal works, *The Architecture of the Well-Tempered Environment* from 1969, and *Los Angeles: The Architecture of Four Ecologies* [fig.7] written after his migration to the U.S. The former extended the significance of Buckminster Fuller affirmed earlier in *Theory and Design in the First Machine Age* to its full implication for the "architecture of well-tempered environment", whereas the latter embarked on the "ecological" consequences for "une architecture autre"

through such an extraordinary case as Los Angeles.

As to the nature of Banham's "une architecture autre", scholars hold diverse and even opposing opinions. Nigel Whiteley concludes it as an "attitude" in line with the post-war *art autre* with its undercurrent of anti-conventionalism, which in British architecture took off primarily with Alison and Peter Smithson's "New Brutalism". [VII] Anthony Vidler, for his part, identifies Banham's real agenda as, in a returning to an "aesthetic tradition", calling for "an architecture that technologically overcomes all previous architecture, to possess an expressive form." [VIII] So far as I can see, such seemingly contradictory positions reflect nothing but different aspects in Banham's path to "une architecture autre". On the one hand, as one might see even in the "New Brutalism", it rested heavily upon the idea of "image" that Banham took on as "one of the most intractable and the most useful terms in contemporary aesthetics" demanding that "the building should be an immediately apprehensible visual entity, and that the form grasped by the eye should be confirmed by experience of the building in use." [IX] Thus not only his praise of Archigram's "Plug-in City" [fig.8] but also his identification of the Smithsons' Hunstanton School [fig.9] as the most emblematic of the "New Brutalism" became well explainable.

On the other hand, Banham's "une architecture autre" indeed assumed an "attitude", either in relation to technology or to the everyday. Vidler recognizes Banham's emphasis

关于班纳姆"另一种建筑／建筑学"的性质，学者的说法不尽相同，甚至截然相反。奈杰尔·惠特里将其总结为与二战之后的反传统主义的"另一种艺术"一脉相承的"态度"，而不是形式美学。[9] 与之不同，安东尼·维德勒认为班纳姆的"另一种建筑／建筑学"本质上是对建筑学"美学传统"的一种回归，其真正议题在于"对一种在技术上史无前例同时又极具表现性之建筑的召唤"。[10] 在我看来，看似矛盾的观点反映的正是班纳姆"另一种建筑／建筑学"中同时存在的不同方面。一方面，正如《新粗野主义》一文所显示的，班纳姆的"另一种建筑／建筑学"对"意象"特别重视，将之视为"当代美学中最为棘手也最为有用的术语之一"。在班纳姆那里，"意象"超越了古典传统的准则，但是它的视觉价值仍在于使建筑"在整体上一目了然，或者在使用体验中获得形式的视觉把握"。[11] 这一点不仅可以解释班纳姆对阿基格拉姆"插入城市"[图8]的颂扬，也为班纳姆将史密森夫妇的汉斯丹顿学校[图9]视为"新粗野主义"的代表提供了某种注脚。事实上，尽管外观上极具密斯气质的汉斯丹顿学校完全没有后期柯布建筑中常见的粗野混凝土材料，但是它在管线设备方面的"意象"表现却在一定意义上构成班纳姆不同于柯布式"旧"粗野主义的"新粗野主义"之"新"的美学维度。

另一方面，班纳姆的"另一种建筑／建筑学"又是一种对待技术和生活的"态度"。维德勒注意到班纳姆对技术的高度重视，并因此将班纳姆的现代主义称为"未来主义的现代主义"。相比之下，班纳姆"另一种建筑／建筑学"对现实生活的关注似乎或多或少被维德勒的"未来主义"议题所淡化。在这一点上，班纳姆不仅将"新粗野主义"视为对当时致力于修正现代主义的"新经验主义"和"新人文主义"的反叛，而且特别推崇史密森夫妇1952年的"黄金巷"和1953年的谢菲尔德大学扩建竞赛方案[图10]，以及他们与英国艺术家帕洛佐和汉德森共同举办的"生活与艺术并行"展览表达的现代生活态度。在班纳姆那里，尽管这两个设计竞赛方案未能取代汉斯丹顿学校在"新粗野主义"中的开创性地位，但是它们似乎最符合"生活与艺术并行"的警告与诉求，[12] 因而也更接近惠特里所谓的"态度"。当然，如果在班纳姆"另一种建筑／建筑学"中有什么真正成为一种超越了"审美传统"

on technology to the extent that he identifies Banham as a historian of "futurist modernism". What Vidler seems to have missed out in this point is Banham's embrace of the everyday. For, being antipathetic to the rise of the "New Empiricism" and "New Humanist" architecture of the time, Banham's account of the "New Brutalism" ended up with a tribute to the Smithsons' competition entries for the City of London's Golden Lane [fig.10] public housing in 1952 and Sheffield University Extensions in 1953. For all the lack of "image" that the Hunstanton School possessed, these two projects, the Golden Lane in particular, may well shed light on what Whiteley refers to as the "attitude" rather than "aesthetic image" in positioning architecture's relationship to an almost formless life world. Still, however, one may have to, once again, turn to *Los Angeles: The Architecture of Four Ecologies*, in which the issues of "formal/aformal", "pure and polished/starkness and directness" or the so-called "warehouse aesthetic/as found" aesthetic once so crucial for the "New Brutalism", and even for *The New Brutalism: Ethic or Aesthetic?* coming out more than ten years later, were largely replaced by concerns that in Banham's theoretical development knowingly or unknowingly transcended the impact of "aesthetics tradition", or "modern picturesque", as Vidler puts it differently.

Archmixing: An "Another Architecture" and Design Research

Now, if the first decade of Archmixing could be identified as a quest for an "another architecture", then its trajectory both resonates with and differs from Le Corbusier and Banham. In the first instance, Archmixing's commitment to challenge the "conventional architecture" is most striking, though like that of Le Corbusier and Banham, this challenging gesture needs certain qualification. Le Corbusier, contrary to what was depicted by Etchells, neither denied the classical values nor withdrew from the brilliant tradition of the vernacular past. What it battled against was the dominant Beaux-Arts architecture that, in his view, had lost contact with classical spirit and vernacular tradition on the one hand, and failed to keep pace with technological development and social transformation on the other. Banham dismissed Le Corbusier's tie with the past, classical or vernacular. For that reason, he even rebuked the "Patio and Pavilion" [fig.11] designed by the Smithsons in collaboration with the British artists Eduardo Paolozzi and Nigel Henderson as too conventional and submissive to traditional values. Yet advocating "une architecture autre", what he felt most uncomfortable with was the "mainstream" architecture of his time, either in the sense of what was regarded as the exhausted modernism, or the "New Empiricism" and the "New Humanist" architecture thereafter. His inclination towards "Futurism" and Buckminster Fuller, the "New Brutalism", the Archigram group, the "Architecture of Well-tempered Environment", Los Angeles and the

7　雷纳·班纳姆：《洛杉矶：四种生态的建筑学》
　　Reyner Banham: Los Angeles, The Architecture of Four Ecologies

的"态度"，那么也许没有什么比晚期在美国完成的《洛杉矶：四种生态的建筑学》更加当之无愧。在这里，无论在 1955 年的《新粗野主义》一文中还是在 1966 年的《新粗野主义：道德还是美学？》一书中仍然占有重要地位的"形式的／非形式的"或者"纯粹精致／粗旷直接"的美学问题被"四种生态"的城市建筑学所取代。"新粗野主义"的"仓库美学"、"恰如身边所见"的"日常美学"也在城市的巨大冲击下丧失了既有的重要地位和意义。

阿科米星：另一种建筑／建筑学与设计研究

　　如果说阿科米星的十年是寻求"另一种建筑／建筑学"的十年，那么这个寻求之路与柯布和班纳姆既有某些共同之处，又无疑存在诸多差异。与柯布和班纳姆一样，阿科米星的诉求是对"传统／既有建筑／建筑学"，或者更准确地说是寄身于当下的"传统／既有建筑／建筑学"的某种挑战。柯布的"（另）一种建筑／建筑学"既没有否定古典的价值，也对优秀的民居传统情有独钟，但是很显然，他强烈反对当时处于统治地位，并且在他看来既丧失优秀的民居传统和古典精神，又与时代的技术和社会

8　阿基格拉姆：插入城市
　　Archigram: Plug-in City

9　史密森夫妇：汉斯丹顿学校
　　The Smithsons: Hunstanton School

"Architecture of Four Ecologies" counteracted that distaste.

Archmixing, for its part, has set out to look for an "another architecture" in the wake of recognition of what they call the "predicament" of architecture today. As it writes: "the difficulties confronting today's architecture lie not in the elusive diversity and flux of changes, but in the inner vacuity and vagueness that the superficial sequins cannot hide. It is increasingly turned into 'single track' architecture. Among so many contradictions caused by such one-dimensioned value system, the most striking one turns out to be the increasingly alienated relationship between the architect as an individual with his or her works and the social mass and their real life, which undermines architecture's momentum forward even worse." [X]

In Archmixing's view, this situation should be ascribed to social-economic factors as much as to the internal causes of the architectural discipline. The former is especially true of the contemporary consumer society in which commercial and investment interests have not only impacted the purpose and method of architecture, but also have profoundly influenced the applications of new materials and technology. Meanwhile, this tendency gets intensified because of a "conventional architecture" that rests on "expression of personal emotions" yet now comforts with the values of consumer society, and turns the profession into a "systematic instruction aiming to stimulate mass consumption". [XI] In other words, this is an architecture that increasingly confines to the

需求格格不入的巴黎美院建筑学。班纳姆批评柯布与古典和传统"调情",也将自己在《新粗野主义》中大加赞许的史密森夫妇参与"这是明天"展览的作品《院子和亭子》[图11]斥为过于传统和缺少艺术性,[13] 但是更为重要的是,他的"另一种建筑/建筑学"是针对战后现代建筑的"主流"与"正统"发起的挑战。他不满足于现代建筑的现状,试图通过对"未来主义"的重新诠释,在新粗野主义、富勒与代马克松住宅、阿基格拉姆、"环境调控建筑学",以及《洛杉矶:四种生态的建筑学》中寻求他所谓的"另一种建筑/建筑学"。

可以认为,阿科米星对当代建筑学"困境"的反思也正是其寻求"另一种建筑/建筑学"的动因。关于这一"困境",阿科米星这样写道:"今天建筑学面临的困难并不在于难以把握的多样性与快速的变化,而在于表面的丰富多彩难以掩盖的内在空泛。建筑学日益成为一种'单一'的建筑学。单向的建筑价值系统造成的诸多矛盾中,最突出的是,作为个人的建筑师及其设计作品与大众及其真实生活之间的关系日渐疏离,这更削弱了建筑学发展的动力。"在阿科米星看来,[14] 造成这一状况的主要原因既有社会经济层面的原因,也有建筑学科内部的原因。前者以当代消费社会为甚,其商业效应和投资利益不仅决定着建筑的目的和方法,而且深刻影响着以"强大的创新能力"为面貌出现的新材料新技术的使用。而在建筑学科内部,以"个人情绪表达的建筑"作为价值系统的"传统建筑学"又在相当程度上顺应了消费社会的需求,导致建筑成为"以刺激大众消费为目的的系统化引导"。[15]

这是一种建筑学越来越受制于"生产-消费"体系的困境。面对这一困境,阿科米星将建筑师能够采取的立场分为三类:"其一是与'生产-消费'体系同步,自觉地成为其中重要的创造力量;其二是坚持原有的文化精英主义立场,远离商业体系,通过选择特定项目和业主来实现建筑理想;其三是在'生产-消费'体系的背景下,关注大众生活与建筑相互作用的新可能,寻找建筑师的新位置,使建筑师的作用更广泛与独立。"[16] 正是从前两个立场的角度,阿科米星对自己以"离合"思想为代表的"前历史",更准确地说是对从庄慎在同济大学的硕士学位论文到阿科米星成立之间的"前历史"进行反思。阿科米星指出,尽管"离合"的思想并非只关注传统形式和空间,

"production-consumption" system, and thereby continues to lock out more complete and compelling possibilities.

In this regard, Archmixing assorts the architect's position into three categories: the first is to keep pace with the "production-consumption" system and consciously become its important creative force; the second is to adhere to the original cultural elitist position, stay away from the business system, and realize architectural ideals by selecting specific projects and owners; and the third is to focus on new possibilities of interaction between the public lives and architecture in the context of the "production-consumption" system in order to find new positions for architects and make the architects' role broader and more independent." XII

It is in connection to the first two categories that Zhuang Shen comes to a reflection on the "pre-history" of Archmixing, or more precisely, a "pre-history" represented by his own course from the master degree thesis at Tongji University to the founding of Archmixing. The master degree thesis, largely a reinterpretation of the Li-he concept, meaning "separation" and "unification", by Chinese 20th century aesthetician Zong Baihua, that in turn was derived from the trigram Li philosophy of Chinese I Ching, concluded with an effort to deal with method issues for today's architects, and in this way "exceeded both conventional issues of form or space and abstract aesthetic philosophy". In Zhuang Shen's self-critique, however, this approach still bore "a tendency to evade

contemporary industrial systems and broader social content. And this is what we've always suspected and wanted to surpass. If an approach is confined to traditional architecture, despite its excellent specialty, its significance will be degraded by the contemporary trend of homogenization. Therefore, whether this approach will work in the future is what we most want to know and try. We believe that a design approach can easily become personalized and confined to traditional architecture if it is only adopted as formal and spatial logic. Nevertheless, if it is adopted as a way of thinking, then it may contribute to the active integration of individuals and society, and conform to the requirements of present social culture." XIII

This leads to Archmxing's move from Li-he to Hun-he. For, if Li-he aims "to perceive and understand the whole from concrete parts", Hun-he, a Chinese expression for mixing, is to be comprehended as "a broader organizational approach" that attempts to get involved issues that conventionally are "not included in the discipline of architecture" and to achieve a "conflation of personal experience, complex background and mass life" as well. XIV In Archmixing, it also triggers an interest in changes in everyday use of both buildings and the city, and its potential to shake off the hegemony of "image architecture". What is more, instead of "what is architecture" or "what is the architect", the conventional way of thinking about the discipline as well as the profession, Archmixing finds more interesting to look into questions like "what is architecture or

或者只是一种抽象哲学和美学认识，而是旨在从宗白华先生关于传统"离"卦美学意义的阐述中挖掘出一种对于建筑师更重要的设计方法，但是"这样的设计方法具有回避当代工业生产体系及更广泛的社会内容的倾向。而这也正是我们一直怀疑并想要超越的。如果一种方法仅是传统建筑学范畴内的，再好的个性也会被当代的同质化趋向消解其意义。因此，这种方式方法在未来是否具有作用才是我们最想要了解并尝试的。我们的看法是，一种设计方法如果仅仅作为一种形式空间逻辑就很容易走向个人化，并局限于传统建筑学的范畴内；而如果上升为一种思考问题的方式，则有可能走向个人与社会的主动结合，契合当下社会文化的要求"。[17] 因此，上述第三种立场不仅是阿科米星试图践行的，也是阿科米星寻求的"另一种建筑／建筑学"的核心。

　　由此带来阿科米星从"离合"向"混合"的转变。在阿科米星那里，如果"离合"是"通过具体的局部感知和理解整体"，那么"混合"则是"走向一种更为广泛的组织方式"。一方面，它试图在建筑中融入更多之前被认为不属于建筑学范畴或者没有建筑学价值的内容，从而获

得一种"个人经验与复杂背景、大众生活的结合"。这导致对建筑和城市的日常状态的兴趣和关注，以及对建筑和城市的日常使用端的变化作为一种能够为"图像建筑"带来改变的建筑学价值的关注。另一方面，与"传统建筑学"致力于询问"建筑／建筑学／建筑师是什么"不同，它更愿意思考"建筑／建筑学／建筑师还有什么用"，相信只有这样"才有可能再发现新的东西"。[18] 换言之，它试图在这样的转变中实现专业的"迂回"，突破建筑学的既有范围，在建筑学与非建筑学的结合中寻求当代建筑／建筑学的立足点和发展动力。或许，这正是 Archmixing 一词的正解：其中 arch 毋庸置疑代表建筑／建筑学，而 mixing 既是"米星"的汉语拼音，又是"混合"的英文单词。根据这一理解，Archmixing 不再是一种巧妙有趣的文字游戏，而是阿科米星寻求"另一种建筑／建筑学"之始的一个简明宣言。

　　这里的"混合"既不意味着随心所欲的拼凑，也不是班纳姆在"新粗野主义"和"独立小组"的艺术展中看到的"意象"。毋宁说，阿科米星的"混合"是一种集理论思考和专业实践为一体的设计研究。作为一个学术领域，

the architect for". Only through such a shift, or a "detour" that moves beyond the conventional boundary of the discipline and combines architecture and non-architecture, "could one see around architecture's own corner". [XV] Here, interestingly, we are arriving at a possible implication of the Atelier's name comprised of arch and mixing, the former apparently stands for architecture, while the latter indicates both phonetic transcription of the Chinese characters and the English word of mixing. But this is more than an artful and funny wordplay. It is, I would like to say, a mini-manifesto that from the outset came to shape much of the true agenda of Archmixing's quest for an "another architecture".

　　More importantly, in the context of Archmixing's development, such a "mixing" demands, first of all, a form of design research made of theoretical thinking and professional practice. In architecture, "design research" was in upsurge during the 1960-70s under the name of "design methods" or "design methodology". The idea was to treat design as a completely rational process, and hope to transform the "black-box" of design thinking into a "transparent-box" conducted by methodological steps and procedures. This rationalist vision soon proved to be problematic and unable to disclose the real feature of architectural design, and led to the fall of "design methodology" as the upmost measure of design research. According to contemporary British scholar Murray Fraser, "design methodology" is about "research of/about design",

and therefore does not make much sense as design research. In Fraser's view, the task of design research is to shed light on "how architecture produces its own insight and knowledge". [XVI] He even rejects Donald Schön's idea of the "reflective practioner" because "it does not fully take into account the vital process of knowledge creation in architecture". [XVII] To Fraser, it seems only "research through/by design" could be truly identified as design research in architecture.

　　Murray's objection of "research of/about design" as design research is reasonable as much it is polemic, for, as I referred to in the another context, when probably conducted, it must be a fertile domain of design research. [XVIII] However, his observation that design research is in essence "a process of inquiry and investigation in which thinking and writing and designing are integrally interlinked throughout" [XIX] does bring about an insight into what underlies Archmixing's quest for an "another architecture". Interestingly, though, while the publication for the ten years anniversary of Archmixing corresponds to theoretical writing and professional practice of the same praxis, they are made as two separate entities, and it is the theoretical part that the present essay is dedicated to.

　　Central to these theoretical writings is, as aforementioned, the present condition of the city and its significance to architecture today. Once again, from Le Corbusier to Banham, the notion of the city and its architectural consequences underwent profound changes. in which the absolute rational

始于 20 世纪 60 年代的"设计研究"最初曾以"设计方法论"的面貌呈现，它试图将设计视为一种完全理性的过程，用理性化的分析步骤和设计过程取代设计思维的"黑匣子"，将这个"黑匣子"变成"透明匣子"。然而这个"透明匣子"并未令人信服地说明建筑设计的真实特点，而只是将之简化为抽象的"过程"和"方法"。这是一度风光无限的"设计方法论"的最大不足，也是它作为一种设计研究不再具有吸引力的原因。当代英国学者莫雷·弗雷泽甚至认为，设计方法不是设计研究，因为它只是"关于设计的研究"。在他看来，"设计研究"的核心应该是"建筑如何生产它的自身认知"。在这样的意义上，似乎只有"通过设计进行的研究"才是"设计研究"。[19]

在我看来，与"设计方法"或者"建筑如何生产它的自身认知"的"设计研究"不同，阿科米星的设计研究显然不只是以"设计进行的研究"，理论思考也是这一研究的重要部分，这从阿科米星过去十年中富有成果的理论写作可见一斑。正如前文所说，这些理论写作关注的重点在于当下视野中的日常城市及其对于建筑学的意义和价值。诚然，从柯布到班纳姆，建筑学对城市的认识和观念已经发生巨大变化。柯布"一种／另一种建筑／建筑学"所热衷的具有完美理性秩序和规划设计的城市被"恰如身边所见"和"四种生态"的城市所取代。在班纳姆的《洛杉矶：四种生态的建筑学》之前，文丘里的《向拉斯维加斯学习》已经问世近十年，而在班纳姆之后，库哈斯从《癫狂的纽约》到《广普城市》的当代城市研究无疑最为引人注目且发人深省。但是，与这些当代城市研究相比，阿科米星的关注点更加微观，因此也更加"日常"。另一方面，与班纳姆最终归结为"意象"的"恰如身边所见"，或者在文丘里那里沦为"符号"的"普通"不同，阿科米星对于"日常"有自己的理解：它首先是一种"非识别系统"，其次是"变化"，而变化又与使用端和城市的"空间冗余"有关。就此而言，当代城市研究中只有塚本由晴及其"犬吠工作室"的工作可以与阿科米星相提并论 [图12]。

如果说阿科米星的理论思考在与设计实践相辅相成的同时又具有完全不同的特质的话，那么在我看来，它在本质上更接近法国哲学家吉尔·德勒兹的工作。在德勒兹那里，哲学的任务是概念性的。不过这种概念性不是分析学派视为哲学研究之核心的概念分析——后者常常导致学究

013

urban order embraced by Le Corbusier was superceded by the concerns for the "as found" and "four ecologies". Banham was far from being alone in this shift. Prior to Banham's *Los Angeles*, Venturi's *Learning from Las Vegas* had already been published nearly for ten years, while some years after Banham, Rem Koolhaas' studies of contemporary cities ranging from *Delirious New York* to *Generic City* made up the most thought-provoking instances in this line. Yet compared to all these precedents, it is the urban phenomena on the micro and thus more everyday level that interest Archmixing most. Moreover, unlike Banham's penchant for the "as found" that ultimately ended up with "images", or Venturi's "ordinary" which in *Learning from Las Vegas* finally became a salute to "sign", Archmixing has teased out an understanding of "every-day world" of its own: firstly as an "unrecognizable system", and secondly as an ongoing process of "change", which of necessity links to the use end and what Archmixing calls "spatial redundancy" of the city. In this respect, Archmixng takes on design research in a way that few contemporaries evince, only Yoshiharu Tsukamoto and Atelier Bow-Bow seem to have provided a more convincing instance [fig.12].

To understand better the theoretical approach of Archmixing, I would parallel it with the work of the French philosopher Gilles Deleuze. In Deleuze, philosophy is a conceptual endeavor, not in the way as Analytic Philosophy takes on with conceptual analysis, but rather, as science extracts prospects and art extracts percepts and affects, philosophy extracts concepts. [XX] His *Mille Plateaux, Capitalisme et Schizophrénie* co-authored with Felix Guattari is a marvelous work of this kind, in which the seemingly platitudinous concepts such as "rhizome", "strata", "body without organs", "desire", "nomad", "war machine", "smooth space", "the striated" and many more have been creatively endowed with meanings, serving as philosophical cornerstones of *Mille Plateaux*.

Now, although not exactly in the same level of sophistication as Deleuze, Archmixing does exhibit ability of working on concepts in Deleuzean manner, from "spatial redundancy" to "unrecognizable system". In an essay entitled "An Altitude of Unrecognizable System: The Architectural World of Geoffrey Bawa", for instance, "recognizable system" is treated as "architectural phenomena that are easily incorporated into the mainstream architectural knowledge system, whose contents bears clear origins and distinctive characteristics, easy to be categorized and analyzed." By contrast, "unrecognizable system" is used "to cover non-mainstream architecture, knowledge systems that are not easily recognized, and architectural phenomena that are of undetermined origin and least distinctive characteristics, difficult to categorize, hybrid or too common, lack artistic creativity and are therefore excluded."[XXI] Seen in this way, Archmixing's interest in Bawa has little to do with the curiosity about his hybrid personal background

型的研究工作，而是概念的创造。换言之，正如科学创造函数，艺术创造感觉，德勒兹将哲学的任务视为创造概念。[20] 他与菲力克斯·瓜塔里合著的《千高原》可谓这种哲学的一部旷世之作，其中的"根茎""层""无器官的身体""欲望""游牧""战争机器""平滑空间""纹理"等看似貌不惊人的概念被创造性地赋予意义，成为构筑哲学"千高原"的基石。依我之见，尽管在哲学思辨的程度上与德勒兹相去甚远，但是阿科米星的"空间冗余"和"非识别系统"等概念完全具有德勒兹式创造性概念的潜质。当然，阿科米星也有完胜德勒兹的地方，比如那篇题为《非识别系统的一种高度：杰弗里·巴瓦的建筑世界》。这是一篇当代建筑学不可多得的美文，它将"识别系统"定义为"那些容易被纳入耳熟能详的主干建筑学知识体系的建筑现象，那些能追根溯源、特别明显、容易归类和分析的内容"。与之相对，"非识别系统"则被用来涵盖"非主流建筑学或者不容易被认识清楚的知识系统，那些来源和特征不明显、不容易归类、边缘、杂交，或者过于普通、缺乏艺术创造性而被排斥在外的建筑现象"。[21] 阿科米星进一步指出，用"非识别系统"来理解巴瓦并不是因为他

个人的特殊性，比如混杂的个人背景，或者其作品透射的"精美品味"，而在于巴瓦在"识别体系"之外糅杂混合的能力及其所能达到的艺术境界。因此，尽管巴瓦的大多数作品并不处在高强度的城市之中，但是它们既是"非识别体系"的一种高度，也是阿科米星寻求的"另一种建筑／建筑学"的一种高度。

阿科米星与建筑学的再征服

从勒·柯布西耶到班纳姆，无论"一种／另一种建筑／建筑学"具有怎样的含义，它们都不是对"传统／既有建筑学"的完全抛弃。毋宁说，它们是"传统／既有建筑学"的再征服。这意味着某些不可避免的矛盾。一方面，正如班纳姆敏锐指出的，柯布的《走向一种建筑》其实"意味着一种一直存在却被遗忘的绝对或者本质的建筑"。[22] 即使柯布对巴黎美院建筑学"深恶痛绝"，但是他仍将巴黎美院建筑理论教授朱利安·加代的"平面是生成器"作为"给建筑师先生的三项备忘"之一。另一方面，尽管对柯布"对布扎传统的吸收细致入微"的"新瓶装旧酒"的本质提出批评，但是班纳姆自己的"另一种建筑／

014

or the "exquisite taste" of his work. Instead, what fascinates Archmixing is Bawa's extraordinary ability of making hybrid a high level of art beyond any "recognizable system". From Archmixing's perspective, without such ability, little can be achieved in getting on a different architecture.

Archmixing and the Reconquest of Architecture

However divergent in meanings, one thing is for sure in both Le Corbusier and Banham: their quest for an "another architecture" was never fully detached from the so-called "conventional architecture". Rather, it seems more appropriate to say that the architecture they standed for was a reconquest of that very "conventional" one or ones. This means some innevitable contradictions. In one aspect, as Banham sharply pointed out, Corbusier's *Vers une architecture* actually "implies, from internal evidence in the book, an absolute or essential architecture, which had always existed and had merely been mislaid." [XXII] Again in another, despite his criticism of Le Corbusier's "rediscovery of the old in the new", Banham himself appeared in no way to get rid of "conventional architecture" completely. Indeed, all three qualities of the new brutalist object he outlined, that is, "1. Formal legibility of plan; 2. Clear exhibition of structure; and 3. Valuation of materials for their inherent qualities 'as found'", [XXIII] did remind much of the classic orthodoxies of high modernism in architecture, if not Le Corbusier's "Three Reminders". And while

such a outline seemed to have faded away in his later *The New Brutalism: Moral or Aesthetics?*, he referred to, among many others, the brick chapel [fig.13] full of "traditional" craftsmanship by the Swedish architect Sigurd Lewerentz alongside with James Stirling's Engineering Building at University of Leicester [fig.14]. In *The Architecture of the Well-Tempered Environment* that, as said before, extended the significance of Buckminster Fuller to its full implication, he nevertheless seemed to hold back the position by recalling the three basic modes of "environmental management" in human history, the "Conservative", the "Selective" and the "Regenerative". [XXIV] Later, Banham extolled F. L. Wright's Baker House [fig.15] for its rich and improved environmental performance, yet pointing out that the architect got it done "without recourse to any technological novelties". [XXV] Admittedly, like Le Corbusier in his *Vers une architecture*, Banham's call for *une architecture autre* is full of contradictions too. But it is right such contradictions that make them real and more convincing.

Similar contradictions and something of creditability hold true in Archmixing too. It turns back on Le Corbusier's heroic modernism and its obsession with the absolute ideal order of the *Ville Radieuse*. It also stands apart from Banham's predilection for "images" and overtly spokesman gesture for *une architecture autre* that led him to force various architects and buildings into his theoretical framework one after another. In particular, it puts its own pre-history of Deshaus under

建筑学"似乎并没有能够与"传统／既有建筑学"彻底一刀两断。他在《新粗野主义》一文中对"新粗野主义"提出的三个定义——合理的平面布置，清晰的结构，节制的细部表现——其实是相当"传统"的建筑学准则。即便这样的定义似乎在后来的《新粗野主义：道德还是美学？》中不再适用，但他又将瑞典建筑师列沃伦茨极具"传统"工艺精神的砖砌小教堂[图13]与斯特林的莱彻斯特大学工程系馆[图14]相提并论。而作为"另一种建筑／建筑学"晚期"高峰"之一的"环境调控的建筑学"也不只是富勒式"未来主义"的一统天下。它对人类建筑"环境调控"三种基本模式——"保温型""选择型""再生型"的总结，以及对赖特以贝克住宅[图15]为代表的"草原式住宅"没有"任何新奇技术"的"丰富而高效的环境改善"的认识都不是无足轻重的过渡性闲笔。确实，与柯布的《走向一种建筑》一样，班纳姆的"另一种建筑／建筑学"也充满矛盾，然而正是这种"矛盾"才使得它们更加真实，同时也更加可信。

　　类似的矛盾以及由此产生的真实与可信也不可避免存在于阿科米星寻求的"另一种建筑／建筑学"之中。一方

10　史密森夫妇：黄金巷设计竞赛方案
The Smithsons: Golden Lane public housing competition entry

11　史密森夫妇等：院子和亭子
The Smithsons *et al.*: Patio and Pavilion

scrutiny for a critique of an architecture predicated on formal aesthetics and "expression of personal emotions". Bearing in mind that all the three co-founding partners and principal architects of Deshaus completed their architectural education from bachelor's degree to master's in China, and in this sense their work may well represent the most excellent fruits of the century-old Chinese "conventional architecture" education, however, we would truly wonder what this could mean for a reconsideration of the so-called "conventional architecture". The fact is, in the meantime of Archmixing's commitment to moving past "conventional architecture" by dedicating to such issues as "everyday world", "change", "unrecognizable system" and urban "spatial redundancy", their architectural practice is still drawing benefits, knowingly or unknowingly, from that very "conventional architecture". To put it straight, without basis laid by "conventional architecture" education, Archmixing could not have come to achieve much of its transition from design research to architectural practice with such creditability.

　　On the other hand, Archmixing's move beyond "conventional architecture" is by no means less radical, not only by the measure of Le Corbusier and Banham, but also in relation to those pioneers in digital architecure that we have today. In this latter respect, we are told that architecture will be doomed to go digital, and along with it the profoundly changes in terms of design thinking, design process, formal aesthetics, spatial

12　塚本由晴等：《东京制造》
Tsukamoto Yoshiharu *et al.*: Made in Tokyo

13　列沃伦茨：圣彼得教堂
Lewerentz: Chapel in Klippan

14　斯特林：莱彻斯特大学工程系馆
Stirling: Leicester Engineering Building

15　赖特：贝克住宅
Wright: Baker House

16　阿科米星：棉仓城市客厅，常州
Archmixing: Cotton Lab Urban Lounge, Changzhou

面，它不仅超越了柯布式现代"英雄主义"以及对理想化"光明城市"的迷恋，也与班纳姆过于迫切成为"另一种建筑／建筑学"之代言人而不断将不同建筑现象装入一个又一个理论框架的姿态以及对"意象"的情有独钟相去甚远。与此同时，它试图摆脱自己大舍时期的基于"个人情感表达"和形式美学的诉求。然而如果说大舍的三位主持建筑师从本科到硕士都在国内接受建筑学教育——在这样的意义上，我们完全可以将"大舍"视为20世纪中国"传统建筑学"教育结出的最为丰硕的成果之一，那么就在阿科米星致力于"日常"、"变化"、"非识别系统"、城市的"冗余空间"之时，就在他们努力让自己在"非识别系统"中实现对"传统建筑学"的超越之时，他们的建筑实践仍在自觉与不自觉之中得益于"传统建筑学"——事实上，如果没有"传统建筑学"打下的基础，阿科米星从设计研究到建筑实践的转化不会如此令人信服。

另一方面，阿科米星对"传统／既有建筑／建筑学"的超越又不可不谓"激进"，其基金程度不仅与柯布和班纳姆相比有过之而无不及，甚至使自诩走在当代建筑学发展"最前沿"的数字化建筑学信奉者的立场相形见绌。一

perception, materials, construction methods, etc. From Archmixing's perspective, however, like all "tech-optimists" in history, this cult of digital technology still focuses too much on "the creation of the building itself including the design and practice of the idea about constructing system", while "the use end of space which has been ignored by traditional Technological Optimists is still not paid attention to." [XXVI] Yet, Archmixing points out, with the burgeoning development of artificial intelligence, an "invisible revolution", which in connection we might see as opposed to Le Corbusier's visual revolution or Banham's aesthetic revolution, is occurring in form of AGV warehousing system or Amazon automated shop. Consequently, Archmixing writes, "stable and 'heavy' things have become increasingly systematic and invisible. The far-reaching impact on life is no longer the presence and the sight that traditional architecture has always attached importance to, but the huge power transmission racks, drainage facilities, the Internet, logistics systems, and the life network of IoT that are always overlooked". [XXVII]

To this end, the modernist strategies such as the Miesian universal space would make little sense to Archmixing, because, I believe, such kind of supposedly one-size-fit-all strategy still remains too obsessed with architectural object itself, be it in the spirit of Wagner's *Gesamtkunstwerk* or in line with Gropius's "total architecture". Nor is Archmixing amused by Banham's mega-structure and his theoretical endorsement

般认为，在可以预期的未来，数字化技术将带来一场深刻的建筑学革命，在设计思维、设计过程、形式美学、空间感知、材料和建造方式等方面全面超越"传统/既有建筑学"。然而在阿科米星看来，如同史上一切"技术乐观派"一样，对数字化技术的顶礼膜拜其实仍然"围绕着建筑本身的创造，包括设计和实施来构建系统理念，却忽视了空间建成后的使用现实、使用后的改变，以及再投入生产，投入消费的无限循环。就此而言，"数字化技术乐观派"并没有真正超越"传统/既有建筑学"重生产端、轻使用端的固有观念。阿科米星因此指出，正如自动导引运输车（AGV）对仓储系统的改变或者亚马逊无人店对消费系统的改变，随着人工智能的不断发展，一场"看不见的革命"（而非柯布的视觉革命或者班纳姆的美学革命）正在发生："稳定的、'重'的事物已日益系统化、隐形化。对生活影响深远的不再是传统建筑学向来重视的在场和可视物，而是那些常常被视而不见（尽管令人想起柯布《走向一种建筑》"视而不见的眼睛"之说）的巨大的电力输送架、排水设施、互联网、物流系统、物联的生活网络等。"简言之，如果要在数字化技术中实现对建筑学的再征服，就必须"将建筑空间的生产端与使用端同等看待"。[23]

在这一点上，阿科米星无意重蹈密斯式"通用空间""以不变应万变"策略的覆辙——也许，在阿科米星看来，密斯的策略还是过于关注"不变"部分的建筑预设，是瓦格纳"整体艺术"或格罗皮乌斯"整体建筑"的另一种表现形式。与此同时，阿科米星也没有像班纳姆那样试图以阿基格拉姆"插入城市"的巨构形式抵抗"日趋无形的计算机化城市"——在这方面，班纳姆的口号是"我们不希望形式追随功能之后变成虚无缥缈"。[24] 相反，阿科米星提供了对数字化技术及其使用端给建筑学带来的属性变化的另一种展望：①单体建筑趋向无形化；②单体建筑趋向片段化；③单体建筑趋向空间内部化。[25] 按照我的理解，无论是"无形""片段"，还是"空间内部化"，上述三点的本质在于建筑的内部化——"内部化"导致建筑的外形不再那么重要，"片段"则应该理解为建筑内部的空间逻辑和使用逻辑不再是同质的整体，而是可以容纳使用变化的异质性存在。有趣的是，这种"内部化"既可以像阿科米星目前的工作室内部力图营造和表达的随意和无形，也可以如同他们在江苏常州完成的"棉仓城市客厅"改造那

of the Archigram group's "Plug-in City", by which, against the theories of "cyberneticists and O and R men" that "a computerized city might look like anything or nothing", he claimed that "most of us want (a computerized city) to look like something, we don't want form to follow function into oblivion." [XXVIII]

Archmixing's idea of how digitalized technology at the use end may alter architecture's prospect is quite different: first, "single buildings tend to be non-morphological"; second, "single buildings tend to be fragmented"; third, "single buildings tend to be spatially internalize". [XXIX] As far as I understand it, whether understood in "non-morphological", "fragmented" or "internalized" terms, the crucial point lies in the internalization of space, for it is through this internalization that the external appearance of a building turns insignificant. It is worth noticing that in Archmixing's practice, such an "internalization" is not necessarily confined to the casual and formless character of the interior of their current studio; it may well be endowed with a strong sense of rituality as their renovation project in Changzhou, Jiangsu Province, called "Cotton Lab Urban Lounge", has succeeded to realize [fig.16].

As the production of Chinese architecture is shifting from the "era of increment" to the so-called "era of stock", wherein renovation of buildings would become much more substantial to architectural practice, Archmixing's "internalized" thinking, which in the most radical form has been turned on as the "Manifesto of Interiority", [XXX] may provide an incisive insight into and wise tactic towards the professional condition that is about to come. What previously looked like a "trivial" matter of architecture seems now fraught with potential. As a point of departure for the discipline, however, the problems raised directly or indirectly by Archmixing still remain to be answered: how would Archmixing fulfill such potential to the extent that it can truly re-conquer architecture as a whole rather than the "interiority" of buildings? How will it surpass the "static system thinking" of the "Technological Optimists" exemplified by Nakagin Capsule Tower and the Metabolism, [XXXI] and bring changes at the use end into architectural thinking through a more dynamic and effective system? How can such "system" overstep what is conventionally attributed to the notion of "function" and "program" in architecture and their affect to architectural space and form, yet without falling back to Christopher Alexander's "Pattern Language" that ever since its birth proved polemic? Compared to what is now known as "feedback design" through "post-occupancy evaluation" as a tool for measuring the spatial effectiveness of built environments and its "closed-loop system" of "analysis-first-evaluation-after", [XXXII] what could architecture really stand to gain by a shift from "what is architecture" to "what is architecture for" that in Archmixing's case has triggered a call for an "another architecture" at the use end?

Forming an alternative strategy in design challenging

样具有强烈的仪式感。[图16]

应该说，随着中国建筑从"增量"时代进入"存量"时代，阿科米星的这一"内部化思维"无疑具有很强的现实对应性以及对即将到来的大量建筑内部改造的实用潜力。但是就建筑学整体而言不可避免的问题是，阿科米星如何在这样的基础上实现建筑学的再征服（而不是内部征服）？它如何克服"中银舱体大厦"和"新陈代谢主义"代表的"技术乐观派"错误的"系统集成"，[26] 以更为切实有效的"系统"将使用端的变化纳入建筑学思维之中？这样的"系统"如何超越以往建筑学中的"功能"和"内容计划"的含义及其与建筑的空间和形式的关系，如何避免亚历山大"模式语言"的局限，成为一个推动建筑学再次向前发展的范畴？相较于过去数十年逐步发展起来的"使用后评估"反馈设计以及相应的"前策划—后评估机制"，[27] 从"建筑／建筑学是什么？"到"建筑／建筑学有何用？"的转变究竟能够在怎样的意义上通过"使用端"触发建筑／建筑学的另一种可能？也许，沿着业已开启的"另一种建筑／建筑学"寻求之路，阿科米星在这些问题上的思考和解答将在下一个十年满足我们的最大期待与想象。

the "conventional architecture" is an undertaking that demands courage and perseverant hardworking bound to confronting with intractable polemics and dilemmas. What it calls for is a more hybrid and more accommodative architecture. Hopefully, along with the trajectory already started in the quest for an "another architecture", the outcome of Archmixing's next decade would be the best we should expect for.

长期从事建筑历史理论和现代建筑理论研究，有大量学术论文发表于国内外建筑期刊杂志。译著《建构文化研究——论19世纪和20世纪建筑中的建造诗学》获2009年第二届中国建筑图书奖。《王骏阳建筑学论文集》第一、二册由同济大学出版社光明城于2017年和2018年出版。近年的代表性论文有《"历史的"与"非历史的"——八十年后再看佛光寺》、"The Everyday: A Degree Zero Agenda for Contemporary Chinese Architecture"等。

Professor of Architecture at School of Architecture and Urban Planning, Nanjing University, China.
He has been published widely in architectural journals and other publications in China and internationally. He is the Chinese translator of Studies in Tectonic Culture: The Poetics of Construction in Nineteenth and Twentieth Century Architecture by Kenneth Frampton. The first and second volumes of his own anthology in architectural theory, history and criticism came out in 2017 and 2018, both published by Tongji University Press. His recent publications include "The 'Historical' and the 'Non-historical' —Towards an Epistemological Reflection Eighty Years after the Discovery of Foguang Monastery" in Architectural Journal, China, 2018, and "The Everyday: A Degree Zero Agenda for Contemporary Chinese Architecture" in Architectural Research Quarterly, UK, 2017.

对谈
Dialogues

葛明✕庄慎：
城市建筑学的核心问题

GE Ming ✕ ZHUANG Shen:
Core Issue on Urban Architecture

1   永嘉路口袋广场，区域模型
Zone model of Pocket Plaza, Yongjia Road

时间：2019 年 8 月 15 日

地点：东南大学建筑学院中大院

葛明（后简称"葛"）：你刚才说阿科米星没有特定的风格，不过我认为还是有一种内在特性的。

作为同行，自然会关心你这些设计所发生的技术、社会背景，但除此之外，我还关心何以你明明不追求风格，但事实上这些设计给人留下了深刻的印象。其背后的原因，我个人的理解是因为你们有一个非常明确的关注点，就是"改变"。你们对"改变"非常敏感，扣住了城市建筑学里的某个核心问题，所以能够产生一种没有风格的方式 [图1]；此外一定又有别的原因，让你们的设计始终是给人留下深刻印象的。这些原因我很在意，也尝试做了一点归纳。

第一点，首先是一种我称之为"结构体"的东西。它既是结构，又像是一个装置，它是一个"物"，包括你们在室内做的一类设计，也包括在建筑上对一个阳台的改变 [图2,3]，等等。这类设计手段熟练，是非常有创造性的。其次，感觉你们十分擅长于用一种"片段"的方式，比如一些老房子改造，刻意把房子做成片段的方式，产生的空间很特别，度也掌握得好。片段一般看似不太能形成一致性，但我认为片段有的时候反而加速形成了一致性。

这类"结构体"和"片段"构成了一个强有力的逻辑，而且你们有越做越熟练的

2　徐汇区龙华街道敬老院立面改造
Facade Renovation for Longhua Street
Elder Care Center, Xuhui district

Time:　Aug. 15, 2019.

Venue:　Zhong Da Building, School of Architecture, Southeast University

Ge Ming (GM): You just mentioned that Atelier Archmixing has no style preference. While I insist that there is a kind of intrinsic feature.

As peers, in addition to naturally paying attention to the technical and social background of your designs, I would investigate why your buildings have made a strong impression though they are not designed with a certain style. I think you've got a very clear concern, the variation, transformation or change. You are very sensitive to "change", which made you stick to some key points in urban architecture [fig. 1]. That's why your works are designed with no style. However, your designs have been impressive for other reasons. I am quite curious about these reasons and tried to make a summary.

Firstly, among these works, the thing that impressed me most is a "structure". I see it as a structure, a device or an "object". It includes the work you did indoors, even a renovation of a balcony [fig. 2. 3]. These are very skillful and mature designs, very creative. Secondly, you are skilled in applying method named "fragment", like renovations of old buildings, dividing the building into fragments, creating special space with perfect moderation. I am deeply impressed. Normally, fragment is less related to unity, but in my opinion, it contributes to unity.

Your strong logic consists of this "structure" and "fragment", and your work is getting more skillful. I am surprised when you dealt with fragment accurately, applied it to an appropriate structure. You have found some design logic on urban architecture.

3　上海文化信息产业园一期B4/B5地块
B4/B5 Blocks of Shanghai Culture &
Information Industrial Park, Phase I

趋势。可以说，大部分情况下能这么准确地切入到一个合适的片段，应对到一个合适的结构体，让我吃惊，觉得你们已找到了某种城市建筑的设计逻辑。

城市建筑，简单来说就需要建筑在城市"之间"，而且能应对快速的变化，或者就像在城市建筑学里经常说的"一个房子是一个小城市，一个城市是一个大建筑"。但如果这类理念只用哲学话语说，而没有找到具体有力的方式去做，其实就可惜了。但如果一个老房子里嵌入一个新的结构体，就有可能让房子变成城市，或者是在城市中构筑结构体，就可能让城市结构之间产生连续，这些就是具体的做法。所以我觉得你们可能已经找到了一种方法，但在看你们的研究和表述的时候，总觉得你们对这点还稍微羞涩了一些。

第二点，拿你们非常有标识性的工作室搬家研究和设计来说，你们常常先找一个现成的建筑，改造、装修做得很少，直接就摆家具，看能产生一种什么样的状态 [图4]。就是说，如何"摆家具"成了一个重要的措施，在我看来这也是你们的一个标志性动作。在一个既有的房子里直接靠摆家具摆出建筑的感觉，而不是靠改造、装修，这一点跨越了通常的分类。这也恰巧是城市建筑学或者是"改变"研究特别需要重视的一种方式。因为城市建筑有时候变更快到改造、装修都跟不上，比如说一个商铺，可能半年一换，难道非要每次都重新装修？能不能靠摆家具就解决问题？同时，这对房子的设计也就提出了新的要求，也要求更讲究，因为像中国园林，一个庸俗的人和一个高雅的人使用它，园林的气质也会不一

4-1 2016-2017年阿科米星虹口工作室，家具布置
Hongkou Office (2016–2017), arranging furniture

4-2 小白楼工作室，平面摆家具模型
Little White House (2018–), arranging furniture in model

023

Urban architecture, to put it simply, the architecture shall stay between the city and resist rapid changes. It is often said in Urban Architecture: "a building is a small city; a city is a large building", I think your logic must have conformed to above similar features. However, it will be a pity if we only talk about these ideas as philosophical discourse without applying them to practice effectively. These concrete working methods include: design a new structure in an old building and turn it into a city or design a structure in a city and make urban structure connected with each other. So, I believe perhaps you have found a new method, but you are modest and prudent to explain it in the research or talk about it.

Secondly, taking several distinctive cases, such as your moving studio program as an example, you often picked an existing building, directly arranged furniture with very simple renovation or decoration. Then you tried to find out what had happened. That is to say "arranging furniture" turns into a significant strategy, for me, this is your identifying operation [fig. 4]. Creating a new building by only arranging interior furniture instead of relying on renovation or decoration, you've thought outside the box. This is exactly a valuable method that needs highlighting for Urban Architecture or research on "change". Because the urban building changes so fast that renovations or decorations can't keep the pace. If the business updates every half year in shops, shall we re-decorate it each time? Is it possible to solve the problem by arranging furniture? Meanwhile, you may need to devote particular care to the new requirements, sometimes may more sophisticate. Like classical Chinese garden, the character of the garden usually relies on the character of the residence. It sounds really abstract, but for Urban Architecture, this is a big topic. Your working philosophy seems close to it: accomplishing the effect with minimum effort.

样。这听上去很抽象，但是对于城市建筑学来说是个大话题。你们做的建筑有这种感觉：用最小的方式来达成效果。

但从另外一个角度来说，我觉得你们还可以更彻底。类似这种"摆家具"或者说"摆环境物"的方式，和"结构体"并用，可能才是最好的状态，会特别放松。约翰·海杜克也做结构体，包括"假面舞会"，它是一种以结构体象征建筑的方式；阿尔多·罗西也是，它嵌在房子里，既是真实的结构体又能使用。这些结构体其实有不少人在做，但你们因为可以与"摆家具"同时推进，就会有突破。

庄慎（后简称"庄"）：嗯！我觉得"结构体""摆家具"这两个概念很形象，提炼切中了方法要害，帮我们总结了工作特征。我们的工作的确有这方面的倾向，我想它来自那些影响我们工作的因素。

关于"结构体"的方式倾向，一是来自城市建筑的现象。我们研究城市建筑的时候发现很多自发性的改造很有意思，它们都讲究有效性，会用尽量有效的建造方式。很多时候自发改造的阳台，自发增加的一个辅助空间，或是一些微小的调整，就是一个局部构筑物或者片段的状态。类似的现象很多，我们观察总结了一些原则，就试着直接用在一些项目设计里，比如桦墅乡村工作室 [图5]。二是因为这种片段式的形式逻辑我们特别熟悉。因为这种形式逻辑其实是一个依附关系，改变的片段附着在原建筑物上面，会提示这是一种变化，原来建筑是一个既有物，新的结构体并不属于原来那个体系，可能是

5　南京桦墅乡村工作室，模型
　　Model of Huashu Rural Studio

024

But from another perspective, you could step forward more thoroughly. To combine this "arranging furniture" or "arranging objects" with "the structure" may achieve the best state, also quite relaxing. John Hejduk also works on structure, including the "masque", the method applying structure to symbolize architecture. And so does Aldo Rossi. The structure is set in the building, and it is real and useful. Many architects are working on these structures, but you are working on these together with "arranging furniture", therefore have achieved a breakthrough.

Zhuang Shen (ZS): Absolutely, "structure" and "arranging furniture" are two vivid and precise concepts. They are the essence of our working methods and the summary of our working characteristics. In our work, we are inclined to these two concepts. This derives from some factors that influence our work. Two things have provided directions for our work on the structure. One is the phenomena of urban architecture. In our research, we found many spontaneous renovations very interesting. They highlight efficiency, tend to applying most effective construction methods. Most spontaneous renovation of balcony, addition of auxiliary space or some tiny adjustments are partial structures or fragments. There are plenty of such cases. Through observation, we have drawn some working principles and applied them to some design projects, like Huashu Rural Studio [fig. 5]. Another reason is that we are quite familiar with this formal logic of fragments, which is actually an attachment relationship. The changed fragments are attached to the original building. They present a change: the original building is an existing object, while the new structure doesn't belong to the original system. It perhaps belongs to another system. The new structure and the original one can form different

另外一个体系，两者可以根据需要呈现不同状态。

关于工作室"摆家具"这件事情，我认为跟我们对城市建筑与空间的看法有关。我习惯把它看成是一个中性的、在时间变化里的自然状态。我对于功能与使用的态度是，不一定让空间来适应我，而是允许我去适应空间。适应的过程中就产生了对它相对轻的调整，而不是重的改变，这形成的结果反过来又影响决定了在其中工作的我们的行为模式。不同的空间，产生的行为模式都不一样。我觉得这也是在那个搬家的过程当中，我们体会到的宝贵的经验，真正关乎使用的某些道理。我们也在工作室搬家的过程当中发现，事实上城市内部空间的腾退非常快，它不断地转化，跟最初设定的使用有时候毫无关系，但是一次次被改变的状态与最初的物质空间积累起来，这就是我们说的"空间冗余"与"中性的建筑"的概念。

葛：关于"结构体"对于房子与城市关系的作用，我常常思考为什么有用，因为结构体的出现有时候会让城市和建筑变得更复杂。这涉及一个有意思的事情，中国的城市快速变化中最缺的就是形制，对比之下，欧洲的传统城市或者城市建筑学则是形制太充分了。中国因为城市化太快而缺少形制，所以有的时候需要些稳定的东西。你们的结构体为什么给人深刻印象？我想是因为它不知不觉提供了一些产生形制的机会，可以让人感觉稳定下来，只不过这个形制或许还需要更多样。

庄：我觉得中国当代城市的这一形制和我们传统建筑学说的典型性不太一

states based on the requirements.

"Arranging furniture" has something to do with our view on urban architecture and space. In my opinion, it's neutral; it's a natural state in changing time. We keep an open mind on functions and use. The space doesn't need to fit our working method. Instead, we will adapt to the space. Then, in the process of adaptation, instead of big change, we make small adjustment, the result of which in turn determines and affects our work. Different spaces cause different behavior patterns. This is the real experience about usage we have learnt from and the working philosophy we applied to those office moves. We also found that the urban interior space changed rapidly. Sometimes the final spatial status has nothing to do with initial design. But when the changes and initial material space are progressively accumulated, the concepts of spatial redundancy and neutral architecture are formed.

GM: I always think why "structure" is useful for the relation between buildings and cities, since sometimes structure makes cities and buildings more complex. What is interesting is that there aren't enough architectural typologies in China's rapid urbanization, while there are too many of them in traditional European cities or urban architecture. Sometimes stable things are necessary because Chinese cities are changing too fast to take shapes. Why your structures are so impressive? I think that's because it is a method to build typologies, to let people feel stable, of course, we may need more diversity.

ZS: This so-called typology in contemporary Chinese cities is different from the typicality in traditional architecture discipline. It was formed by repeated accumulation of quantities. There are many variable architectural phenomena

样，它是由数量的重复积累和变化形成的。城市中的很多变化的建筑现象，不断地出现在各类局部中，每个都有相似的内在形成逻辑，但形式各不相同，没有一个是可以称为最典型的。我想这其实就是我们俗称的一种典型的"涌现"现象。

葛：是的。另外，我自己也喜欢结构体，比如说坡法的使用[1]，但方式跟你可能不一样，你的结构体来源和手段更多样，更愿意出人意料。而我的那种像是重锤，希望抡到后来水平能提高，让重锤看起来有点轻。你的好像是一会儿轻一会儿重，这可能是由你坚持的这种城市建筑的状态来决定的，这是我的理解。

接着继续说"摆家具"，刚才你的话使我有了更深的印象，基本上也肯定了我对你的观察。我写过一篇《日常生活——空间的方法》[2]的文章，里面涉及空间类型学，空间类型学必须跟地点有关。比如说，你在现有的工作室中创造了很多的角落空间，其实就是利用一种地点产生了空间类型学。你们恭城路工作室的相邻房间都有门洞门槛 [图6]，显然不太想让人过去，但又是可以跨越的，还有虹口工作室突然出现的桥 [图7]，在我看来这些都很有意思。所以就我的理解，等将来时间久了，"摆家具"相对于结构体可能是一种更加具有创造力的方式。

"摆家具"还与另一个概念相关。我看了你们的许多项目设计，有几个项目我特意区分出来了，像这种的我将之称为"大平面"。平面大的时候该怎么处理呢？巴瓦有巴瓦的大平面做法，巴拉干、布扎也都有各自的处理方式。但是在城市建

6　徐家汇工作室，连通的洞口
　　Connecting holes, Xujiahui Office

7　虹口工作室，连接合伙人工作室和公共办公区
　　的"桥"
　　"Bridge" addition between the principals' office
　　and the main workplace, Hongkou Office

in the city, constantly happening in all kinds of parts. Each phenomenon contains similar internal formative logic, while different in forms, thus none of them could individually be seen as the most typical. This is what we referred to as an emergence of typicalities.

GM: Yes. Besides, I like structure, but the methods I applied are different, as the use of slope method[1]. Your structure is more varied and unexpected in origin and methods. But my method is more like a heavy hammer, wish it can look lighter when I can use it more skillfully. In my opinion, your design methods applied to structure are more varied, perhaps resulting from the condition of urban architecture you stick to.

Let's move back to "arranging furniture". What you just mentioned has left me a deeper impression, which made me sure that I understood you correctly. In my article "Everyday Life Design Methodology of Space"[2]. I discussed spatial typology. In my understanding, spatial typology must relate to place. For instance, you've created many corner spaces, resulting in various spatial typologies in one place. There are door openings and thresholds between adjacent rooms in your studio on Gongcheng Road, Xujiahui [fig. 6]. Obviously, the designer didn't want people to go from one into another, but it is possible to stride across. The bridge in your Hongkou Studio [fig. 7] has a similar effect. All these spaces seem very interesting to me. In my opinion, with more time, "arranging furniture" may grow into a more creative method compared with "structure".

"Arranging furniture" is also relevant to another concept. I've checked many of your designs and intentionally separated some of them. I call these cases "large plan". How to deal with plan of large scale? Geoffrey Bawa, Luis Barragán, Beaux-Arts

筑中间，不可能做到那么诗意，我觉得你们可能不知不觉创造出了一种城市建筑中大平面的办法。它有建筑学的意义，有创造力。之前你对"改变"的各种研究中，感觉提性能这点多一些。我想性能是重要的，但可能不是核心，类似塚本由晴说的行为也不是核心。我在系统地看了你们设计的各个工作室平面后，非常振奋，刚才的《日常生活——空间的方法》里提到了空间类型学，城市建筑里的大平面问题要面对的正是这个感觉。

庄：之前你说的"摆家具"，现在我们讨论的"大平面"，这两者和我们在工作中探讨的"内部"主题有关系，也在相关的设计里面有运用。一是所谓"大平面"以何种形式呈现。比如金山岭艺术接待中心设计 [图8]，最初使用设定为售楼部，后来我们建议业主做一个多义空间。用一个中性的大空间来鼓励未来的布置多义化，同时用来创造与周围风景的新关系。另外，还有一种不是大平面的"内部"。比如 YoungBird 室内空间的改造 [图9]，这个房子里原本的两个房间是完全隔离、没有关系的，但是我们对空间做了一次手术——选择的位置比较特别——在空间高低最纠结的地方将局部用体积减法切开了，切开之后会形成一个在不同内部、内外空间之间的空洞，这使各部分相互关联起来。这是对既有内部的一种"破坏"，是另外一种方式。构筑物"依附"也好，在"大平面里摆家具"也好，把完整的东西"破坏"也好，对我们来说都是本质上一致的手法。

8　阿那亚金山岭艺术中心，概念模型
Conceptual model, Art Center of Aranya, Jinshanling

027

may have their own way. But urban buildings are difficult to achieve such poetic. In my opinion, you've unconsciously invented a method of dealing with "large plan" for urban buildings. It's creative and meaningful for architecture discipline. Before, the performance was most frequently mentioned in your researches. I think performance is important but should not be taken as a core issue, and neither is the behavior mentioned by Yoshiharu Tsukamoto. I am really encouraged after systematically investigated the "large plan" designed in your studios, I think the space typology discussed in "Everyday Life: Design Methodology of Space" is exactly what the "large plan" in urban architecture deals with.

ZS: Both "Arranging furniture" and "large plan" are related to the "'interior" issue in our work, both strategies have been applied to relevant designs. One application is in which way the so-called "large plan" is presented? For instance, the Reception Center of Aranya [fig. 8] was originally designated as a sales house. Later, we suggested the client to turn it into a multi-purpose space. Providing a large neutral space to stimulate future various arrangements, meanwhile defining a fresh relationship with the surrounding landscape. The second application concerns plan with moderate size. For example, in the Interior Renovation of YoungBird New Office [fig. 9], although the two rooms inside were totally separated, we rearranged the space in a very special position, where intriguing space heights meet. We partially cut this area and form a hole connecting different interior, between inside and outside, thus different parts connect with each other. This is a destruction of existing interior space, also a different working method. Whether it is the attachment of structures or "arranging furniture in large plan" or "destruction" of the whole

9　YoungBird室内空间改造
Interior Renovation of YoungBird Office

葛： 我理解的处理大平面的核心并不只是空间分割，还包括类似"摆家具"的方式，这其实跟产生新的模式有关系。比如说对于一个大平面，在布扎里就是服务与被服务的关系，路易斯·康就会用平面分割的方法。但在一个大平面中，像你们特意把很多房间打通，留下很多角落、很多门槛，表面是不方便、方便并呈，其实是表达了空间的意义——这种方法在我看来都可以称之为"摆家具"，这事很有力量。

> **庄：** 我理解虽然我们用的词不一样，但是我们讲的意思是一样的。这个事情是一个蛮微妙的东西，它既有一些暗示，同时又有错位。

葛： 对，这种方式不只是空间分割，更不是装修。现代建筑中也有这种情况，密斯·凡·德·罗的设计在某些方面其实就是"摆家具"，但他还是古典的做法，是用家具来完成一个构成，所以并不特别应对城市建筑中的大平面问题，大家也不觉得这一方法好用。但我始终觉得"摆家具"本身可以是一种建筑设计的突破。

> **庄：** 我明白你的意思，我们的工作有一块是"向内部进发"。

葛： 我自己也有个研究，称之为"桌子空间"[3]。其实就是摆桌子，摆得让人感觉不一样，以桌子为中心来做。桌子有点碍手碍脚，但是实际上桌子又最常用。

> **庄：** 我想这跟你前面讲的"物"的概念是有关的。比如说桌子是个普通物，而通过设计摆放它被赋予了不同的意义，比如说碍手碍脚或是顺畅，但它同时本身还有桌子"本体"这件事，我觉得这个可能跟你刚刚讲的"结构体"的精神一致。

thing, all these methods are essentially unified.

GM: In my understanding, the key for dealing with "large plan" concerns not only spatial separation, but also methods including "arranging furniture". This has something to do with producing new modes. For example, in the Beaux-Art system, the large plan consists of the relationship between "serve and served" spaces, while for Louis Kahn, it consists in plane segmentation. But in your designs, you intentionally knocked through many rooms, left many corners and thresholds, which juxtaposed convenience and inconvenience. In fact, all these have expressed the significance of space and I call this working method "arranging furniture". It's quite powerful.

> **ZS:** Although we are explaining with different words, now I understand we are referring to the same thing. It is subtle. and contains hints and dislocations.

GM: Exactly, this is neither spatial segmentation nor spatial decoration. It also happens in modern architecture. Actually some of Mies van der Rohe's designs were "arranging furniture", but his methods are classic, applying furniture as spatial composition.. This is nct a suitable solution for arranging large plan in urban architecture, and we don't think his methods work really well. Nevertheless, I always find that "arranging furniture" is a breakthrough of architectural design.

> **ZS:** I know what you are talking about. Part of our work is "heading for interior".

GM: "Space of table"[3] is one of my own researches. Put simply, it concerns how to make difference through arranging tables, here tables were taken as the core issue. Tables stand in the way but they are actually most commonly used.

> **ZS:** This is related to the concept you mentioned before, the *Thing*. For example, through designed placement, the ordinary table is given special meaning. No matter the table stands in the way or not, table is table. It's the same as the

葛：接下来的话题是关于你刚才介绍的研究框架。我在一开始就讲述了这一观点：你们做的工作之所以跟很多艺术家、网红建筑师不一样，是因为你们有某种内在的一致性，你们所关注的快速等话题还同时结合了建筑学中的一些基本问题。当然建筑学的基本问题有些会发生改变，但有些不需要改变，我觉得这是你们的工作非常重要的价值。

比如在城市建筑学中，研究一层平面是最基本的方法之一，柯林·罗、阿尔多·罗西、昂格尔斯都做过这方面的研究。城市里存在大量的一层平面，按照普通的观念来说，一层其实不好用，到处被人偷窥，但是有的时候又是最抢手的，因为商业价值最高，所以如何正确理解这样的城市空间？一层平面太重要了，公共、私密……机会全在这里，是一个研究城市建筑学基本问题的切入对象。

从这个角度，我会更在意你们工作室的作品中那些在"改变"中有稳定内容的项目。这些稳定的东西之所以有特点，是因为它们是在有了"改变"思维之后稳定的东西。你们的这些项目大部分都是这样，所以我觉得它们很棒，我觉得还可以进一步凸显这种研究的建筑学意义。

   庄：平时做设计的时候，我们会用很多设计方法，这些方法被我们当作实现目的的手段，大部分情况下它们是隐形的。同时，大部分时间这些方法是组合的、灵活的，我们觉得，将不同的方式进行组合是一种创造性的设计方法，这些被应用的、组合的方式，既有新的也有旧的，我想，那些你认为稳

"structure" you mentioned before.

GM: The next topic goes to the research framework you have just introduced. I would like to repeat my point, your work is different from that of many artists or internet star architects, because there is some inherent consistency in your work and the topics you concerned, like speedy, are combined with some basic issues in architecture. Certainly, some of these basic issues will change but some don't need change. This is the most important value of your work.

Like in Urban Architecture, one of the basic architectural methods is to research the ground floor. Colin Rowe, Aldo Rossi and Oswald Mathias Ungers have all made researches on this field. Ground floors are everywhere in the city. As common sense, the ground floor is too exposed, but it is also very popular since it produces commercial value. How to understand this kind of urban space? The ground floor is so important, public, private... full of opportunities, it is a good starting point for examining the basic issues in urban architecture.

From this perspective, I will care more about those projects you have contained stable things in "changes". These stable things are characteristic because they are formed by thinking of changes. Most of your projects are like this and they are really great. It's necessary to further emphasize the architectural significance of these researches.

   ZS: We usually apply various design methods in our work. They are used to achieve our purpose and are invisible in most cases. Meanwhile, in most chances, they can mix and are rather flexible. It is a creative design strategy combined by various methods. Both old and new approaches are put into application and combination. I suppose, so-called stable gene you have

定性的基因就是在这样的组合应用中被保留下来的。

葛： 在我的观察里，你们不断在呈现如何达到稳定和变化之间的平衡。它或许是一种灵活应变的策略，看到什么就能快速地找到一招以解决这个问题，但又有所不同。因为你们长期关注日常变化，处理相关问题，所以作品中逐渐产生了一种出人意料的质感，这确实让人对你们所提倡的这种城市建筑学充满期待。

庄： 城市建筑学在中国的确有非常好的可以观察、实践的条件，它形成的速度、数量非常大，而且里面又有各种复杂变化的因素。

葛： 是的，可能没有哪个地方有比这里更快的、更大的变化。以此为核心来处理一些事情，然后寻找对建筑学本身的一种理解，这与欧洲或者其他地方的状况是不一样的。面对这种快，其实我们要做的事情是从日常到日常，然后突然地呈现形制。改变一次就增加了一次形成形制的力量，城市的改变才有价值。

你们的不少方案有这种感觉。但是有的方案，有时候可能因为特别想探讨技术的变化、对性能的理解、方法上的变化，或新概念的提出等，在过程中反而会有一定的磕绊。这些内容有时候会助力你的设计，有时候会对你形成限制，让你走向一条分岔的路。有的房子带有一种犹豫，我也觉得这是一种非常真实的实验状态。但是我建议不妨把有些分叉砍掉，但是又不要砍光，分叉的力量再集中一点。我想这样的话可能就会形成一种推进。

庄： 我最想听到的就是这些建议，对于我们来说，目前这是一个阶段性的小

10   2016年城市研究：逆向还原，城市内巷分析图解
2016 Urban Study: "Analytic Restoration", axonometric of Urban Inner Lane

found was retained in this process.

GM: As far as I am concerned, you are keeping to present the balance between stability and change. It can tackle the problem in a clear-cut, seems like a flexible measure, and it is also different. Through constantly dealing with everyday change, your work gradually achieved some kind of unexpectation. I am really looking forward to the Urban Architecture you advocated.

ZS: The conditions of Chinese Urban Architecture you concerned are very suitable for observation and practice. Urban buildings are developed rapidly and accumulated in huge volumes. They also contain a variety of complex change factors.

GM: You are right. Changes in other fields are less notable than in the urban facilities in China. Based on these results, we carry out our work and obtain understandings of architecture itself. This is totally different from the situation in Europe or anywhere else in the world. Facing such a fast change, we must be stick to everyday and create our own typology. Every time change happens, the power of the form grows stronger, which makes urban change valuable.

Many of your designs have given me such feelings. While some designs were stuck in the process because too much technical changes and understanding of performance were discussed, because working methods were changed or new concept was proposed. Sometimes these factors contribute to your design, sometimes limit you and force you to make choice. They created a dilemma for you, a real experimental state. But I recommend that we make choices, with fewer choices, become more focus while maintain the diversity. Then our work can be pushed forward.

ZS: I have long hoped to hear these advices. For us, this publication is a period-

结，最需要的就是建议，也让我们以后的工作更有效地聚焦。

葛：我觉得分叉不是你的劣势，是你的优势。因为你是一个擅长与分叉打交道的人。你的设计中也会有很多中国的元素，包括离合、景致、行为等，一个善于分叉的人才能面对"变"的问题，有柔韧的姿态。就像是一棵树，枝多了以后才能够应对变，但是长得太满了的话就要适当修剪。我觉得你跟华老师一样有一种知识分子的状态，所以对于这种分叉总是愿意以一种平和的心态来面对。

庄：我们想整理清楚自己的认知结构框架，也是为了防止某种倾向：我们经常跟日常的城市现象、城市建筑打交道，其实很容易沉溺进去，没办法跳出来 [图 10、11]。这有好处也有坏处，坏处就是作为实践者，你一下子被这种状态所俘获，沉醉于自己做的那些动作里，会没办法让自己的认识变得更加冷静一点，这个是我觉得不行的地方。你得有一个指导性的东西，能够在认知的高度，或者是在设计研究的高度重新跳出来。这也是我后来慢慢坚持习惯就这些方面写一些东西的原因。

葛：对于城市建筑学本身，对于"快""改变""限制"产生的一些事情，我觉得你们已经有了一种基本的格局，这是这十年来特别有价值的地方。如果要我说期待的话，就是刚才提到的那种从日常转到日常中形制的感觉是否可以更清晰，这也是对当代中国有价值的地方。还有就是反复提到的"大平面"，它的背后就是城市建筑学的一个核心。此外还有一个密度问题，人与建筑之间的密度，人与人

11   2016年城市研究：逆向还原，四川北路日本海军特别陆战队司令部旧址
2016 Urban Study: "Analytic Restoration", Japanese Special Marine Command Former Site, North Sichuan Road

ic summary. What we need most are advices, which will make our work more efficient and focus.

GM: To make a choice is not your weakness. It's your superiority because you are good at making choice. There are many Chinese elements in your design, including separation and unification, landscape and behavior, etc. Only flexible person, person who knows how to make choice well can handle "changes". Just like a tree, it can adjust change with enough branches, but if there are too many branches, it's necessary to cut and trim. Ms. Hua and you are intellectual professionals. You prefer to make these choices with grace and poise.

ZS: We want to clearly shape our cognitive frame in order to avoid some tendency: since we often work with everyday urban phenomena and urban architecture, we are easy to get trapped in the mindset and fail to think out of the box. [fig. 10–11] This would have the advantages and disadvantages. The disadvantages lie in: as a practitioner, you get trapped in this state all at once and get indulged in this work, which makes you fail to take a rational look. You need to know how to guide the work. You should jump out from the reality based on a cognitive latitude or a design research perspective. This is why later I slowly get used to write something on this.

GM: You´ve already created a basic structure for Urban Architecture, for something related with "fastness", "change" and "restriction". This is the most valuable thing you´ve achieved in last ten years. If I am supposed to raise further expectations, that will be, if the typology "from everyday to everyday" could be clearer, this is of much value to our country. Besides, the "large plan" we repeatedly mentioned, the core of urban architecture is right behind it. Furthermore, the topic of density,

之间的密度。这些话题的探索，其实不可能是一个工作室所能完成的，而是现在中国建筑师需要共同思考的。对于它，坦率地说，大家还非常不敏感，像你们工作室一样有这种敏感度的非常少见。

庄：我觉得建筑师可能应该主动去认识这样一个事情。中国的建筑师，我觉得不一定说要创造所谓的中国建筑，而是说他们面临的条件具有中国的独特性，别人没办法进来研究，但其中应该可以得出普适性的研究。你有这个条件，所以就应该去做这个事情。

葛：是的，这需要大力提倡。我觉得中国的建筑教育应该有一些使命。庄老师，你有没有想过，将来你要是收弟子，准备传授他什么？举个例子，如果让你带研究生，你准备让他写什么？

庄：哈哈哈，我从来没有想过这个问题，太突然了。你今天提的这个问题可能会对我的下一个十年有影响。你讲的其他问题有的我也想过，但这个问题我真的是一点都没有想过，可能因为我不是老师……

葛：我提这个问题其实跟你的主题"改变"有关系。改变有的时候是时间的改变，你想，有一个弟子去传承，就需要一个试图让你的工作历史化的过程，但不是把你变成一个纪念碑。

庄：如果我以后真的有一个弟子，我希望他能够持续地对这个东西有反思、质疑，这个是我一定会要求的。

032

the density between people and architecture, between different people. The explorations on these topics couldn't be completed by only one studio. All Chinese architects should take this responsibility. To be frank, most of us are not so sensitive to this, but your studio is ahead of us, which is rare.

ZS: I think architect should actively realize that it isn't necessary for Chinese architects to create so-called Chinese architecture. But the conditions for local practices are of Chinese characteristics. Architects can do universal researches on them. Architects from other regions may have limited chances to fully understand these conditions and achieve useful guidance, while Chinese contemporary architects possess convenient access to all these. So, of course, we should do this kind of research.

GM: You're right. This shall be strongly encouraged. China's architectural education should have a clear mission. Have you ever thought if you accept a disciple, what will you teach him? For example, if you are a postgraduate tutor, which thesis topic will you give your student?

ZS: (Laughing...), I haven't stopped to think about this. Perhaps, your question will affect me in the next ten years. I've thought about some of your questions, but I've never thought about this question at all. Maybe it is because I am not a professor...

GM: In fact, My question is related to your theme "change". Sometimes change happens as time goes by. If you want a disciple to inherit, it is actually to historicize your work, but it doesn't mean that you need to be converted into a monument.

ZS: If I do have a disciple in the future, I wish he can keep reflections and queries on this. I'm sure I will ask him to do that.

葛明

东南大学建筑学院教授 、副院长。

主要设计作品：威尼斯国际建筑双年展中国馆之——"默默"，2008 年；如园，2010 年；微园，2014 年；春园，2018。

主要研究领域：建筑理论，设计方法，教学法，发表《体积法》《结构法》《不定形法》《黑》《微园记》等论文；参编《园林与建筑》《建筑研究》等著作。

GE Ming

Professor, Vice dean of School of Architecture in Southeast University, Nanjing.

His main works include "Murmur" as one of the Chinese Pavilions in 11th International Architecture Biennale in Venice (2008), Ruyuan Garden (2010), Weiyuan Garden (2014), Spring Garden (2018).

His main research fields include Architectural theory, Design methodology and Pedagogy. He has published papers on methods from space, typology, conceptual architecture, garden and so on.

034

鲁安东 × 庄慎：
设计如何适应未来改变
LU Andong × ZHUANG Shen: How Can Design Adapt to Future Change

1   棉仓城市客厅 内部
Interior, Cotton Lab Urban Lounge

时间：2019 年 8 月 15 日
地点：南京金银街某咖啡馆

鲁安东：(后简称"鲁") 中国在技术上并不一定先进，但是中国有一种使技术迅速社会化的条件，所以使得某些可能性在中国更早、更快地变成了一种具体实践。你的建筑实践虽然是在一个自我世界的范围里，但它具有实验性，甚至不应只是被看作在中国本地的实验性。在中国本地，你的建筑很多时候反而会被认为是在处理问题。你确实是在处理真实的问题，只不过你认为的这个真实跟大多数建筑师理解的已经不太一样了。但是如果从一个更大的范围来看，这种对真实问题的处理已经构成了一种实验。所以我觉得从超越本土的视角来看，这些对他人应该是非常有启发的事情。

庄慎：(后简称"庄") 我们感兴趣的的确是发生在建筑、技术与人们使用之间的普遍性的问题，而不仅仅是地方性、本地化的问题。

鲁： 这个事情比较有趣的就是这里。人跟环境的交互方式带来一种日常性，我们关注的这种技术甚至是媒体的日常化，从负面的角度来说是对人的异化，从正面的角度来说是使用端的改变，在我看来二者是一样的。这样的一个状态才是真实的，才是设计的起点。

庄： 没错。从这里回到开始设计之前，技术或其他因素的变化带来改变，原来的建筑方式、观念可能不再适用，但是它们带来的新东西是否好，我们也

Time: Aug. 15, 2019
Venue: Cafe on Jinyin Street, Nanjing

Lu Andong (LA): China is not a technologically advanced country, but in this country, there is a condition for the rapid socialization of technology, which turns certain possibilities into concrete practices earlier and faster in China. Although your architectural practice is within the scope of a self-world, it is experimental, and should not even be regarded as an experiment merely in China. In China, on the contrary, people may feel that your building is quite often a solution. Actually, you're dealing with real problems, but the reality in your mind is different from what most architects understand. On a larger scale, the approach to "real" problems has become an experiment. So I think, from a perspective beyond the native land, it should be very enlightening to others.

Zhuang Shen (ZS): Yes, what we are interested in is universal architectural issues between architecture, technology and people's use, not just specific problems of regionalism and localization.

LA: This is probably the most interesting thing. The way people interact with the environment brings about a kind of everydayness. We are concerned about the daily use of this technology and even the media. The negative: it brings alienation to human beings, the positive: the user's end has changed, while for me there is no difference between these two points. Such a state is the real and the starting point of design.

ZS: That's right. Back to the beginning of the design, changes in technology or other factors may no longer apply to the original building methods and concepts, but we do not necessarily know whether the new things it brings are

不一定知道。如果我们不理解它的规律、基础的东西，就没办法做客观的评价。我认为我们首先要做的不是设计，而是基础研究。

鲁：你是先有想法再实践还是先实践再总结？

庄：二者是交织的。基本上是在"处理问题—解决问题"与"发现现象—思考现象"，两者之间来回地工作。我曾思考，20世纪90年代后我们国家的建设量这么大，但为什么没有像《向拉斯维加斯学习》《癫狂纽约》《东京制造》这样的思考？这个问题其实挺刺激人的，说明我们缺乏对于现象的发现习惯。

鲁：在其他一些发展中国家，比如南美，他们的建筑工业、建筑技术跟中国相差不多，但是他们在回应问题方面会自觉得多，你觉得他们在技术手段层面和你刚刚说的那个层面的思考是一样的吗？

庄：没有对南美的建筑做过研究，但应该是不一样的。南美洲当时大量、直接运用普适的现代主义的设计思想与方法工具，中国没有出现这样的应用时期。自经济快速发展与城市化以来，我们快速地进入了中国式的商品化或者是消费化的年代，以至于20世纪90年代以来，中国建筑师们来不及产生同时也缺乏思考问题的方式或方法工具。我们当时面对大量设计的时候，把各种能借鉴的方法都用上了，所以很混乱。但是现在想来，我觉得当时的工作环境其实挺宽松的，所有的业主对你的唯一要求就是"新"，但其实是一直没有系统的工具能应用，也没有新的工具来对付实际中面临

good or not. If we don't understand its rules, basic issues, we can't make an objective evaluation. I believe the first thing to do is not designing, but basic research.

LA: Do you have ideas before starting a practice or start to practice and then make a conclusion?

ZS: Alternately. It is a kind of work back and forth between dealing with problems, solving problems, discovering and thinking about phenomena. I have thought that with the huge amount of national construction since the 1990s in China, why there have been no thoughts like those in *Learning from Las Vegas*, *Delirious New York*, and *Made in Tokyo*? In fact, this problem is quite discouraging; it reveals that we are not used to discovering phenomena.

LA: In other developing countries, like South America, their architecture industry and architectural technology are similar to China's, but they are much more conscious in responding to problems. Do you think their way of thinking is at the same level of the technical method as you have just mentioned?

ZS: I haven't researched architecture in South America. It should be different. At that time, a large number of universal modernist design ideas and methods were directly applied in South America, but there was no such period of application in China. Since the rapid economic development and urbanization, we have rapidly entered the era of Chinese-style commercialization or consumerization, consequently Chinese architects didn't have time to make such applications since the 1990s, and they even lacked ways or tools to think about problems. When we were dealing with a large number of designs, we were applying every method we could, so it was very confusing. It now appears that

的特别情况。

鲁： 在 2000 年左右比较直接地对这种快速增长进行回应的是都市实践建筑事务所。我觉得像深圳这种快速扩张的都市需要对其都市性有所表达，都市实践满足了这个需求，因此被选择。而且它对问题的回应在当时实际上是非常实在的需求。另外，我比较感兴趣的是，比如在 2000 年之后那几年，大家都会觉得都市是非常有趣的，但是为什么现在建筑师对于新的数字媒体带来的交互变化这类事物不再感兴趣了呢？这跟都市一样，都是建筑学不可回避的前提。为什么当代建筑师不像二十年前对城市感兴趣那样对这些东西感兴趣呢？

庄： 拿中国的情况来说，一方面可能是建筑设计被使用得太过专业化。这种专业化其实已经不知不觉地成为了一种商品化。在建设量急增而且快速进入到商品化的空间生产之后，它们的确消解了建筑的意义，让大家不去思考这件事情。因为有很多事要做，很多业主的要求、市场的要求要去满足，大家自动地被裹挟着去做了。另一方面，我觉得当时的学界、研究者实际上也是很失落的，他们甚至一直到现在都还处于有些失语的状态，我不知道这样描述是不是准确。如果说市场化、商品化的东西里面没有任何建筑学价值，那剩下的哪些里面又有建筑学价值呢？哪些是真正的方法？实际上，我们是缺少新的研究方式，老工具检索不到研究内容。我们自己没有研究，外国人的也没有现成可用的，因为我们遇到的那些问题有的在国外不是问题，有的他们就没有碰到过。所以反过来看，我觉得整个学术研究、对设计的研究处于

the working environment at that time was quite relaxed. The only requirement of all the clients was "new"; in fact, there have been no systematic tools, nor new tools to deal with the special situation in reality.

LA: Around 2000, it was URBANUS Architect who responded more directly to this rapid growth. I think a rapidly expanding city like Shenzhen needs to express its urbanity, and URBANUS was chosen because they successfully met this demand. What they responded to was actually a very concrete need. In addition, what I am more interested in is, for example, after 2000, all architects thought the city was very interesting, but why are we no longer interested in interactive changes brought about by new digital media? Like the city, this is an unavoidable premise of architecture. Why aren't contemporary architects interested in these things as they were interested in cities twenty years ago?

ZS: In China, perhaps the architectural design is too utilitarian and professional. In fact, this professionalization has unconsciously become commoditized. After the rapid increase of construction volume and the rapid entry into a commercialized space production, the significance of architecture has indeed been dispelled, which makes us stop thinking about this. Because there are many things to do, we had to satisfy many clients' requirements, market requirements automatically. On the other hand, I think the academic circles and researchers at that time were actually very disappointed, and even now they are a bit wordless. I don't know whether this description is accurate or not. If there is no architectural value in marketization and commercialization, then where is it? What are the real architectural methods? In fact, we lack new research methods and old tools cannot retrieve research content. We haven't studied it and no

一种防守状态。防守状态最容易陷入往后看或者往别人那里看的情况。所以我觉得学界对实践的指导是失语的。那么，实践建筑师呢？按理说实践建筑师应该更容易发现东西，因为他们在第一线干嘛！但他们当时是被裹挟着在做那些空间设计。一直到现在实践建筑师还在干的很多事情，我觉得是商品、媒体、流量促成的。虽然那样的工作空间实际上很狭窄，从法兰西风格的豪宅一直到卒姆托式的空间，都可以被这个体系消费，最终变成一种同质化的东西，但很多建筑师可能觉得沿着某种"经典传统"成长的方式，是一条在市场竞争的生存压力下的有效的成功之道。也许这从侧面回答了为什么当代建筑师对新的东西不感兴趣。

但我认为新的东西是未来的，它是未来的生产爆发点，对一个发展体系来说它必须以新的范式出现。我们的学校或者主流价值还在讲之前的东西，反应太慢。但是变化其实已经在发生了，你能感觉得到。

鲁： 我在南京大学开过一门研究方法课，一上来就让大家讨论什么是"现实"，但同学们常常对此无动于衷，我觉得挺有趣。"现实"是什么？"现实"有很多不同层次的定义，这其实是一个立场问题，但是大部分人没有想过"现实"也是别人眼中的那些事。有些人认为"现实"是一种客观的东西，从科学的角度看是现实生活，但是从社会的根源看，"现实"在多大程度上是物质的？多大程度是稳定的？多大程度上是个人化的？比如对于一个患有严重精神疾病的人来说，"现实"是非常个人的。所以最终这些其实都是价值判断。显然，对你来说，你

corresponding foreign research was applicable, because some of the problems we encounter are not their problems, or they have never had such problems. See it in another way, I think the whole academic research and design research are playing a role as defenders, which is most likely to get caught up in referring to previous research or other's research. So I think the academic guidance to practice is helpless. So what about architects? Is it reasonable to say that architects should find things more easily? Because they are working in the first front! But you have to know they were forced to make those space designs. Up till now, the architects are still doing a lot of things required by commodities, media, and traffic volume. Although the workspace is actually very narrow, from the French style of luxury houses to Zumthor-style space, all can be consumed by this system, and eventually they become homogeneous. But many architects felt that according to a certain "classical and traditional" growth mode, it's an effective way to obtain success and survive in the market competition. Perhaps this is part of the answers to why contemporary architects are not interested in new things.

But I think new things belong to the future, it is the flashpoint of future production. For a development system, it must appear in a new paradigm. Our academy or mainstream values are still talking about old things. They failed to keep up the trend. But you can feel changes are happening.

LA: I taught a research methodology course at Nanjing University. I asked students to discuss what reality was at first, but I found it interesting that the students were often indifferent to it. What is "reality"? "Reality" has many different levels of definition, which is actually a matter of standpoint, but most people did not think

相信的并作为起点的现实，其实跟很多年前已经完全不一样了。

庄：你讲的现实是有一种复杂性在里面的，我同意。对我来说"现实"更多地是要跳出既有的专业范围冷静地去看这一件事。

我们的设计教育体系其实是抽掉了一些部分，比如建筑与社会经济、技术发展之间的关系，这部分不太教，但很重要，是判断设计的重要因素。事实上当你开始站在一个更大的体系中，对现实的认知就不同了。

鲁：事实上，你会不会认为需要先具备作为一个好建筑师的基础能力，再去获得一些比如社会性的、消费主义这样的视角，这些是要有先后次序的？

庄：可能是这样的。我觉得把自己放到一个更加中性的角度去看待建筑的时候，我已经是一个很成熟的建筑师了，基本上已经有了建筑形式语言，它像锚一样稳住你的工作。

鲁：有件事我一直很困惑。我觉得建筑学在根本的层面上是行动主义的。行动能力是要被训练的，所以我们专业训练做这件事。但是由于建筑学的能力训练自带价值观，这其中就存在一定风险。在训练了几年之后，你可能已经被这个系统同化了，如果等到研究生阶段或者工作之后再开始进行反思，会不会太晚？可能很多人工作之后也关注社会，但是他的专业技能带给他的价值或者认识的判断已经固化在血液里了。你也是这么经历过来的，为什么你能够反思修正前面那个阶段的东西？

庄：一方面是发现旧的方式没法解决现实的问题，旧的价值观在现实中令人

2　棉仓城市客厅"屋中屋"
House in House, Cotton Lab Urban Lounge

that "reality" is also what others see. Some people think that "reality" is an objective thing, from a scientific point of view it is real life, but from the root of society, to what extent is "reality" material? To what extent is it stable? To what extent is it personal? For example, for a person with severe psychiatric illness, "reality" is very personal. So these are all value judgments. Obviously, for you, the reality you believe in as a starting point is not the same as it was many years ago.

ZS: I agree that the reality you're talking about is complex. For me, the "reality" is more about thinking it calmly, thinking it outside the box of existing expertise. In fact, in our architectural design education system, the relationship between architecture and socio-economic or technological development is neglected. However, this part is very important, it is key for judging designs. In fact, when you stand in a larger system, you will find a different "reality".

LA: In fact, do you think there is a proper order, which means it is necessary to have the basic ability to be a good architect first, and then to get broader perspectives such as sociality or consumerism?

ZS: Maybe. When I treat architecture with a more neutral perspective, I am already a very mature architect who possessed a confident formal language of architecture. It can stabilize your work as an anchor.

LA: I have long been puzzled by one thing. Basically, an architect should be an activist. Actionability is to be trained, so we specialize in this training. However, since professional architectural training contains one's own value, you may find it risky. After a few years of training, you may have been assimilated by the system. For example, is it too late to start reflection at the post-graduate stage or at work? Maybe a lot of people pay attention to society since they start to work, but the value

怀疑。另一方面，我自己有一种倾向，把建筑学的设计方法当作手段。恰好我做设计的手法基因是那种注重原则，但形式方法多变、手段很灵活的方式。这种手法会促成思维方式。这种方式天生有一个小基因，它为了整体关系或者解决问题能够灵活运用手段，它不会迷信于某种具体特征。

鲁： 手段不存在绝对性。

庄： 对。这会为我们现在的很多工作带来非常好的基因，相对而言它是一种为目的而开放的方法。

鲁： 这有一定的相对主义，会对你的设计造成麻烦和困扰吗？

庄： 我觉得会对识别性造成麻烦和困扰。在如今的媒体和读图时代，强烈且令人印象深刻的形式是非常重要的，在这方面我们的这种方式天然属于弱的，因为它无法为建筑师形成符号式的积累。

鲁： 你觉得棉仓 [图1–图4] 有可识别性吗？

庄： 有，但是无法重复。识别性对于一家事务所的意义是能够重复，最后成为一个文化的 logo，这需要有形式的积累和固化。棉仓当然有识别性，它对于一个单纯空间是有识别性的，但它不是可重复的形式。棉仓能够指导以后实践的是隐含在背后的逻辑，我对这个隐含在背后的逻辑更感兴趣。

鲁： 这十年来，你觉得从哪一个建成项目开始，你的思想真正被融入了实践，你关于"改变"的想法真正成为了那个项目的内核，或者说被容纳在那个项目中？

庄： 2014 年前后我们做了一系列关于局部立面的改造 [图5,6]，而且我们都做

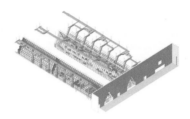

3　棉仓城市客厅，室内新建舱体和管道
Two chambers and air ducts, Cotton Lab
Urban Lounge

formed by his professional skills or the judgment of his knowledge has begun to circulate in the blood. Now that you've experienced all this, why your reflection can correct things from the previous stage?

ZS: On the one hand, I found that the old method failed to solve practical problems, and it is doubtful whether the old value works in reality. On the other hand, I prefer to see architectural design methods as means. It happens that my designing philosophy is that paying attention to principles, being flexible in form and method. It contributes to the way of thinking. This method inherits a little gene, which can be used flexibly to solve problems or overall relationships without sticking to particular characteristics.

LA: There are no fixed means.

ZS: Exactly, it will bring very positive factors to many of our current work. Relatively speaking, it is an open method satisfying the purpose.

LA: This is something similar to relativism. Will it cause trouble and puzzle to your design?

ZS: I think it will cause trouble and puzzle to identify. In today's media and visualized era, strong and impressive forms are very important. In this respect, our methods are born weak, because they cannot form a symbolic accumulation for architects.

LA: Do you think the Cotton Lab Urban Lounge [fig.1 – fig. 4] is recognizable?

ZS: Yes, but it can't be duplicated. For a studio, the significance of recognizability is to repeat and finally become a logo, a cultural identity. This requires formal accumulation and solidification. Of course, as a simple space, Cotton Lab Urban Lounge is recognizable, but its form is irreproducible. What Cotton Lab

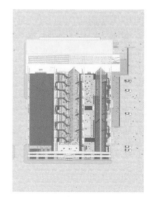

4　棉仓城市客厅，轴测图
Axonometric drawing of Cotton Lab
Urban Lounge

5　衡山路890弄（衡山和集）8号楼外立面改造
Facade Renovation for No.8 Building, Lane 890 Hengshan Road, Shanghai

6　斜土社区活动中心立面改造
Facade Renovation for Xietu Community Center

7　台州路桥商业建筑，模型
Model of Taizhou Luqiao Commercial Building

出了一些不同的花样。后来有了室内项目之后我开始反思，这些促使我对局部和调整这件事有了一个感性的认识。

鲁： 如果把立面改造和室内改造作为一种项目类型，这种局部化改变了市场或者社会，因此在社会的运行机制中，已经在以局部的方式去操作建筑。

庄： 对。你会觉得你找到了一种方法，不仅仅是理论上的想法，这种方法是能够介入这些事情的。而且你找到了对象，破除了曾经要做一个完整建筑的执念。我觉得一旦这类事情发生，你就会知道自己在建立某种方式，而且是跟别人不同的方式。

鲁： 你处理立面改造的方法和处理室内改造的方法是相同的吗？还是你会再定制一种新的方法？

庄： 它们有统一的地方。比如用局部来改变整体，或者把房子当成一个既有物来做，其实这种基因很早以前就存在。我记得在大舍的时候做的路桥传统小商业建筑改造 [图7]，其实最后是把建筑单体当一个规划做，某种意义上它是用了组织的方法，也是混合的方法。我们当时做了很多这样的东西，但这是观念式的，当时做得很生硬，比如嘉定博物馆新馆 [图8]，也没有脱离对房屋中心的认知。

后来开始做这些片段以后，深入到了内部、局部，我就意识到了时间性的概念。房子是既有物，它可以积累，可以在原始的基础上改变。你会发现你的概念或者是想法其实只是植根于一个局部，而不是对一个完美房子的展现。

Urban Lounge has contributed to future practice is the logic behind it. Actually, I am more interested in this hidden logic.

LA: In the past ten years, in which completed project your design philosophy was really incorporated into practice? Your idea became the core of that project, or was adopted in that project?

ZS: Around 2014, we completed a series of facade renovation programs [fig. 5–6]. It was in the same year, we were commissioned some partial facade reconstructions, all of which have actually achieved diverse designs. Later, after we had interior renovation projects, I began to reflect, which prompted me to have a perceptual understanding of part and adjustment.

LA: If we regard facade reconstruction and indoor renovation as two project types, this partial change has changed the market or society. That is to say in the operation mechanism of society, partial reconstruction has been a new type of architectural project.

ZS: That's right. You may feel that you have found a way to get involved in these things, not just a theoretical idea. And you find the object and start to break away from the idea of dealing with a whole building. I think once this happens, you will know that you are establishing a certain method, a different way from others.

LA: Will you adopt the same method in facade reconstruction and indoor reconstruction? Or will you customize a new method?

ZS: They are unified. For example, to change the whole with parts, or to see the building as an existing thing. In fact, this idea existed a long time ago. I remember the reconstruction of traditional small commercial buildings in Luqiao,

你能够用一个局部去响应一个整体，当然也能够破坏一个整体。如果把这件事和我们的城市研究放在一起看，你会发现它们有很多典型的相同之处。从那时候开始，我就觉得我们有自己的工作对象了。

鲁："工作对象"这个词很有趣，因为对象塑造方法。你有没有想过画一张图，看一下你到底处理过哪些对象？

庄：基本上会集中于三种东西：局部、片段、内部。新建的建筑和改造的建筑都可以用同样的方法。

鲁：昨天我跟几位建筑师讨论了这件事，当时有几个问题他们没有同意我的观点，我刚好可以问一下你。第一，你是否认为建筑适应未来变化的能力是有强弱之分的？有的建筑更适应，有的建筑不适应。比如框架结构其实适应能力很强，它的变化很多，这种能力是建筑本身的能力。

庄：那当然。

鲁：第二，能不能通过设计去加强建筑适应未来变化的能力？

庄：我认为是可以的。建筑适应未来的能力一方面跟它本身的物质程度有关系，另一方面，我之所以觉得可以通过设计与调整去改变这件事，是因为我们生活在一个更大的系统里，物质空间越来越显得只是其中的一部分。所以我认为，当一个设计可以引入系统其他部分的力量时，当然可以通过设计加强或者改变建筑适应未来变化的能力。

鲁：这就是一个很重要的区分点。昨天没有人同意我的观点，因为他们认为未来

8　嘉定博物馆新馆
　　Jiading New Mesuem

Zhejiang Province I did in the Atelier Deshaus period [fig. 7]. In fact, we treated a single building as a planning unit. In a sense, it used the method of organization, this is also a method of mixing. We did a lot of similar projects then, but this one was conceptual. While at that time, the concept was still rigid, like the design of Jiading New Museum [fig. 8], and I still held the recognition on building as the core.

Later, when I devoted to fragments, my work was extended to the interior and the part, and I realized the concept of timeliness. The building is an existing thing, which can be accumulated and changed on the original basis. You will find that your concept or idea is actually related to a part, not a whole perfect building. You can respond to a whole with a part, and of course, you can destroy the whole. Considering our urban studies, you will find there are many typical similarities. From then on, I realized that we had our own working objects.

LA: The term "working object" sounds interesting, because the method to be adopted usually is determined by object. Have you ever thought about drawing a picture to see what objects you've dealt with?

ZS: In this direction, we will basically concentrate on three things: parts, fragments and interiors. These can be applied to new buildings as well as reconstructed buildings.

LA: Yesterday I happened to discuss this with several architects. They didn't agree with me on one thing. I want to ask you right now. First of all, do you think some buildings are easy while the others are difficult to be adapted to future changes? Some of them are more adaptable, and the others are not. For example, the frame structure is actually highly adaptable, it changes a lot. This ability is a natural

会有变化，且未来的变化建筑师无法想象，所以你现在做的任何增加适应性变化的努力是徒劳的。

　　庄：现在不去想象或者还只是从自己原来的学科氛围里去推论，那当然会跟你没有关系。但是建筑师需要去想象，因为我觉得建筑师应该对未来的变化承担更大责任。

鲁：我完全同意。其实重要的是你对于建筑能做什么的认识是不同的，你会认为这是你的责任的一部分。

　　庄：对。建筑学难道不应该有一些更主动的东西吗？

鲁：再问你一个问题，也是一个重要的区分。从刚才的描述中，你最终造出来的物质性的干预，在我看来其实是一种带有基础设施性的东西，它支持一些变化，所以它本身是一种支持性的工具。就像桌子一样，你并不会把这张桌子看成美丽的雕塑，而是看成支撑我们聊天的工具。那么你是否认为一个建筑应该体现建筑师的情感，体现一种感性层面的东西？

　　庄：这正是有趣的地方。我觉得我们自己的工作在某种程度上是走在边缘的，甚至再往前走就虚无了，这产生的变化会和原有的建筑学方式产生很有意思的冲突，这种冲突会带来新的张力。

鲁：我一直有一个疑惑，我觉得由于你关注这一点，所以你对于变化、不确定性和偶然性容忍度非常高。我看你很多的决策，至少那些非关键性决策，经常是临场做的，比如忽然觉得涂某个颜色挺好的 [图9]，当然这是在你的整个认知中的，

property of building itself.

　　ZS: Of course.

LA: My second question is: is it possible to strengthen the building's ability to adapt to future changes through design?

　　ZS: I think so. On the one hand, this ability is related to its material, on the other hand, I think it can be changed by design and adjustment because we live in a larger system, where material space is increasingly showing only a part of it. So I think when a design can introduce other power of the system, of course, such ability can be strengthened or changed by design.

LA: This answer is totally different. No one agreed with me yesterday because they thought there would be changes in the future and these changes were unpredictable, so any efforts you were making to increase adaptability are futile.

　　ZS: It certainly has nothing to do with you if you don't imagine or only infer from your original academic atmosphere. But architects need to imagine because I think architects should take great responsibility for future changes.

LA: I couldn't agree more. The important thing is that your understanding of what architecture can do is different, and you will see it as part of your responsibility.

　　ZS: Right. Shouldn't architecture have something more proactive?

LA: One more question, also an important distinction. Based on what you have just described, the material intervention you eventually created is, in my opinion, an infrastructural thing that supports some changes so that it can be seen as a supportive tool. Like this table, you don't see it as a beautiful sculpture, but as a tool to support our conversation. So do you think that a building should embody the architect's emotion and express perceptual thinking?

没有问题。我好奇的是，如果你不是在那一天那个时刻面对那个决策，如果换一天、换一种心情，你是不是会得到一个不一样的设计判断？

庄： 完全可能。

鲁： 你会认为这种随机性是你设计的必然结果或者说是一种设计特征的表达，还是会认为这是失控的部分？它是积极的还是消极的？

庄： 这与我们在设计中处理形式的方法有关，当某个因素引发了一个需要的修改的时候，我会迅速地检视整体。我们的设计原则往往是非常明确的，但是具体方式是很不固定的。

鲁： 所以你只要在检测中兼容就可以了？

庄： 是的。比如我们在需要做一个决定的时候，如果我把某个地方改了，可能会把另外一个地方也改了。我会迅速把整个设计拆解，至少在思想上拆解一遍，从逻辑上拆解一遍，然后再组成一个新的逻辑，这其中的变化因素很多，哪天心情好或者不好、忙或者不忙都可能造成不一样的结果，但是最后都会形成一个新的整体。

鲁： 这件事很有趣。有的设计系统里每一个设计决策都可以从方法原理中推导出来，在某个时刻做的决策是唯一的，如果换一个时间、地点得到的结论相同，这才是一个好的设计方法。

庄： 我不是这样的。我的设计方法是枝状和返回式的，属于多元式的，比如要想达到一个目标，我可以同时想出好多种方法，瞬间就会想不同的路径，

9　宝山贝贝佳欧莱幼儿园
Renovation of Baoshan Beibeijia Olion Kindergarten

ZS: That's why it is so interesting. I think to some extent we are working in the edge zone and our work even will be meaningless if we continue stepping forward. The changes will provoke interesting conflicts with the original architectural methods. Such conflict will bring new tension.

LA: I've always had a doubt, just because you focus on this, you have a very high tolerance of change, uncertainty and contingency. I found that many of your decisions, at least those not critical ones, are often made on site. You would suddenly decide on a certain color for painting [fig. 9]. Of course, the decision is still within your whole recognition. It's a right decision. What I am wondering is, if you were deciding on a different day and with a different mood, will you get a different design judgment?

ZS: Entirely possible.

LA: Do you think this randomness is the inevitable outcome of your design, or is it an expression of design features, or is this part out of control? Is it positive or negative?

ZS: It has to do with the way we approach form in design, and when something triggers a change, I will quickly review the whole. We are working with clear design principles, but with a very unstable specific method.

LA: So you just have to keep the change compatible with the whole in the review?

ZS: Yes. For example, when making decisions, if I change one place, I may change another. I will quickly disassemble the whole design. At least disassemble it in my mind, with logic. Then a new logic is formed. There are many changing factors. Like how are you feeling, how busy you are, all these factors may lead to different results. No matter how different the results are, a new whole will be eventually formed.

LA: This is very interesting. In some design systems, every design decision can be

当推进路径受阻的时候就会回到原来那个地方再重新开始，所以它引出的结果会不一样，这是训练出来的。[图 10]

鲁： 这个方法其实对你来说很重要。

庄： 对，这是一种思维方式。这是一种发散式思维和整体式思维融合在一起的方法，它对于各种因素与关系特别敏感。

鲁： 可以叫做实时动态调整。

庄： 我觉得逻辑性要很完整。

鲁： 我想起学生时代，大多数建筑学的学生会在某个时刻被一些现象打动，比如一个窗户的光斑投影在某个地方，这类由建筑支撑的诗意景象成为他们的建筑要追求的东西。那么在你的设计方法中，这部分还有吗，还是它们会在某个地方出现？

庄： 我的形式思考能力很具象，我跟我们很多学生和手下的设计师说，设计时一定要具体地想问题，比如你设计一条走道也好，一个楼梯也好，你要想象它的使用场景，是什么人在用，怎么用，在怎样的环境里用。

鲁： 你并不是想象几点钟那个地方会有什么样的光？

庄： 有时候也会，但这不是我的目标，我不会单注意一种行为、一个时刻，而是会把它纳入到一个更大的整体里去，否则你的设计就特别干。其实具体性对我们现在的状态来说是一种均衡 [图 11、12]，因为我们现在想事情其实挺枯燥的，倾向于站在很冷静的系统的角度上去想建筑。我自己的情境感挺强

10　设计思路图：不断生发和选择的过程
Design process diagram: continuously diverging and organizing

046

deduced from the method and principle. The decision made at a certain time is unique. If the same conclusion is drawn at a different time and place, this design method is proved to be a good one.

ZS: This is not my philosophy. My design method is branch-like, return-like, more specifically, multivariate. For example, if I want to achieve a goal, I can think it in many ways at one time, I think of different methods in an instant. When the plan is hampered, I will go back to the start point and restart. This will lead to different results. I am trained to have my own style. [fig. 10]

LA: This method is actually very important to you.

ZS: Yes, it's a way of thinking. This is a way of combining divergent thinking with holistic thinking, which is particularly sensitive to various factors and relationships.

LA: We can call this a real-time dynamic adjustment.

ZS: The logic inside should be fully complete.

LA: I recall that in my school days, most students of architecture would be moved by some phenomena at some time, such as the spot projection of a window somewhere, and this kind of poetic scene supported by buildings became their pursuit. So, is this part still being included in your design method? Or will it appear somewhere?

ZS: My thinking ability on the form is very specific. I told many of the students and designers that we should think about specific problems when designing. For example, if you design an aisle or a staircase, you should imagine usage scenarios. Who is using it, how to use it, and the surrounding environment when using it. [fig. 11–12]

的，但如果真要把它变成一个目的去营造建筑，我觉得是很腻味的，我现在不太喜欢陷入场景氛围的设计。

鲁：我觉得场景其实有几个不同的意思，你说的其实是使用情境。

庄：我觉得设计师应该知道自己在创造什么，用什么样的方法，能自由驾御方法。

鲁：我想提一个比较具体的问题。从你的价值观到你思考建筑的方式，再到你的工具都很完整，你现在是一家事务所的负责人，你如何保证手下的员工都跟你处于同一个价值体系中，且能够贯彻这些？

庄：组织。这跟做建筑是一样的，你想选什么材料、能够凑成什么东西，你的工作室里有不同的人才，他们做事的方式是不一样的，你如何把他们当作元素组织起来，再把工作分解，最后你要能够总控。

对我们事务所来说，观念很重要，并且它很多时候体现在策略上。现在我在事务所做的工作往往更多的是策略，有好的也有不好的，最后的完成度不一，但是也会逼着你把策略变得更清楚、更有特征。在关键策略上你能够从不同的层面切入，方法不一样，带来的结果也不一样，比如棉仓就是如此，我们最近有个项目也是如此。

鲁："当你说"策略"的时候，你已经把策略和具体的措施分开来了，是吧？策略是更加带有纲领性质或者原则、哲学层面的结晶，你明显是把它当褒义词用的，对吧？

11　嘉北郊野公园北游客中心，室内
Interior of North Visitor Center of
Shanghai Jiabei Country Park

11　嘉北郊野公园北游客中心，室内
Interior of North Visitor Center of
Shanghai Jiabei Country Park

12　港城广场展示中心，茶室
Exhibition Center of Harbor City Plaza , Teahouse

047

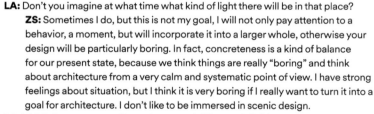

LA: Don't you imagine at what time what kind of light there will be in that place?

ZS: Sometimes I do, but this is not my goal, I will not only pay attention to a behavior, a moment, but will incorporate it into a larger whole, otherwise your design will be particularly boring. In fact, concreteness is a kind of balance for our present state, because we think things are really "boring" and think about architecture from a very calm and systematic point of view. I have strong feelings about situation, but I think it is very boring if I really want to turn it into a goal for architecture. I don't like to be immersed in scenic design.

LA: I think the scene actually carries several different definitions. What you are talking about is situational use.

ZS: I think designers should be fully understood what they are creating, which methods they are adopting, and how they can fully control such methods.

LA: I would like to ask a more specific question. The working value, the way you think about architecture and your working instruments are complete, you are now in charge of an architectural office, how can you ensure that your employees are in the same value system and they are stick to this?

ZS: By establishing a good organization. Like architecture, you need to decide what materials to pick, what you are going to build. There are different talents in your studio. They work in different ways. You need to organize them, assign the work to every one of them and of course, you are the general controller. For our studio, ideas are very important, and they are often reflected in working strategies. Now most of my job is making strategy. There are both advantages and disadvantages. Though these jobs are accomplished at different levels, it forces you to make a clearer and more featured strategy. While implementing strategies, you

庄：当然是当褒义词用的，这是我们的工作方法。说"策略"比较文绉绉的，其实就是想法，还不是概念，是可操作的想法。

鲁：你觉得你所有项目里完成度最好的是哪个？

庄：其实我觉得我们现在的完成度好像也一般。你说的完成度是指工程完成度还是想法完成度？

鲁：我就是想诱导你暴露出你潜意识里的完成度是哪一个。

庄：我觉得工程完成度国内跟国外已经没有差距了，国内做得越来越好。我们现在已没办法在这一点上去跟大的机构竞争，所以我们要从其他角度去获得优势，就像田忌赛马。

鲁：你最想做的建筑类型是什么？博物馆吗？

庄：不。而且我还没有准备好。如果无法在一个新建筑中体现出我的工作方法，那对我来说是没有意义的。在这一块我们还不成熟，因为我们对我们工作方法的自如的使用是基于既有建筑天生的前置条件的，它们与复杂的城市有诸多关系。

鲁：每种方法是有适用领域的吗？

庄：我觉得对于一个事务所来说，方法要有统一性，而且从基础研究的角度来说，观念认识和方法需要有通识性。我觉得我们需要时间去应用、试验方法。

鲁：我想起了你的一个破绽。南京桦墅那个长鼻子大眼睛的房子的做法是不是你

can get involved from different levels. The different methods you adopt, the different results you obtain. Like the Cotton Lab Urban Lounge and one of our recent projects.

LA: When you say "strategy", you have already separated strategy from specific measures, right? Strategy is more programmatic or philosophical. For you, obviously it is a positive word, right?

ZS: Of course, it's how we work. The word "strategy" is more literary, actually it's an idea, not a concept, an operable idea.

LA: Among the projects you did, which project was fully completed?

ZS: Actually, I think all the projects are normally completed. Are you referring to the completion of project or idea?

LA: That's what I want you to tell me. Subconsciously, which completion you are referring to.

ZS: As for the completion of project, I think there is no difference between China and foreign countries, local design companies are doing better and better. On this point, we don't have the confidence to win big companies. That's why we need to gain other advantages, like Tianji's horse racing strategy.

LA: What type of architecture do you most want to do? Museum?

ZS: No. I'm not ready for that. It doesn't make sense to me if I can't apply my working methods to a new architecture. We are still immature in this area, because many of the methods we grasped and skillfully applied are based on the natural properties of existing buildings. They have all sorts of relationships with complex cities.

LA: Can each method be applied to a certain area?

ZS: I think for a studio, the working method should be unified, and from the

莫名其妙产生的想法？［图13］

庄：没有。你觉得那是开玩笑吗？难道是因为我写了一些POP（通俗）的文章？

鲁：我是觉得你做这件事的整个策略，其实跟乡建是不兼容的。但是在那个地方那个房子又被视作乡建。

庄：对。我对乡建一点兴趣也没有。桦墅最终虽然被使用了，但我觉得这是资本下乡，一阵风就走了，所以我并不认为它的功能有多成功，但是它用的手法完全是有我们特征的手法，揭示场地、依附、调整、组织等。

鲁：我觉得在你的这批乡建项目里，黎里跟你的策略最兼容［图14］。改变局部，具有一种对于真实生活的兼容性。黎里这个想法是很贴切的，但是双栖斋［图15］和桦墅其实很难让人信服，它们对于你的手法实验当然有用。不过，回顾你这十年的逻辑，这都是一些拓展。

庄：我觉得黎里更像一个调整，它在调整的过程中把空间序列组织起来，比如从窄小黑暗的弄堂进入。这些其实很有美学性，运用到了关系。双栖斋也是如此。

鲁：是的。你现在再来看这三个项目，最动人的部分都是"破绽"，对不对？双栖斋的光影和曲线，还有桦墅的庭院。

庄：我觉得这三个项目体现的是存在于我们手法里的基因。从我们现在的角度再去理解这几个项目，显然它们已经不是我们现在要做的方向了。

13　南京桦墅乡村工作室，分解轴测图
Decomposition axonometric drawing,
Huashu Rural Studio

049

perspective of basic research, the concept of understanding and methods need to be general. We need time to apply and test our method.

LA: Now I am thinking of an exception. Huashu Rural Workshop in Nanjing was designed with a long nose and big eyes [fig. 13]. Did this idea turn up in your mind suddenly?

ZS: No. Do you think that's a joke? Is it because I wrote some POP articles?

LA: I think the whole strategy of this project is incompatible with rural construction. But in that place, Huashu Rural Workshop was regarded as rural construction.

ZS: You're right. I am not interested in rural construction at all. Although Huashu Rural Workshop was finally used, I think it more likes capital gets into rural place, just a whim. I don't think its function is successful, but the method applied in Huashu is branded with our own characteristics, revealing the site, dependence, adjustment, and organization, etc.

LA: I think the rural construction project LILI (Suzhou) [fig. 14] is most compatible with your strategy. Change parts, to be compatible with real life. LILI is very close to your real strategy. By contrast, Twin Trees Pavilion [fig. 15] and Huashu Rural Workshop are less convincing. They are certainly useful for experiment on your strategy, but reviewing your logic in this decade, these are exceptions.

ZS: I think LILI (Suzhou) is more like an adjustment, in the process of which the spatial sequence was organized. You know, entering from the narrow dark alley. These are actually very aesthetic, the logic of relationship was applied. So is the Twin Trees Pavilion.

LA: You're right. Now when we take a look at these three projects, the most moving parts are "exceptions", right? The light, shadow and curve of Twin Trees Pavilion and

14 黎里，屋顶
LILI, On the Roof

鲁：你早期做过一段时间这个东西。我比较感兴趣的是，比如经过十年，现在回顾的时候，你会不会回过头去思考这几个项目？现在怎么看待它们？

庄：我们的工作方向与方法是过去所有的因素促成的，这个过程是积累变化的，幸运的是我们一直在有意识地试图用一些线索来组织那些不同的东西。我们就是在这个环境中一边干活一边想问题的团队。

其实这十年中最让我觉得有些小成就的是积累，在这个过程中没有失去我想去做的事。我们不跟风，而且我是天生的怀疑论者，对流行的东西我总是不自觉地要怀疑一下。平时的点点滴滴可能不会察觉，但是回过头来整理的时候会让我们觉得还是有一个挺有意思的积累过程，我希望接下来也能够如此。

鲁：工作室的搬迁计划就和刚才的三个工作对象一样，是另外一根线索。这根线索其实也讲了很多故事，包括你的立场、头脑发热，等等，我觉得很有意思。你们搬了有五六次了吧？

庄：十年搬了六个工作室 [图16]。

鲁：观察一下这些，自己有反思、有变化吗？

庄：有。其实搬工作室的事一开始是没有计划的，我们没有那么高的策划能力。但是真正做起来之后就把它纳入到整个工作的一部分了，好或者不好，总之就是折腾呗，所以这件事变得越来越有意思。搬工作室这件事从一开始的头脑发热，到后来变成了一个故事，这里面也有各种复杂的考量。我觉得

15 双栖斋
Twin Trees Pavilion

the courtyard of Huashu Rural Workshop.

ZS: I think our working philosophy was vividly applied to these three items. To understand these projects from our current perspective, we are sure that they are not we are currently working on.

LA: In the early stage of your career, you worked on this. What I'm interested in is, for example, when you look back on the past ten years, will you think about these projects again? What do you think of them now?

ZS: Our work direction and methods are influenced by all the experienced factors in the past. It is a process of accumulation and changes. Fortunately, we have been consciously trying to organize different things with some clues. We keep on working and thinking in this environment.

In fact, in the past ten years, I obtained the sense of achievement through accumulation. In this process, I am still working on what I loved. We never follow others, and I'm an innate skeptic. I always subconsciously take a skeptical attitude on fashion. You may not care about dribs and drabs in daily life, but when looking back, you will found that it is a very interesting process of accumulation. I hope this status will remain unchanged in future.

LA: The move of the studio is another clue, just like the three work objects. It tells a lot of stories, including your position, crazy ideas, etc. That's interesting. How many times have you moved your office? Five or six?

ZS: Six times in ten years [fig. 16].

LA: Think about these moves. Do you have any reflection Have you been changed?

ZS: Yes. Actually, moving studios was not in our plan at first. We didn't have such high planning ability. But when it was put on the agenda, we regarded this

对于我们来说，最重要的是对于使用空间的真实性的理解，不是站在别人的角度而是站在自己的角度去感同身受。我不知道我们的员工怎么样，至少对我自己来说是这样的。

鲁：员工觉得怎么样？老板疯了？

庄：没有，他们觉得还可以。这也验证了我们的想法，人是可以适应空间的。

最近这一次可能会有本质性的变化，因为我们要移动办公了，具体会怎么变化，好不好，我还不太清楚。现在我们的员工可以自行决定来或者不来坐班。

鲁：你的整个策略的关注点在原来传统建筑学的框架里，总体来说是空间和使用范畴，但这件事其实跟其他几个建筑的重要范畴关系不大，比如物理性能和舒适度。当你在追求改变、适应不确定性的时候，事实上会不会牺牲了比如声环境、热环境？

庄：关于舒适度的问题我做过考虑。其实我觉得舒适度这件事是值得反思的。人文主义、现代主义等说建筑是为人，建筑应该更呵护你、使你感到更舒适。很多商业口号、消费口号也是这样说的，它是为你度身定做，为你的舒适性做考虑，而这也正是你所需要的。建筑也是这样，我们被告知好的建筑能够让你感到舒适，它照顾到你的身体对光、声、暖等的舒适感的需求。我想问，谁说这是最好的建筑？你的适应性呢？你对自然的抗争呢？作为生

16-1 长顺路工作室，室内
Changshun Road office, Interior

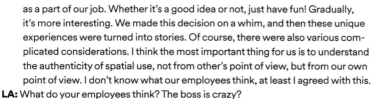

as a part of our job. Whether it's a good idea or not, just have fun! Gradually, it's more interesting. We made this decision on a whim, and then these unique experiences were turned into stories. Of course, there were also various complicated considerations. I think the most important thing for us is to understand the authenticity of spatial use, not from other's point of view, but from our own point of view. I don't know what our employees think, at least I agreed with this.

LA: What do your employees think? The boss is crazy?

ZS: No, they are fine. This also tested our idea that people can adapt themselves to space.

Recently, we are planning a big change, mobile office. No one knows whether this is a good idea or not. Now they can make choice, sitting in the office or working in somewhere else.

LA: Your working strategy keeps its focus in traditional architecture, generally speaking, space and usage, but this has little to do with other important areas of architecture, such as physical performance and comfort. When you seek changes and adapt yourself to the uncertainty, will you actually put other factors aside, like acoustic environment and thermal environment?

ZS: I have considered comfort. It deserves reflection. According to humanism, modernism, etc., "architecture serves people". It takes more care of you and make you feel more comfortable. Just as many marketing slogans express. The architecture is tailored for you, aims to offer you more comfort. This is exactly what you need. In architecture, we are told that a good building can make you feel comfortable. It takes care of your body's comfort of light, sound, warmth etc.. I am curious about who defines this as the best building. What about

16-2 徐家汇工作室，室内
Xujiahui Office, Interior

物提升生存的能力呢？这些都到哪里去了？

鲁：你夏天不开空调吗？

　　庄：开空调啊。人们的生活越来越舒适，但是如果因此认为建筑一定要变得更舒适，为此技术化需要更精确，那我要打一个大大的问号。即使是在可以完全控制的情况下，这样的要求也应该打一个问号，比如有个全智能的建筑，它为什么要把不舒适的情况排除呢？我觉得这是完全说不通的。我们曾经设想过不舒适的建筑，做过一些方案，虽然没有建，但是我们用过这样的手法。[图17]

鲁：是什么样的？很有意思，你应该做个展览。

　　庄：还不成系列。很多东西只是在一味地迎合你，但迎合你的不一定是最好的。

鲁：其实我有一个关于现实的困惑。很多时候你知道他们（业主或使用者）想要的、认为对的其实是不对的，但你服务于他们，他们构成了一个现实，但是你有你相信的东西，那么这时候你怎么继续相信你相信的那些呢？

　　庄：我觉得我们的工作不是传教，你也没办法强迫别人去用不舒适的东西。但是我们讨论这样的事的时候，至少从建筑师的角度来说，我觉得我们可以对任何已经发生的事情进行重新定位和反思。有了这样的认知之后，你就会发现更多的可能和手段，至少在方法上会有更多可能性。设计者可以站在更加广泛的角度看待这件事。

052

the adaptability? Struggle against nature? Ability to increase survivability as creature? They are also very important and shouldn't be neglected.

LA: Do you use air conditioning in summer?

　　ZS: Yes, I do. People' are enjoying more comfortable life, but this doesn't mean that the architecture should be more comfortable or more accurate technology should be applied to architecture. Though everything is under full control, we doubt if such requirement is necessary. For example, there is a smart building, why its uncomfortable factors should be excluded? This doesn't make sense. We had designed some uncomfortable buildings. Although these buildings were not actually built, we tried such design method. [fig. 17]

LA: What were they like? Interesting, you should make an exhibition.

　　ZS: Those were still individual cases. Many designs went all the way to satisfy you. But it doesn't mean they are the best designs.

LA: In fact, in my mind I have a puzzle about reality. Many times you know what the client/user want and what they think right actually are wrong. But you are working for them and they form a reality. But you believe what you believe, then at that moment how do you go on believing what you believe?

　　ZS: I don't think our job is to instruct and influence others by our word and deed, and you can't force others to use uncomfortable things. When we talk about this, at least from the architect's point of view, we can reposition and reflect on anything that happened before. With this recognition, you will find more possibilities and means. At least there will be more possible methods. Designers can consider this from a broader perspective.

LA: The uncomfortable architecture you just mentioned is very interesting. Since

鲁：我觉得你刚才说的不舒服的建筑很有趣。由于某种不舒服使你要去适应自然，假如你从历史的角度看，可能它对你基因的贡献更大，会比你现在感觉舒服更好，是吗？

庄：对。

鲁：如果我们认为人跟物之间存在一种更加复杂的、会不断演化的"用"的动态关系，这难道不是现代主义建立起来的真正核心吗？

庄：怎么讲？

鲁：为什么杰弗里·斯科特写现代主义是人文主义？我觉得因为现代主义最核心的东西就是它确认了建筑和人之间的"用"的关系。人在建筑里是真实存在的，是一个有身体的人。

庄：像这样从人的角度去考虑建筑，抛去功利，单纯为人或者社会，这是一个向好的意愿，建筑同时存在与冷峻的经济生产之间的关系，这两个建筑的关系很有意思。这个时代也面临着这样的问题，我们正处于经济、技术变革的过程中，要再次去思考这个问题。

鲁：我再问最后一个问题。回忆一下你在学生时代对古代园林的兴趣，在手法主义背后的离合、关系，你当时对人有兴趣吗？

庄：当然，但是它跟现在的点是不一样的，当时我注意到传统文献里，园林、传统民居建筑会大量涉及非常具体的人事、情感方面的叙述。我记得当时还引用了《项脊轩志》中"庭有枇杷树，吾妻死之年所手植也，今已

you feel uncomfortable, you have to adapt yourself to nature, if you look through the historical angle, perhaps this discomfort contributes more to your genetic evolution than keeping you comfortable, right?

ZS: Yes.

LA: If we think there is a more complex and evolving dynamic relationship of usage between human and things, isn't it the real core of modernism?

ZS: I am all ears to your explanation.

LA: Why did Geoffrey Scott see modernism as humanism? That's because the core of modernism is that it confirms the "use" relationship between architecture and human. Man does exist in architecture, a real man with body.

ZS: It is a good intention to think about architecture from the perspective of human beings, refusing to be utilitarian, with the purpose of benefitting human beings or society. However, there is other relationship between architecture and economic production. These two relationships are very interesting. At the present age there are also similar problems. Facing economic and technological changes, we need to think about this again.

LA: Last question, just refresh your memory, the interest you took in Chinese traditional gardens in student age, you are researching separation and unification, researching relationships beyond mannerism, were you also interested in human at that time?

ZS: Of course, but it is different from my present point of view. At that time, I noticed that in the traditional literature, gardens, traditional residential buildings usually involved a lot of very specific narrative on people and things. I once quoted the chapters in Xiang Ji Xuan: "The loquat tree I planted in the courtyard the year my wife passed away has grown up now to give shade." This descrip-

亭亭如盖矣"这样的章句，非常具体。我一直认为园林是不能用抽象的方式来研究的。

鲁：确认一下，你是一个人文主义者，不是一个技术主义者。

庄：我对技术也很感兴趣啊。[图18]

18　鲁安东（右）对谈庄慎（左）
Dialogue between Lu Andong (right)
and Zhuang Shen (left)

tion was very specific. I have always believed that we shouldn't study gardens in an abstract way.

LA: Just make sure that you are a humanist, not a technician.

ZS: I am also interested in technology. [fig. 18]

鲁安东

南京大学建筑与城市规划学院教授，南京大学—剑桥大学建筑与城市合作研究中心主任、南京大学可沟通城市实验室主任。

曾任剑桥大学沃夫森学院驻院学者、德国德绍建筑研究所客座教授、澳大利亚昆士兰大学访问教授、美国宾州州立大学亨利·鲁斯访问学者，担任英国 *Architectural Design (AD)*、《建筑学报》、《时代建筑》、《建筑师》等学术期刊客座主编。2015 年发起"格物工作营"，2015-2018 年发起"南京长江大桥记忆计划"，2017 年在纽约新当代美术馆举办"红色未来主义"专题展览，2018 年主持了伦敦设计双年展中国馆并获得特别荣誉奖。

LU Andong

Professor in School of Architecture and Urban Planning, Nanjing University, Director of the University of Cambridge-Nanjing University Research Centre on Architecture & Urbanism and Director of the Communicable City Laboratory.

He was a Fellow of Wolfson College at the University of Cambridge, Guest Professor at Dessau Institute of Architecture (DIA), Germany, ATCH Research Fellow at the University of Queensland, and Henry Luce Foundation Visiting Scholar at the Pennsylvania State University. He acted as guest-editor for academic journals including *AD, Architectural Journal, Time + Architecture*, and *The Architect*. He initiated the Investigate-It Workshop in 2015 and the Memory Project of the Nanjing Yangtze River Bridge (2015–2018). He curated a series of research-based exhibitions, including: Red Futurism (New Museum, New York 2017) and the Chinese Pavilion (London Design Biennale 2018) receiving Honourable Mention Award.

论文
Articles

设计研究"改变"的纲要
Design Research Outline on "Change"

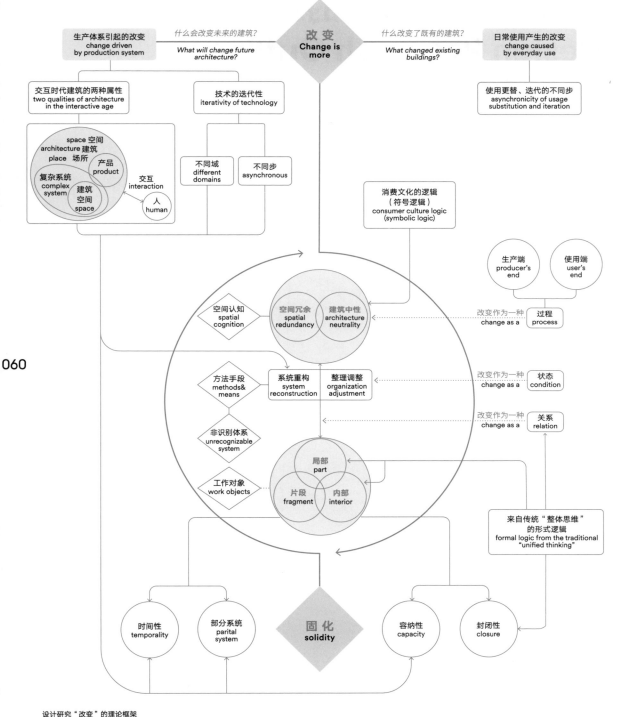

1

设计研究"改变"的理论框架
Theoretical Framework for Design Research on "Change"

本书选编的11篇论文，包括9篇中文论文和2篇曾独立发表的英文论文，是阿科米星建筑设计事务所于2012—2018年间在国内外专业期刊中陆续发表的设计研究论文。这些文章虽然完成于不同时期，但相互之间有共同的内在联系，即围绕着"建筑改变"这一核心问题，各有侧重地在具体的主题里描述我们各阶段工作的大致轮廓。这篇纲要是对阿科米星整体工作与思考的框架梳理和系统阐述，以帮助读者更容易阅读这些文章，并获得更为清晰和完整的理解。

设计研究"改变"的背景

我们希望阿科米星的工作有探索性。通过实践与设计研究能够观察捕捉到还未被意识或重视到的、具有普遍性的建筑学认知原理与方法。

这些愿望的外在原因是，我们认为城市与城市建筑将是我们实践工作的重点。城市建筑在城市里占用有限并相互关联制约的资源，随着社会经济、文化生活的变化而变动，实践需要新的认知理论。内在原因是我们认为当代建筑学需要新的基础研究，认为建筑学正处在一个改变与面对未来的时期。这样的感觉并非只是一种直觉，也来自我们实践的切身体验。我们之所以觉得做这样的设计研究会有所收获，跟我们长期在国内实践密切关联。参与、目睹了中国数十年的社会经济的发展，城市化的快速增长与变化，我们认为中国当代城市化的时空压缩情况是独特的，完全可能在此基础上获得一些新认知和新启示。

这也是将"改变"确定为阿科米星日后工作方向的认知切入点的由来和背景。

我们做此系统性的大框架梳理，目的是在自己的工作中能养成一个积累整理的习惯。因为我们将多元复杂的日常城市建筑作为实践与研究对象，容易沉溺其中，中性的理论框架有助于使我们的设计研究避免个人式的趣味与偏好，也避免仅仅是发展应用既有的设计认知与原理，或仅仅是证明或完善已有的理论。

改变是建筑的"自然"属性

改变是事物的"自然"属性，它不仅属于城市和建筑，它也属于万事万物。我们生活在一个变化的状态当中——这也是建成环境身在其中的世界。

The eleven articles selected and compiled in this book are from the design research papers published continuously in domestic and overseas professional periodicals by Atelier Archmixing from 2012 to 2018. Although these papers have been completed at different times, they share echoing concerns. Through emphasizing the core issue "architectural change", they have profiled our work at different periods under specific themes and with various focuses. This outline is a structural organization and systematic elaboration on the overall work and reflection of Atelier Achimixing. We hope it will help the readers to gain clearer and more comprehensive understanding.

Background for the Design Research on "Change"

We hope the work at Atelier Archmixing would be full of explorations. Through practice and design research, we hope to observe and capture those covered or neglected architectural cognition and method with universal meaning.

The apparent reason why we have these hopes is that urban areas and urban architecture will be the major focus of our practices. Urban architecture takes limited and inter-related resources in the city. They would change when the socio-economic and cultural life changes. That's why new practices ask for new cognitive theories. The inner reason lies in that we think contemporary architecture needs new basic researches. Now we feel architecture is in a period of change to face the future. Such a feeling is not just an instinct. It comes from our practice experiences for many years in China, and we believe such kind of design research would be rewarding. After witnessing the quick social-economic development and the rapid urbanization in China within decades, we think the time and space compression in contemporary Chinese urbanization is unique, it can form a solid basis for new architectural cognition and inspiration.

That's why we decided to take "change" as the main focus for Atelier Archmixing's future work.

To cultivate a habit of gathering and organizing work experiences, we provided here a systematic theoretical framework. We don't want to be overwhelmed when we take the diverse and complex everyday urban architecture as the subject of our practice and research. A neutral theoretical structure may avoid our indulging in personal tastes and preferences during design research. It can also prevent us from developing and applying only those ready-made design cognitions and theories, or satisfying in proving or improving current theories.

Change is "Natural" to Architecture

Change is the "natural" property for objects. This property is hidden not only in cities and buildings but also in everything. We live in a state of constant change, so as the world of the built environment.

改变是既有建筑学的认知盲点

改变发生在万物之中，普遍到建筑学不再试图思考其专业属性。久而久之，这也成为建筑学的一个认知盲点。

这并不是说建筑学只关注那种固定的状态。建筑学以往的研究、工作的思维方式与关注点，习惯放在从概念预设到如何把它实现。即使其中重视变化的部分，大多也是设计可以预期的变化或者是希望控制的变化，会归纳其类型。这不知不觉形成了一种固化的思维。面对那些意料之外的，或不受原来概念控制的变化——那些往往要发生在建成之后的使用过程中，由其他力量和因素推动形成的变化，既有建筑学是缺乏认知的。

改变是一种对于常识的专业反思

10 年来，阿科米星的实践与设计研究工作背后一直有隐含的内在逻辑，线索可以追溯到成立之前主持建筑师庄慎的初始工作经验。这些不同时期、不同层面、不同程度的认知与实践由于不曾间断的设计工作与思考习惯，慢慢积累发展。最后归结为更为明晰的切入点。

"改变"就是这样一个常识式的切入点。

城市与建筑的改变是一种独特的常识，这样的独特性是指：一方面，改变是一种显性的物质变化，它与物质和使用的变化有关，我们沉浸在它的显而易见之中却早已忽视它。另一方面，改变是一种隐性的控制力量，它发生于社会生活与生产体系的变化推动之中，是系统力量的结果，我们同样沉浸在其中但很难察觉。

而建筑学如果能在常识层面产生出新的认知与方法，那一定是件令人兴奋的事。

改变有两个问题：什么改变了既有的建筑？什么会改变未来的建筑？

我们这一代建筑师，大概都会身处这样一种过程中：感觉到建筑学的转变过程可能在发生。这样的处境自然带来某种焦虑状态，回看现代主义建筑运动兴起的 20 世纪初和反思现代建筑思想爆发的 20 世纪六七十年代，当下的年代是相对疲弱的。在看似丰富的变化之下是建筑学游离于社会生产、社会大众的边缘化状态。空间制造的刺激性增大，但信息的爆炸也导致感知的疲软。空间需求，体验度的供给超出了人类生物体能够承受的限度，既有空间

Change is a Cognitive Blindspot of Current Architecture Discipline

Change happens in everything. It is so universal that architecture field no longer consider its academic meaning. With time, it has become a cognitive blindspot in architecture discipline.

This doesn't mean architectural field only cares about the fixed state. The former architectural researches, thinking patterns focus more on the concept creation and its execution. Even when we pay attention to changes, we usually design those predictable or managable changes. In either way, we will categorize them. Without noticing, a fixed mindset is formed. When faced with unexpected or uncontrolable changes, which are mostly present after construction due to other powers and factors, the existing architecture discipline lacks knowledge.

Change is a Professional Reflection on Common Knowledge

For a decade, there is always a hidden logic behind the practice and design research at Atelier Archmixing, which actually roots in Zhuang Shen, the principal architect's early working experience far before Archimixng was founded. Based on continuous design and thinking, these cognition and experience at different times, different levels and different degrees have gradually accumulated into a clearer breakthrough.

"Change" is such a breakthrough point of common knowledge.

Change in cities and buildings is an unique common sense. In one aspect, change is an obvious physical modification which is related to the change of object and its usage. We are so immersed in its obviousness that we have ignored it. In the other aspect, change is a hidden controlling power. It appears in the development of social life and production system, a result of systematic power. We are too immersed to detect it.

If architecture discipline could make cognitive and methodological breakthrough on a common knowledge level, it must be exciting.

Two Questions Concerning Change: What Changed Existing Architecture? What Will Change Future Architecture?

For architects of our generation, most have the sense that transformation is taking place in the architecture discipline. This situation will naturally bring anxiety. When we took a retrospect on the early 20th century when modern architecture movement thrived, and the 1960s and 1970s when the reflection of modern architecture exploded, we may find the current age is relatively weak. Behind the seemingly rich changes, architecture discipline is actually straying away from the social production and mass population. Even though the spatial stim-

价值的过剩是我们这个时代面临的普遍状态。一切预示着系统性的改变将要发生，种种景象仿佛再现了一个典型的转变时期的图景：一个复杂系统正在走向自身的末期，将要被另一个新的系统跳跃迭代。

"什么改变了既有的建筑？什么会改变未来的建筑？"有关改变的两个问题引导我们对当下与未来的建筑改变进行研究。关注改变会把设计研究的注意力引导向当下与未来的空间使用端，这与传统建筑设计研究集中于生产端完全不同。

建筑学将要面临的问题是未来建筑会怎样改变，这些改变将带来与传统建筑学价值观与内核之间的矛盾问题。进一步，更重要的是要问这样的改变给人类社会究竟将带来怎样的影响？是好是坏？正是基于此，我们认为首先要研究的正是"改变"本身的原理。

什么会改变既有的建筑？

什么会改变既有的建筑？既有建筑改变的主要原因是日常使用，是使用的迭代与建筑物质变化的不同步引起了改变。

进入后工业社会以后，消费系统本身不鼓励空间寿命与空间使用相匹配，而是鼓励空间的快速更迭。当代的建筑空间设计呈现出多样的变化，但表象之下空间逻辑实质同质化。这也使传统的建筑设计方法和工具失效，需要找到新的认知与方法。

对中国建筑师而言，情况更为特殊。中国社会的这种变化尤其突出，经济发展推动的产业使用更迭，社会生活与习俗的巨大变化在过去几十年里呈现高度压缩状态。这样的状态正是中国当代建筑设计广阔的实践场所与研究空间。然而，中国本土各类设计企业中的实践建筑师在这股洪流的裹挟下，投身于生产与生意之中，却没有太多时间开展深入的建筑学反思和讨论。他们使用的概念往往是对西方相关建筑话语的二手消费。而另一方面，学院内的研究者与理论学者，大多又因为较少涉及如此广泛的第一手实践，而倾向于回旋在传统的学说与历史的启示之中。我们很遗憾地看到，因为中国建筑界尚未形成产业发展与建筑文化研究的互相配合，结果是，在数十年的建筑空间积累之后，本土原创性的建筑理论研究与设计研究都处于碎片化状态，尚缺乏对于嘈杂无序的空间堆积背后有没有建

ulation is increasing, the information explosion would leave us insensible. Space and experience have overflown to a degree human being could not bear. The excessive value of existing space is what we commonly face now. All these hint that a systematic change will occur. All these seem to reproduce the landscape of a typical transformation period: a complicated system is extincting and will be replaced by a new one.

"What has changed the existing architecture? What will change the future architecture?" These two questions will guide our research on current and future architectural change. A focus on change will bring the attention of design research to the use end now and in the future. This is totally different from the traditional focus on the production end.

The question architecture discipline faces is how the future architecture will change. Since these changes will generate conflicts with traditional architectural values and core issues. The further question is what kind of influence has this change brought to our society? Is it positive or negative? Based on these questions, we put the priority on examing the principle of "change" itself.

What Will Change Existing Architecture?

The reason why current architecture changes is due to daily use. Change occurs when usage updates fail to catch the pace with the physical change in buildings.

After post-industrialization, consumption system doesn't encourage a coordination between the life span of space and its use. Instead, it encourages rapid spatial updates. On the surface, contemporary architectural space design looks diverse, but in essence, the space logic underneath is homogenized. This homogenization has made traditional architectural design methods and tools invalid as well, so we need to find new ways of cognition and method.

For Chinese architects, the situation is even more special. Due to rapid industry updates pushed by economic development, spatial homogenization in China is even more prominent. Great changes in social life and customs in the past decades have been highly condensed. Such a situation has formed a broad stage for Chinese contemporary design practice and research. Having thrown themselves in production and business in such a whirl, local architects have no further strength to dig into reflections and discussions on architecture discipline. The concepts they rely on are mostly secondhand knowledge from the western world. On the other aspect, the researchers and theorists in colleges tend to circle in traditional theories and historical revelations since they relatively have less firsthand practice. It is pitiful that since there hasn't formed a coordination between industry development and architectural cultural research, after decades of space accumulation, original architectural theoretical research and design research are all fragmented. Few systematic architectural reflection on the chaotic spatial

筑学内容的系统深思。其中，日常空间与城市的改变显然正是这样被忽视的、可能产生新内容和新方向的领域之一。

什么会改变未来的建筑？

什么会改变未来的建筑？主要是生产体系更新引发的改变，技术的迭代与建筑的物质变化不仅不同步，而且会在不同领域引起改变。人机交互时代的建筑，有两种属性与技术相关，一方面，空间、建筑、场所是容纳科技产品、复杂信息系统的场所；另一方面，建筑本身也是一个可以被技术赋能的复杂系统。正因为如此，技术的发展对建筑的影响增大了。

这部分的改变是未来的，也是未知的，某种程度上是一种努力的预见。建筑学相对于其他技术的迟缓发展是由其体系决定的。生产体系更倾向于在敏感端发生变化，比如在工厂的生产端与个人的消费端。此时，普通的建筑总是反应迟缓。这并非是因为建筑的沉重，而是因为建筑在社会生产体系中处于相对的末端。以往，建筑主要是一种综合技术与社会文化、艺术的物质空间，而现在，这样的

属性正渐渐被其作为生产体系中的一个角色所替代。相应地，建筑师的作用也在悄悄地发生着变化。当建筑师意识到自己是正变化的生产体系里的一员时，传统的文化与价值体系还未及时地更新调整，这就造成了现在的建筑师社会地位的尴尬：既非属于传统，也非属于未来，既非属于文化艺术，也非属于市场技术。

空间冗余与中性的建筑

改变形成了空间冗余，冗余不仅是物质的，同时也是符号的。空间冗余就是空间与空间文化在时间上的改变积累。

不断改变的建筑是中性的。建筑的中性也正是空间冗余在时间历史中的切面属性，是用时间历史的视角来看空间冗余。

阿科米星的研究始于空间的传统美学研究，继而关注消费文化逻辑、建筑空间混合，逐步向大众文化和日常城市研究方向发展。空间冗余是我们 2014 年提出的建筑认知概念。这个概念的主要意图是将建筑与城市空间放在一个时间的维度里去理解。将建造与使用共同作为设计的前

accumulation has achieved. Everyday space and urban change are obviously one neglected area where new content and direction may emerge.

What Will Change Future Architecture?

What will change future architecture? Changes occur mainly because of updates in production system. Updates in technology never keeps the pace with the material change in architecture. Their changes happen in different fields. In the era of human-computer interaction, two architectural properties are related to technology. In one aspect, space, architecture, and place are where scientific products and complex information system are contained. In the other aspect, architecture itself could be a complicated system endowed by technology. Consequently the influence on architecture due to technological development has increased.

This part of change belongs to the future. It is uncertain. To some extent, it is also a prediction. Compared with technological development, the architectural development is rather slow because of its system. Production system tends to change on the most sensitive ends, such as the production end in factory and individual consumption end in everyday life. Normal architecture usually react slowly. It is not because architecture is heavy, but because architecture lies at the relatively far end in social production system. In the past, architecture is a physical space combining technological,

social, cultural and artistic issues. But now this property is gradually replaced by a role in production system. Architects' role has also changed into a part of the changing production system. Since the traditional culture and values haven't updated, contemporary architects are facing an embarrassing social situation. It is neither traditional nor futuristic; neither cultural-artistic, nor market or technology oriented.

Spatial Redundancy and Neutral Architecture

Change has led to spatial redundancy. Redundancy is not only material, but also symbolic. Spatial redundancy is the change and accumulation of space and spatial culture along time.

The ever-changing architecture is neutral. Such neutrality is also an aspect of spatial redundancy in time and history, which allows us to view spatial redundancy from the perspective of time and history.

This cognitive concept about architecture—spatial redundancy was raised by Atelier Archmixing in 2014 based on our researches from traditional aesthetics in space, consumption culture and logic, mixture of architectural space, to our attention to popular culture and everyday urban research. The main intention of this concept is to place architecture and urban space in a time dimension and put construction and use together as design preconditions. In this way, we open a dimension for cognition and design method, which would be

提，这就为设计的认知与方法打开了一个扩展的维度，我们认为这也是对于建筑更完整的认知。时间变化的维度带来的空间理解完全不同于传统固化或预测式的空间判断。

整理、调整与系统重构

使用引发的改变主要体现在建成后的日常使用对空间的整理与调整上。生产体系引发的改变主要体现在对空间与建筑的系统重构上。

阿科米星的设计项目包含城市中大量日常普通功能类型的房屋改造以及新建工程，还有不少属于局部的设计、轻质的调整和有效的改造。这类项目的状态与我们在城市研究里看到的建筑的自然使用和改变的状态完全一致。这种整理与调整的方式也成为我们事务所的主要设计方法。另一方面，新的技术发展与生产消费系统的模式改变也势不可挡地带来建筑在大的社会生产体系里的重新定位。

局部、内部、片段

经过调整与重构的建筑与空间，产生了新的局部、内部和片段的自治。

局部、内部、片段，这三者有含义重叠的地方，但它们都在表述一个概念。这个概念不是这三者各自能够独立完成定义的。局部更像是总的描述，但更倾向于物理形体；内部更倾向于空间，而且更具有维度意味；片段则偏向于时间与系统。局部具有自治性。内部有两种属性：一是内部的容纳性，内部可看作一个中性空间，可容纳差异性系统；二是内部的封闭性，内部即一个体系，封闭体系就意味着等待破坏，被打破这也意味着系统的重建。片段具有时间性，片段与局部不同，局部是物理性的，而片段有时间性与部分系统性。

局部与内部在传统的整体思维里也是重要的对象。比较有意思的是，在传统空间美学里，认识整体的局部方式，是一种通过破坏整体，从局部感知整体的思维方式。

局部、内部、片段，是由空间冗余引起的，也与空间冗余相一致。局部、内部、片段正是空间冗余的一个侧面，也是它的一部分。

我们能够越来越肯定的是，这三者将成为我们未来工作的重要领域。

what we think a more complete cognition. Such spatial understanding brought about by change in time is totally different from traditional fixed or predicted judgement on space.

Organization, Adjustment and Systematic Reconstruction

Change due to use is mainly shown in spatial organization and adjustment caused by daily use after the building was built. Change from production system is mainly embodied in systematic restructure of space and architecture.

The projects Atelier Archmixing takes part in mostly include ordinary building renovation and new construction. There are also many partial designs, light adjustments, and effective renovations. The state of these projects are totally the same as those under natural use and change we see in urban study. This organization and adaptation have also become our major design methods. What's more, mode change in new technological development and production-consumption system have inevitably reoriented architecture in the social production system.

Parts, Interior, Fragments

After adjustment and reorganization, buildings and spaces generate fresh autonomy in parts, interior, and fragments.

Parts, interior and fragments are overlapped in meaning but they express the same concept which couldn't be defined independently by each of three terms. Parts is more like a general description but focuses more on physical shape; interior directs towards space and is meaningful in dimension; fragments tilts to time and system. Parts are autonomous. Interior has two properties: one is its inclusiveness. The inside could be treated as a neutral space and could tolerate differentiated systems. The other is that interior is closed, it is a system. Being in a closed state means this state is waiting to be destroyed or broken through; in other words, it means the system needs to be reconstructed. Fragments are featured timeliness. Different from parts which is physical, fragments have to do with time and is partially systematic.

Parts and interior are also essential in traditional thinking of unity. More interestingly, in traditional Chinese aesthetics, the way of learning parts from the whole is also the way of breaking the unity and sensing the whole through parts.

Parts, interior and fragments result from spatial redundancy and also coherent with it. Parts, interior and fragments are one side and also one part of spatial redundancy.

What we are sure about is all these three aspects will be the important fields in our future work.

Structural Relationship in the Frame

The three groups of concepts each targets an area in Atelier Archmixing's reflection and practice in architecture. Spatial redundancy and neutral architecture is our spatial cog-

框架中的结构关系

空间冗余与建筑中性，整理、调整与系统重构，局部、内部与片段，这三组概念分别对应阿科米星建筑思考和实践中的空间认知、方法手段和工作对象。

从"改变"这个主题角度来看，空间冗余、建筑中性意味着改变作为一种过程。整理、调整、系统重构意味着改变作为一种手段和存在状态。局部、内部、片段与空间冗余、建筑中性的关系，意味着改变作为一种关系。

本文由庄慎为本书撰写，作为全书理论文章的引言。

nition. Reorganization, adjustment and systematic restructure are our working methods. Parts, interior and fragments are the objects of our work.

Seen from the theme "change", spatial redundancy and architectural neutrality is change as a process. Reorganization, adjustment and systematic reconstruction is changed as a method and state of existence. Parts, interior and fragments in relation to spatial redundancy and architectural neutrality is change as a relation.

This outline was written by Zhuang Shen as the introduction of the following theoretical articles.

2

选择在个人与大众之间
Standing Between
the Individual and the Public

1   科幻电影《我，机器人》中具有自主意识的NS-5型机器人Sonny
The self-aware NS-5 robot Sonny in sci-fi movie *I, Robot*

作为一名职业建筑师，工作不仅是一份维持生活的职业，同时也意味着一种直接的经验和责任：丰富建筑学在当代的价值，充实建筑师自身的价值，探索更多可能性。如今，艺术和文化的创造越来越受到经济系统的控制，建筑领域也不例外，这里充满了困惑与迷茫，消融与突变，危机与可能。在这一过程中，职业实践中最多也最艰难的就是选择。

当代建筑的困境：个人与大众的分离

我们认为今天建筑学面临的困难并不在于难以把握的多样性与快速的变化，而在于表面的丰富多彩难以掩盖的内在空乏。建筑学日益成为一种"单一"的建筑学。单向的建筑价值系统造成的诸多矛盾中，最突出的是，作为个人的建筑师及其设计作品与大众及其真实生活之间的关系日渐疏离，这更削弱了建筑学发展的动力。

造成建筑、建筑师与大众分离的原因是多方面的。在商品社会里，关于建筑的一切都变成了商品。从重要的公共项目到普通的商品住宅，建筑直接产生的利润和间接创造的经济和社会效益成为衡量其成败的主要标准。城市管

理者将建设活动视为经营城市的资本，希望每幢建筑都成为独树一帜的形象工程，创造"毕尔巴鄂效应"[1]，用建筑吸引旅游者和投资者，扩大城市的竞争力和影响力。房地产投资商则热衷于把所有财力和智力的投入都转化为卖点，追求利润最大化。在这样的实践中，投资者的利益决定着建造的目的和方法。与此同时，新技术、新材料的使用也被纳入以生产—消费为目标的体系。就像日新月异的工业产品[2] [图1]，其技术处理已不再冰冷无情，而是愈发人性化，结合着具有无穷想象力的审美趣味，这也是未来建筑的写照。目前，如何运用新技术、新材料的主要推动力是消费引导，它是一把双刃剑，一方面解放了强大的创新能力，另一方面则充满了市场经济的利益至上原则。

以上一切表明：建筑发展的动力从以往对大众生活的理解和关心转向以刺激大众消费为目的的系统化引导。在这一过程中，设计很大程度上已经转变为生产和包装空间商品的艺术，是文化产业的一部分。建筑艺术原有的自主性与社会性逐渐为消费逻辑所取代，制造差异和时尚成为创新的主要内容。同时，以市场为导向的艺术创造必然偏向于资本与权贵的利益，非但未能促进社会的公平与和

For a professional architect, work is more than earning a living; it means a direct experience and responsibility: exploring the values and possibilities of architecture in the contemporary era, and enriching the values and possibilities of architects themselves. Today, the creation of art and culture is increasingly controlled by the economic system, and architecture is no exception. In this process, making choices is the most common and difficult part of professional practice.

The Dilemma of Contemporary Architecture: the Separation of Individuals from the Public

We believe that the difficulties the architecture is facing today lie not in the diversity and rapid changes that elude our grasp, but in the inner emptiness, that richness and colorfulness on the surface have difficulty concealing. Architecture is increasingly becoming "uniform" architecture. Among the many contradictions caused by a one-dimensional architectural value system, the most prominent is that the increasing dissociation of individual architects and their designs from the public and their real lives, which further puts a brake on the development of architecture.

There are various causes for the separation of architecture and architects from the public. In commodity society, every-thing about architecture is a commodity. The direct profits and indirect economic and social benefits generated by ar-chitecture in areas ranging from important public projects to

ordinary commodity housing are the dominant measures of its success. Urban administrators regard construction activities as the operating capital of their cities. They want each building to be a unique image project, pursuing the "Bilbao effect"[1], creating "Wow Architecture" to attract tourists and investors, and expand the competitiveness and influence of their cities. Real estate investors are keen to turn all financial and intellectual input into selling points to maximize profits. In this practice, the interests of investors dictate the purpose and method of construction. On the other hand, the use of new technologies and new materials has also been incorporated into a system geared towards "production-consumption". Just like in the case of ever-changing industrial products[2] [fig. 1], its technical treatment is no longer cold and ruthless, but increasingly humanized, combined with infinitely imaginative aesthetic taste. This is what future architecture looks like. At present, the main driving force behind the use of new technologies and new materials is consumption-oriented. It is a double-edged sword. On the one hand, it unleashes a strong capacity for technical innovation. On the other hand, it is governed by the "economic interests first" principle in the market economy.

All of the above shows that the driving force behind the development of architecture has shifted from understanding and caring for the public lives to systematic guidance aimed at stimulating mass consumption. In this process, the design

谐，反而加大了社会的分裂与隔离。这种情况导致的建筑的单一性，就是当代建筑所面临的与大众生活分离的困境。

最后，相对于现代主义时期被视为时代英雄和社会先锋的崇高地位，今天建筑师的社会地位和理想抱负明显下降了。通过规划现代城市和为工人阶级设计社会住宅，现代主义建筑师得以把个人理想和大众需求相结合。但是今天，以赢利为目的的商业项目成为建筑实践的主要内容，建筑师与经济系统从对立走向合作，最典型的就是，曾经被现代主义先锋所排斥的商业领域，现在已经成为前卫建筑的实验地。在库哈斯、赫尔佐格与德梅隆、扎哈·哈迪德、伊东丰雄、安藤忠雄、皮亚诺、斯蒂文·霍尔等国际明星建筑师与 PRADA、CHANEL、KENZO、HERMÈS、LV 等顶级时尚品牌的高调合作中，这种商业与艺术的联姻，或者说奢侈品牌成为建筑艺术最大赞助商的趋向彰显无遗。建筑师在利益上与社会中上阶层保持一致是现实社会发展的表现，而不利的一面就是其对普通大众的物质精神生活缺乏了解的条件和动力。更进一步，因为现代主义的乌托邦理想在现实中存在诸多弊端，今天的建筑师大多

认同其社会身份已然从改革社会的激进分子转变为改良局部环境的技术专家。以资本为导向的设计倾向于将创造限定在技术和美学范围内，建筑师的个人理想与大众利益的关系是间接、消极和被动的。

建筑师作为组织者：个人与大众之间的价值取向与策略

对于建筑学越来越受到"生产—消费"体系影响这一事实，我们觉得建筑师能采取的立场大体可以分为三类：其一是与生产—消费系统同步，自觉地成为其中重要的创造力量；其二是坚持原有的文化精英主义立场，远离商业体系，通过选择特定项目和业主来实现建筑理想；其三是在生产—消费体系的背景下，关注大众生活与建筑相互作用的新可能，寻找建筑师的新位置，使建筑师的作用更广泛与独立。

第一种选择是主动的，也是主流。如果现实允许，我们很支持这种选择。其核心在于产品的品质，关键在于建筑师与社会经济、技术、生产水平的协同合作。作为当今建筑发展的主要动力，这种自上而下的方式主要起到引导消费主义生活方式的作用，使大众被动接受对生产—消费

has largely been transformed into the art of producing and packaging space commodities and has been part of the cultural industry. The autonomy and sociality of architectural art have been gradually replaced by the logic of consumption. Making differences and creating fashion has become the main content of innovation. Meanwhile, market-oriented art creation is inevitably biased towards the interests of capital and the bigwigs. Instead of promoting social fairness and harmony, it has increased social fragmentation and segregation. The uniformity of architecture caused by this situation is the dilemma contemporary architecture is facing architecture is separating from the public life .

Finally, compared with the lofty status of architects who were regarded as heroes and pioneers in the modernism era, the social status, and ambition of today's architects have obviously declined. By planning modern cities and designing social housing for the working class, modernist architects were able to combine personal ideals with popular demand. But today, profit-oriented commercial projects have become the main content of architectural practice. The relationship between architects and the economic system has changed, from confrontation to cooperation. As the most representative case, the business domain once rejected by pioneers of modernism has now become the testing ground for avant-garde architecture. The marriage of business and art or the trend of luxury brands becoming the biggest sponsors

of architectural art is evident in high-profile cooperation between international star architects (Koolhaas, Herzog & de Meuron, Hadid, Toyo Ito, Tadao Ando, Peano, and Steven Holl) and top fashion brands (PRADA, CHANNEL, KENZO, HERMS, and LV). As a result of social development, the interests of architects and the upper-middle-class have remained the same. It has caused a lack of condition and motivation to understand the material and spiritual life of the general public. Further, because of the many drawbacks of modernist utopian ideals in reality, instead of regarding themselves as radical social reformers, most architects now identify themselves as technologists who specialize in improving local environments. Capital-oriented design tends to confine creation to the limits of technology and aesthetics. The relationship between architects' personal ideals and public interest is indirect, negative and passive.

Architect as Organizer: Values and Strategy Between the Individual and the Public

Regarding the fact that architecture is increasingly influenced by the "production-consumption" system, we could roughly divide architects' positions into three categories. The first group keeps pace with the "production-consumption" system and consciously serves as its important creative force. The second adheres to the original cultural elitist position, stays away from the business system, and realizes architec-

体系有利的价值系统，而不是深入大众生活去理解和发现其物质精神需求并设法满足。同时，在中国，由于社会管理系统和物质技术条件的整体不足，各个地区发展极不均衡。在工程实践中经常会碰到理想与现实产生冲突的问题，品质某种程度上取决于运气：要么没材料没技术，要么有材料没技术，有材料有技术的状况则非常难得。这大概也是中国会出现那么多"山寨"建筑的重要原因吧。

第二种选择是对商业体系的反抗。在本质上，持这种态度的建筑师的精英意识与大众的文化和鉴赏力是相排斥的。然而，精英主义的立场同样面临被消费的处境，阳春白雪的高雅品位成为与其他大众化风格形成差异的策略，甚至被当作身份地位的符号象征成为建筑营销和城市经营的策略，这也是国际明星建筑师在全世界广受追捧的重要原因。这些单纯从某种专业领域来看具有价值的建筑作品，甚至可能导向一种将资本和权力，以及迷人的环境资源作为实现职业理想的唯一途径的误区。

第三种选择是不回避生产—消费系统的影响，也不将个人限定于专业领域，而更关注现实本身，并希望从巨大的变革和冲突中寻找建筑与社会生活结合的新机会。这种

选择认为，个人与大众之间应该形成一种双向作用，既不是由上至下的强制作用，也不是自下而上的纯粹自发行为，而是通过建筑师的主动参与形成一种良性互动关系。其目的在于既能与社会发展保持一致，也能有益于改善大众生活和社会环境。总之，选择在个人与大众之间的价值取向，这就是笔者的主张。

今天的建筑学最要紧的不是固守以往的经验与位置，而应致力于探寻新的策略和原则。这种新的普遍的方式不会存在于原来的系统与范畴之中，而会存在于不断消融的各种系统与范畴之间。高雅文化和通俗文化之间从来没有像今天这样具有相互交织融合的可能性，而这就可能成为当代建筑发展的契机。

对于建筑师而言，他们最为关心的是，能否找到一种广泛适用的设计策略，使立场的选择不致沦为空洞的口号。现在，这种选择既是一种价值的选择，同时也是一种策略的选择。通过上面的比较可以看出，这种选择根据国内的情况，一方面弱化了第一种选择中技术和品质的限制，另一方面选择社会文化领域的切入点使其更有适应性与开放性。对于建筑师来说，价值界限消融与转变预示了

tural ideals by selecting specific projects and clients. The third focuses on new possibilities of interaction between the public lives and architecture in the context of the "production-consumption" system in order to make the architects' role broader and more independent.

The first is an active and mainstream choice. If reality permits, we highly support this choice. Its core lies in the product quality, and the key point is the collaboration between architects and social economy, technology and production level. As today's main driving force behind the architectural development, this top-down approach mainly plays a role in steering the public towards a consumerist lifestyle, making the public passively accept a value system beneficial to the production-consumption system rather than go deep into the public lives to understand, discover and try to meet their material and spiritual needs. Meanwhile, in China, due to the inadequate social management systems and the limit of substance and technologies, the development among different regions is uneven. The conflict between ideals and reality is common in construction practice. To some extent, good quality grows more dependent on luck: You may have neither materials nor technologies, or you have only materials but no technologies. It is rarely found that you have both materials and technologies. This is probably an important reason why there are so many "copycat" buildings in China.

The second choice is to resist the business system.

In essence, the architects who hold elitist mentality are exclusive with the public culture and taste. However, elitism could also be consumed. Highbrow refined taste has become a strategy to differentiate from other popular styles. It is even regarded as a symbol of status and has become a strategy for architectural marketing and city management. This is also an important reason why international star architects are widely sought after all over the world. These architectural works are valuable only when judged from the perspective of particular expertise. This may even lead to a misunderstanding that capital and power, as well as fascinating environmental resources, are the only way to achieve career aspirations.

The third choice is to neither shy away from the effects of the production-consumption system nor limit the individual to a field of expertise. One shall pay more attention to reality and find new opportunities for integrating architecture and social life in the midst of dramatic changes and conflicts. This choice holds that there should be a two-way interaction between the individual and the public, which is neither a top-down imposition nor a purely bottom-up spontaneous action. It shall be a positive interaction through architects' active participation. Its purpose is not only to keep pace with social development but also to improve the public lives and social environment. In conclusion, we suggest choosing a value orientation between the individual and the public.

For today's architecture, the most important thing is not

建筑师可以成为另外一种角色，既不是参与创造者，也不是对立反抗者，而是积极组织者，是另一种意义上的积极参与者。今天，在中国，建筑实践活动具有很大的不确定性，社会文化背景又相当复杂，建筑师作为一位组织者，积极主动地分析、理解现实条件，并在此基础上有效组织各种设计要素和技术可能性，是一种开放的设计策略，因为这种组织的方式是建立在既有的范畴、界限和物质内容，比如技术和材料之外的，可以涉及不同的设计要素，采用不同的系统模式，也能带来不同的效果。因此这种方式具有广泛的适用性和很大的灵活性。通过组织当代建筑面临的各种关系，建筑师可以重构建筑与社会大众之间的交流和融合，这既是建筑全面的价值所在，也是建筑师的独立的社会价值所在。

从离合到混合：用组织的设计方式联系个人与大众

对于建筑事务所来说，组织者是一种可能的角色选择与策略。相应地，组织也可以视作一种可能的建筑设计方式。从笔者的个人经验来说，组织的方式经历了一个连续的发展转变与选择的过程。这种方式最早表现为"离合"

的方式，进而拓展为"混合"的方式。这也是建筑师个体的思考方式试图与社会不断结合的过程。

起初，笔者关心的是传统问题：从十几年前研究传统庭院[3]开始，希望理解其原理及其在建筑学、美学等方面的精神，用以指导设计，使其具有中国本土精神。正是通过这一时期学位论文的研究，尤其是接触了宗白华先生论著中关于传统"离"卦美学意义的阐述[4]，笔者发掘出"离合"这种可以转化为建筑设计方法，而非只关注传统形式和空间，或只是抽象哲学和美学认识的思想。这一思想对实践产生深刻影响的原因是，它并非一种固定的建筑设计的艺术原理或法则，而是一种对建筑师而言更重要的思维方式。

显然，那是一种走向自我内心与体验的方式。在相当一段时间里，笔者也曾希望运用这种方式进行具有本土精神的单纯建筑设计，在这个基础上研究建筑与叙事、体验、情境、氛围的关系。但建筑师社会理想的诉求使我们一直不愿完全走入关注建筑师个人情绪表达的建筑。我们欣赏柯布西耶、哈桑·法赛、查尔斯·柯里亚，还有那些获得阿卡汗建筑奖[5]的建筑师们。这种愿望如此强烈，致

to cling to past experiences and what it used to be. We shall try to explore new strategies and principles. This new and common approach will not exist in the original system and category but will exist among various systems and categories that are constantly disappearing. Today, there is an unprecedented mixing and fusion of highbrow culture and popular culture. This may become an opportunity for the development of contemporary architecture.

For architects, the primary concern is whether a widely used design strategy can be adopted so that taking a stand no longer remains an empty slogan. It is a choice of values and strategies. Through the above comparison, it can be seen that this choice is based on the domestic situation. On one hand, it weakens the limitations of technology and quality as mentioned in the first choice, on the other hand, it is more adaptable and open-ended, taking social culture as a cut-in point. Since the value boundaries disappeared and changed, architects can fit into another role, neither as participants in creation nor as mavericks, but as active organizers or active participants. Today, in China, architectural practice is fraught with huge uncertainties. The social and cultural background is extremely complex. As an organizer, the architect should apply open-ended design strategy based on active analysis and comprehension of the practical conditions. On this basis, he effectively organizes various design elements and technical possibilities. This organizational approach is based on

existing categories, limitations, and materials. In addition to technologies and materials, it is also able to involve different design elements, adopt the different system and achieve varying effects. Therefore, this approach is very applicable and flexible. By organizing the various relationships that contemporary architecture is facing, architects can reconstruct the communication and integration between architecture and the public. It is the overall value for architecture and also, the independent social value of architects.

From Separation and Unification to Mixing: Using Organizational Design Approach to Connect the Individual and the Public

For architecture firms, to be an organizer is a possible choice and strategy. Accordingly, the organization can also be regarded as a possible approach to architectural design. Based on our own experience, the organizational approach has undergone a process of continuous development, transformation, and selection. This approach first appeared as a "separation and unification" approach and then expanded into a "mixing" approach. It is also a process in which an individual architect tries to integrate his way of thinking into society.

At first, we were concerned about traditional issues: We started studying traditional courtyards[3] more than two decades ago with the hope of understanding the principles behind them and the spirit they embody in terms of architec-

使我们一度对建筑学与建筑师的现状深感失望……

变化是从着手商业项目开始的。商业项目与住宅，这两个在中国关系到最大部分人群日常生活的领域，以前我们接触得很少。是商业项目促使我们真正认真地开始关注当今社会及消费文化的逻辑、大众文化的现象与规律，并认识到关乎建筑师社会理想的现实对象与内容。

于是，慢慢尝试着将离合的方式与当代文化逻辑联系在一起，开始展示出一种更广泛的可能性。

我们一直深感佩服的是冯纪忠先生的见解："设计要如何走向世界？不是自己走向世界，是作品自然而然地走。走向自己的内心愈深，则走向世界的前景愈宽。"[6]他是对的，令建筑师始终坚持的激情，只能来其自我认同。

离合：一种思考问题的方式

一切要从"分离"开始。[7]

分离是一种认识世界的方式。在笔者看来，分离作为目的、作为形式逻辑是次要的，重要的是作为一种手段。

分离就是用来感知整本的手段。离而合，这是中国式

的逆向思维方式，也是中国式的主观思维方式。

在文徵明为苏州拙政园绘制的三十一景之《瑶圃》[图2]上，连续的风景中那道篱笆将空间隔断为内外，从而向观画者提示内外两部分空间原本为一体。值得一提的还有这幅画的构图，前后左右直接截断，反而使得空间超越画幅的边界，在观画者的感知中蔓延开来。篱笆与画幅均是作为分离的手段而出现，整本空间的感觉才是篱笆与画幅作为分离的最终目的。

再如，"抽刀断水水更流"，因为割断，反而更强烈感觉到水的长流不息。再比如，"遥知兄弟登高处，遍插茱萸少一人"，正因距离的远才显感情的近。

传统文艺理论中所谓化实为虚，化虚为实，按我们的理解，论述的都是永恒与感知点的关系。其中，"虚"即根本、整本、一、无常、永恒、哲学的终极、生命的意义、灵光一现的真理。而"实"则是令人开悟的那一事、一物、一处情境、一曲音乐、一道光线。而连接起这两者的是主体。那个实即分离的整本。因此，中国传统的认知方式中，"一"，即整本，始终是个潜在的背景，因为这个，万物才存在意义。而让万物与虚无的整本联系在一起的是主体的

072

ture, aesthetics, etc. Then we will be able to use them to guide design and localize them in China. It is through a study on dissertations during this period, especially Mr. Zong Baihua's treatise on the aesthetic significance of the traditional trigram "Li"[4], we invented the "separation and unification". It can be transformed into an approach to architectural design instead of focusing solely on traditional forms and spaces or abstract philosophical thinking and aesthetic ideology. The reason why this thought has a profound impact on practice is that it is not a fixed artistic principle or rule of architectural design. It's a more important mode of thinking for architects.

Obviously, it's a way of looking into one's own heart and experience. For quite some time, we also hope to adopt this approach to carry out simple architectural design with a local spirit, and on this basis, to study the relationship between architecture and narratives, experiences, situations, and atmospheres. But the pursuit of architects' social ideal made us reluctant to embrace architecture that gives attention to architects' personal emotional expression. We admire Le Corbusier, Hassan Fathy, Charles Correa, and architects who won the Aga Khan Award for Architecture[5]. This desire was so strong that once we were deeply disappointed with the current situation of architecture and architects...

The change began with commercial projects. We had little contact with commercial projects and residences. In China, these are two areas relevant to most people's daily life. It was

commercial projects that prompted us to seriously pay attention to the logic of today's society and consumer culture, to the phenomena and principle of popular culture, and to find out real objects and contents relating to architects' social ideals.

Thus, the separation and unification approach was slowly linked to the logic of contemporary culture, demonstrating a wider range of possibilities.

We have been deeply impressed by Mr. Feng Jizhong's insights: "How can design obtain the world approval? It does not mean that an architect shall be world-renowned. It means that the work shall be carefully designed by the heart. The deeper you go into your heart, the brighter prospect you will have to achieve success in the world."[6] He is right. For architects, the secret of always being passionate is to get self-identification.

Separation and Unification: A Mode of Thinking

Everything begins with "separation"[7].

Separation is a way to know the world. In our opinion, it's more important that we regard separation as a means than a purpose or a formal logic.

Separation is a means of perceiving the whole. Reunion after separation is a Chinese-style reverse way of thinking and a Chinese-style subjective view of thinking.

In the *Garden of Jade* [fig. 2], one of the 31 scenes painted by Wen Zhengming for the Humble Administrator's Garden in

2　文徵明绘《瑶圃》
Garden of Jade, painted by Wen Zhengming

Suzhou, the fence in the continuous landscape separates the space into the inner and outer parts. The author is suggesting to the viewer that the two parts were originally a whole space. It is worth mentioning that the picture is cut up in all directions. This makes the picture overflowing with a sense of space. People are able to imagine the extended space out of the picture. Both the fence and the frame are used as means of separation, and the ultimate purpose of such separation is to create a sense of the whole space.

Another example is selected from classical Chinese poetry: "water flows even faster when you cut it with a sword". It means that with each cut by a sword, you may feel a steadier water flow. Another example, as a Chinese classical poem said: "I know my brothers would, with dogwood spraying in hand, climb the mountain and think of me from far away." It is the long-distance separation that makes people feel emotionally closer.

Turning a void into a solid and vice versa in the traditional literary theories is, according to our understanding, about the relationship between eternity and the point of perception. "Void" is the foundation, the whole, one, impermanence, eternity, the end of philosophy, the meaning of life, and an inspiring truth, while "solid" is a case, an object, a situation, a piece of music or a ray of light that enlightens. The subject is the actually separated whole that connects the void and the solid. Therefore, in the traditional Chinese way of cogni-tion, "one", namely the whole, is the underlying backdrop throughout; only in this backdrop things are meaningful. What connects all things to the empty whole is the subject's experience and emotion. Therefore, for Chinese people, everything is emotional. Every human being, from nobility down to common people, carries such emotion.

The separation-unification relationship not only reveals the understanding of the relationship between the whole and the part in Chinese traditional culture but also emphasizes the necessity and importance of personal experience in the process of understanding the whole through the part. "Unification" is subjective imagery, and becomes meaningful only through human's intervention and perception. For exam-ple, the Chinese classical poem by Wang Wei: "Sauntering along till the end of the brook, I take a rest and watch the clouds appear." The poet's thoughts flew to the air when he came to the end of the road. Is the space here separated or connected? Of course, it is connected. The end of the road is the starting point of his thoughts. The action of cutting off seems to imply separation, but the goal is finally reached through experiencing eternity. Only in this way can parts acquire meaning in the whole process.

Separation and Unification: A Holistic View of Architecture

The whole is perceived through separation; the whole

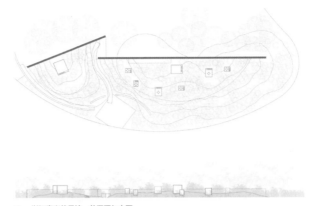

3　浙江嘉兴竹里馆，总平面与立面
General plane and elevation of the House in the Bamboo Grove, Jiaxing, Zhejiang

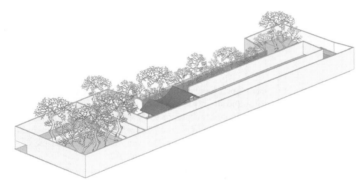

4-1　四川青城山八大山房，鸟瞰
Aerial view of Badashan Villa, Mount Qingcheng, Sichuan

4-2　四川青城山八大山房，水院
Water courtyard of Badashan Villa, Mount Qingcheng, Sichuan

体验与情感。所以，在中国人的眼中才会万物有情，这样的情感上至王侯大夫，下至黎民百姓，莫不如此。

离合关系不仅揭示出中国传统文化中对整本与局部之间关系的理解，更强调了个人体验在通过局部了解整本的过程中的必要性和重要性。"合"是一种主观意象，只有通过人的介入和感悟才能获得意义。例如，王维诗："行到水穷处，坐看云起时。"在前路断绝之处，思绪勃然漫游至无穷辽阔。此处的环境究竟是阻隔还是连接？当然是连接了。前路的断绝正是思绪的起点，断了似乎是隔远，却因体悟永恒而真正亲近了目标。这样局部事物才会因整个过程而获得存在的意义。

离与合：建筑中的整体观

通过分离的手段获得整体的感知，通过具体的局部的感知理解整本，因为整体的存在，具体的事物获得意义，个人体验在元素关系、局部与整体关系的认识中起到决定作用。离与合这种相辅相成的关系在我们的好些设计项目中采用。在运用这种方式的过程中，个人的经验与感悟是设计的关键，好比写诗，格律人人通晓，诗意却大相径庭。

案例1：竹里馆（2003年设计，未建[图3]）。"竹里馆"是一处掩土社区会所。建筑的大部分被掩盖在竹林下，一些外露的玻璃小室为竹林所包围，它们是一些茶室、阅读室，让使用者获得"独坐幽篁里"的感觉。在这里，建筑显然是弱的，不光是因为形态小巧轻盈，或是其分散的空间造成体验上的时间多样性，更因为其本身形态与空间被刻意设计为不具独立感与完整性。群体也是如此，看似是个群落，但彼此之间不能形成完整的关系感。只有依靠竹林的加入，才能形成完整的整体环境体验感。

案例2：青城山八大山房（2008年设计，未建[图4]）。这个住宅的设计要回答这样一个问题，一个要以远处青城山为景观的住宅，在住宅外到处可以看到山的情况下，该怎么办？方案中，住宅的中心是一处水庭院，这个安静庭院别无他物，只有同处一院的青城山片断与其水中倒影。为强化这个庭院的体验，整体空间的引导采用了欲扬先抑的方式，通过长时间曲折深奥的空间过渡才能到达这里，转过墙来，先是山水中的虚像，再是山的虚实叠合景象迎面而来。如果没有远处的山，庭院空自等待，就失去了生命与意义。因为有这样的关系存在，建筑可以看作本身是

is understood through the perception of specific parts. Concrete objects acquire meanings because of the existence of the whole. Personal experience plays a decisive role in the understanding of the relationship between elements, and between parts and the whole. The mutually complementary relationship between separation and unification has been used in many of our designs. In the process of adopting this method, personal experience and perception are the keys to the design. Like poetry writing, everyone is familiar with metrical patterns, but the poetic flavors are quite different.

Case 1: House in the Bamboo Grove (designed in 2003, unbuilt [fig. 3]). House in the Bamboo Grove is an earth-sheltered community clubhouse. Most of the building is covered by the bamboo grove. Some exposed glass rooms are surrounded by bamboos. They are designed tea rooms and reading rooms where people can get the feeling of "sitting alone in the bamboo grove". Here, the building is clearly weak, not only because it is compact and slim in form, or its dispersed space causes temporal diversity in experience, but also because it is so designed as to lack a sense of independence and integrity. The same thing also happens in communities. It looks like a community, but these buildings can't achieve a sense of wholeness. Only combined with the bamboo grove, can people feel this wholeness.

Case 2: Mount Qingcheng Badashan Villa (designed in 2008, unbuilt [fig. 4]). In designing this house, we have

to answer this question: What should we do if we want to see Mount Qingcheng in a distance everywhere outside a house? A water courtyard was designed in the center of the house. This is a pure and quiet courtyard with nothing but a part of Mount Qingcheng and its reflection in the water. In order to better immerse visitors in the courtyard, the whole space was designed by sharp spatial contrast. Only through a long and tortuous space transition can visitors get access to this courtyard. When they turn the corner, they would first see the reflection of the mountain in the water and then an overlap between the mountain and its reflection. If there is no mountain in the distance, the courtyard would lose its vitality. Because of this, the building is regarded as incomplete. It is a part of the whole scenery.

Case 3: Jiading New Town Urban Planning Exhibition Hall (designed in 2009, completed [fig. 5]). The renovated and expanded building consists of two distinct parts, the renovated original building and new additional structures with new functions. The whole building is designed in an overlooking position, connecting to the park green land in front. This sizable building shows its relationship with the scrub in another way - balance. Without park trees, the building would appear unbalanced from the perspective of architecture.

This is a characteristic approach, but on the other hand, there are limitations. So far, this approach has shown a tendency to evade contemporary industrial systems and broader

不完整的，只是从整体中被分离出来的一部分。

案例3：嘉定新城城市规划展示馆（2009年设计，已建成 [图5]）。这个改扩建建筑由明显的两部分组成，一部分为原有建筑的改造，另一部分为根据新增功能要求所作的加建。整体建筑是有姿态的，这种眺望的姿态将建筑与前面的公园绿地连接起来。这个硬朗的大体量建筑用另外一种方式显示了它与低矮树丛的关系，那就是均衡。如果没有公园树丛的平衡，单从建筑而言，其形态是失衡的。

这是一种有特征的方法，但另一方面，这样的方式也存在很大局限。迄今为止，这样的设计方法具有回避当代工业生产体系及更广泛的社会内容的倾向。而这也正是我们一直怀疑并想要超越的。如果一种方法仅是传统建筑学范畴内的，再好的个性也会被当代的同质化趋向消解其意义。因此，这种方式方法在未来是否具有作用才是我们最想要了解并尝试的。我们的看法是，一种设计方法如果仅仅作为一种形式空间逻辑就很容易走向个人化，并局限于传统的建筑学范围内；而如果能上升为一种思考问题的方式，则有可能走向个人与社会的主动结合，并契合当下社会文化的要求。

从离合到混合：走向更为广泛的组织方式

按照法国社会学家鲍德里亚的说法，消费体系中，一切能指与所指之间固有的关系断裂了，漂浮在空中的能指与所指任意结合，唯独不再与真实结合。[8] 这就是消费逻辑。这样的状态渐渐变成了我们的生活：电视、互联网、还有各类消费品。在史无前例的可能性之前，选择的任意性使建筑设计像流行商品般具有一种特有的虚无忧伤的色彩，"一切坚固的东西都烟消云散了"。[9] 这种情绪同样从1982年OMA为拉维莱特公园竞赛做的规划图 [图6] 上传达出来，画面伤感的情绪后面看不见的是弥散在一切中的、仿佛控制着未来又超越以往的无边理性。

关于建筑的一切仿佛也落在这样的逻辑之中。消费逻辑使一切建筑的风格与内容变得快速而短暂，失去了固有的意义，同时，在这种系统之中，个性成为一种风格符号，传统的真实与品质的含义早就被改写，从而成为所谓的"边缘性差异"。[10] 一切在价值上变得如此同质。

如果没有因此而陷入文化价值虚无主义中的话，消费逻辑在我们看来也有积极的具有启示意义的另一面。

一方面，传统等级与界限的消除，对建筑师来说，意

social content. And this is what we've always suspected and wanted to surpass. If an approach is confined to traditional architecture, despite its excellent specialty, its significance will be degraded by the contemporary trend of homogenization. Therefore, whether this approach will work in the future is what we most want to know and try. We believe that a design approach can easily become personalized and confined to traditional architecture if it is only adopted as formal and spatial logic. Nevertheless, if it is adopted as a way of thinking, then it may contribute to the active integration of individuals and society, and conform to the requirements of present social culture.

From Separation and Unification to Mixing: Towards a Broader Organizational Approach

According to French sociologist Jean Baudrillard, in the consumption system, the inherent relationship between all signifiers and signified is broken, and signifiers in the air can be freely combined with signified, except that they are no longer combined with the reality.[8] This is the logic of consumption. This state is gradually formed in our life: TV, the Internet, and a variety of consumer goods. In the face of unprecedented possibilities, the arbitrary nature of choice makes architectural design take on the peculiar color of nothingness and sadness, similar to those fashion products. "Everything solid has vanished."[9] This sentiment was also found in the planning chart drawn by OMA in a 1982 design competition for the Parc de la Villette [fig. 6]. What's hidden behind the sadness is the infinite rationality which scatters in everything and seems to control the future and transcend the past.

Everything about architecture seems to be related to this logic. The logic of consumption makes all architectural styles and content fleeting and transient, losing their inherent meaning. Meanwhile, in this system, personalities have become style symbols, due to this, the traditional meaning of truth and quality has been transformed into the so-called "marginal differences"[10]. Everything has become so homogeneous in value.

The logic of consumption would be positive and enlightening for us if it had not been trapped in cultural nihilism.

On the one hand, for architects, the elimination of traditional hierarchies and boundaries means that there will be broader perspective and many valuable and important tasks suddenly appear: to pay attention to all walks of lives and cultures at all levels in cities, to get inspiration from them, especially those spontaneous, common and popular ones that don't belong to elegant culture or commercial system. The mainstream culture, non-mainstream culture and all kinds of subculture should be viewed equally and in light of development, thus new architectural possibilities are able to be found among them.

5-1 嘉定新城规划展示馆，总体模型
Overall model of Urban Planning Exhibition Hall, Jiading district, Shanghai

5-2 嘉定新城规划展示馆，建筑与景观的关系
Scene of Urban Planning Exhibition Hall, the relationship between
architecture and landscape

6 OMA/库哈斯设计的拉维莱特公园概念图
Concept plan of the Parc de la Villette, designed
by OMA/Koolhaas

味着视野可以变得更加开放，突然有很多重要的工作值得去做：去关注城市中真实存在的各个阶层的生活，各种层次的文化，尤其是其中不属于高雅文化范畴的，也不属于商业系统的，自发的、普通的、大众的东西，从中获得启示。用同等的、发现的眼光去看待主流文化、非主流文化、各种亚文化，在它们之间寻找建筑新的可能。

另一方面，在既有建筑价值系统消融，原有的一切变得模糊而不确定的情况下，一种新的确定性则清晰地显露出来，那就是这种系统组织逻辑本身。永恒不变的已不再是固有的某种形式，而可能是某种模式。在实践中选择尝试组织的方式，一方面是想回避中国相对落后与不均衡的工业生产体系，而选择充满差异的复杂社会内容；另一方面也有在不确定中寻找确定的想法。

但是，如果单纯遵循消费逻辑，那这种组织混合的方式同样存在很大局限性——很容易成为商业体系的一部分，从而彻底丧失其广泛的适用性与建筑学的普遍意义。在这种情况下，离合的思想方式对于避免陷入商业模式的组织起到了很大的作用。从离合的角度来看，混合的各个部分互相作用使对方分离，通过分离，原有的整体意义被强化

了，各部分又融合为新的整体。如同文徵明拙政园图中的另一幅《小飞虹》[图7]所示：建筑掩映于树木之中。从离合的角度来看，完整的建筑及路径被分离为几个部分。它们是怎样联系为整体的呢？从一处到另一处究竟发生了怎样的故事？当中失落的片断是靠我们个人的想象来完成的。这里，作为目的和活动空间的建筑和路径被视为整体，与之性质迥异的树木成为分离整体的介入物——异质体。

如果从混合的角度来看，建筑与树木彼此混合，互相成为彼此分离的手段，故事也同样发生了。不同属性，跟主体关系存在很大差别的事物——建筑、路径和树木被当作同等地位的组织要素，共同构成整体。换言之，混合意味着各类元素互为离合，其中，元素的确定不再受制于传统固有的内容，而变得更为自由，并形成一种更广泛的离合形式。

由于离合的方式是一种整体意义上的思想方法，由此衍生的混合这种方式就是源于建筑师主观意愿的混合——一种有目的的指向整本的混合，也是个人经验与复杂背景、大众生活的结合，而不是随心所欲的任意拼贴或拼凑，跟商业化的无序混和有着本质区别。这种有目的、有

078

On the other hand, even as the existing architectural value system disappears and things become blurry and uncertain. A new certainty is clearly revealed, it is the organizational logic of the system. What's eternal is no longer an inherent form, perhaps it will be a model. By trying the organizational approach in practice, on the one hand, we want to avoid China's relatively backward and unbalanced industrial production system, and choose complex and variegated social content. On the other hand, we intend to seek certainties in uncertainties.

However, if we simply follow the logic of consumption, this organized mixing approach will also be very limited. It can easily become part of the business system, thus it will completely lose its broad applicability and universal relevance in architecture. Under this circumstance, the thinking of separation and unification plays a very important role in avoiding getting trapped in an organization under a business model. From the perspective of separation and unification, various parts of the mixture are separated from each other through interaction, the meaning of the original whole is strengthened through separation and then various parts are newly integrated. As shown in *Little Flying Rainbow* [fig. 7], another picture painted by Wen Zhengming for the Humble Administrator's Garden, the building is nestled among the trees. From the perspective of separation and unification, the complete building and path are separated into several parts. How are they

connected to form a whole? What happened from one place to another? The missing stories require people's imagination. As the purpose and activity, the spaces, the building, and path in the picture are regarded as a whole, and the trees (as a different nature) is the intervening object that separates the whole - the heterogenic body. From another perspective of mixing, if the building and the trees are mixed and separated from each other, a story also happens. Things of different attributes, which are also very different from the subject, such as the building, the path, and the trees are equally treated as organizational elements that together form the whole. In other words, the mixing approach means that various elements are separated and also unified. The determination of elements is no longer subject to traditional inherent content. The elements can be determined more freely. The form of separation and unification becomes universal.

Since the separation and unification approach is a holistic way of thinking, the mixing approach derived from it is an approach generated from the architect's subjective wish - a purposeful mixing oriented to the whole, a combination of personal experience with complex backgrounds and public lives. It is not a random mixing and is essentially different from commercialized random mixing. This purposeful, organized mixing is the result of the association between the separation and unification approach and contemporary social reality. Its significance lies in the fact that it enables architects to

7 文徵明绘《小飞虹》
Little Flying Rainbow, painted by Wen Zhengming

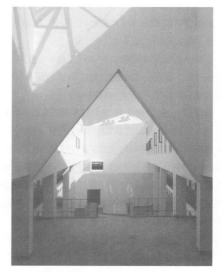

8 东莞理工学院计算机系，内庭院
Scene of the inner courtyard of the Department of Computer Science and Technology, Dongguan University of Technology

9-1 重庆商业街 设计意象
Concept sketch of Chongqing Commercial Street

9-2 重庆商业街 鸟瞰图
Aerial view rendering of Chongqing Commercial Street

组织的混合是离合方式与当代社会现实相关联的结果，其意义是使建筑师得以采用主动与个人的方式参与社会文化实践，成为积极的组织者。

关于有组织的混合，在实践工作中我们不断试验各种可能性，下面是一些实际工程与展览的记录，分别根据不同的情况考察了组织混合的各种可能性。

案例1：东莞理工学院计算机系（2002年设计，已建成[图8]）。这个项目组织的是错位的环境体验——理性的计算机系与感性的不属于此地的内部空间。这个建筑是个特殊的例子，设计时间较早，当时完全不是从混合而是从情境的角度出发的。现在看来，可以看作是一处情境错位产生的混合。这个建筑有着类似阿尔瓦罗·西扎设计风格的形态，修道院式的围廊，白色雪山意象的楼梯间与街道式的室外楼梯等。这一个个片断全部不符合计算机系这类建筑的固有印象，而无关的两者却戏剧化地混合在一座建筑之内。这展示了混合的另一种可能性：建成的情境与建筑的固有含义之间产生关系，而不再需要采用不同的几种类型、风格或者情境。

案例2：重庆商业街（2004年设计，未建[图9]）。这里组织混合的是社区中心的感觉——熟悉的购物场所与聚落的社交空间。在这个项目中，我们将众多的零售商业与重庆的城市地貌形态混合在一起，一方面形成了众多路径的商业业态，另一方面在高容积率与高密度的条件下还给社区绿化聚落构成众多公共空间。这两者的混合是相互促成的，同时由一个共同的愿望——居民熟悉的家——整合在一起。一方面，我们希望透过迷宫式的聚落产生寻找，一旦熟悉了，你才是本地人，而本地人的感觉就是家园的感觉；另一方面，每一个零售店的环境与空间都是不同的，这样的差异设计是形成特征与记忆的开始。

案例3：台州路桥商业建筑（2005年设计，未建[图10]）。这也是较早的一次尝试，组织混合的是建造方式。不足200平方米的房子是两栋与传统风貌核心区协调的新商业用房，必须符合对于传统风貌区新建工程的大多数要求。当时面临一个有趣的情况，建筑师不懂古建构造，懂古建构造的施工公司不懂风貌保护原则，只会做仿清式假古董房子。于是，这个小房子被规划成两部分，一部分是建筑师规划并负责具体设计的墙；另一部分是建筑师规划由专业古建修缮公司负责深化设计并施工的传统建筑。这样的

participate in social and cultural practice actively and personally. They turn to be active organizers.

With regard to organized mixing, we have been experimenting with various possibilities in practice. The following are the records of some projects and exhibitions. We have examined the possibilities of organized mixing according to different situations.

Case 1: Department of Computer Science and Technology, Dongguan University of Technology (designed in 2002, completed [fig. 8]). This project aimed to organize and mix mismatched environmental experiences - The rational computer science faculty and emotional inner space which is really antipathetic. This building is a special case. It was an early project designed from a situational perspective, the perspective of mixing was not considered. Now it can be regarded as a mixture of situational mismatches. With a monastery-style corridor, a stairwell with white snow-capped mountain imagery and a street-style outdoor stair-case, the building looks similar to Alvaro Siza's design. All of these pieces subverted the fixed image of computer science faculty, and these two irrelevant things are dramatically mixed in the same building. This demonstrates another possibility of mixing: The situation after completion relates to the inherent meaning of the building. Consequently, it is unnecessary that the designer picks different types, styles or situations.

Case 2: Chongqing Commercial Street (designed in 2004, unbuilt [fig. 9]). This project aimed to organize and mix feelings in a community center—a familiar shopping area and social space in settlements. In this project, we mixed many retail businesses with Chongqing's urban landform. On the one hand, commercial activities are accessible through many routes; on the other hand, a lot of public space is made available in the settlements for community greening despite its high plot ratio and density. These two parts interact in the mix and are integrated together by a common aspiration - a home familiar to residents. On the one hand, we want to take actions like pathfinding through maze-like settlements. You can only qualify as locals after you have become familiar with the place. Being local makes you feel like at home; on the other hand, the environment and space of every retail store are different, and such differentiated design is the beginning of the formation of characteristics and memories.

Case 3: Luqiao Commercial Center (designed in 2005, unbuilt [fig. 10]). This project is also an earlier attempt, and it aimed to organize and mix the mode of construction. Two new commercial buildings with an area of less than 200m² are located in the core area with traditional features. The design had to meet the requirements for most new projects in this area. We then had an interesting challenge. The architect knew little about historic building structure, while the construction company knew historic building structure well but was ignorant of the principles for style and feature

10 台州路桥商业建筑，模型
Model of Luqiao Commercial Center, Taizhou, Zhejiang

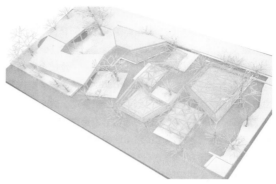

11 上海青浦新城仁杰会所，模型
Model of Renjie Club, Qingpu district, Shanghai

12-1 昆明文明街"漫游的庭院"，鸟瞰
Aerial view of the "Promenade Courtyards", Renewal of Kunming Wenming Street, Yunnan

12-2 昆明文明街"漫游的庭院"街景
Street view of the "Promenade Courtyards", Renewal of Kunming Wenming Street, Yunnan

12-3 昆明文明街"漫游的庭院"，内院
Courtyard view of the "Promenade Courtyards", Renewal of Kunming Wenming Street, Yunnan

组织方式产生了满足各方需要的新旧融合的新建筑。设计的关键在于对当代和传统的不同建造方式的混合组织。

案例4：仁杰会所（2006年设计，已建成 [图11]）。这里组织混合的是社区中的公共活动场所——社区消费空间与公共活动空间。这个项目试图将两类社区使用的空间混合在一起，一类是餐饮，另一类是社区活动。这个项目建成了，但从本来的愿望来讲不成功，原因并不在于施工的粗糙与后期商业的修改这些跟美观相关的问题，而在于两个与组织本意矛盾的地方：一是商业业态的使用与小区居民无关；二是公共空间最终失控而缺乏真正的公共使用。这再次让我们感到在组织混合的设计策略中，模式把握的准确性至关重要。

案例5：昆明文明街（2006年设计，未建 [图12]）。这个项目组织的是大众的休闲消费生活，包括各种层次的休闲活动，从市井的到高雅的，以及当代商业消费活动。这个风貌区改造最大的挑战是如何使原有的市井空间在贵族化的商业改造与复古风格化的习惯思维之间具有存留之地。我们研究了原有的城市结构、功能与空间组织，确定采用灵活的混合策略，其中值得一提的是将原来的孤立庭院转化为串连的漫游庭院这一策略。根据这一构想保留的巷道不受太多商业干扰，结合原来庭院建筑的虚实逻辑，使商业活动的多元性与不确定性成为串连起来的新公共空间——庭院活动变化的混合因素。我们希望通过这样的混合将室内外空间的使用潜力尽可能发掘出来：地皮价格高昂的室内空间为贵族化的商业地产功能所占据，而室外的公共空间通过管理则可以提供给那些只能承受微薄租金的市井业态与流动摊贩使用。这是一项极其复杂，需要各方面观念协调、管理统一进行的计划。作为建筑师，提出这样理想主义色彩较浓的建议可能有点一厢情愿，更可能面临最终的失败。但无论如何，我们愿意尝试下去。

案例6：朱氏会所（2007年设计，未建 [图13]）。这个设计组织混合的是多个侧面的家庭生活。这个私人会所的组织是蒙太奇式的，差异性与戏剧性就是建立整体性的原则。

案例7：嘉定秋霞圃西侧地块的三个方案。对于秋霞圃西侧地块的工作，我们一直将它置于混合组织的模式之下研究。以下是其中三个有代表性的方案。

一是嘉定秋霞圃西侧地块城市设计研究（2008年设计 [图14]）。对于地块的初始研究方案是在没有任务书的

preservation. It could only construct fake antique houses in Qing Dynasty. As a result, the small house was divided into two parts. A wall planned and designed by the architect, and a traditional building planned by the architect, designed in detail and constructed by the professional historic housing repair company. By this organizational approach, new buildings with the integration of old and new were constructed to satisfy all parties. The key to the design lies in the organized mixing of the contemporary and traditional construction mode.

Case 4: Renjie Club (designed in 2006, completed [fig. 11]). This project aimed to organize and mix places for public activities in the community—consumption space and public activity space. The project intended to mix two types of community spaces, one for catering and the other for community activities. Though the project has been completed, it failed to express our original intention. This is not because of aesthetic issues like construction quality or commercial modification in the later period. There are two reasons that contradicted the organizational intention: first, the commercial activities are irrelevant to community residents; second, we eventually lost control of the public spaces, which are not really for public use. This once again brings into focus the importance of accurately picking the mode in design strategy involving organized mixing.

Case 5: Kunming Wenming Street (designed in 2006, unbuilt [fig. 12]). This project aimed to organize and mix the public leisure consumption, including leisure activities at various levels, from the vulgar activities to elegant ones, as well as contemporary commercial expense. The biggest challenge in the transformation of this area is how to preserve a space for the original civil area satisfying in the meantime the aristocratic commercial transformation and retro-styled habitual thinking. We studied the original urban structure, functions and space organization, and decided to adopt a flexible mixing strategy. One strategy is worth mentioning, the originally isolated courtyards were transformed into a cross-linked courtyard system. According to this idea, preserved lanes will not be subject to an excess of commercial interference. Considering the logic of void and solid, a new public space was linked by the diversity and uncertainty of commercial activities—the mixing factors on changes in courtyard activities. With the help of this mixing approach, we hoped to maximize the potential of indoor and outdoor space as possible as we can: boutique commercial activities were arranged to move into expensive indoor spaces. For those common commercial activities or mobile stall vendors who can only afford small rent, they were arranged to move to outdoor public spaces. This is an extremely complex plan that requires the coordination of many ideas and centralized management. As architects, we may have indulged in a bit wishful thinking by proposing this overly idealistic plan, which is likely to fail. Whatever it may be, we will keep on trying.

13　上海青浦新城朱氏会所 模型
Model of Zhu's Club, Qingpu district, Shanghai

14　嘉定秋霞圃西侧地块城市设计，商业与园林混合模型
Model for the plot west to Qiuxia Garden in Jiading, Shanghai, mixing the commercial space and garden functions in urban design

Case 6: Zhu's Club (designed in 2007, unbuilt [fig. 13]). This design aimed to organize and mix multiple aspects of family life. We decided to adopt a montage organization for this private club. The principles for establishing integrity consist in differentiation and dramaticism.

Case 7: Three plans for the plot west of Qiuxia Garden in Jiading (Completed). We have been studying the plot west of Qiuxia Garden under the mode of organized mixing. The following are three representative plans.

Ⅰ. Urban design research for the plot west of Qiuxia Garden in Jiading (designed in 2008 [fig. 14]). The initial research plan for the plot was carried out without specifications. The plan envisages a mix of two functions: commercial space 、 and traditional garden, namely the public use of contemporary cities and the styles and features of traditional cities. Commercial space is a new public space for citizens, and the traditional garden is planned to be the new entrance of Qiuxia Garden, with part of it being an extension of the north section of the historical Garden. The commercial part and the garden can be connected in any combination. Two different parts influence each other, bringing a brand new experience. What makes us most excited about the plan is the mixing of popular commerce and an elegant garden, which were originally two unrelated spaces.

Ⅱ. Implementation plan for Jiading Museum (designed in 2009, completed [fig. 15]). When the plot was finally designated

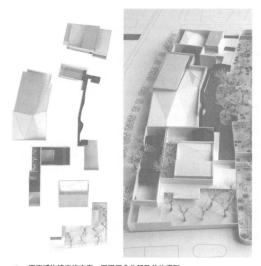

15　嘉定博物馆实施方案，双园概念分解及总体模型
Dual garden concept in the implementation plan for Jiading New Museum, Shanghai

情况下进行的。方案设想混合两部分功能：商业与传统园林，也就是当代城市的公共使用性与传统城市的风貌。商业空间是新的市民公共空间，传统园林部分是秋霞圃的新入口，其中一部分是秋霞圃北园的扩展。商业与园林两部分可以任意组合联通，其巨大的差异性形成相互影响的新体验。这个策划最令我们感到兴奋的地方在于将大众化的商业与高雅的园林混合，这原本是不可能相提并论的两个世界。

二是嘉定博物馆实施方案（2009 年设计，已建成[图15]）。当这个地块的最终功能被确定为博物馆，在沿用上述的混合策略时，一个新的问题出现了，那就是差异体验的程度。博物馆展示空间与传统园林，同样是具有文化气质的建筑体验，原有的差异度模糊了。于是，我们把两部分都策划为园林，一部分是传统园林，另一部分是当代的地景园，从而形成带来不同感受的双园，新的整体形成了。

三是嘉定博物馆过程方案（2009 年设计[图16]）。这个过程方案值得一提的地方在于通过它，混合组织的方法展现了适应广泛的一面，这个方案的结果是纯净的，不再有任何直接的形式符号痕迹。组织混合的内容涉及不同的

空间体验与感性，包括在街道上不断看到园林局部而产生的对于园林的富于情感化的片断城市记忆和博物馆内部的展示体验。最终的方案由两种类型的体验空间相间混合而成：其一是室内经过策划布置的文物展示；其二是从城市角度对秋霞圃景致的片断连缀，依据氛围的处理命名为"聆听的视觉"。设计的出发点是建立城市、园林与博物馆之间的恰当关系，这种关系是以人的体验为基础的，建筑因为这样的关系存在而具有意义。

案例 8：上海文化信息产业园 B4/B5 地块（2009 年设计，已建成[图17]）。在一个由独立办公单元构成的场地内，如何解决高密度和高容积率要求与大量公共空间需求之间的矛盾？如何组织并激发户外活动和公共交流？因为在这里工作的将是从事信息科技和文化创意行业的年轻白领。以上两个问题是这个项目最主要的出发点。"悬挂的庭院"这一设计策略虽然简单但十分有效。通过将原本位于底层的庭院抬升至二、三、四层，解放了很多地面，基地内的公共区域大大增加了。跟层高一样高的方孔铝板包覆着悬挂的挑院，形成了空中庭院，从内部看有足够的私密感，又不会阻挡与外部环境之间的视线和声音交流。镂

for a museum and the above-mentioned mixing strategy was applied, a new problem arose: how different should these two experiences be designed? Since the museum exhibition space and the traditional garden both send out similar architectural experience with cultural characteristics, their differentiation was diluted. Consequently, both parts were designed as gardens, a traditional garden, and a contemporary landscape garden. Different gardens, different feelings, a new whole was thus created.

III. Process plan for Jiading Museum (designed in 2009 [fig.16]). It is worth mentioning that through this plan, the organized mixing approach became widely adaptable. The results of the plan are pure, free of any traces of direct formal symbols. The approach involves different spatial experiences and perceptions: emotionally rich fragments of urban memory on gardens and exhibition experience in the museum. The final plan lied in a mixture of two types of experience space: a planned indoor exhibition of cultural relics and some successive fragments of Qiuxia Garden from an urban perspective. It was entitled "Vision audible" according to the atmosphere processing. The plan was designed to establish a proper relationship among city, garden, and museum. The relationship is based on sensory experience, which made the architecture meaningful.

Case 8: Block B4/B5 in Shanghai Cultural and Information Industry Park (designed in 2009, completed

[fig. 17]). Since young white-collars who dedicate to the IT industry and cultural creation will work here, in this place composed of independent office units, how to eliminate the conflict between the requirement for a high density and high plot ratio and the demand for a tremendous public space? How to organize and encourage outdoor activities and public communication? The project aimed to answer these two questions. The "hanging courtyard" concept is simple but effective. The courtyard originally located on the ground floor was elevated to the second, third and fourth floor. Huge ground space was released, while public space was significantly amplified. The elevated courtyard was wrapped with square hole perforated aluminum sheets with a height the same as each storey. It seemed like there was a courtyard in the air. Standing inside, people may obtain enough privacy. Their view to the outside would not be blocked and vocal communication would not be interrupted. With its hollowed-out surface, the boundary between indoor and outdoor spaces turned to be less apparent. The public, semi-public and private spaces constitute whole encouraging various activities and communications.

Case 9: Shuangding Road Kindergarten in Jiading New Town (designed in 2010, completed [fig.18]). This project aimed to organize buildings and outdoor activity spaces for children A conventional kindergarten design usually separates the building and the playground. We gave up this approach

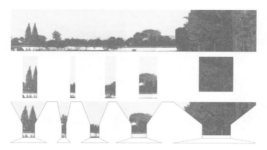

16-1 嘉定博物馆过程方案"聆听的视觉",叙事概念
"Listening Vision" narrative concept in the process plan for Jiading New Museum

16-2 嘉定博物馆过程方案"聆听的视觉",沿街邂逅园林
"Listening Vision" encounter garden along the street in the process plan for Jiading New Museum

17-1 上海文化信息产业园B4/B5地块"悬挂的庭院"概念图解
Conceptual diagrams of the "hanging courtyard", B4/B5 Blocks of Shanghai Culture & Information Industrial Park, Jiading district, Shanghai

17-2 上海文化信息产业园B4/B5地块,外观
Exterior view, B4/B5 Blocks of Shanghai Culture & Information Industrial Park

17-3 上海文化信息产业园B4/B5地块,内景
Interior view, B4/B5 Blocks of Shanghai Culture & Information Industrial Park

19-2 诸暨剧院，夜景
Night view of Zhuji Theater

19-3 诸暨剧院，文化公园
Zhuji Theater Cultural Park, inner yard

19-1 诸暨剧院，鸟瞰
Aerial view of Zhuji Theater, Zhejiang

18-1 嘉定新城双丁路公立幼儿园，模型
Model of Shuangding Road Public Kindergarten, Jiading District, Shanghai

18-2 嘉定新城双丁路公立幼儿园，活动区
Image of the activity area of Shuangding Road Public Kindergarten

空的界面模糊了室内外空间的界限，也将公共、半公共和私密场所组合成一个整体，鼓励着各种形式的活动和交流。

案例 9：嘉定新区双丁路幼儿园（2010 年设计，已建成 [图 18]）。这个项目组织的是建筑与儿童户外活动空间。为了在有限的基地内提供充足且高品质的游戏场地，设计摒弃了建筑与场地分离的习惯做法，而是将两者进行整合，同时还将不同性质的游戏场地——微地形和活动操场整合在一起：主体建筑贴北边布置，底层低幼空间的屋顶和南向整个基地都成为户外活动空间，包括大面积游戏场、多层草坡，还有嵌入首层作为托儿班单元活动区的椭圆形庭院，从而最大限度地提供了健康阳光的户外活动空间的面积和类型。建筑与场地融为一体。

案例 10：诸暨剧院（2011年设计，已建成 [图 19]）。这个设计有意将管理的公共领域（剧院）和开放的公共领域（城市文化公园）组织在一起，使不同类型的公共活动在一起发生，从而营造真正的公共文化氛围。传统的集中式剧院很难在不割裂基地环境的情况下创造自身的领域感，为此我们选择了内含城市空间的模式，用架空的圆环圈起

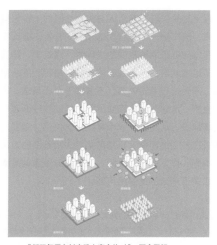

20-1 成都双年展东村实践之离合体·城，概念图解
Conceptual illustration of Urban Acrostic under the Chengdu Biennial - Dongcun Practice

20-2 成都双年展东村实践之离合体·城，街景意象
Street view Image of Urban Acrostic under the Chengdu Biennial - Dongcun Practice

in order to obtain sufficient and high-quality playgrounds in a limited space. The kindergarten is designed to integrate both of them. Furthermore, various playgrounds like micro-topography and play fields were integrated. The main building was located on the north, and the roof of the ground-floor space for young children and the southern part of the base was designed to be outdoor activity space, including a large playground, a multi-layer grassy slope, and an oval-shaped courtyard embedded in the first floor as an activity area for nursery class. In this way, the kindergarten was provided with maximum healthy and sunny space for outdoor activity and plenty of space types. The building and the site finally integrated into a whole.

Case 10: Zhuji Grand Theatre (designed in 2011, completed [fig. 19]). This design intentionally put a managed public area (theatre) and an open public area (urban cultural park) together, so that different public activities might take place in the same area. A true public cultural atmosphere was created. In a traditional centralized theater, it is difficult to create a sense of domain without splitting the environment. For this reason, we adopted a mode that contains urban space. The theater and the cultural square are circled by an overhead ring, inside there are leisure services like landscape restaurants and cinemas. The urban green park extends inside while the film and television functions extend outdoors. Between the ring and the theatre, there was space for people to enjoy open-air

剧院和文化广场，圆环中包含了景观餐厅、电影院等休闲服务功能，城市绿地公园延伸进场地，影视功能则由室内延伸到室外，在圆环和剧院之间可以观看露天电影和室外演出，激发丰富多彩的群众活动。"剧院中的公园"和"公园中的剧院"这样混合不同性质公共空间的方式形成了特殊的领域感和场所感。

案例 11：成都双年展东村策略之离合体·城（2011 年设计 [图20]）。这个设计组织的是不同类型的城市生活场所。成都东村作为当代中国新城建设普适模式的一个案例，整体配套齐全、指标完善，却因可感知范围功能单一、空间隔离，而使人居生活受到阻碍、城市缺乏生机。我们的策略是通过对城市、社区、公共设施空间的多次分解和重构，将原本分离的田园、城市和建筑转变为混合的生活场所，以增进公共聚集和交融的完备性与多样化，营造富有活力的宜居环境。对于中国快速城市化带来的生存环境与城市生活之间的冲突，我们认为靠传统的田园策略和理论化的乌托邦思想是无法解决的，发掘城市归属感的产生途径并利用其自发衍生的力量或可成为改善之道。

结语

以上是关于选择在个人与大众之间的一些思考、策略与实践。选择是一个过程，也是一个开始。在现实社会文化的等级与界限消融转变的过程中，建筑学、建筑师的新意义是否能从寻找一个独立的位置开始呢？不从属于生产体系，不受控于消费体系，不留恋于个人表达，不局限于理论空谈，从新的社会现实出发，像那些令人尊敬的前辈建筑师那样，从现实世界中寻找新的价值，用发现的眼光看待正在发生的现象，坚持用实践去检验新的方法。

毕竟，作为一名建筑师，他的职业决定他需要设想的是一切关于未来的美好的可能。

本文作者系庄慎、华霞虹，最初发表于《建筑师》2012 (6)：43–51。论文初稿完成于 2009 年 4 月，当时庄慎仍为大舍建筑设计事务所的合伙人。应董豫赣老师的邀请，大舍参加其策划的"青年建筑师'从'丛书"计划。本文是为该书所写的文章之一，后由于种种原因，书至今尚未出版。2011 年作者对文章进行了修改，并增加了新的案例。

movies and outdoor shows. Varieties of public events were encouraged in this place. "Park in the theatre" and "theater in the park", this way of mixing different kinds of public spaces creates a special sense of domain and sense of place.

Case 11: Separation and Unification in City, Chengdu Biennial – Dongcun Strategy (designed in 2011 [fig. 20]). This exhibition design aimed to organize and mix different types of urban living places. As a model of new town construction in contemporary China, Chengdu Dongcun boasts a complete set of supporting facilities and scores well on various metrics. However, since the perceivable areas have single function and the spaces are isolated, the life here was disturbed and lack of urban vitality. In order to enhance the completeness and diversity of public gatherings and interfusion, creating a vibrant livable environment, we decided to repeatedly deconstruct and rebuild the urban area, community, and public facility space, transforming previously separated rural areas, urban areas, and buildings into a mixed living place. With regard to the conflict between the living environment and urban life brought about by China's rapid urbanization, we believe that it cannot be solved by traditional countryside strategies and theoretical utopian thoughts. It is necessary to explore how to create a sense of belonging to the city and take advantage of the power arising spontaneously from it. Perhaps, this is a solution to the problem.

Conclusion

In this paper, we have discussed some thoughts, strategies, and practices about staying between the individual and the public. Making choices is a process and a beginning. As social and cultural hierarchies and boundaries are disappearing and changing, can architecture and architects find an independent position to stand? Neither yield to the production system nor subjected to the consumption system. Neither be obsessed with individual expression nor indulge in empty talk.

We decide to learn from those respectful older generations, sticking on the current social reality to seek new value, examining the everyday circumstance to discover fresh design principles and testing new approaches with persistent practice.

After all, as an architect, we are destined to envision all the wonderful possibilities for the future.

The paper co-authored by Zhuang Shen and Hua Xiahong was firstly featured in The Architect, 2012 (6): 43–51. The first draft of this paper was completed in April 2009, when Zhuang Shen was still a cofound partner at Atelier Deshaus. At the invitation of Prof. Dong Yugan, Atelier Deshaus participated in his "Young Architects 'From' Series" program. This article is one of the articles written for the book, and for various reasons, the book has not yet been published. In 2011, we revised the article and added new cases.

3

非识别体系的一种高度：
杰弗里·巴瓦的建筑世界
An Altitude of Unrecognizable System: The Architectural World of Geoffrey Bawa

1　杰弗里·巴瓦
Geoffrey Bawa

2　新议会大厦外观
New Parliament Complex

斯里兰卡建筑师杰弗里·巴瓦（1919—2003 [图1]）出生于富裕家庭，早年从英国剑桥毕业，本当子承父业担任律师，在欧美游历数年后，欲定居意大利，后因在家乡购下庄园而发掘出对建筑的兴趣，当他从伦敦建筑联盟学院毕业回国开始建筑实践时已是 38 岁高龄。在其后40 余年的职业生涯中，巴瓦建成了斯里兰卡新议会大厦（1979—1982 [图2]）等重要作品，其中最有影响力的要数住宅和旅馆。

虽然身处边缘，或者正是因为边缘，包括南亚地区特殊的地理气候和历史文化背景[1]，本人极其混杂的血缘关系[2]，所受的西方教育和欧美文化的影响，曾经的欧洲合作者和大量西方仰慕者在英文世界的推荐等诸多因素综合，巴瓦的建筑成就获得了不同方面的肯定：他曾荣获2001 年阿卡汗建筑奖终身成就大奖，肯尼斯·弗兰姆普敦将他列为"批判的地域主义"建筑师，马来西亚建筑师杨经文则称其为"亚洲建筑同仁心目中最初的英雄和大师"。

学术界对巴瓦的认识呈现以下几种倾向：褒扬的声音认为，巴瓦的工作属于地域主义或地域现代主义，是现代性和地方性的高度融合，或者说他的工作与自然气候、手工精神、地方文化等主题关联紧密，是"地方的神明"。批评的看法一种认为，巴瓦的工作属于西方设计文化与殖民地文化杂交的产物，本质上没有太深刻的内涵；另一种认为，巴瓦的工作主要是为精英阶层与上流社会服务，缺乏更广泛的价值和意义。

从笔者角度来体会，这些带有西方中心参照倾向的评论或多或少都是一种对巴瓦复杂工作的标签化，在这些标签后面的是一个建筑学的识别体系。然而，笔者认为，从这些我们已经习惯的角度去认识和讨论巴瓦建筑工作的价值，难免形成相对标准化、表面化的理解，同时也忽略了因其历史地理位置和个人经历的特殊性，巴瓦建筑世界的独特性与不可复制性，这最终也会削弱学习和发展其经验的开放性和可能性。这是笔者对以往研究的疑虑，也是试图寻找新的视角来解读巴瓦作品及其意义的最大动力。

以非识别体系为研究视角

研究者眼中的巴瓦与巴瓦眼中的自己

对于巴瓦传奇的人生和艺术作品，迄今已有相当丰厚

Sri Lankan architect Geoffrey Bawa (July 23, 1919–May 27, 2003 [fig. 1]) was born in a wealthy family. When graduating from Cambridge University, he worked as a lawyer, following his father's footsteps. After traveling in Europe and the U.S. for several years, he intended to settle in Italy. Later he bought an estate in his hometown and thereupon discovered an interest in architecture. He was already 38 years old when he returned home to begin his architectural practice after graduating from the Architectural Association School of Architecture (AA). Over the next 40 years of his career, Bawa completed important works such as the New Parliament Complex (Kotte, 1979–1982 [fig. 2]) in Sri Lanka, while his most influential achievements are residences and hotels.

Although he was on the margins, or precisely because he was on the margins, Bawa's architectural achievements have been extensively recognized, thanks to the special geography, climate, historical and cultural background of South Asia[1], his extremely mixed-blood relations[2], the influence from Western education and European and American Culture, his former European partners and a large number of Western admirers' recommendation in the English world. He won the Chairman's Award of the 2001 Aga Khan Award for Architecture (only four persons have won the award since 1978). Kenneth Frampton identified him as a critical regionalist Malaysian architect Ken Yeang called him "the first hero and guru in the hearts of Asian architectural peers".

The academic community has various comments on Bawa and his practice: Those who compliment him believe that Bawa's work belongs to Regionalism or Regional Modernism, representing a high degree of integration of modernity and locality, or his work is closely associated with natural climate, craftsmanship and local culture, showcasing "the genius of the place". One critical view is that Bawa's work is a product of hybridization between western design spirit and colonial culture without any profound meaning in essence. Another critical view is that Bawa's work is mainly for the elite and the upper class, lacking broader value and significance.

From our point of view, these comments which undoubtedly have a western-centered tendency are more or less labels put on Bawa's complex work. Behind these labels is the mainstream architectural recognition system. However, we believe that discussing the value of Bawa's architectural work from conventional perspectives will easily lead to standardized and superficial understandings. Meanwhile, by doing so, we have ignored the particularity of Sri Lankan geographical location and history, ignored the uniqueness of his personal experience and the non-replicability of Bawa's architectural world. This will ultimately undermine the openness and possibility of studying and developing his experiences. These doubts towards previous studies are also the primary motivation driving us to interpret Bawa's works and their significance from a fresh perspective.

的研究成果。在其基金会的网站上[3]，综合不同研究者的观点，英国学者大卫·罗布森[4]将其不同时期的作品总结为四个代表性的特征：开端的热带现代主义、早期的当代乡土、成熟时期的地域现代主义和文脉现代主义。总体而言，在这些研究者看来，巴瓦作品的核心价值似乎在于对地方性和现代性矛盾的调和，作为修正的、多元化的现代主义在南亚地区的一个重要代表，巴瓦的设计对同质化的国际式现代主义构成了批判和挑战。

对于被加诸的这些标签，巴瓦自己往往采取顾左右而言他的态度，保持一种怀疑，却也不直接说拒绝。他不愿意被贴标签，不仅是因为时时都希望突破原来的自己，更是因为他并无意于证明什么设计的理论或原则。巴瓦对理论极端不信任，又不愿意谈及他的方法和所受的影响，使人们更加无法透过标签看到本质。他曾写道："当人们感受到乐趣，就如同我在设计和建造房屋时所感受的一样时，我发觉根本无法用分析的、条条框框的方法来描述其确切步骤……我深信建筑是无法用言语来解释的……我一直喜欢看建筑，但难得喜欢阅读建筑说明……和其他人一样，我认为建筑无法完全解释清楚，必须去体验。"

对比两者，研究者的标签无疑建立在我们所熟知的专业话语系统之上，很容易识别。而巴瓦的语焉不详就很难被纳入既有的体系，如何来发现其中的价值和可能呢？这些标签和反标签背后所展示的识别与非识别的建筑世界，是本文要讨论的内容。

识别体系与非识别体系

我们姑且用"识别体系"来指代容易被纳入耳熟能详的主干建筑学知识系统的建筑现象，那些能追根溯源、特征明显、容易归类和分析的内容。与之相对，用"非识别体系"来涵盖非主流建筑学或者不容易被认识清楚的知识体系，那些来源和特征不明显、不容易归类、边缘、杂交，或者过于普通、缺乏艺术创造性而被排斥在外的建筑现象。

在我们看来，巴瓦的建筑世界所具有的非识别性，植根于其复杂的个人经历、经验，以及斯里兰卡特殊的历史地理、社会文化的综合影响。

选择另一个角度来理解巴瓦的工作，一方面是因为巴瓦的建筑具有特殊的代表性与典型性，另一方面，或者说

Unrecognizable System as a Research Perspective
Bawa in Researchers' and His Own Eyes

A lot of research has been done on Bawa's legendary life and art works. The website of his foundation[3] contains the views and opinions of different researchers. British scholar David Robson[4] summarized his works in different periods into four representative characteristics: Tropical Modernism in the beginning, Contemporary Vernacular at the early stage, and Regional Modernism and Contextual Modernism during the maturity period. Generally speaking, in the eyes of these researchers, the core value of Bawa's works seems to lie in the reconciliation of the contradictions between locality and modernity. As an important representative of revised and pluralistic modernism in South Asia, Bawa's design constitutes a disapproving critique of and a challenge to homogeneous international modernism.

For all these labels, Bawa often maintained a sense of skepticism, but he didn't deny them outright. He did not want to be labeled, not only because he always wanted to go beyond himself, but also because he had no intention of proving any design theory or principle. Bawa's extreme distrust of theory and his reluctance to talk about his methods and the influences exerted on him make it even more impossible for people to see the essence through labels. He once wrote: "When one delights as much as I do in planning a building and having it built, I find it impossible to describe the exact steps in an analytical or dogmatic way. I have a very strong conviction that it is impossible to explain architecture in words… I have always enjoyed seeing buildings but seldom enjoyed reading about them… Architecture cannot be totally explained but must be experienced."

By comparing the two, we find that researchers' labels are undoubtedly based on the professional discourse system we are familiar with and are easily recognizable. Given Bawa's evasiveness, it is difficult to include him in the existing system. How to discover the value and possibility in it? Behind these labels and anti-labels are a recognizable architectural world and an unrecognizable architectural world, which are what this paper is going to discuss.

Recognizable System and Unrecognizable System

Let's use the "recognizable system" to refer to architectural phenomena that are easily incorporated into the mainstream architectural knowledge system, whose contents bear clear origins and distinctive characteristics, easy to be categorized and analyzed. In contrast, we use the "unrecognizable system" to cover non-mainstream architecture, knowledge systems that are not easily recognized, and architectural phenomena that are of undetermined origin and lest distinctive characteristics, difficult to categorize, hybrid or too common, lack artistic creativity and are therefore excluded.

更大的目的是要发掘大量还未被纳入建筑学研究的日常世界的价值。那些无从被标准化、类型化、识别化，那些非典型的普通日常建筑，基本不会进入主流建筑学的讨论与关注范围。即便讨论，往往要么被视作高级层面的建筑学的一种通俗演绎版、山寨消解版，要么作为一种原生态的建筑现象，无法从中萃取有规律、有价值的方法。巴瓦的工作建立起了糅杂的、非类型化的建筑世界的一种高度，值得研究者与实践者去比较和思考它与其他非识别体系建筑之间的关联。

图纸的世界与生活的世界

巴瓦的建筑世界不仅建立在现实的生活与空间、室内与室外的交融当中，也建立在图纸与实物、意象与真实的穿越之中。如果你第一次阅读巴瓦的设计图纸，那些把建筑结构体、各种植物、手工艺品乃至工业产品都不厌其烦地绘制出来的平面图和剖面图会给你留下极端深刻的印象。这些具体与抽象并存，还充满想象的意象的图纸，不仅准确再现了为各种物品所包围的生活空间，而且很好地揭示出相应的价值观念、艺术手段和生活姿态。

跟艺术家及团队的合作

巴瓦无疑是一个有着人格魅力的组织者，这不仅表现在他后来驾驭各种建筑体系的能力上，也体现在他组织合作的能力上。这些颇具艺术性和神秘气质的图纸并非出自巴瓦本人之手。他自己用圆珠笔绘制的图纸虽然相当准确，却远远谈不上美观，更没有超越技术表达的意义。巴瓦事务所的图纸全部是手下绘图员的作品，尤其是其中一位后来成为艺术家的员工拉奇的功劳。但是创造这种画风的则是一位澳大利亚艺术家唐纳德·弗兰德。1957—1962年，唐纳德曾在巴瓦哥哥比维斯的庄园居住了 5 年，创作了《科伦坡城》《加勒城》等著名作品，为比利弗庄园设计了个洛可可风格的大门。在此期间，他也教会了巴瓦的绘图员们这种独特的全景画风格的绘图技巧。

巴瓦的成就是不能跟活跃在他周围的事务所合伙人、员工以及众多艺术家分割开来的。在事务所里，这个据说没有实际技能，不会画图，对园艺知之甚少，对建造没有切身经验的人是团队的中心人物。他指挥、鼓励、哄骗、激发那些擅长做这些事的人，使他们忠心耿耿。他将他们聚集起来，启发他们，鞭策他们，担任他们的精神领袖。

In our opinion, the unrecognizability of Bawa's architectural world is rooted in his complex personal experiences, and the combined influence of Sri Lanka's particular historical geography and social culture.

We choose to understand Bawa's work from a different perspective, not only because Bawa's architectural works are representative and typical in a special way, but also because we intend to explore the value of numerous everyday phenomenon that has not yet been incorporated into architectural research. Those typical and ordinary everyday buildings, which cannot be standardized, categorized and recognized are thus seldom discussed and noticed in the mainstream architectural discourse. Even when being discussed, they are often regarded as a vulgarized or copycat version of the high-level architecture, or as a primitive architectural phenomenon, and no valuable approaches can be extracted. Since Bawa's work has brought the mixed, uncategorized architectural world to a new level, it is worthwhile for researchers and practitioners to compare and think about its association with other buildings in the unrecognizable system.

World of Drawings and World of Life

Bawa's architectural world is built not only on a blend of real-life and space, connecting space between indoors and outdoors, but also on a transcendence between drawings and reality, or the imagery world and physical world. If you read Bawa's design drawings for the first time, you'll be greatly impressed by the plans and sections carefully illustrating not only architectural structures but also species of plants, handicrafts and even industrial products like Rolls–Royces. These drawings are both concrete and abstract, full of imaginary images, not only accurately reproducing the living space surrounded by various objects, but also revealing the related values, artistic means, and life attitudes.

Cooperation with Artists and Teams

Bawa is undoubtedly an organizer with a personality charm, which is not only reflected in his ability to control various architectural systems, but also in his ability to organize cooperation. These artistic and mysterious drawings were not created by Bawa himself. Although his drawings with a ballpoint pen are quite accurate, they are far from being aesthetically pleasing and convey no meaning beyond technical expression. The drawings of Bawa's firm were all the works of his drafters, especially one of the employees (Laki Senanayake) who later became an artist. But it was Donald Friend, an Australian artist, who created this drawing style. For five years from 1957 to 1962, Donald lived in Brief Garden, an estate of Bawa's brother, Bevis Bawa, where he created famous works such as "the City of Colombo" and "The City of Galle", and designed the Rococo style gate of Brief Garden.

通常，他会先想出一个主要概念，并提供一条发展路线，接下来就一直充当严厉的评判者和仲裁者，直到取得理想的结果。当然，也总是他，到现场去驱动项目，对工匠做最严格的要求，不断修改调整直至最终。因此，"他就是那位为设计吹出最后一口仙气的人"。

跟巴瓦紧密合作的艺术家除了前面提到的拉奇以外，还有艺术家芭芭拉·桑索尼和蜡染艺术家艾娜·德·席尔瓦，而后者还是他第一个重要作品的业主。德·席尔瓦住宅（1960—1962）的图纸也是这种独特画风的早期代表。

对自然／人工，想象／理性的编织

巴瓦事务所的图纸绝对不只是技术符号，它们是整个生活世界的详实描绘。无论是建筑的结构、构件，还是室内的家具、庭院的陈设，地面不同材质的铺砌，品种不同、大小各异的树木都被同样精心地描绘出来，自然与人工，想象与理性平等地被编织在一起，构成一幅具体而复杂的艺术品。

在德·席尔瓦住宅中，女主人收集的石柱、石磨，乃至小乌龟都在平面和剖面图中找到了恰当的位置 [图3，4]。

在33弄自宅（1960—1997）中，两台不同年份生产的劳斯莱斯汽车像雕塑一样守候在入口处，这些机械时代的产品，连同走廊边手工的瓦罐、房间内富有质感的地毯，都是生活空间的重要构成元素。在赤壁之家（1997—1998 [图5]）的剖面中，垂直陡峭的悬崖、连绵的大海、垂直的松林与椰林被如实地描绘出来，和穿插其间的水平屋顶构成交织和对比。

巴瓦事务所的图纸不光是对生活世界的真实再现，甚至还会加入想象的意象。卢努甘卡庄园（1948—1997）水门边是一头水泥塑的美洲豹，静静地蹲在那里守候湖面，豹子尺度不大，按照实际比例并不能在总平面图上反映出来。但是拉奇用类似古代地图表意的方式，在水岸边大大地画了一头豹子侧身像，把这个内容标识了出来。

因为充满了地理历史的复杂性、热带的植物、具象的充满物质的细节，这些图纸呈现出一种独特的异域风情，同时也将现代的手法，空间和构筑方式融解其中。

被物包围的世界

更重要的是，这些画的表现方式也准确地体现了巴瓦

During this period, he taught Bawa's drafters this unique panoramic style of drawing.

Bawa's achievements would have been impossible without the support of the firm's partners, employees and many artists around him. In the firm, this man who was said to have no practical skills, know nothing about drawing, know little about gardening, and have no personal experience in construction was the central figure of the team. He directed, encouraged, cajoled and inspired those who were good at doing these things, making them loyal to him. He brought them together, inspired them, whipped them, and served as their spiritual leader. Usually, he would first come up with a major concept and provide directions, then act as a rigorous judge and arbiter until the desired results were achieved. Of course, he was always on the scene to drive the project, demanding that artisans comply with the most stringent requirements, and constantly modifying and adjusting until the end. Therefore, "he was the one who gave the finishing touch to the design".

Artists who worked closely with Bawa, in addition to the Laki mentioned earlier, included female artist Barbara Sansoni and batik artist Ena de Silva, who was also the client of his first important work. The drawings of the Osmund and Ena de Silva House (1960–1962) were also an early representative of this unique style of drawing.

Weaving Together Natural and Artificial, Imaginary and Rational

The drawings of Bawa's firm are definitely not just technical symbols. They are a detailed depiction of the entire living world. The structure and components of the building, indoor furniture and courtyard furnishings, different paving materials, and trees of different varieties and different sizes are all meticulously depicted. "Natural" and "artificial", and "imaginary" and "rational" are woven together equally to form a specific and complex piece of art.

In the case of the Osmund and Ena de Silva House [fig. 3, 4], the stone pillars, stone mills, and even the tortoises collected by the mistress find the right place in the plans and sections. In the case of the 33rd Lane Residence (Colombo, 1960–1997), two Rolls-Royces manufactured in different years guard the entrance like statues. The mechanical-era products, along with handmade cans along the corridor and textured carpets in the room, are important components of living space. In the section drawing of the Pradeep Jayewardene House (1997–1998 [fig. 5]), the vertical steep cliff, the rolling sea, the vertical pine forest, and the palm forest are faithfully portrayed, interweaving and contrasting with the interspersed horizontal roof.

The drawings of Bawa's firm are not simply a true representation of the living world, as they also contain dreamed images. Guarding the watergate of the Lunuganga Garden

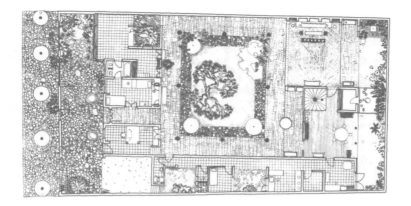

3　德·席尔瓦住宅平面图
Plan of the Osmund and Ena de Silva House

4　德·席尔瓦住宅庭院
Courtyard of the Osmund and Ena de Silva House

5　赤壁之家剖面
Section of the Pradeep Jayewardene House

作品的独特氛围，那就是一个被物品所包围的品位生活的世界，这种倾向在 33 弄自宅有典型的呈现，事实上起源于更早期的案例：德·席尔瓦住宅。德·席尔瓦夫妇斥巨资在市中心购买了一块不大的转角基地建造自宅。这是一块较难处理的基地，艾娜前面咨询过四位建筑师，直到她的朋友比维斯·巴瓦将弟弟介绍给她。艾娜起初对巴瓦有点反感，因为曾见过他开着劳斯莱斯呼啸于街巷间。不过见面后尤其是设计不断深入后，两人成为最好的朋友与合作伙伴。巴瓦的设计很好地理解了艾娜希望开放空间的意图，更重要的是他敏锐地捕捉到了女主人的特殊需求。巴瓦自己回忆道："我记得和艾娜聊天，看她为所有自己喜欢的东西簇拥着——她想要的全部无非就是砖墙和一个屋顶。平面的生成主要是由于她，因此也就是我，想得到一处内部情况不会让邻居一览无遗的私家宅第。"

巴瓦之所以敏感，因为这也是他自己想要的世界。纵观巴瓦的建筑世界，物，尤其是手工之物包围着使用者。巴瓦只是为这些富裕阶级审美品位的物的世界带来了新的图景？还是更具意义？分析巴瓦的作品呈现，我们认为，它并不刻意寻求器物背后深度的思辨含义，却选择用大量

丰富、直接的感官体验来建立一种精神的享受。

被现代主义

无论是早期的"热带现代主义""当代乡土"，还是后期的"地域现代主义"和"文脉现代主义"，研究者对巴瓦作品的认识主要是以地方性和现代性的对立统一为关键切入点的。其中，"现代主义"大部分被放置在核心位置，而热带、乡土、地域、文脉则主要作为修饰词加入，以揭示其作品跟标准化、同质化的国际式建筑之间的差异，也强调出巴瓦的设计是对传统现代主义的一种纠正或补充，显示出了更为进步和多元的意识形态和设计理念。

而在笔者看来，这种过度强调现代主义的立场对巴瓦的作品来说有点"被现代主义"的尴尬。从人文主义到文艺复兴到现代主义再到后现代主义，西方文化中心主义的线性进步史学观和设计思想意识形态所推崇的以现代主义为正确方向，其他作为补充和完善的观念束缚了现当代建筑学的视野。回到创作主体本身的状态去讨论其价值观念、设计策略和具体手法，采用认识非识别体系的眼光去分析巴瓦的建筑，可能更接近其工作的意义。

(Bentota, 1948–1997) is the concrete sculpture of a leopard, quietly crouching there looking at the lake. The leopard was not large in size, and could not be reflected on the general plan according to the actual scale. But Laki has put a leopard guarding the water in a way similar to ancient ideographic maps.

Filled with the complexity of geographical history, tropical plants, concrete material-filled details, these drawings present a unique exotic style, integrating with modern techniques, spaces and construction methods.

A World Surrounded by Things

More importantly, the expression of these drawings also accurately reflects the unique atmosphere of Bawa's works, namely a world of taste and life surrounded by things. This tendency is typically presented in the 33rd Lane Residence. In fact, it originated from an earlier case: Osmund and Ena de Silva House. Ena de Silva and her husband Osmund spent a huge sum of money to buy a small corner site in the city center to build their own home. It was a difficult site to deal with. Before her friend Bevis Bawa introduced his brother to her, Ena had consulted four architects. At first, Ena was a little resentful of Bawa, for she had seen him whizzing through the streets in his Rolls-Royce. However, after the meeting, especially as the design progressed, the two became the best friends and partners. The space designed by Bawa represented a good understanding of Ena's desire for open space and, more importantly, he was keenly aware of the special needs of the mistress. Bawa recalled: "I remember talking to Ena, seeing her surrounded by all the things she liked. All she wanted was brick walls and a roof. The plan came about largely because of she, and consequently, I wanted a private compound that would not be overlooked by the neighbors."

Such sensitivity of Bawa stemmed from the fact that this was also the world he wanted. Throughout Bawa's architectural world, things, especially handmade things, surround the occupant. Did Bawa just bring a new picture to the world of things catering to the aesthetic tastes of the affluent classes? Or is there something more significant? After analyzing Bawa's works, we believe that they do not deliberately seek the deep speculative meaning behind the artifacts, but choose to establish a kind of spiritual enjoyment using a large number of rich and direct sensory experiences.

Being Branded as a Modernist

Whether it is the earlier "Tropical Modernism" and "Contemporary Vernacular" or the later "Regional Modernism" and "Contextual Modernism", researchers' understanding of Bawa's works is mainly premised upon the unity of locality and modernity in opposition. "Modernism" is mostly placed in the core position, while "tropical", "vernacular", "regional" and "contextual" are mainly added

相对主义的立场

虽然在 AA 学习的是现代主义建筑，虽然因所处时代以现代生活需要和现代技术为基础，巴瓦作品中现代的空间、形式和技术占据了大部分的比重，但有必要指出的是，追求现代主义既不是巴瓦设计的出发点，也不是其目标。甚至在巴瓦的头脑里，现代性并不因为代表了时代精神而具有比传统形式、乡土或古典更先进的意义。巴瓦不是站在现代主义立场上的南亚地区的传播者和延续者，相反，他本质上是个相对主义者，他自己对"地域主义"的认识可以很好地说明这一点。

巴瓦认为，在某个特殊的场地中满足特殊的需要所产生的结果自然就是地域的，这并非刻意为之。他反对将地域主义与现代化（普世文明）对立起来的说法。因为在他看来，所谓的地域性并不是由表面形式决定的，因此，某些地区的泥棚跟美国采用工业材料建造的住宅具有同样的地域性效果。

在主流的建筑学识别体系中被归类和对比的概念，在相对主义者巴瓦的眼里，其价值和地位是一样的，无论是乡土（地域）或现代，东方或西方，自然或人工，手工或技术……它们都具有同样的价值，需要同等对待，也可以同样地运用于新的设计中。比如，巴瓦在他大量的设计中，因为气候的缘故，都采用了改良后的瓦坡屋顶，这几乎成为其建筑的一个重要形式特征；但在最后的赤壁之家中，为了空间环境体验的需要，他很自然地采用了平屋顶的结构。出于与环境融合的需要，坎达拉玛酒店（1991—1994）同样在最后取消了坡屋顶。

拿来主义的策略

斯里兰卡拥有多民族、多信仰交融的传统，本土历史文化丰富，还先后被欧洲三国殖民长达 450 年，独立后，政治、经济、社会也起伏不定，因此，地方建筑文化的渊源和建造的条件都复杂多变。巴瓦本人深爱欧洲文化，剑桥毕业后曾有近四年时间完全在远东和欧美游历，他尤其偏爱意大利。在最终走上职业建筑师道路后，去欧洲游历也是他每年的保留曲目，参观最新建筑是他的爱好之一。成名后，巴瓦在印度、印度尼西亚、新加坡等国都接到过委托。总体而言，巴瓦具有非常复杂丰富的经历，其所受文化影响也颇为复杂。更进一步，巴瓦从事建筑业的初衷

as modifiers in order to reveal the differences between his work and the standardized and homogenized international architecture, emphasizing that Bawa's design is a correction or complement to traditional modernism and presents a more progressive and pluralistic ideology and design philosophy.

In our opinion, this kind of overemphasis on modernism is a bit embarrassing for branding Bawa's works as a modernist. From humanism to Renaissance to modernism and postmodernism, the linear progressive view of history and design ideology, resulting from Western cultural centralism are a kind of bondage. Concepts that taking modernism as the right direction and others as complements and improvements hamper architectural vision. By going back to the creator himself, analyzing Bawa's architectural works from the perspective of the recognizable and unrecognizable systems, based on which to discuss his values, design strategies, and specific techniques, we have a better chance to comprehend his contribution.

Relativist Position

Having studied modernist architecture at AA, living in an era with modern life, technology, and spaces, the majority of Bawa's works concern modern forms and technologies. It is necessary to point out that the pursuit of modernism is neither the starting point nor the goal of Bawa's design. In Bawa's mind, modernity even has no advanced meaning than traditional forms, vernacular or classical just because it represented the spirit of times. Bawa was not a modernist communicator and a continuator in South Asia. On the contrary, he was a relativist. His own understanding of "regionalism" provided a piece of evidence.

Bawa believed that regionalist design results from meeting specific demands for a specific site. He objected to the idea of pitting regionalism against modernization (universal civilization). In his view, the so-called regionality was not determined by superficial forms, so mud huts in some regions had the same regional effect as houses built with industrial materials in the United States.

In the eyes of the relativist Bawa, various concepts classified and contrasted in the recognizable system of mainstream architecture all have the same value and status, be it Vernacular (regional), Eastern or Western, natural or artificial, manual or technical. For example, because of the tropical weather, Bawa used improved tiled pitched roofs in many projects, which turned into his important architectural feature. Whereas in his last work, the Pradeep Jayewardene House, he naturally adopted a flat roof structure to accommodate the need for a space environment experience. The pitched roof design of the Kandalama Hotel (1991–94) was also canceled for the sake of integration with the hilly environment.

是有能力为自己修建适用的庄园，以及像他表妹建议的"还可以去烧别人的钱实现自己的想法"。设计对他而言，既非谋生必需，亦非受某种社会责任的驱使，完全是兴趣所致，所以他没有思想包袱，对不同的原型在使用时也没有高下的成见。

正因为如此，尽管认为"经过四十余年的实践，巴瓦成功地为自己的祖国斯里兰卡创建了一系列革命性的建筑原型"，连大卫·罗布森也不得不承认，"要确定巴瓦所受的影响其实很困难。因为（巴瓦）自己曾谈到过就有英国的乡村住宅、意大利的花园、格兰纳达的阿尔罕布拉宫以及拉贾斯坦的堡垒，还承认欠下了僧伽罗古典和乡土建筑的人情。不过，他也受到现代建筑运动的两位英雄密斯·凡·德·罗和勒·柯布西耶的影响，他们的作品在巴瓦那些乍看非常传统的建筑中得到了响应。"

巴瓦的很多作品来自不同文化的建筑原型。比如巴瓦最重要的公共建筑，在斯里兰卡民主社会主义共和国建立后，受总统亲自委托设计的新议会大厦，其像帐篷一样的铜屋顶是根据传统的康提式屋顶结构抽象而成的，而整体则是一个彻头彻尾的现代结构平面。

实用主义的方法

在针对不同的项目选择具体的形式时，大到空间组织，小到材料构造，巴瓦的原则基本上是实用主义：以现实为依据，以结果为导向，来源或形式本身具体如何并不重要，只要适用，都可以自由采用。

在刚刚结束AA的学习回斯里兰卡实践的初期，巴瓦并没有太多的职业经验和形式技巧，其作品很大程度上受到老师马克斯韦尔·弗莱（1899—1987）和简·德鲁（1911—1996）的影响。弗莱夫妇当时正主持热带学院，并在北非和印度进行现代主义实践，这种实践是从国际式现代主义衍生出的热带版本——拒绝传统的风格，除了为热带地区特有的气候所提供的遮阳系统外，完全采用体现功能的抽象形式和现代化的技术与材料，其典范就是柯布西埃的昌迪加尔。巴瓦早期的作品也主要采用平屋顶、混凝土框架结构、厚重的墙体和遮阳等，如主教学院教学楼（1960—1963）。

但实践数年后，巴瓦意识到，对以充沛的阳光和雨水著称的南亚气候来说，坡屋顶在排水、隔热、通风、遮荫等各方面的性能均优于平屋顶。因此，1959年在为加勒

Bringing Strategy

Sri Lanka has a very complex multi-ethnic and multi-faith tradition. It has a rich indigenous history and culture and 450 years of European colonization. Since independence, it has undergone political, economic and social ups and downs. As a result, the origin of local architectural culture and the construction conditions behind it are complex and changeable. Bawa loved European culture, particularly fond of Italy. He spent nearly four years traveling in the Far East and Europe after graduating from Cambridge. After he eventually embarked on a career as a professional architect, traveling to Europe was a must for him every year. Visiting the latest buildings was one of his hobbies. Since he became famous, Bawa had been commissioned in India, Indonesia, Singapore, and other countries. Overall, Bawa had been exposed to very complex and rich experiences and cultural influences. What's more, Bawa pursued architecture as a profession with the intention of building a suitable estate for himself and "realizing his own ideas with others' money" as suggested by his cousin. He took up design not driven by the necessity to earn a living or by certain social responsibility, but purely out of interest, so he was unburdened by ideological baggage and unbiased in his approach to modern, vernacular and classical prototypes.

That's why, despite believing that "after more than four decades of practice, Bawa has succeeded in creating a series of revolutionary architectural prototypes for his motherland Sri Lanka", David Robson had to admit that "it is difficult to determine what influences Bawa has been exposed to, because (Bawa) himself has talked about British country houses, Italian gardens, the Alhambra in Granada and forts in Rajasthan, and admitted that he owes a debt of gratitude to Sinhalese classical architecture and vernacular architecture. But he has also been influenced by two heroes of the modern architecture movement: Mies van der Rohe and Le Corbusier, whose works are echoed in Bawa's architectural works which seem to be very traditional at first glance."

Many of Bawa's works may come from architectural prototypes of different cultures. For example, in the case of the most important public building designed by Bawa, the New Parliament Complex which was commissioned by the President himself after the establishment of the Democratic Socialist Republic of Sri Lanka, its tent-like roof was abstracted from the traditional Kandyan roof structure, while the whole building has absolute modern structural plan.

Pragmatist Approach

When choosing specific forms for different projects, from spatial organization to structure and materials arrangement, Bawa basically adhered to pragmatism. The source or form itself is not important. As long as it is applicable, it can be used freely.

6　阿尔弗莱德前街2号内院
Inner courtyard of the House for Dr. Bartholomeusz

的德·席尔瓦医生设计住宅时，他用一个完整的长坡屋顶覆盖了这个处于陡峭斜坡上的基地。在以后的职业生涯中，坡顶成为其大量作品的必备要素，这一方面使其作品具有了明显的地域和传统的特征，另一方面其作品也变得不再纯粹，与环境更为融合而不是形成强烈反差。

在1960年代初期，由于国家政治的原因，进口物资受限，也正是在这样的条件下，巴瓦开始开发、利用、改进传统的材料和工艺。这种对当地资源的探索与其说是向地域主义转型的自觉行为，不如说是被现实条件限制所激发的职业本能。值得一提的是他在阿尔弗莱德前街2号住宅（后来成为巴瓦工作室，1961—1963[图6]）中所作的两处技术革新：一是采用抛光的椰树杆加上花岗石柱础、柱头做所有的廊柱，这样的柱子与传统的木柱相比显得更纤巧修长，上下收分比较微妙；二是采用葡萄牙筒瓦覆盖在波形水泥板上的双重瓦顶做法，既有利于防水和隔热，又避免屋顶太重。这种屋顶做法在此首获成功后，巴瓦在后期多个作品中都如法炮制。更有意思的是，这种屋顶做法后来成为了斯里兰卡地区坡屋顶的习惯性构造，广为流传。

这种实用主义的方法并不仅限于对地方传统和工艺

7　卢哈纳大学
University of Ruhuna

In the early days of his practice in Sri Lanka after finishing his studies at AA, Bawa did not have much professional experience and was deficient in formal skills, and his works were largely influenced by his teachers Maxwell Fry (1899–1987) and Jane Drew (1911–1996). Frye and his wife were presiding over the Tropical Academy and practicing modernism in North Africa and India. This practice is a tropical version derived from international modernism—rejecting traditional styles. Except for the sun-shading system provided for the unique climate of the tropics, it completely adopts technologies and materials that embody the abstract and modernization of functions, just like Le Corbusier's Chandigarh. Bawa's early works used flat roofs, concrete frame structures, thick walls and sunshades, such as Bishop's College (1960–1963).

After years of practice, Bawa realized that pitched roofs outperformed flat roofs in drainage, heat insulation, ventilation, shading and other aspects in the South Asian climate, known for its abundant sunshine and rainwater. Therefore, in 1959 when he designed the house for A.S.H.de Silva, a doctor in Galle, he covered the site on a steep slope with a complete long, pitched roof. In his subsequent career, the top of the slope became a necessary element of a large number of his works, which on the one hand gave his works distinct geographical and traditional characteristics, and on the other

的发掘和利用，也涉及对现代的标准化手段的灵活运用。一个典型的例子是在南方省马特勒兴建的卢哈纳大学（1980—1988 [图7]）。这是一个面积超过 4 万平方米的大项目，30 公顷用地分布在三座陡峭的山丘上。为了简化工作，基地被纳入平面 3 米×3 米，竖向 1.5 米的网格系统中，所有的建筑基本都放在这一南北向的正交网格中，所有节点也尽量标准化，只有局部会根据地形调整。建筑的构造是最直接的那种：砖墙白色粉刷，波形水泥板上覆半圆形筒瓦。各式连廊和庭院将建筑群连成整体，景观或收或放，灵活多变。在跨越三座小山丘的校园里，50 栋单体在形制、材料、标准细部上都只有有限的类型，但总体却形成了非常丰富的空间和景观效果，除了高低错落、尺度各异外，自然也被有机地整合到建筑中，因此每个区域都具有独特性。

糅杂的构筑体系

这种对待物的世界的态度、相对主义的立场、拿来主义的策略、实用主义的方法使巴瓦获得了很大的创作自由度和灵活度，也为其作品赋予了极端丰富和复杂的特征，

无论在空间、形式、材料、构造上都是不同的内容相互纠缠和融合，形成一种糅杂的构筑体系，而这种含混的样貌也可以体现为很多层次的时间性表达。不同时空的文化遗产在此共同留下痕迹，而自然在时间脉络中对建筑的作用也被组织其间。

方盒子与庭院、材质及装饰细部

虽然常常为筒瓦的坡顶和热带的植物所遮掩，除坎达拉玛酒店这样需要跟随山体结合的少数案例以外，巴瓦的建筑其实全部建立在正交的网格系统内，建筑主要是基于功能排布的大大小小的方盒子，加上热带地区连接实体空间或休息的敞廊。其空间类型和组合方式都是有限且简单的。

然而，通过庭院与半室外空间的介入，这些简单的方盒子和正交网格结构体呈现出丰富的空间体验和不同的调性。比如艾娜·德·席尔瓦住宅的庭院处在中央，加上四周围廊，面积几乎是建筑占地的四分之一，彻底奠定了其集中内敛的个性。而在巴瓦自宅中，大大小小的庭院跟建筑或开或闭的空间完全是一种没有主次的交融关系，均质，弥散，尺度亲切，色调幽静。新议会大厦则通过不同

hand made his works no longer pure, more integrated rather than in sharp contrast with the environment.

In the early 1960s, imports were restricted for political reasons. It was under such conditions that Bawa began to develop, utilize and improve traditional materials and crafts. This expioration of local resources is not so much a purposeful conscious act of transforming to regionalism as a professional instinct to cope with the constraints of realistic conditions. It is worth mentioning that he made two technological innovations in the House for Dr. Bartholomeusz (Geoffrey Bawa's Office, 1961–1963 [fig. 6]): One is all the columns made with polished palm poles plus granite pillars. Such columns are more slim and slender than traditional wooden columns and curve more subtly from the bottom upward. The other is the double tile roofing practice of laying Portuguese tiles over corrugated cement sheeting, which is not only conducive to waterproofing and heat insulation but also avoids overloading the roof. After his initial success with this roofing practice, Bawa did the same for a number of his works later. More interestingly, this roofing practice later became a customary practice for pitched roofs in Sri Lanka and was widely adopted.

This pragmatist approach is not limited to the exploration and use of local traditions and crafts, but also involves the flexible use of modern standardization methods. A typical example is the University of Ruhuna, Matara (1980–1988 [fig. 7]).

It was a large project covering an area of more than 40,000 square meters. The 30-hectare site straddled three steep hills. In order to simplify the work, the site was incorporated into a grid system (3m×3m horizontally and 5m vertically). All buildings were basically placed in such north-south orthogonal grids, all nodes were also standardized as much as possible, and only parts were adjusted according to the terrain. The construction is the most direct: whitewashed brick wall and corrugated cement sheeting covered with semi-circular tiles. All kinds of corridors and courtyards connect the buildings into a whole, and the landscape changes constantly as it swells and shrinks. On the campus straddled three small hills, 50 single buildings differ little in shape, materials, and standard details, forming a very rich whole. Nature is organically incorporated into randomly scattered buildings, different in size, so each area has achieved its own uniqueness.

Mixed Architectural System

Thanks to his attitude towards the world of things, the relativist position, the bringing strategy, and the pragmatist approach, Bawa enjoyed great flexibility in the creation, his works endowed with extremely rich and complex features. No matter it is in space, form, material or tectonic aspects, different contents intertwine and merge with each other, forming a mixed architectural system. This ambiguous

大小的建筑体量和庭院，形成端庄的空间序列，主次有别又相互统一。

而在旅馆的设计中，巴瓦则更为注重整体流线的组织，往往会在到达入口前通过一系列的轴线转折和空间序列，欲扬先抑，在望穿秋水的渴望中将震撼突然带给来访者。如果只选一个项目来说明巴瓦酒店设计的精髓，那无疑就是坎达拉玛酒店。这个作品中，空间序列的组织，形式、空间与环境关系的营造已达到炉火纯青。业主原本选择的基地就在锡吉里耶（斯里兰卡古城，狮子岩）的古老山崖脚下，5世纪迦叶波国王在此建造了城堡。但对巴瓦而言，该基地过于直白，缺乏惊喜，他更倾向于选择富有戏剧性、神秘而不确定的场所。于是一行人驱车在城郊转悠，巴瓦用楞杖在远远的群山中选择了10公里以外一片巨石嶙峋的山地，在此可俯瞰古老的坎达拉玛大水库（4世纪建造），也可远眺皇城和18世纪的丹布勒佛教壁画石窟。后业主和设计师又经直升机、吉普车等多次考察，最终选定了一块看似无法抵达的山脊作为新基地。巴瓦很快确定了脑海中的图景：从丹布勒出发向东几公里，需穿过密密的丛林，通过蜿蜒的、长长的、为树林包裹的引道，几乎180°的回转来到在暮色中唯一温暖的接待空间，又逐渐被引至休息区，浩瀚的水库，远处隐约的狮子岩剪影。无论对从那个古城回来，还是将去那个古城参观的游客来说，这都是一种令人叫绝的空间叙事。酒店入口楼层以上均为公共区域，以下则是客房，顺着山体水平蜿蜒展开，面向水库，视野开阔却又足够隐秘。建筑最初采用坡顶并与山体完全贴合，最终则采用平顶，平面增加了转折以获得更好的景观，形式被弱化到极点。走廊体系被精心设计，其节奏，开合角度与视野时刻配合着行人与景观的关系。当夜晚来临，走在热带雨夜开敞的室外走廊内，人为无限的自然所吞噬，那种紧张而刺激的震撼感很难用语言来描述。这不是一座被看的建筑，而是一处看风景的营地。[图8, 9]

增加巴瓦作品复杂度的还有他对材料和细部的灵活使用。地方的或是现代的，古典的或是当代的，在巴瓦手下并无太大区别，可以并置在空间中。比如碧水酒店（1996—1998[图10]）的柱子，首层是混凝土方柱，浅色的粉刷，楼上则用精巧的木柱支撑起多层瓦铺就的坡屋顶。在阿洪加拉遗产酒店（1979—1981），入口大厅里十几根柱子形成开敞的入口空间，柱子间距并不均匀，还刷成了不同

appearance can also be reflected in many layers of temporal expression. Careful organization of cultural heritages from different eras and regions leave traces, nature engraves on buildings with its knife of time.

Square Boxes and Courtyards, Materials and Decorative Details

Although often covered by semi-circular tile roofs and tropical plants, Bawa's buildings are all built in an orthogonal grid system except for a few cases such as the Kandalama Hotel that need to be integrated with mountains. Most of the buildings are square boxes of various sizes arranged based on functions, connected with open corridors perfect for rest in the tropics. The spatial types and their combinations are both limited and simple.

However, through the intervention of courtyards and semi-outdoor spaces, these simple boxes and orthogonal grid structures present a rich spatial experience and different atmosphere. For example, in the Osmund and Ena de Silva House, one-quarter of the whole site is occupied with open spaces, the courtyard in the center, surrounded with galleries, the inward and reserved character was determined. In Bawa's own private residence, courtyards of various sizes mingle equally with rooms and corridors, solid and void disperse homogeneously, creating a friend scale and a tranquil tone. For the New Parliament Complex, diverse buildings and courtyards are arranged according to hierarchy, forming an elegant and coherent relationship.

In the case of hotel design, Bawa focused more on the circulation. After a rhythm of repressing and turning, the visitors' curiosity has been stimulated, will the entrance start to emerge. If only one project is selected to illustrate the essence of Bawa's hotel design, it is undoubtedly the Kandalama Hotel. This work showcases a marvelous skill in spatial organization, creating perfect connections between the architectural form, space, and the natural environment. The client has originally chosen a site at the foot of an ancient cliff in Sigiriya (an ancient city in Sri Lanka, the Lion Rock), where King Kasyapa built his castle in the 5th century. But Bawa was expecting a more dramatic, mysterious and uncertain site. Therefore, the group drove around the outskirts of the city. Bawa pointed at a mountainous site strewn with jagged rocks 10 kilometers away in the distant mountains with his walking stick. The new site overlooks the ancient Kandalama reservoir (built in the 4th century) and gives distant views of the palace and the 18th century Dambulla Cave Temple. After making several inspections in either a helicopter or a jeep, the client and the designer finally selected a seemingly inaccessible ridge as the final plot. Bawa quickly rendered the picture in his mind: A few kilometers east of Dambulla, after traveling through a dense jungle and a long, winding approach in the forest and making a turn of almost 180 degrees, visitors come

的绿色，而柱子本身带有精巧的柱头和柱础，这种柱子形式在斯里兰卡的殖民地时期建筑中俯仰皆是，放在这个总体现代的流动空间中，你并不会觉得繁琐，反而有一份亲切和放松感。巴瓦在坎达拉玛酒店走廊中将柱子刷成了迷彩色。除了中间接待大厅的柱子是跟环境对比强烈的白色圆柱以外，其他公共空间的方形混凝土柱不是被刷成深灰色，甚至黑色，就是抹了草绿色，十足是迷彩服的隐身效果。只有你在廊中行进时，才会深切体会到这一简单手段是多么的高明和准确：柱子仿佛在空间中消失了，所有的注意力都被引向外面的丛林、碧水、远山乃至天空。

材料的时间性表达

时间在巴瓦的建筑世界里是一个与众不同的要素。像33弄自宅和卢努甘卡庄园，这些属于他自己的生活空间，都是他花了数十年去兴建，去改变。在巴瓦看来，建筑"就是不断地被使用，再使用，必要时被移动甚至取代的东西"，换言之，建筑就如同生命，生老病死是常态。巴瓦甚至不会费心去记录这些变化的过程，他更把这些看作是自然的一部分。

8 坎达拉玛酒店外观
Exterior of the Kandalama Hotel

to the only warm reception space in the twilight and are gradually led to a lounge where they see the vast reservoir and the faint silhouette of Lion Rock in distance. This is an amazing spatial narrative for visitors, no matter they are coming back from or going to the ancient city. Above the entrance floor of the hotel are all public areas and below are guest rooms, which are spread out horizontally along the mountain and overlook the reservoir, affording a wide view while providing sufficient privacy. The building was originally designed to have a pitched roof and fit perfectly with the mountain. Finally, the flat roof was used, with the plane turned to get a better view. The form was weakened to the extreme. The corridor system was meticulously designed, and its rhythm, opening, and closing angles and view are always in line with the relationship between pedestrians and the landscape. The intense and exciting thrill brought about by walking in the open outdoor corridor on a tropical rainy night, swallowed up by the infinite nature is beyond words. It is not a building to be seen, but a place embracing nature. [fig. 8, 9]

Bawa frequently juxtaposed contrasted elements, local or modern, classical or contemporary bears no difference. The flexible use of materials and details further enriched his work. For example, in the Blue Water Hotel (1996–1998 [fig. 10]), the first floor uses light-colored concrete square columns, while upstairs applying exquisite wooden columns to support a pitched roof covered with multiple layers of tiles.

9 坎达拉玛酒店走廊
Corridor of the Kandalama Hotel

10 碧水酒店走廊
Corridor of the Blue Water Hotel

11 卢努甘卡的客房敞棚
Open corridor outside the rooms of Lunuganga

12 卢努甘卡的景观
Landscape of Lunuganga

因此，巴瓦能预见到自然跟建筑融合的可能性毫不奇怪。坎达拉玛酒店在建设前后均饱受争议，一方面因为这本是一块佛教圣地，不希望被人破坏，另一方面，该建筑体量庞大，又是粗犷的混凝土结构和平屋顶，虽倚靠山崖顺势蜿蜒，但在建成之初光秃秃的，非常扎眼。是时间和自然慢慢修复了这个现代主义建筑的"大伤疤"。数年后，当绿色的藤蔓吞噬整个结构体后，建筑被完全吸收为山崖和自然的一部分，生活其中如同生活在丛林里，设计师的用心终于实现。相信这绝非偶然的结果，已经75岁的巴瓦肯定具备这样的预见能力。

不仅如此，这样的观念更为糅杂的体系成为巴瓦自然而然的选择。在其用一生经营的卢努甘卡庄园建筑中，你可以看到各种各样的建筑元素糅杂在一起，由于组织得极其自然，很难分清究竟属于什么风格，哪种体系，却呈现出一种总体的感觉。这种总体的感觉和庄园的气质是匹配的，需要仔细去辨别才会发现丰富的元素。对巴瓦来说，他对处理不同体系的技巧似乎已经驾轻就熟了，传统的材料、现代的材料，简单的方式、复杂的方式，符号形式、意象形式、抽象形式，他都可以轻易地糅杂在一起使用。

例如，从庄园东侧入口经一个隐秘的堑道横穿庄园的肉桂山，来到西南角一组客房，建筑靠南端有个东南亚典型的室外棚屋。这个棚屋采用混凝土框架，但柱子抹面有的用水泥砂浆，有的却用涂料。屋架和屏风均为木质，但屏风下面是一块本色抹光面的水泥板台面，茶几也是一块很大的预制水泥板，上面用棕榈叶印出花纹。灯是黑色铁艺的，门是木质的，茶几边坐的地方又是一个水泥墩子，地面则是砖铺的。这个空间的建造形式、选用材料看似很随意，是一个非常混合的体系，然而身临其境，你体验到的是整个空间和氛围，它和外部景观一样混杂，也一样舒适。[图11]

这些杂糅的体系产生出某种时间的、历史的感觉，仿佛这些建筑生来就拥有自然的历史。

世俗中的精神空间

如果说巴瓦那些来源和特征都含糊不清、充满混杂元素与体系的作品，其生成有什么必然的凝聚力的话，那就是他极端个人化的价值观念和生活方式——一种世俗生活与精神空间的高度融合。

More than a dozen columns in the entrance hall of Heritance Ahungalla (1979–1981) form an open entrance. The columns are set in changed gaps and painted in different greens, all bearing exquisite heads and foundations. This arrangement of columns can be found everywhere in Sri Lanka's colonial architecture, and in this generally modern flowing space, instead of feeling cumbersome, it gives a sense of intimacy and relaxation. Bawa painted the columns in camouflage colors when designing the corridor of the Kandalama Hotel. While the white round columns in the middle reception hall are strongly contrasted with the environment, square concrete columns in other public spaces are painted dark grey, black or grass green to create a flawless invisible effect similar to that of camouflage clothes. Only when you walk in the corridor will you deeply appreciate how clever and accurate this simple means is: the columns seem to have disappeared in space, and all the attention is directed to the jungles, the blue waters, the distant mountains, and even the sky.

Temporal Expression of Materials

Time is a distinctive element in Bawa's architectural world. For example, he had spent decades to build and change his 33rd Lane Residence in Colombo and the Lunuganga Garden in Bentota, which were his own living spaces. Bawa saw buildings as " things that are constantly used, reused, moved or even replaced when necessary." In other words, buildings are born, grow old, get sick and die like living beings. Bawa didn't even bother to document these changes, and he saw them as part of nature.

Therefore, it is not surprising that Bawa could foresee the possibility of nature and building integration. There had been much controversy before and after building the Kandalama Hotel. On the one hand, for a Buddhist holy site, any activity might cause undesired damage. On the other hand, the massive and bare building with a rough concrete structure and a flat roof would inevitably leave an unpleasant view even if it wound along the cliff. Time and nature slowly repaired the "big scar" of this modern building. A few years later, when green vines engulfed the whole structure, the building was completely absorbed into the cliff and nature. Living in this hotel was like living in the jungle. The designer's intention was finally realized. We believe that this was not accidental, but had been foreseen by this 75 -year-old architect.

Moreover, such a mixed system is a natural choice for Bawa. In the Lunuganga Garden to which he has devoted his entire life, you can see a variety of architectural elements mixed together. They are organized so naturally, just like a whole. It is difficult to distinguish the origins of these styles and systems. Such a feeling of wholeness matched with the temperament of the estate. Only through the exercise of careful discernment can abundant elements be discovered and classified. Bawa has demonstrated a good mastery of the skills

建筑在其间扮演了与那些手工器物同样的角色，为相应的人、相应的生活而定制，其中有些还会随着时间、习惯的改变而不断调整。说到底，对于巴瓦来说，劳斯莱斯的古典气质，手工标志与澎湃的发动机组合在一起才是美丽的。为此，他的建筑需要真正居住、使用才能辨析其中简单直接的原则。如果仅仅作为旁观者，有时感觉他的建筑奢侈而甜腻，或者折中而模糊，似乎缺乏鲜明的类型或者宣言式的立意。批评者因此验证，这样的建筑不过是现代主义建筑的地方实践或者边缘化的模仿应用，巴瓦只是这样的实践当中具有艺术高度的一员。唯有我们抛开这些不假思索的主义与风格、类型与血缘的条条框框时，才能从一个普通建筑师的角度去真正接近巴瓦，去理解他那些隐藏于改变、糅杂的建筑世界之下的真实想法与目的。

以身体愉悦为基础的精神揭示

事实上，巴瓦作品所体现的整体感觉每个都是明确的，细节与局部、与整体相呼应，每个细节的考虑在形式与结果方面都思路清晰。巴瓦找到了古典与现代方式相会的地方：用一种简约甚至极少的叙事方式，将人投入景观

的画面，又拉出到精神的享受之中。[图12]

在卢努甘卡主屋的南露台上，孤零零地放了一张桌子与一把椅子，桌面是白色的水泥抹面，上面向心印着几个大片热带植物叶图案装饰。这是巴瓦的早餐桌。巴瓦在这里一个人享受早餐时，视线可以正对向肉桂山与两边丛林形成的如画美景。看到这样的设计，在感觉奢侈震撼之余，自然也会明白，对巴瓦而言，所有物质的组织是为了身心的愉悦。在自己的住宅和庄园数十年的不断更改尝试中所形成的认识与结果，巴瓦总会运用到其他的项目中。[图13]

在遗产酒店项目中，经过入口弯弯折折的绵长小径，一侧伴着低低的风雨檐廊，绕过入口纵向伸展的椰林水池，终于来到接待大堂。这是一处开敞的大厅，阴影遮蔽下，海面凉风阵阵袭来，热带骄阳下的烦躁一扫而光，通体舒畅。此时，透过大堂内逆光的圆柱阵列，就像透过长焦距的镜头一样，远景被过滤拉近，只看见蓝天下，排列成一条直线的海浪迎面而来，触及沙滩时，浪线无声地腾起一道整齐的白墙，一次接着一次，和着一直在的凉风。[图14]

而在巴瓦最后一个公共建筑作品——碧水酒店中，设计师驾驭建筑形式与体验的技法更臻于老道和内敛，这种

104

required to deal with different systems. He could mix materials of tradition and modern, methods either simple or complex, symbolic, intentional and abstract forms together with ease.

For example, in the Lunuganga Garden, starting from the east entrance, you travel across the estate's Cinnamon Hill through a secret passage, arriving at a group of guesthouses in the southwest corner. At the south end of the building, you will see an outdoor hut in a typical Southeast Asia style. The hut has a concrete frame, its columns covered with different coats, some in cement mortar, some in the paint. Both the truss and the screen are made of wood, but under the screen is a naturally polished cement table top. The tea table is also a large precast cement slab, which is printed with patterns of tropical leaves. The lamp is made of black wrought iron, the door is made of wood, beside the tea table is a concrete block for sitting, and the ground is paved with bricks. This space, the construction forms materials seem casually selected, creating a very mixed system. However, when you are standing inside, what you experience is the whole space, mixed and comfortable, just as the external landscape. [fig. 11]

These mixed systems produce a sense of time and history, as if these buildings were born with natural history.

Spiritual Space in Secularism

If Bawa's works, which have unclear origins and characteristics and are filled with mixed elements and systems,

owe their creation to any necessary cohesion, it must be his extremely individualized values and lifestyle—a high degree of integration between secular life and spiritual space.

Buildings play the same role as handcrafted objects, customized for the corresponding people and their life, some of which are constantly adjusted over time and with the change of habits. In the final analysis, for Bawa, Rolls—Royce's classical temperament, handmade logo, and raging engine are beautiful only when they are assembled together. For this reason, his buildings need to be truly inhabited and used in order to identify their simple and straightforward principles. From a bystander's point of view, sometimes it feels that his buildings are extravagant and sugary or compromised and vague, seemingly lacking a distinct type or a manifesto-style vision. Critics thus claim that such buildings are merely local practices or marginalized imitative applications of modernist architecture, and that Bawa is only one artistically aspiring follower of these practices. Only when we let go of the constraints of these unconceived doctrines and styles, types and bloodlines, can we really approach Bawa from the perspective of an ordinary architect to understand his real ideas and purposes hidden under a changing, mixed architectural world.

Spiritual Revelation Based on Physical Pleasure

In fact, the overall feeling embodied in Bawa's works is clear, details, parts and the whole echo each other. Every

极具简约色彩的情感激发已有了更不动声色的做法。碧水酒店被构想为一座"城市的广场",用来供城市的中产阶级进行社交。与之匹配,巴瓦设计了一种庄重克制的调性,只使用了正交的柱网体系。经过精心的安排,普通的重复节奏的柱廊与柱网空间所具有的冷静极简控制了整个酒店的气氛。

以完美艺术为目标的生活享乐

巴瓦并非禁欲主义者,但他更倾向于艺术化的生活方式,避免物质与欲望在中产、富裕阶层可能产生的低俗与堕落,使之成为一种世俗生活中的艺术典范。

在其亲自监督建成的最后一个作品——赤壁之家中,巴瓦在各种建筑形式间自如游走的能力得到了最明显的证实。在此,巴瓦采用的不是具有地方传统意义的坡顶结构,而是一个简约棚屋的钢结构平顶形式 [图15]。诗人迈克尔·翁达杰为之赋诗《赤壁之家》,没有比这更合适的文字来说明设计的意图:建筑与它所服务的生活艺术是如何重叠,从而建筑成为了艺术。诗文如下:"美蕊沙没有镜子。海在树叶间,浪在椰林里,古老的语言在马尾松

的臂弯里,传统啊传统,代代相传。祖父种下的凤凰树浴火重生,兀自穿出屋顶,无拘无束。房屋如同一张打开的网。其间,夜晚聚焦于一个呼吸,一个脚步,一个物品或姿势,我们却无法依附其上。只有在夜晚感知中,那些或长、或短、或困难的时刻。在那,即使在黑暗中,也没有一条地平线没有树木,唯有那树叶间船只的微光,只余一步便消弥于无形。"

如果说有什么作品代表巴瓦的精神,体现他对待世界的态度,那么一定是他的两处宅邸:位于科伦坡的33弄自宅和位于本托塔的卢努甘卡庄园。

位于科伦坡郊区一条支弄上的自宅是巴瓦的建筑试验田。这条街道尽头原来有一排四幢僧侣居所,巴瓦用十年时间逐一盘下,于1968年启动全面改整。原来的支弄被改造为入口长廊,内部粉刷成白色,旁边点缀着一系列小天井。长廊将大大小小的居住空间串联起来,尽头是后花园一株高大茂盛的素馨树。经过近四十年的持续改造,原来平房的状貌几乎不存,任意、如画的品质跟强烈的秩序与构成如影随形,内、外的意义消失殆尽,柔和的光线与家居器物共同营造出一种略略偏暗的质感氛围,从明亮的

detail is well thought out in terms of form and result. Bawa found a place where classical and modern approaches meet: using a simple and even minimal narrative approach to throw people into the landscape and then pull them into spiritual enjoyment. [fig. 12]

On the south terrace of the main house of the Lunuganga Garden, there is a solitary set of a table and chair. The table has a concrete white plaster top, which is decorated with several patterns of large tropical plant leaves converging towards the center. It is Bawa's breakfast table. When Bawa enjoyed his breakfast alone here, he could look directly at the picturesque scenery of the Cinnamon Hill and the jungles on both sides. In addition to being awed by its luxuriousness, people who see the design will naturally understand that for Bawa, all the material organization is for the pleasures of the body and mind. Bawa would always apply these understandings and results derived from decades of constant attempts to change in his own residences and estates to other projects. [fig. 13]

At the entrance of Heritance Ahungalla is a long winding path. On one side of the path are low-hanging eaves. Walking along the path and around the longitudinally extending palm forest pond at the entrance, you finally come to the lobby. It is an open hall. In the shade, bombarded by a stream of cold breezes blowing from the sea, you feel happy and relaxed from head to toe. The anxieties you suffered under

the scorching tropical sun totally swept away. At this point, through an array of columns in the lobby that filters and magnifies distant scenes like a long-focus lens, you see waves moving in a straight line towards you under the blue sky. Upon touching the beach, the waves rise silently to form a neat white wall time and again, in keeping with the constant breezes. [fig. 14]

In Bawa's last public building work—the Blue Water Hotel, the designer's skill of controlling the architectural form and experience was more old-fashioned and restrained. A more quiet approach was taken to a very minimalist emotional stimulation. Blue Water Hotel was conceived as a "city square" where the city's middle class could socialize. Correspondingly, Bawa designed a solemn and restrained tone, so only an orthogonal column network system was used. Through a thoughtful arrangement, the calm and minimalist nature of the common rhythmic colonnade and column network space controls the temperament of the entire hotel.

Enjoyment of Life Aiming at Perfect Art

Bawa was not an ascetic, but he preferred to an artistic lifestyle. He avoided the vulgarity and depravity that materials and desires may produce in the middle and affluent class by making them an artistic example of secular life.

In his last work the Pradeep Jayewardene House,

13　巴瓦的早餐桌
Bawa's breakfast table

14　遗产酒店的大堂
Lobby of Heritance Ahungalla

15　赤壁之家
Pradeep Jayewardene House

室外进入，情绪自然会宁静下来。这一闹市中的宅邸，不仅是巴瓦建筑修补术技巧的数十载结晶，也是一处真正的栖居之所。[图16]

没有卢努甘卡就没有作为"亚洲建筑师心目中最初的偶像与大师"的巴瓦，没有体会卢努甘卡的趣味就无法理解巴瓦设计中精妙的空间与体验组织。卢努甘卡是巴瓦建筑世界的起点，是其空间、形式和意境的实验室，更是其灵感源泉和精神家园，也是灵魂归宿（2003 年巴瓦去世后骨灰撒在庄园核心区）。巴瓦把空闲的时间全部奉献给了卢努甘卡，他人在斯里兰卡时，几乎每个周末都在此度过。卢努甘卡庄园是巴瓦半个多世纪不断改造的结果，其灵感来自世界范围内他曾探访过的众多园林（意大利、英国、西班牙、亚洲其他国家包括中国苏州园林等），但却不尽相同。早在 1947 年买下这两座庄园后不久，巴瓦就先把 1930 年代建造的平房改造成了居住主屋，两处主要景观也基本成形：向南眺望，可见远处小山上矗立的佛塔；北侧露台则临湖而建，水畔一株高大茂盛的素馨树（实际上是两棵，用人工合为一体）蔚为壮观，遒劲的枝桠间是断臂西方少年的石像，背后碧蓝的湖水波光粼粼。

卢努甘卡的重点在园林，室内仅用于睡觉，用餐往往在不同的外部空间进行。这里也是巴瓦的建筑试验田，每当其设计理念有所突破和转变时，这里似乎总是恰好也在大兴土木。卢努甘卡庄园就是巴瓦本人，它的气质就是巴瓦的气质。卢努甘卡是拥有人格的，巴瓦在世时，随之生长活跃着，巴瓦去世后，保持着静止的美丽，如同停止了生长改变的生命。世界上历经数百年不断改变生长的建筑不在少数，卢努甘卡的独特在于，它只属于一个人，是一个人用了几十年设计营造的结果。

巴瓦的启示：非识别体系的高度与可能
非识别体系的一种高度

本质上，巴瓦的建筑世界是一个难以复制的独特案例。出身上流社会，接受良好教育，衣食无忧，为了打理建造自己的庄园，从而走上建筑道路，巴瓦被认为主要是为上流社会的精英服务的就不足为怪了。但换一个角度，正是因为这样的个人背景，巴瓦的工作一开始就是把建筑设计本身当成一种手段的。他听从表妹的建议以高龄学生的身份去欧洲学习建筑时，目的无非是这样不仅可以烧自

Bawa's ability to move freely between various architectural forms was most evidently demonstrated. Here, instead of using the local traditional pitched roof structure, Bawa used the steel structure of a flat-roofed minimalist hut [fig. 15]. Poet Michael Ondaatje once wrote the poem "House on a Red Cliff" for it. There is no more appropriate text to illustrate the design intent: how architecture overlaps with the art of life it serves and thus becomes an art. The poem reads as follows: "There is no mirror in Mirissa. The sea is in the leaves, the waves are in the palms, old languages in the arms of the casuarina pine, parampara, parampara, from generation to generation. The flamboyant a grandfather planted having lived through fire lifts itself over the roof, unframed. The house an open net where the night concentrates on a breath, on a step, a thing or gesture we cannot be attached to. The long, the short, the difficult minutes of night, where even in darkness there is no horizon without a tree, just a boat's light in the leaves, last footstep before formlessness."

If there is any work that represents Bawa's spirit and reflects his attitude towards the world, then it must be his two residences: the 33rd Lane Residence in Colombo and the Lunuganga Garden in Bentota.

The private residence located at a branch lane on the outskirts of Colombo was Bawa's architectural test field. At the end of the street, there was once a row of four monk's residences. Bawa bought them one by one over a decade and started a comprehensive transformation in 1968. The branch lane was transformed into an entrance corridor with a white-painted interior and a series of small patios beside it. The corridor links up living spaces of various sizes, ending with a tall and lush Jasmine tree in the back garden. After nearly 40 years of continuous transformation, the original bungalows had changed almost beyond recognition. A random and picturesque quality goes hand in hand with a strong order and composition. "Inside" and "outside" have become meaningless. Soft light and household utensils together create a slightly dark atmosphere, which naturally calms your mood as you enter from outside on a bright day. The downtown mansion is not only the culmination of Bawa's building repair techniques over a period spanning decades but also a real dwelling. [fig. 16]

Without Lunuganga, there would be no Bawa as "the first idol and master in the minds of Asian architects". Without experiencing the fun of Lunuganka, it is impossible to understand the subtle space and experience organization in Bawa's design. Lunuganga is the starting point of Bawa's architectural world, the laboratory of his spaces, forms and artistic conceptions, the source of his inspiration and his spiritual home as well as the destination of his soul (Bawa had his ashes scattered in the core area of the estate after his death in 2003). Bawa had devoted all his free time to Lunuganga, where he spent almost every weekend while he was in Sri

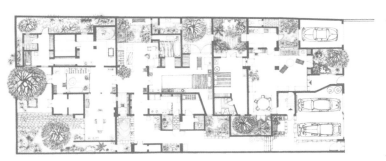

16　科伦坡的33 弄巴瓦自宅平面图
Plans of the 33rd Lane Residence

Lanka. The Lunuganga Garden is the result of more than half a century of continuous transformation by Bawa, inspired by the many gardens he had visited worldwide (gardens in Italy, Britain, and Spain, and gardens in other Asian countries including gardens in Suzhou, China). Shortly after buying the two estates in 1947, Bawa first converted the bungalows built in the 1930s into the main house. The two main landscapes were basically formed: looking south, you can see the Buddhist pagoda standing on the hill in the distance; the northern terrace was built near the lake, a tall and luxuriant Jasmine tree (actually two, combined artificially) by the water presents a magnificent sight, among its vigorous branches, is an armless stone statue of a Western boy, with the turquoise lake behind it sparkling. The focus of Lunuganga is on gardens. Indoor spaces are only used for sleeping, and meals are often taken in different outdoor spaces. It was also Bawa's architectural test bench. Whenever there were any breakthroughs and changes in his design concepts, the place was always bustling with construction work. The Lunuganga Garden is Bawa himself, and its temperament is Bawa's temperament. Lunuganga has a personality. When Bawa was alive, it grew vigorously. Since Bawa's death, it has maintained the beauty of stillness like a living thing that has stopped changing and growing. There are many buildings in the world that have been changing and growing for hundreds of years. Lunuganga is unique in that it belongs to only one person and is the result of decades of design and construction by this one person.

Bawa's Revelation: Height and Possibility of the Unrecognizable System

Height of the Unrecognizable System

Essentially, Bawa's architectural world is a unique case that is difficult to replicate. Given that Bawa was born into the upper class, was well-educated, did not have to worry about food and clothing, and embarked on architecture in order to build an estate for himself, it's not surprising that Bawa was considered to be mainly serving the elite of the upper class. But on the other side of the coin, it was precisely because of such a personal background that Bawa's work began with architectural design just as a means. When he followed his cousin's advice to study architecture in Europe as an older student, his aim was not only to play with architecture with his own money but also to play with architecture with others' money. By "playing with architecture", he intended to create a spatial environment in which he could enjoy life. Therefore, in Bawa's view, the architecture he studied was more like a means of opening up a life of practice, and then the various changes and developments produced through application became his own personal conscious methods and understandings. This may also be why when the label "regional modernism" was foisted upon him, he evasively denied it. Obviously,

己的钱玩建筑，还可以顺便烧别人的钱玩建筑。所谓"玩建筑"就是想弄出一个自己生活享受的空间环境。因此，在巴瓦看来，他学习的建筑学更像是一种开启生活实践的手段，而后运用中产生的各种各样的变化与发展，到后来就成了专属他个人的自觉的方法与认识了。这恐怕也是为什么当被贴上"地域现代主义"这样的标签时，他自己要语焉不详地否定了。显然巴瓦是一个极具艺术品味与修养并享受生活的人，这样的特质结合了成熟自如的建筑学技巧与组织，才能将个人化的经验转化为高度个人化的建筑艺术，形成独特的建筑气质。当考察家庭财富、个人品味、才智修养、社会情况等多种因素相遇结合的可能性时，你不得不承认，巴瓦确实是一个独特的例子。那么，去认识这么一个个人化的例子仅仅是为了欣赏其精美的品味吗？

开放与发展的可能

全球化的文化和生产体系使现当代建筑学的语境主要在可识别、可类型化的系统中展开。交流、传播的模式更使类型化与模式化、易被解读的建筑学成为宠儿。由此形成的主体结构的封闭倾向，使建筑学越做出开放的姿态，

却越暴露出自说自话、陈词滥调的窘境。在笔者看来，建筑世界是广阔而丰富的，标准语言之外还有丰富而有活力的天地。不过，这个世界又是如此模糊，事到临头，习惯总让我们回到原来的语言中。唯有强烈的直觉告诉我们：真实普通的日常世界里有着未被建筑学识别重视的力量。也许这些力量并不是没有被意识到，而是难以被萃取；也许只是我们还没有信心能预见到结果。巴瓦，这个远在印度洋岛国的建筑师，他的这些基本上是喃喃自语的封闭作品，却似乎可以成为某种启示和参照。巴瓦的建筑世界展示给我们一个关于识别体系之外、糅杂混合的体系可能达到的一种艺术境界。这是一个单纯由建筑师独立指挥所创造的世界，有别于社会合力自发形成的日常现象，它为我们在寻找识别体系之外的建筑学拓展之途中标记了一个高度。

本文作者系庄慎、华霞虹，最初发表于《建筑学报》，2014 (11): 27-35。本文作者衷心感谢有方旅行组织了"变化即永恒：巴瓦的启示"旅行。作为首次旅行的策划人和旅行手册的研究者及行程设计者，我们有机会更深入地研究巴瓦的设计文献并亲历现场体验。

Bawa was a person who had great artistic taste and enjoyed life. Only when such qualities are combined with mature and dexterously executed architectural skills and organization can they transform personal experience into highly individualized architectural art to form a unique architectural temperament. When examining the possibility of family wealth, personal taste, intellectual accomplishment, social conditions and other factors meeting and combining with each other, you have to admit that Bawa is indeed a unique example. So, is it just for the sake of appreciating his exquisite taste that we acquaint ourselves with such a personal example?

Possibility of Exploiting and Developing

A globalized cultural and production system makes the context of contemporary architecture mainly unfold in a recognizable and categorizable system. This mode of communication has further popularized these categorized and modelized architecture that is easy to interpret. Consequently, with this close main structure, the architecture discipline is put into such a dilemma that the more it shows an open attitude, the more exposed it is to self-talk and clichés. In our opinion, the architectural world is vast and rich. Beyond the standard language, there is a prosperous and vibrant world. However, the world is so vague that habits always drive us back to those conventional languages at the last minute. Only a strong instinct tells us that there are forces in the real and ordinary everyday world. They have not been recognized and taken seriously by architecture discourse. Perhaps these forces have already been noticed, but they are difficult to extract; perhaps we just don't have the confidence to anticipate the results. Bawa, an architect far away in an Indian Ocean island country, seems to provide some inspirations and a frame of reference through his basically self-talking works. Bawa's architectural world shows us an artistic realm that can be reached by a mixed system outside the recognizable system. It is a world created by an architect as the sole commander. It is very different from everyday phenomena spontaneously formed by social synergy, but it has marked a height in our search for approaches to expand architecture outside the recognizable system.

The paper coauthored by Zhuang Shen and Hua Xiahong was first featured in *Architectural Journal*, 2014 (11): 27–35. The authors would like to thank Archiposition for organizing the architectural trip: "Change is Everlasting: Inspiration from Geoffrey Bawa". As the first curators and researchers of this program, they enjoyed the opportunity to study Bawa's design literature more deeply and experience it on the spot.

4

日常 · 改变 · 非识别体系
Everyday, Change and the Unrecognizable System

1   莫干山庾村文化市集蚕种场改造，小展示馆
Small exhibition hall, Silkworm Hatchery Renovation, Mogan Mountain
Yucun Culture Market

作为在国内受教育、在国内设计建造的本土建筑师团队，阿科米星建筑设计事务所一直将快速城市化和全面市场化视为实践的语境，将纷繁复杂的中国城市（城乡）现状视为设计的出发点，也是自己身处其间，无法忽视的日常环境。在这样的实践环境中试图发现一些建筑学的新经验，一直是我们工作的动力，其中越来越吸引我们的正是那看上去问题无穷，然而又生机勃勃，仿佛蕴藏着巨大力量的日常城市与建筑。

关注日常城市

首先，我们认为今天建筑学正"日益成为一种'单一'的建筑学。单向的建筑价值系统造成的诸多矛盾中，最突出是，作为个人的建筑师及其设计作品与大众及其真实生活之间的关系日渐疏离，这更削弱了建筑学发展的动力"。为此，我们曾提出"选择在个人与大众之间"[1] 的立场，并认为"应该关注日常的城市与建筑。用同等的、发现的眼光去关注城市中真实存在的各个阶层的生活、各种层次的文化"[2] 尤其是其中普通、大众、自发的东西，并从中获得启示。

其次，相对于"建筑／建筑学／建筑师是什么"，我们更关心"建筑／建筑学／建筑师还有什么用"。因为在我们看来，前者主要涉及体系化的经验，关乎出生和血统是否纯正，而后者却意味着更为开放的边界，具备更多适应和突破的可能性，更可能产生因地制宜的结果，有时候或许也是生存的唯一选择。经过这么多年快速的城市化，目前，中国的城市化正在向更广阔、更深入的方向发展，我们面临的是全新的状况，无法从他处获得可以直接运用、参考的经验。同时，面临的城市发展状况也相当复杂，好或不好的事同时存在。但我们主张乐观地将其视为发掘建筑学新方向的一个机会。

最后，我们认为自己是城市建筑师，也很喜欢这种状态。日常的城市和建筑既是我们运用设计方法、建筑技术等去实践的对象，也是我们可以研究和学习的对象，二者在实践当中会相互作用。日常城市离我们很近，并不学术，难以抽象。城市里有交通的拥堵、雾霾、噪音等令人不舒服，但是在这样不舒服的地方，什么东西吸引了你，什么东西让你选择在此定居？无论是美学、文艺，还是社会学、经济学都很难解释清楚。城市天生有某种吸引我们

Since its establishment in 2009, Atelier Archmixing has concentrated on "ordinary" programmes in Shanghai and its neighbouring cities, towns, and villages of the Yangtze River Delta. The everyday world is where we live and work, where our designs perform and have influence. It is also something we study within the Atelier through the process of moving to different premises each year, a practice that began out of necessity and has continued by design.[I] Learning from the everyday world with a fresh and reflective eye is crucial for both recognition and action. Whether from participant observation, or from various design experiences, we have drawn a similar view that the essence of our surrounding space is ever changing, and its different conditions should be seen as neutral. Working from this position, we tend to treat historical traces and present requirements equally. The current built environment is seen as no more than a particular moment of spatial accumulation and transformation, in which both what is designed and built to plan—that which has long been valued as the core of architectural practice, especially since the modern movement—and its later adaptation, adjustment, and modification—that which has usually been categorised as everyday life and excluded from design field—are considered to be of equal value within what are just frozen seconds of architectural activities.

Spatial Redundancy: Discovering the Neutral Essence of the Built Environment

We use the term "Spatial Redundancy"[II] to describe this everyday status of the contemporary urban built environment, which includes the modification, accumulation, repetition, superabundance, residue, and dislocation of vast material spaces and cultural symbols. These phenomena have long been judged as "leftover", "excessive", or "overflow". In our opinion, such evaluations and attitudes are too negative to guide architectural practices in the everyday context. When examining without prejudice, those impure, inefficient, and imperfect spectacles are not harmful; to some extent, they are inevitable and even useful. Just as in the field of information technology, where wasted spaces and desired redundancy are used for error detection and correction to avoid emergency failure, spatial redundancy exposes the natural state of an urban built environment of complexity and coexistence.

Viewed over a longer historical timeframe, spatial redundancy reflects the dynamic evolution of spatial changes and accumulations of both materials and symbols, resulting from the negotiation of different powers. It also emphasises the general character of the built environment that gradually emerges over time, a shared and sophisticated condition inhabited by different individual buildings through processes of congestion, superposition, and modification, free from the lonely isolation that a freshly completed project has to bear.

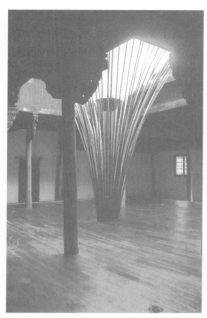

2 富春江走马楼加建竹结构伞状屋顶
Addition of a bamboo structure umbrella roof, Fuchun
Kosa Zoumalou

3 衡山坊8号楼立面改造
Facade Renovation for No.8 Building, Lane 890 Hengshan
Road, Shanghai

5 徐汇区龙华街道敬老院立面改造
Facade Renovation for Longhua Street Elder Care Center

4 双栖斋
Twin Trees Pavilion

a   Informal additions to residential facade
不断"溢出"的住宅立面

b   Different elements added to a residential facade
住宅建筑立面的不同元素

c   Mainstream architectural design is a linear process
between goal and building
主流建筑设计是目标与建筑之间的线性过程

d   Architectural practice involves a recurrence of goal,
concept, building, use and change
建筑实践包括目标、概念、建筑、使用和变化的反复循环

的力量存在，而这就是我们关心日常城市和建筑的原因。

　　传统的建筑学往往认为建筑本身应该是完整的，可以单独拿出来，作为一个实践或研究的对象。但是在不断的实践中，我们发现其实不然，日常城市与建筑是可以用不同的层面来实践的，它有很多中间的状态存在，建筑学的应用可以是局部的、变化的，不是一个非常完整的体系。这是一种开放的方法，也与局部和变化有关。

　　比如我们实践的一个案例是要改建一个屋顶 [图1]——将莫干山乡间两个普通坡顶小屋改造成一个绿色产品的小展示厅。[3] 为了充分利用原有的房子，节约造价，我们设想构造一个有厚度的屋顶，把这个形态与光线均很独特的空间直接作为展示小屋。富春俱舍走马楼改造案例则是为一个传统的院宅加一个顶 [图2]。因为这个老宅要改变使用功能，需要封闭以便安装空调。但是原有的木屋架不能用作新屋顶的承重结构。于是，我们设计了一个独立钢柱的伞结构，覆面的构造是可开启的塑料薄膜。关于这类局部改造，我们也有在城市里的案例。比如衡山坊8号楼立面改造项目是城市中常见的商业表皮改造 [图3]，但我们希望做得有所不同。因此，在普通的青砖中，加入了一种相

同尺寸的会发光的"青砖"，使这个白天低调融合的历史建筑在夜幕降临时呈现出令人惊艳的变化。这些琐碎的，或者是片断的工作，就都属于城市建筑中常见的局部更改的应用型工作。

　　日常的城市中建筑之间的关系是多种多样的，而城市始终是一个背景。因此，建筑学与日常生活建立联系并不困难，有时我们会通过组织的方式，把建筑组织到更大的环境里去。双栖斋 [图4] 坐落在苏州旁边一个古镇的深处，空间十分内向，却一点也不孤立，因为其设计用到了整体的叙事组织：从外面的停车场开始，穿街走巷，慢慢接近这个不起眼的房子，打开这扇木门时，一个独特的空间被展示出来。这就是这个设计的完整想法，漫长的行走和最后的惊喜是我们用心组织过的，它并不见得高深，却能给人带来快乐和与众不同的体验。

改变即日常

　　有一部关于跑酷的电影，展示了一群跑酷族在巴黎的上空，在城市屋顶间像野猴子一样跳跃，城市环境仿佛自然丛林。在我们看来，这部电影形象地展现了人与城市的

Spatial redundancy is not necessarily a global phenomenon. It happens more frequently in regions with high time-space compression in urbanisation. Taking China as an example, due to the rapid economic growth of the last four decades, urban material spaces have quickly generated, a large number of which are mutations resulting from discontinuous economic and social development. Besides the worldwide celebration of China's rapid urbanisation, there are also fierce debates about the rapid change, decay, and even death of Chinese contemporary architecture. In short, spatial redundancy is a widespread condition of the contemporary Chinese built environment, and also a common situation that local architects must deal with.

By taking spatial redundancy as a neutral state, we have developed a different insight into what time and change mean for the built environment. Architecture is no longer a destination achieved by the execution of an original concept. It is instead an endless recurrence consisting not only of concept and construction, but also of use and change, which may initiate new rounds of design and construction. The influence of the built environment is reflected in its interaction with users, who will accept, adjust, integrate, or struggle with and modify spaces so that they meet their own requirements. In the everyday world of these developing regions with dense populations like East Asia, there are overwhelming scenes of these kinds of architectural activities, the majority of which

are informal constructions for housing. Residents apply various available materials, structures, and technologies to build additional facilities on the surfaces of their dwelling structures: drying racks, planting frames, air conditioners, balconies, kitchens, bathrooms, pigeon houses, and so forth. These proliferating spaces are the traces of outflowing living functions or the adjustment of limited spaces to domestic evolutions [fig. a, b]. This is exactly why, where and how urban spaces are constantly accumulated and modified, and through which the everyday world of spatial redundancy is gradually shaped.

Therefore, it is necessary to replace the mainstream notion of "stable architecture" with the concept of "dynamic architecture" or "changing architecture". In developed countries, especially those of Europe and North America, rooted in the spirit of architectural modernism, the purity and integrity of a new building are highly valued and the ideal state of completion may be carefully preserved for a considerable time period. By comparison, in rapidly growing countries like China, there are, already—during the design and construction phases—numerous more unpredictable and uncertain aspects, including irrational and unscientific planning, extremely tight budgets and deadlines, half-industrialised-half-handcrafted building techniques, not to mention all of the uncontrollable eventualities following completion. Taking all of these potential changes into

相互适应关系，或者说人对城市的适应、发现、使用和调整。如果我们抛开美学、文艺、采风的心态去看，会发现在城市中随处可见这样的现象。我们的城市，其未来的命运如何？它在学者的研究里，更真实地存在于我们周围。设计师的思维习惯使我们很容易把建筑想象成永恒的事情，对设计对象呵护备至，事实上，大部分日常建筑都会被调整，会被不断改动。房子都是有寿命的。今天的建筑师建成一个房子会想要赶紧去拍照片，如果不拍完照片，好像没有完成，拍完了照片，对建筑师来说作品仿佛就算完成了。然而你会发现，建筑师完成不久的房子就有可能会被改动，被重新利用，甚至拆除。对于原来的房子，有人觉得好，有人觉得不好，在我们看来，这才是真实的状况。只有重新适应这些房子时，建筑学的意义才变得更加明晰，或者说更加有吸引力。

中国的城市化，有很多地方是需要被调整的。因为以往的快速城市化是简单粗暴的、生产式的、批量化的，对一些基本和重要的问题关注不够，比如说个人、身体、社会性选择等问题，因此它必然会被再次改变和改造。快速城市化之后的调整和改善，是我们需要考虑的。在阿科

米星建筑设计事务所近年的工作中，这类项目越来越多：最初是老的房子要改造，逐渐地新的房子也开始要被改造，有时候房子还没建完也要叫你改造，甚至还有房子还在图纸上就要被改造了。比如上海徐汇区龙华街道老人院这个项目 [图5]，就属于最后一种状况。业主要求我们帮忙美化立面，这并不困难，但经过研究我们发现了一个更有意思的切入点，或者说更本质的问题：这座老人院是按照医院的平面模式设计的：中间内廊，两边房间，阳台相互孤立，老人们在此长时间居住，几乎没有交往和透气的空间。于是，我们决定把阳台打通并连接起来，形成一条户外的交流公共走廊，并在走廊中设置了一些悬挑的休息平台院子；同时争取在每个闲置的屋顶增加一个临时的阳光房，供老人看电视、打麻将等消遣娱乐。最后的结果是，立面设计的委托演变为使用空间的调整和改造，显然后者更有积极意义。

日常建筑、日常城市给我们的另一个启发是建造的有效性。民间的施工，人们能够拿到的就是简单的材料，但这些材料在解决问题的工程中被利用得很直接，而且往往与使用的寿命相匹配，为了达到时效性与经济性、功

consideration is crucial for designing in a context of spatial redundancy. In this case, the building should be seen as a dynamic process requiring the ongoing revision of objectives, strategies, and consequences, rather than the pursuit of an ideal moment of completion that would best fulfil the initial assignment—the approach typically learnt from schools of architecture. [fig. c, d]

Spatial Redundancy or Pragmatic Efficiency

If "Spatial Redundancy" is the neutral essence of the built environment that we are examining, are there any architectural principles we can identify embedded in it? Based on our everyday experience, seemingly passive spatial redundancy could be transformed into pragmatic efficiency. As soon as the building is completed, users will begin to adjust it and its surrounding environment, according to the present conditions and resources. The building enters into an independent state, free from its initial meaning as a newly completed structure. These kinds of adjustments focus on the part instead of the whole, with pragmatism and effectiveness the most important principles. Existing conditions, together with the constant accumulations of reality, become the starting point for changing urban and architectural spaces, which will never return to their initial state. Moreover, subsequent users will gradually adapt the existing space to render it compatible with their own spatial requirements. In short, fitting, or

adjusting the old space to suit the new user could achieve functional efficiency.

"Apple Apartment", a nickname for an ordinary residential tower in Shanghai, serves as a typical example of positive urban spatial redundancy. Although the building's appearance is largely preserved just as it was when completed, almost 80% of the original residences have been replaced by E-commerce shops. The functional adjustment is rather simple. Since the plan of each residence is close to that of a small office unit, the dwelling tower is straightforwardly transformed into vertical streets with numerous shops selling digital products. The silent facade towards the city street is a perfect mask to hide extensive illegal functional and spatial transformations within the urban public sphere.[III] [fig. e, f]

It is natural that the urban building is constituted by numerous such continuous "independent" moments. When taking the evolution of these buildings as the basis of our research and design, we tend to treat the existing urban spaces of different times, different origins, and different features as equivalent, because they are all immediate circumstances with a common system of meanings, just as different life forms co-exist in the natural world. From this standpoint, we can also draw the following conclusions, that architectural change is not necessary for progress, and spatial redundancy could be neutral.

"Change means progress", "change is for progress":

6　莫干山蚕种厂改造，竹棚
Bamboo shed, Silkworm Hatchery Renovation, Mogan Mountain
Yucun Culture Market

7　安龙森林公园东部码头小镇商业建筑，模型
Model of Commerciall Building at East Dock Town in AnLong Forest Park

e　Street view of "Apple Apartment", Shanghai
实业大厦的街景视角

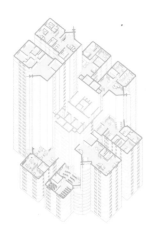

f　Functional analysis of "Apple Apartment"
实业大厦的功能分析

g　Fuchun Kosa Zoumalou
富春俱舍走马楼

h　Interior space Renovation of Shanghai YoungBird office
YoungBird 室内空间改造

能性之间的平衡，这样的建造一定要是有效的。比如我们2013年建成的莫干山蚕种场场地改造案例 [图6]，就需要充分地考虑时效性。事实上，我们需要做的是一个有点临时性的工作：给整个场地做一个先期的改造，以便吸引更多的人来关注，更多的资本来投入。虽然没有很多的预算，却要面对几千平方米待改观的场地。完成后半年，那个地方有的留、有的拆，再去看那边的情况时，作为设计师，心情还是挺复杂的，虽然一开始就已经有了心理准备。

蚕种场原始的室外场地是不规则的，如何处理这些场地？比较多种可能性后发现，场地最大的问题是每个局部都缺乏中心感。我们的策略就是要给每个不同的地方创造不同的中心感，并确定搭建一系列竹棚子，构成大大小小中心空出场地、具有明确形状的领域，每个竹棚除了中间的空间由连续线条封闭出边界以外，其他的形状和线条都是开放的，正是通过这样的开放性，室外空间的不规则形态被弥合起来。建成后，这些竹棚有效地把场地结合起来，地面坡度、竹棚、房屋、公共空间等都被有机地组织在一起。这个设计将一些基本的建筑学原理在日常的状态

里加以运用，反而更有意义了。

这种有效性不仅体现在空间的组织上，还体现在制图和施工的方式上。因为现场太复杂，这个项目最初并未绘制精密的图纸，而是做了一个大比例的模型，搬到现场作为施工样板，同时派驻现场建筑师，选竹子，现场指导，指挥工人搭建。所谓的施工文件，其实就是模型加施工要点的规则，列成表格，并且这些也不是一下子写出来的，而是开始建造以后慢慢整理出来的，同时也会补充节点的详图，过程很灵活，也很有效。因此，所谓有效性，不仅指结构、细部等环节，也包括整个建造的有效性，以及工作方式的有效性。日常的工作和专业的工作，有时候我们容易割裂开来，但事实上总是混合在一起的，当你熟悉了这些以后，方法自然就会很灵活。

面积大，周期短，施工方法也必须简单有效。在几千平方米范围内，如何在钢架上放置这几千根竹子？如何定位？如何快速调整？太复杂了不仅费力，也费钱。最后有效的做法实际上是在现场跟工人商量出来的，先用一根钉子把竹子和钢架直接固定在一起，便于转动调整，然后再固定另一端。

117

these are dominant value systems of modern society, including the architectural field. In the everyday built environment, we witness various kinds of change. Some involve vigorous large-scale urban construction and updating, some concern the natural replacement cycles of life and death, and then there are those prevailing everyday transformations, often banal, and even illegal. However, mainstream architecture tends only to stress those revolutionary creations that appear to have complete independence, clear concept and novel form, and are usually the results of abundant manpower and material resources, elaborate planning, and construction. Everyday changes of evolutionary significance are largely ignored. Even if noticed, they are seen as meaningless, without any potential to guide new designs.

On the contrary, Atelier Archmixing prefers to see change as an objective process that is largely outside a particular set of values or priorities. It is neither the upgrading that modern society has become accustomed to, nor the designers' obsession with progress and revolution. Architectural change is, in our view, of neutral essence. That is why, in a series of urban and rural regeneration projects, we took existing buildings as a neutral base, and saw our own work as an adjustment over a short period of time in response to new use requirements. These projects are of diverse purposes and backgrounds. Some of them involve updating urban and rural interior spaces. For example, Zoumalou of

Fuchun Academy [fig. g] transformed a historic house with an open courtyard into an enclosed bar and reception for a rural resort. A new umbrella structure combining bamboo and Polyurethane films was juxtaposed with richly carved wooden beams enclosing the vernacular yard. For the Young Bird magazine, we renovated the interior space of a former piano factory into a cutting-edge office space [fig. h]. Some of them are small renovations of simple and ordinary buildings or structures in both urban and rural areas. For example, the Twin Trees Pavilion modified a village pigpen into a relaxing pavilion in a historic town near Suzhou [fig. i]. We have also built a temporary reading pavilion on the pavement of central Shanghai's fashion venue, Xintiandi, which is a product of extremely intense processes: 15 days' design, 15 days' preparation, 5 days', construction and another 16 days' existence. [fig. j]

We have undertaken facade renovations for old buildings in an urban context [IV] In the last three years, Atelier Archmixing has designed and built five such projects successively in different areas of Shanghai, arising from various kinds of opportunities. The five facade renovation projects are: SVA Comprehensive Office Building, Xuhui [fig. k], No. 8 Building, Hengshanfang [fig. m, n], Xietu Street Community Centre [fig. l], Longhua Elderly Care Centre (2013–2016) and Removal Renovation of Chen Huacheng Memorial in Baoshan (2014–2015). Due to their different functions, sizes, locations,

i   Twin Trees Pavilion, Jiangsu
双栖斋

j   Temporary Reading Pavilion in Xintiandi, Shanghai
上海新天地临时读书空间

k   SVA Office Complex, Xuhui district, Shanghai
SVA综合办公楼

l   Facade Renovation for Xietu Community Center, Xuhui district, Shanghai
斜土社区活动中心立面改造

m   Quietly integrating with the historical context during the daytime, Facade Renovation for No.8 Building, Lane 890 Hengshan Road, Shanghai
衡山路890弄8号楼白天与周围历史建筑融为一体

n   Distinguished from its surrounding by lighting up during the evening, Facade Renovation for No.8 Building
衡山路890弄8号楼夜晚时分璀璨的外立面

此外，有效性也不能忽略对材料耐久性的不同需求。建筑都是有寿命的，有一定的时间性。在莫干山场地改造中所使用的竹子，如果不做特殊处理的话，寿命是一年左右；同样，那些钢构件也会生锈腐蚀。鉴于这个项目本身的临时性目的，一年基本上就完成使命了，所以，竹子和钢架的连接节点并不需要很永久，只要能比一年时间长一点就可以了，所以最后采用了非常简单的直接用钉子钉这样的构造。事后讲来好像很玄妙，但在我们的日常生活中，量体裁衣的道理司空见惯。另一个细节是钢结构的基础，最后采用了一个"大长钉"的基础，先把它锤到地坪里，然后把方钢焊在上面。实际场地的条件并不一样：有的地方混凝土很厚，有的表面看上去是混凝土，实际上只有很薄的一层，因此没有办法做一个统一的精确的基础，而且要一一定位太麻烦了。我们没画图纸，只有大致的规划，需要最便捷的施工方法。这样做相当于一个小桩打进去，地上还露一节，也不费什么钱，弄错了可以再打一个。总结起来，我们认为，在学校里学到的建筑学原理是简单而学术的，当你接触到各种实际的工业体系、材料体系、建造体系时，需要面对复杂情况，并将原理转化为有

效的实际做法。

最后，日常的城市和建筑也带给我们一种时间差异感的力量，这会导向形式，可能是一种混合的体系。有时受到很多规范或者体系的限制，我们很容易把很多混合的体系过滤掉，这很可惜，至少在观念上，我们不应该排斥和忽视这样的体系。我们正在设计的一个面对湖景的商业建筑就是有意识使用两个体系的案例［图7］。我们对商业建筑的理解是，它总是要不断地改变。因此设计时，我们做了一个很舒服的平台，平台是钢木结构的体系，作为商业空间的附加物，上面还能够再搭建，满足丰富的使用需求。平台下面的商业建筑实体，其实将来充满了变数。这个看似永久的建筑外观，它可能是暂时的、会随着使用被不断调整的；而那部分看似临时的平台，反而恰恰是相对永久性的。

非识别体系的建筑

日常的建筑、日常的城市让我们产生兴趣与关注的就是它不断改变的状态，这对我们的实践是有启发的，从中，我们希望发现更多的"建筑师还能干什么"，或者"还

purposes, budgets and preconditions, the designs adopted correspondingly diverse strategies.

Unrecognizable System: Taking Adjustment and Application as Design Strategy

Through processes of global industrialisation and modernisation, architecture seems to have become, like many other modern disciplines, a dominant recognisable and categorisable system. In the context of globalisation, homogenised mechanisms of economic and cultural production, and techniques of digital media communication and transmission, contemporary architecture tends to celebrate even more those practices and theories that are highly-legible, styled, and branded. In our view, beyond this classified and customary system, there is another rich and active sphere in the everyday world that needs to be discovered.

We use the term "Recognisable System" to identify those architectural phenomena and design canons that are typically included in established architectural discourse; they usually have obvious features, and can be readily traced to a particular source, classified, and analysed. By contrast, we would like to coin "Unrecognisable System" to describe non-mainstream architectural experiences that are hard to recognise and classify due to their opaque origins and qualities, including marginal, hybrid building spectacles, and others that are rejected because of their randomness, ordinariness, and lack of artistic innovation. This term not only identifies the characteristics of the everyday world, especially that of developing regions with discontinuous economic and social progress like modern China, but also highlights a largely underestimated source and long-ignored resource for developing new architectural principles and design strategies.[V]

Instead of selecting and quoting from the legitimatised lexicon of the "Recognisable System" in order to guarantee a pure and clarified building character, this new approach advocates applying all kinds of concepts, forms, and techniques without prejudice, using and mixing them flexibly, liberating them from their origins and inherited meanings, be they of the mainstream or periphery. On account of its diverse sources, features, and methodologies, this approach can be roughly summarised as the design strategy of the "Unrecognisable System". It aims to engage with the reality of "Spatial Redundancy" and to shape the future of such conditions in a way that maintains their character.

This approach, which is rooted in and leads to a further architectural understanding of this "Unrecognisable System", prefers adjustment to innovation in urbanism. Today's society relies heavily on innovation, taking it to be the strongest driving force in production and consumption. The endless upgrading of lifestyle symbolised by the accumulation of electronic products has become a worldwide fashion that influences all social activities, including urban development.

能给建筑学带来哪些新鲜的东西"。

　　然而，这些无从被标准化、类型化、识别化，或者说非典型的普通日常城市和建筑，基本不会进入主流建筑学的讨论与关注范围。即便讨论，往往要么被视作高级层面的建筑学的一种通俗演绎版、山寨拷贝版，要么作为一种原生态的建筑现象，无法从中萃取有规律、有价值的方法。究其原因，更大程度上是一种观念的束缚。

　　如果我们用"识别体系"来指代容易被纳入耳熟能详的主干建筑学知识系统的建筑现象，那些能追根溯源、特征明显、容易归类和分析的内容，与之相对，用"非识别体系"来涵盖非主流建筑学或者不容易被认识清楚的知识体系，那些来源和特征不明显、不容易归类、边缘、杂交，或者过于普通、缺乏艺术创造性的建筑现象。全球化的文化和生产体系使现代建筑学的语境主要在可识别、可类型化的系统中展开。交流、传播的模式更使类型化与模式化、易被解读的建筑学成为宠儿。因此形成的主体结构的封闭倾向，使建筑学越是做出开放的姿态，却越暴露出自说自话、陈词滥调的窘境。而在笔者看来，建筑世界是广阔而丰富的，标准语言之外还有丰富而有活力的天地。不过，这个世界又是如此模糊，事到临头，习惯总让我们回到主流的可识别的现代建筑语言中。唯有强烈的直觉告诉我们：真实普通的日常世界里面有着未被建筑学识别重视的力量。也许这些力量并不是没有被意识到，而是难以被萃取；也许只是我们还没有信心能预见到结果。然而我们也可以从世界范围一些经常处于边缘的建筑师那些糅杂混合，却达到了高超的艺术境界的作品中，看到识别体系之外的建筑学可能的高度，而这些可以，也应该被用作我们对建筑学进行新的探索和拓展的有益参考。

本文作者系庄慎、华霞虹，最初发表于《新建筑》2014 (06): 16–19。本文英文稿并非翻译，而是庄慎、华霞虹发表于 A&HCI 收录的英国杂志《建筑研究季刊》(*Architectural Research Quarterly*) 2017, 21(3): 222–233 上的英文论文《向日常世界学习》" Learning from the Everyday World "。

Here innovation takes the form of systematic "heavy" actions, such as vast-scale demolition and construction, tactics with strong visual impact and significant theoretical developments. Contrary to these kinds of innovation, which are characterised by mandatory intervention and substantial transformation, Atelier Archmixing advocates a strategy of adjustment, gentle intervention, and subtle control in the built environment. Although it is true that, after decades of rapid urbanisation, regeneration programmes are becoming as widespread and as important as new constructions, this turn to adjustment need not only be limited to repairing and correcting errors and mistakes of many years of brutal redevelopment. Instead of a passive project of clearance, adjustment is a positive action of organisation and utilisation. Through gentle gestures towards existing buildings and urban spaces, the design strategy of adjustment aims at making the best use of original features, enmeshing them with the new requirements, reorganising the whole program to satisfy the new users. Although it may result in characters that are hybrid, temporary and ordinary, this design strategy is effect-oriented and thus rather satisfying.

　　The facade renovation programme of Longhua Elderly Care Centre (2013–16, Xuhui District, Shanghai) designed by Atelier Archmixing is a good example. This is a nursing home located in a dense residential area in central Shanghai. The original plan was poorly organised, in the manner of a hospital, without public spaces. The designer successfully persuaded the client to refocus the brief from surface beautification to spatial intervention. Continuous balconies of varying sizes were built out from the exterior walls and glass meeting rooms were installed on the empty roofs where residents could watch television, play cards, chat, or just sunbathe. These sunny new communal spaces, fabricated from light and inexpensive structures and materials, resemble the informal additions and modifications typical of the Shanghai urban context. Whether from the perspective of programme or design strategy, these activities of adjustment are soft and not easily categorised, but they have effectively and efficiently solved functional problems. Moreover, these subtle changes are exactly where a true architectural identity, both rooted in and benefiting the local quality of life, can be develop.[VI] [fig. o, p]

　　Besides the tactics of adjustment, the design strategy of "Unrecognisable System" also emphasises its methodology of application. Since the changes and adjustments of everyday urbanism often focus only on partial and short-term interests and results, it is more practical and efficient to apply flexible strategies and methodologies instead of systematic frames. Appropriate words, concepts, forms, materials, and technologies should be selected and applied according to their efficiency instead of their purity and consistency with the mainstream architectural system. On one hand, the current everyday built environment characterised by spatial redundancy is an impure situation, resulting from an overall

o   South facade of Longhua Street Elder Care Center
徐汇区龙华街道敬老院南立面

p   Comparison of facades before and after renovation,
Shanghai Longhua Elder Care Center
徐汇区龙华街道敬老院立面改造前后效果图对比

plan and professional design, supplemented by spontaneous everyday modification, most of which are informal activities. It is impossible to settle concrete problems by fitting into guidelines of orthodoxy. On the other hand, as a modern profession and discourse in a developing country, Chinese architecture draws on various origins and influences in its evolution, but there remains hardly any original theories or methods domestically produced. Absorbing nutrition from different sources is necessary and important.

What, then, is the guideline for applying this knowledge about our "Unrecognisable System" in new design and regeneration projects? First, in an age with various and differentiated building purposes and technologies, we should actively select strategies of different origins and functions to achieve specialised and appropriate consequences. Furthermore, choosing different strategies according to their efficiency could result in unique forms. Last but not least, taking the uncertainty of the contemporary Chinese built environment, for example, the half-industrialised-half-handcrafted building technologies into consideration, exploiting opportunities within this hybrid and ever-changing situation, and applying strategies flexibly with a view to the overall result, these attitudes can lead to positive results.

A noteworthy example is the renovation programme of Chen Huacheng's Memorial (2014–15, Baoshan district, Shanghai), designed by Atelier Archmixing. The biggest challenge for this project was how to transform a supplementary facility in this everyday urban park with an irregular plan into a serious memorial hall for a national hero without sacrificing the public affinity for it. Familiarity and Quietness are two features we wanted to embody in this commemorative structure. Continuous open galleries were employed to give the humble structure a formal and decent appearance, rhythmic spatial order, and an appropriately serious atmosphere. Open boundaries that integrate with the surrounding environment also sustain everydayness. In order to avoid visual shock to everyday users in this park, the design applied not only traditional building forms and tectonics, but also common materials and modest treatments. The exterior walls and concrete columns were covered with plain cement, the timber columns, beams and rafters were all painted dark, and the modern, precisely connected details of timer and steel structure were oiled to black. In this way, Atelier Archmixing takes a position that, when renovating ordinary buildings in everyday contexts, it is important to restrain design power and desire, placing emphasis on application instead of creation, in the conviction that these approaches offer new potential to explore the intrinsic strength of everyday life. [fig. q, r]

From Ordinary to Ordinary, From Everyday to Everyday
Atelier Archmixing is not alone in exploring architectural guidelines drawn from the everyday world in order to resist

q Axonometric drawing of the Renovation of Chen Huacheng Memorial
宝山陈化成纪念馆，轴测图

r Eastern stages to hillside of Chen Huacheng Memorial
宝山陈化成纪念馆东侧前往后山的廊子

122

the elitism embodied in architectural modernism. Publications such as *The Death and Life of Great American City* (Jane Jacobs, 1961), *Architecture without Architects* (Bernard Rudofsky, 1964), *Learning from Las Vegas* (Robert Venturi, Denis Scott Brown, Steven Izenour, 1972), *Delirious New York* (Rem Koolhaas, 1978), *Architecture of the Everyday* (Steven Harris and Deborah Berke, 1997), *The Structure of the Ordinary* (N. J. Habraken, 1998), *Everyday Urbanism* (John Chase, Margaret Crawford and John Kaliski, 1999), *Incomplete Urbanism* (William Lim, 2012), and many others advocate the re-examination of urban disorder to discover an essence of contemporary architecture different from the modernist orthodoxy.

As a contemporary Chinese architectural studio practising in a context of rapid urbanisation and its aftermath, where "Spatial Redundancy" is a common situation, the search for an alternative approach outside the "Recognisable System" is inevitable and necessary to achieve pragmatic effectiveness and efficiency. In our view, the enduring questions include: what and how can architecture achieve and contribute today? And is it possible for Chinese architects to seek out original design strategies and methodologies from the heterogeneous everyday world in contemporary China? Instead of pursuing extraordinary landmarks or monuments with idealised permanency, we therefore prefer to start from the ordinary conditions of the local built environment, applying various

concepts, technologies and approaches without prejudice to achieve a product of "Unrecognisable System". The results may be ordinary in appearance and ephemeral in existence, but this is a consequence of the decision to restrain design power and avoid showcasing exaggerated formal or tectonic innovations. In our view, ever-changing is the essence of the everyday built environment and also its source of diversity and vitality. Under the hegemony of globalisation and its homogenising power, "an authentic contemporary Chinese architectural identity will emerge and develop only from the solid soil of reality",[VII] which is constituted mainly through the ordinariness of everyday life.

The paper coauthored by Zhuang Shen and Hua Xiahong was firstly published in *New Architecture*, 2014 (6): 16–19. The English paper is not a translation, but an English paper "Learning from the Everyday World" coauthored by Zhuang Shen and Hua Xiahong published in *Architectural Research Quarterly*, 2017, 21 (3): 222–233.

空间冗余
Spatial Redundancy

5

空间冗余是当代城市的普遍状态，是当下建筑学实际面对的普遍状态，而我们则把它当作我们建筑学实践研究的既有现实和出发点。

空间冗余的定义

冗余的字面解释是多余，不必要的重复，通常会被联系到无用、低效和有待精简。选用冗余来描述当代建筑现象具有特定的意义。作为信息理论、计算机科学、工程学，乃至生物学中的专门术语，冗余的影响可负可正。一方面，冗余可能造成低效、破坏和不必要的浪费，[1] 一般来说应该在设计中尽量避免；但另一方面，冗余也可能是专门设计的保障措施，重复的软件或硬件配置，不仅可以降低突然遭受致命破坏所带来的风险，[2] 而且因为不需要过于纯净严密的环境条件，或者说容错能力更强，实施起来也可能更加便捷可靠。这表明，很多看似消极的事物也可能具有积极合理的一面。

在习惯中反思，用新鲜的眼光打量既有。我们认为，这正是研究城市与城市建筑时需要被重视的认知态度。也因为如此，我们用"冗余"来描述城市建筑空间的重复、

多余、残留、错位等状态。这些现象通常会被冠以"剩余""过量""溢出"等带有无效价值意味的判断词，我们却认为，这种通常被当作不纯净、不高效、不完美的状态，某种程度上并非多余，而是必然的、必需的，它们可以被看作复杂、共存的自然状态。引入"空间冗余"这一新概念，一方面是为了纠正旧有的、量化的价值评判，另一方面也是为了将物质空间中文化符号的积累意义也纳入其内。简言之，空间冗余是一种城市常态，它既是物质空间上的，也是文化符号上的。

同样值得反思的是，专业领域对于类似"空间冗余"这样的"多余"现象的刻意回避和忽略，我们认为是不良的、阻碍前进的，至少也是缺乏价值的，这种认知同建筑学科过于受发展与进步的现代思想主导有关。我们研究空间冗余，是希望从另一个角度审视城市建筑的生存规律，将建筑学放置到更长远的历史周期、更广泛的存在状态下进行审度和反思。

在现代社会的生产消费体系中，在现代技术的支持下，在当下越来越纷繁快速的城市活动与日常生活中，空间冗余在建成环境中突显出来。其既涉及城市物质空

Spatial redundancy is a general state in contemporary cities. It is actually what contemporary architecture is commonly facing. We take it as the reality and starting point for architectural practice and research.

Definition of Spatial Redundancy

The word redundancy literally means surplus and unnecessary repetition. It is usually associated with characteristics such as useless, low-efficient, and to be refined. There is a special meaning in picking redundancy to describe contemporary architecture. As a technical term in information theory, computer science, engineering, and even biology, the influence of redundancy can be both negative and positive. On one hand, redundancy could result in low-efficiency, destruction, and unnecessary waste which should normally be avoided as much as possible in design.[1] But on the other hand, redundancy perhaps could serve as specially-designed protective measures. Redundant software or hardware not only lower the risks brought by sudden deadly breakdown, but are probably more convenient and reliable in use, since they can survive in less pure or rigorous environment or they have a higher tolerance to errors.[2] This shows that negative things might have positive and reasonable sides.

To reflect on the ordinary things, to consider the existing things with a fresh eye. This is exactly the cognitive attitude we emphasize when studying cities and urban architecture.

It is also out of this reason that we pick "redundancy" to describe recurrence, surplus, residue, dislocation in urban architectural space. Usually, these descriptions carry unworthy connotations such as being "leftover", "overdue", "overflowed", but we think this state is not redundant, but unavoidable and necessary, although it is usually treated as less pure, less efficient, and imperfect to some degree. They can be seen as a complex and co-existing natural state. By introducing the new concept "spatial redundancy", on one hand, we hope to rectify the old and data-driven judgments; on the other hand, we want to include the acquired meaning of cultural symbols in physical space. In a word, spatial redundancy is a common phenomenon in the urban area, from the perspective of both physical spaces and cultural symbols.

It is also worth reflecting that the phenomenon such as spatial redundancy in specialized fields is deliberately avoided, neglected. Spatial redundancy is regarded as inadequate, impeding or at least useless. This cognition has unduly succumbed itself to the dominance of modern developing and progressive ideologies in architecture. By studying spatial redundancy, we hope to inspect the survival rule of urban architecture from another angle. Through putting Architecture into a longer historical period and a broader circumstance, the study aims at academic inspecting and reflecting.

In the production-consumption system of modern society, with support from modern technology, facing the in-

间和符号的激增和改变，也涉及当代建筑学实践与理论的不断生产和发展：信息、知识、理论过剩，设计语言自我演变，持续不断地产生新的多余、碎片与自说自话的形式，各种意义指涉断裂、错位的存在物。这些都构成了方便的条件，让我们通过对日常建成环境，尤其是像上海这样具有典型表现的城市的观察，去研究空间冗余，从中发掘的特征和规律或可成为建筑学理论和实践具有启发的方向。

空间冗余：时间向度上的变化与积累

时间性是建筑和城市的固有属性，但其意义在不同的历史阶段不尽相同。

时间性曾经是单体建筑和局部城市空间中层层累积的痕迹，建筑史中此类案例可谓屡见不鲜，比如，那些利用历史遗迹，经过漫长周期修建的、各部分风格不尽相同的教堂，那些在中世纪致密的城市肌理上兴建的城市广场和林荫大道，等等。时间具体而绵延，空间充满矛盾性和复杂性。现代主义时期主张确定的计划和精确的目标，建筑最理想的状态是凝固在实现概念的瞬间，只有这样才能实现建筑的纯粹性和完整性。时间变化对物质空间的影响被忽略，至少是被淡化了。在这样的思想观念作用下，单体建筑和局部空间被抽象成代表凝固点时刻的孤岛，时间的连续感只能由这些孤岛连接起来的虚线构成。在当代建筑的城市化状态中，个体和局部的孤立属性又发生了改变：城市活动的密度不断增加，城市建筑日常使用的变量增大，改变和调整日益频繁，在时间向度上加速积累空间的变化，从而形成了空间冗余。

我们对空间冗余的研究，就试图以当代建筑或城市空间诞生之后的状态作为出发点。通常，作为实践者，城市规划师和建筑师们关心的是从设计开始到建造完成的周期，检验结果和目标的吻合程度，以此印证设计工作的必要性和合理性。而建成以后的时间性，则往往被设定为一种可预期的状态，不论是以超越时间、达到永恒为理想目标，还是以有计划、可把控的变化为主要动向，建筑学者们在概念上完成了建筑的纯净性。然而，建筑物和城市空间的真正生命周期，无论是对使用者还是周边环境的影响，事实上都始于建造完成以后，体现在使用者的具体要求及其变化与建筑物的斗争与融合，

creasingly fast-paced and various city activities and daily life, spatial redundancy is highlighted in the built environment. It touches upon the booming and changing of urban spaces and symbols as well as the continuous growth and development of contemporary architectural practice and theory: excess information, knowledge and theories, self-evolvement in design language all contribute to a fresh wave of redundancy, fragments, self-talk, and various meanings related to broken and misplaced existence. These all conveniently enable us to study spatial redundancy by observing the routine built environment, especially a typical city like Shanghai, and to illuminate architectural theory and practice through studying its patterns and features.

Spacial Redundancy: Change and Accumulation Based on the Temporal Dimension

Temporality is inherent in architecture and city, but its meanings change at different historical stages.

Temporality embodies itself in the continuous accumulation in a single building or partial urban space. There are numerous similar cases in architectural history: the churches with parts in different styles restored over a long period on previous historical sites; the city squares and avenues built on condense urban texture in Middle Ages, etc.. Time is tangible and extending. Space is contradictory and complicated. During the Modernism period, it was urged to make definite plans and accurate goals because the ideal state of a building was at the moment of achieving the concept. Only then could people realize the purity and completeness of the architecture. The impact of change in time on physical space was neglected, or at least weakened. Under the influence of this ideology, single buildings and partial urban space are abstracted into isolated islands representing the moments. Time continuity can only be sensed through the dotted line connecting these islands. In urbanization of contemporary architecture, the isolation of single building and partial space has changed: increasing urban activities, transformed usage of urban buildings, frequent changes and adjustments have accelerated spatial accumulation as time goes on. Then spatial redundancy is formed.

Our research on spatial redundancy sets the status after the born of contemporary architecture or urban space as the starting point. Usually, as practitioners, the concerns of the urban planners and architects lie in the project cycle (from design to construction) and how well the result meets the goal, to assess the necessity and reasonableness of their design. The temporality of the building after construction is intended to be predictable. No matter the architects aim to make the architecture eternal, or aim to make planned and controllable changes, they conceptually achieve purity of architecture. However, the real life cycle, the impact on users and surroundings of architecture and urban space actually starts after

接受与调整之中。纵使建筑师努力提高设计功能的精确性与使用的弹性，后续的生活依旧很难全盘遵循计划。由于时间发展的绝对性，积累和变化是建筑存在的常态。基于这样的视角，设计和建造不再是确定的因果诉求，而是转化为一种过程，起点和终点均成为动态的瞬间，短暂性和不确定性成为必然。

所谓空间冗余，关注的就是这种在历史中逐渐形成的建成环境的整体特征。它既是历时性的——反映了动态生成过程，是在不同力量的博弈中，在较长的周期内完成的物质和符号空间的不间断的改变和聚集；它也是共时性的——反映了这种累积、叠加和变化随时呈现出来的复杂状貌，以及这些状貌背后的共同特征——摆脱了作为新建物的初始意义后的独立状态。正是这种历时性与共时性的同时并存构成了空间的冗余状态。

在考虑时间向度上的变化与积累情况之后，我们今天习以为常的建筑价值判断，即建筑和城市的功能与它们的实体空间之间确定的关联及对应方式，将被一一突破。既有的物质空间和符号意义成为一种中性的存在，在后续的改变和调整中可以等同视之。这是一种新的价值视角与工作研究的出发点。

我们关注上海的城市建筑研究，正是因为，在冗余空间的研究内容里，上海可以作为一个典型的对象。其一，同样是时间向度的积累和变化，也可进一步区分为徐变和突变两种状态。前者在较长时间内循序渐进地完成，具有较好的计划性和延续性，后者因为种种原因缺乏长期的计划，或者实施过程鲜有连贯性。跟社会不同阶段的工业化相对同步的欧美城市的现代化发展很大程度上可以归为徐变。比如纽约的城市规划控制，在曼哈顿这么高密度、拥挤，全盘私有化的城市里，虽然表面变化多端，各自为政，但仅仅是考察它那些有效且系统的私有化公共空间，就会发现这是建立在分区制度上的一个经过长时间积累控制建设的旧有计划。[3] 在中国近代以来的城市发展中，突变的状况比比皆是。比如像上海这样的城市，从开埠以来，经历过租界和国民党政府时期的土地开发私有化，新中国成立以后的土地国有化，改革开放以来高速的房地产开发，新时期新常态中土地新的转型与城市内部的改造，这一切都发生在不足 180 年的时间内，其中最大的城市与建筑的改变分别发生在 20 世纪初和 20 世纪末前后的

the construction. It is reflected in the user's requirements and changes; in their clash and combination, tolerance and adjustment with the architecture. Even if the architects strive to improve the accuracy and flexibility in design, it is hard to follow their plan in the future. Accumulation and change are constant in architecture due to the absoluteness of time. From these perspectives, design and construction are no longer linked by certain causality, but are turned into a process in which both their start and end become dynamic moments, making transience and uncertainty their definite properties.

By studying spatial redundancy, we pay attention to the overall features in the built environment formed gradually with the historical development. It is diachronic, reflecting a dynamic process in which physical and symbolic spaces are constantly changing and combining under the competition of various forces within a relatively long period. It is synchronic as well, reflecting the complicated but commonly-featured appearance as a random result of accumulation, combination, and change. This common feature is an independent state after the buildings get rid of their initial meaning. Historic and synchronicity coexisting, spatial redundancy is thus formed.

After considering change and accumulation along time, the conventional architectural evaluation systems, which believe the accurate associations between the architectural and urban functions and their physical space, will be broken one by one. The current physical space and its symbol will become neutral and can be treated equally in subsequent change and adjustment. This is a new perspective and our starting point for research.

The reason we pay attention to urban architecture in Shanghai is that Shanghai could be taken as a prototype for studying spatial redundancy. Firstly, we need to clarify that accumulation and change along time can be further divided into two states: incremental and abrupt. The former is relatively better planned, extended and thus accomplished gradually in a rather long period; the latter is due to lack of consistency in implementation or lack of long-term planning. Modernization in European-American cities where industrialization took place relatively at the same time as social development could be to a great extent called incremental change. If we take a look at the urban planning in Manhattan, New York, we will see the city is highly condensed and privately-owned, although the city appears varying and incompatible. But if you only examine its systematic and effective privately-owned public space, you will discover this is an ancient plan based on the zoning system and has gone through long-time accumulation, control, and construction.[3] In recent decades of urban development in China, abrupt changes occurred everywhere. Take Shanghai as an example: after its establishment, it went through privatization of land in the period of foreign settlement and Kuomintang government; it went through nationalization of land after P.R.C was

两个 30 年。经济社会发展的不连续性造成了很多突变的城市空间。

其二，因为时空高度压缩，中国城市的空间冗余更为典型，状况也更复杂。一方面是快速增长产生的积累、错位、重复、大量堆积甚至闲置，另一方面是因为不科学、不连续的规划，粗放管理而导致的错误、不适用，快速的调整和改变的需要。与增长同样备受瞩目，但饱受诟病的是中国建筑的快速改变、衰败和消亡。在这样的语境下，将经过历史积累和改变而形成的复杂的建成环境作为我们研究和实践的出发点，就变得更加迫切和具有普遍性了。

空间冗余：建成环境的自然属性

空间冗余并非局部的、偶然的不完美，而是以城市为代表的人类建成环境的普遍状态，既不可避免，也无法消除。客观条件和主观动机的复杂性和矛盾性，两者在时空中的持续作用，都会造成这种绝对的状态。很大程度上，它是无法控制的，也并不存在去除冗余，实现纯净完善的终极目标。在我们看来，城市的变化与冗余状态仿佛生长中的珊瑚礁，不停地产生，不停地固化。城市建筑呈现出

的自然状态就是指将城市的既有空间与物质存在看作是一种即时的自然状态，不同时间、不同来源、不同性质的空间和物质同时并存，具有同等的意义。

无论何种学科，伴随着时间的前行，越来越多以往不受关注，不受重视的内容被发掘出新的意义，从而推动着学科知识和实践策略的拓展。从勒·柯布西耶对飞机、轮船的赞美，文丘里夫妇主张向波普文化学习[4]，到库哈斯从拥挤文化[5]、垃圾空间[6]中发现新的城市生长规律，等等，都是这样的新视角。我们越来越关注的则是这种以冗余为特征的自然、完整的城市与建筑状态。

一直以来，专业领域非常重视建筑从概念到图纸到建成的过程，并将之视为建筑学研究的核心，完美的城市应该是尽可能广泛、持久地实现和保持设计的理想状态。然而，城市中的建筑一旦产生，就进入到一种"被城市化"的状态。所谓的"被城市化"，其实就是使用者利用现状条件或既有资源，对城市环境与建筑物进行再调整的过程。这种调整是局部的，有效性是其最大原则，城市空间与建筑的既有条件与不断累积的现状成为每一次改变的新基础，空间的冗余就在这样的情况下逐渐累积。

founded; it experienced rapid real-estate development since reform and opening-up; it experienced land transformation and urban internal transformation during economic renovation; all these changes happened within 180 years and two greatest urban and architectural changes occurred in the 30 years at the beginning and the end of the 20th century. Inconsistency in economic and social development has led to numerous abrupt changes in urban space. Secondly, since these changes occurred within such short periods and limited space, spatial redundancy in Chinese cities is even more conspicuous and complicated. On the one hand, as a result of the rapid growth, accumulation, misplacement, repetition, pile-up, and even disuse caused redundancy. On the other hand, it has been due to mistakes and misfit resulted from unscientific, discontinuous planning and rough management and the need for fast adaptation and change. As conspicuous as this growth, fast change, decay, and destruction of Chinese architecture are much-criticized. In such a context, it becomes even more urgent and generally applicable for us to base our research and practice on the complex built environment formed through historical accumulation and change.

Spatial Redundancy: a Nature of Built Environment

Spatial redundancy is not a partial or accidental imperfection. It is a common situation in the built environment exemplified by cities. It is absolutely unavoidable and irremovable. This absolute state results from the constant interaction between complicated and contradictory objective conditions and subjective motivations in time and space. To a great extent, it can't be controlled and it's impossible to remove redundancy and obtain purity and perfection. To us, urban change and redundancy are like coral reefs. They are constantly produced and solidified. When we describe urban architecture as natural, we see existing spaces and materials as current natural beings. These spaces and materials from different times and origins and of different nature could co-exist and share equal value.

No matter in which disciplines, as time goes on, content that so far has received little attention and importance has increasingly been explored to find new meanings. In this process, disciplinary knowledge and practical strategies have been enriched. This new perspective can be found in the praise of airplanes and ferries from Le Corbusier; in the claim by the Venturis to learn from pop;[4] in the discovery of new urban growth patterns by Koolhaas after he studied the Culture of Congestion[5] and Junkspace,[6] etc.. We are delivering increasing attention to the natural and complete urban and architectural state featured by redundancy.

The professionals always put great emphasis on the linear design process, from concept to blueprint then construction. They regard this process as the core of the architectural study. A perfect city should reach its expected

具有冗余特征的空间在这样的利用中不会再回复到其产生的初始状态，后续使用者将根据自己的需要选择保留或者修改既有空间。更重要的是，后续的使用者会在利用中逐渐适应并发现既有空间对其使用的匹配性。这样一来，空间的冗余不再是一种消极的多余，而是成为利用的一种效率。这样的活动并非只出现在普通民众的个体行为之中，而是遍及社会生活的各个层面。因为通常没有设计专业的目的和手段介入，这种"被城市化"以使用和调整为主要内容，其结果大部分是无序混杂的，甚至不乏庸俗丑陋。对此，主流建筑学迄今尚未加以研究，即使关注，也常常被当作是"反乌托邦"的，只能用于批评，不值得提倡，至少不可能从中获得系统的启发。然而，对我们来说，这种所谓的"被城市化的建筑"，恰恰是建筑的自然完整状态，其价值不应该被排除与忽视。

随着全球城市化程度的不断提高，"被城市化的建筑"及其构成的城市空间是未来建筑实践的重要领域。将这种城市的自然状态及其演变当作我们研究与工作的基础，意味着将历史的痕迹和当下的需求等同视之，接受绝对状态的冗余，将其作为新的设计的出发点和结果。这种将既有

空间看作是自然状态的视角，也可以被看作是适应于建成环境的变化积累过程的随时定格的一种方法，无论是从设计到建造的过程，还是此后的使用、调整和改变，不过都是这样的瞬间凝固。

改变 vs. 进化

空间冗余，以空间的不断改变为特征。

这种改变更大程度上是一种没有价值偏向的客观属性，既非我们今天已经习以为常的更新换代，也不是设计师念念不忘的进步与革命。

就像歌德在《浮士德》中所描述的，现代社会将发展作为唯一正确的方向，孜孜以求，不惜代价。今天建筑学的理念和方法很大程度上也建立在这样的进步观念的基础上。然而，单向度的进步思想不仅会屏蔽多样的传统沉淀，也容易无视复杂的现实可能，表面上可能壮观刺激，长久下去却只能留下片面、单调的结果。比如，后现代时期提出的"建筑的复杂性和矛盾性"就源于对现代主义建筑过于纯净的进步建筑价值观的反思和批判。而中国当代建筑的大拆大建，其合法性也建立在"发展是硬道理"的

aim in the design and should widely and durably maintain this state. However, once urban buildings are built, they will be urbanized. This will happen when the users utilize current conditions and existing resources to adapt to the urban environment and buildings. Such adjustment is partial and is principled by effectiveness. The existing and accumulating conditions of urban space and architecture offer new foundations for every change, spatial redundancy is then slowly piled up.

Space featured in redundancy under such usage will not return to its initial state when it was first completed, because users will keep or adapt the existing space based on their needs. What's more important, during usage, future residences will gradually adapt themselves and discover how well the space coordinates with their usage. In this way, spatial redundancy is no longer a negative surplus, but contributes to efficiency in use. Such activities appear not only among ordinary individual behaviors but permeate every aspect of social life. Their results are mostly orderless, even vulgar and unattractive because the focus of "being urbanized" is mainly on using and adjusting without professional objectives and means. Mainstream architects so far have not researched this. Sometimes, even if they shift their attention to it, the phenomenon is usually treated as dystopia. It has always been used for criticizing and is not worthy of being popularized, or at least won't be expected to produce systematic inspirations.

But we believe that this so-called "urbanized architecture" is precisely the natural and complete status of architecture. Its value should not be rid or neglected.

With the development of global urbanization, "urbanized architecture" and the urban space it constitutes are important for future architectural practice. To base our research and study on the natural state and changes of these urban areas means to treat equally historical imprints and current needs, to accept the absolute state of redundancy, and to take it as the starting point and the end of new designs. This perspective sees the existing space as natural. It can also be compared as a way to take a snapshot randomly during the process of changing and accumulating in a built environment. Early design, construction process, later usage, adjustment, and change are all these snapshots mentioned.

Change vs. Progress

Spatial redundancy, characterized by ever-changing space.

This change to a greater extent is objective and with no value preference. Neither is this change the replacement we usually do, nor is it an improvement or revolution desired by designers.

Just as how Goethe described in *Faust*, in modern society people diligently strived after development at all cost, which is their only correct mission. The ideologies and

指导思想基础上。

"改变意味着进步"和"改变是为了进步"潜移默化地影响着现代社会的整体价值观念，今天，建筑学的主流思想和方法也十分强调这种意义和价值的评判。虽然在建成环境中，我们可见的改变多种多样：既有轰轰烈烈的大规模城市建设和更新，也有建筑本身的生老病死、自然更替，更普遍的还有无孔不入、乏善可陈的日常改造，甚至是违章搭建。但是，主流建筑学的讨论主要集中在具有进化意义的、完美独立、概念清晰、形式新颖的创造上，即使没有突出的艺术创新，至少也是投入大量人力物力，精心规划和建设的成果。而生活中的这些断断续续、缺乏特征、或好或坏、非进化式的改变，即使被注意到，也会认为是无意义的，不值得讨论的。

研究空间冗余，关注这些日常的改变，挖掘其规律和特征，反思其价值和潜力，尽管一时还难以获得精确的、体系化的认识，但是对我们而言，只有先抛开先入为主的价值评判，才可能从进化的思想束缚中解脱出来，去寻找建筑学的新方向和新方法。

调整 vs. 创新

空间冗余，促使我们去思考调整这种策略。

经过多年的快速城市化积累以后，当下和未来中国建筑实践或是继续创新，刺激新的空间生产与城市化，或是对或新或旧的城市和建筑空间进行利用和调整。当然，后者并不等同于在新增建设用地控制越来越严格的情况下，对城市内部存量空间进行改造和更新，也不止是要对数十年粗放型发展造成的缺失和错误进行整改和补救。如果说创新趋向于一种强制性介入和重型改变的话，调整的立场则基于顺应性介入和弱的控制。

调整是一种司空见惯的空间实践，可能是因为旧有空间与使用需求不匹配，可能是出现了新的需求，可能是基于某种外力，也可能仅仅是自然的兴衰。调整无时无刻不在建成环境中发生着作用，可能出于设计师之手，也可能完全是民间自发。跟全新的系统化创造和生产不同，调整或许并没有显著的改变，因此也不容易产生明显的进步，甚至都难以被注意到。但调整是对旧有和新增资源的价值的发掘和利用，并在此基础上进行灵活有效的组织。

今天的社会更推崇创新。因为在以经济增长为主导的

approaches in today's architecture rely, to a great extent, on such an idea of progress. The legitimacy of those destructions and constructions in China is also based on the ideology "development is the hardcore idea". Nevertheless, people who focus narrowly on progress may not only block out diverse traditions formed through time, they are also more likely to neglect the complex possibilities in reality. Their design may look magnificent and exciting, but as time goes on, it will turn to be unilateral and boring. An example could be seen in the idea of "contradiction and complexity in architecture" during the post-modern time. This idea originated from reflection and criticism on the excessively pure progressive philosophy of modernism architecture.

"Change means making progress"; "to change is to make progress". These mindsets are unconsciously influencing the overall values in society. Today, the mainstream ideas and approaches in architecture also emphasize judgment on these mindsets. Although in built environments, we see different changes: massive urban construction and renovation, the life cycle of buildings, banal everyday adjustments, or even illegal construction. However, the discussions on mainstream architecture focus mainly on creations that are progressively meaningful, perfect, independent, conceptually clear and new. Even if there are no artistic breakthroughs in these creations, they are at least supported with huge resources, carefully planned and managed. But for the changes that are

continual, featureless, neither good nor bad and non-evolving in life, even if they are noticed, they would be considered as meaningless and unworthy of discussion.

Even though within a short period of time, it is hard for us to acquire accurate and systematic knowledge by studying spatial redundancy, monitoring these daily changes, exploring its patterns and features and reflecting on its values and potentials. To us, only when we get rid of preoccupied judgments, can we free our mind from progressiveness-based ideas and set out to look for new directions and approaches in architecture.

Adjustment vs. Innovation

The existence of spatial redundancy urges us to think about the strategy of adjustment in architectural practices.

After rapid accumulation in urbanization through years, current and future architectural practices in China either keep innovating to stimulate fresh spatial production and urbanization, or keep utilizing and adjusting existing urban and architectural space. With an even stricter control over adding construction sites, the latter certainly contains not only changing or renovating urban spatial capacity, but also rectifying and modifying the deficiencies and mistakes resulted from decades of under-planned development. If innovation tends to impose interferences with heavy changes, then adjustment is complementary interferences of lighter control.

Adjustment is common in spatial practices, maybe due to

生产消费体系中，创新是发展的重要动力，像电子产品那样永无止尽地更新换代已经成为主流的生活方式。这种创造倾向于系统式的"重型"行为，动辄提出系统化、令人耳目一新的解决方案。这不仅涉及城市空间的大拆大建，也包括醉心于强烈的视觉冲击和宏大的理论建树，对于实用但不显著的微小改变缺乏兴趣。

当空间冗余成为常态时，调整并非只是被动的规整和清洁的工作，更是一种积极的组织和利用的行为。具体的实践主张采用"轻改变"的策略，对既有空间仅实施轻微操作，充分利用前期资源，与新的使用提出的具体需求紧密结合进行整理，强调实效，包容混杂、临时、普通等特征。

在经历时空高度压缩的城市增长和更替阶段以后，基于中国人口多、资源少，总体经济水平有限的现状，针对空间冗余的调整将成为我们不可避免的工作内容，不抱成见地进行实践，态度和动作虽轻，成果却未必不佳。

应用 vs. 引用

日常城市的改变与调整通常只关注局部或临时的利益

和效率，倾向于灵活有效的策略和手段，往往信手拈来，少有章法。具体如形式、材料和建造，抽象如概念、原理和方法，一概不问出处，不求系统。这种基于实用主义的应用策略是日常城市变化与积累的主要法则，它源于空间冗余的既有现实，也造成了未来的空间冗余。

今天的主流建筑学更重视的是引用的方式，即在可以归类的系统里进行较为确定的选择，有清晰的价值导向和概念，有纯净的风格和形式，有可辨的技术和方法。至少那些可以被归入可识别系统的，具有正统性、目标性、纯粹性的被赋予了合法的也是更高的价值，对于理念混杂、特征模糊的日常应用现象则缺乏足够的兴趣，以及关注和研究的意识。

然而，除了极少部分以外，空间冗余是一种不纯粹的状态，其中既包含计划统筹和专业设计的结果，也有不受约束的日常改变的产物，本身具有很大的复杂性和多变性，如果先入为主地引用确定的模式，很可能或者不适用，或者产生僵硬的结果。更进一步，中国的建筑学科先天具有来源和所受影响多样混杂的特点，其演化、现状和目标也较少自主性和连续性，尚未形成原创性的理论和方

the incoordination between existing space and demands, maybe due to new demands, or because of some outside forces, or maybe just because of the natural life cycle. It forever exerts its influence on the built environment. This influence maybe comes from designers or citizens. Different from systematic creation and production, the adjustment may not result in a conspicuous outcome, the improvement would not be easily produced or even noticed. But the purpose of the adjustment is to explore and make use of existing and newly-added resources and to conduct flexible and effective organization.

People are anxiously seeking innovation in today's society because innovation is the driving force for the development of production and consumption system dominated by economic growth. Endless upgrading and renewing of electronic and electrical products have become a mainstream lifestyle. This kind of innovation is more of heavy-handed change, raising systematic and totally new solutions. It involves both sweeping construction and deconstruction in urban space as well as the creation of strong visual impact and grand theory. But it takes little interest in practical but trivial changes.

When spatial redundancy becomes normal, adjustment is not only passive regulation and clearing. It is a positive organization and utilization. In practice, it is suggested to make "light changes", which means people only bring slight changes to existing space and make full use of previous resources;

closely adapt the space to new requirements; focus on being effective, tolerant, temporary and ordinary.

Since urban booming and alternation have happened in highly condensed time and space in China, based on the fact that there is a huge population, limited resources, and restricted economic situation in our country, we see adjustments targeting spatial redundancy as our necessary job. The accomplishment might not be bad if we could unbiasedly practice with moderate attitude and action.

Application vs. Quotation

Usually, people who make daily changes and adaptations in cities are only concerned with partial or temporary interest and efficiency. They tend to adopt flexible and effective strategies without fixed rules. Such strategies with no origins or systems can be found in concrete fields such as form, material, and construction, or in abstract fields such as concept, theory, and approach. Neither origin or system is asked. Applications based on pragmatism is the major principle of everyday urban change and accumulation. They are derived from reality while creating potentials for future spatial redundancy.

Nowadays mainstream architectural studies put much more emphasis on quotations. People prefer to choose in a categorizable system with clear guiding values and concepts; pure styles and forms; discernible technologies and approaches. At least those included in recognizable systems

法，将之纳入一个系统的框架是不现实的，也是不必要的。针对这种情况，没有预设地将各种理念、技术和手段视为等价之物进行选择，不深究其背后特定的意义，不追溯其来源的正统与乡野，灵活、糅杂地加以应用，是我们认为现实和可能的实践方式。相对于已经确立的建筑学系统，这种策略以及由此获得的结果可以不甚严密地被称为"非识别体系"。[7] 如果冗余是我们所研究的城市与建筑空间的特征总结的话，非识别体系就是针对空间冗余所采取的设计方法以及相应的结果的描述。

本文作者系庄慎、华霞虹，最初发表于《时代建筑》2015 (5): 108–111。

are legitimate, goal-oriented, pure and highly-valued. But they are not applicable in featureless daily phenomena of hybrid ideologies, which mainstream field are less motivated to research.

However, in most cases, spatial redundancy is impure. It is highly complicated and variable because it is a result of both previous planning, professional design, and out-of-control daily adjustment. If we are preoccupied with certain theories, it is very likely the theories won't apply or lead to misfit. Furthermore, it is unrealistic and unnecessary to fit architecture in our country into a systematic frame because this discipline is inherently diverse in origins and influence; its development, current situation, and future goal are relatively lack in motivation and continuity; there have not been original theories and methods formed. In this context, we think it is practical if we treat all theories, techniques, and approaches equally without paying too much attention to the legitimacy of their origins, and using them flexibly and holistically. Compared with established architectural systems, this strategy and its results can be loosely termed as "unrecognizable system"[7]. If redundancy is the summarized characteristics of urban and architectural space we study, the unrecognizable system is to describe the design of spatial redundancy and its result.

The paper coauthored by Zhuang Shen, Hua Xiahong was firstly published in *Time+Architecture*, 2015 (5): 108–111.

6

城市内的工作室
Work Within the City

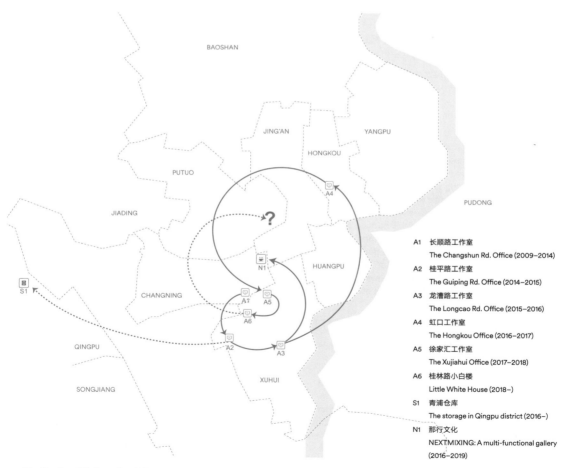

A1 长顺路工作室
    The Changshun Rd. Office (2009–2014)

A2 桂平路工作室
    The Guiping Rd. Office (2014–2015)

A3 龙漕路工作室
    The Longcao Rd. Office (2015–2016)

A4 虹口工作室
    The Hongkou Office (2016–2017)

A5 徐家汇工作室
    The Xujiahui Office (2017–2018)

A6 桂林路小白楼
    Little White House (2018–)

S1 青浦仓库
    The storage in Qingpu district (2016–)

N1 那行文化
    NEXTMIXING: A multi-functional gallery
    (2016–2019)

a   "New Year, New Office" map, Shanghai
    "一年一个工作室" 搬家地图

工作 / 工作室

作为在上海的建筑师事务所，这座城市不仅是工作与日常生活的场所，也是我们一直感兴趣的研究课题所在。伴随着阿科米星的工作视野越来越关注城市内部的空间问题，工作室也成了我们用来直接观察城市建筑内在空间并在其中实践的好地方。我们的工作室一直很简单，但在过去六年间（2009—2015），事务所的工作室经历了几次选择、停留和搬迁，由此，我们也留意观察了日常的使用与房屋之间一些有意思的关系。

沉浸在社区 / 安定的工作室

阿科米星的第一个工作室[1]开始于2009年盛夏，我们租下了老式居民区内一间闲置的小型托儿所的一层空间并加以改造。这个原来作为小区配套的托儿所，现在二楼是经营化妆品的公司及其仓库，三楼则是一处群租宿舍。房屋所处的居民区很有上海本地特点，是1980年代上海中心城区外迁扩散的产物。本是标准化的多层住宅，经过20多年，住宅楼随处可见居民自行搭建和改造后生机勃勃的成果。

工作室原本的内部格局基本未动，保持原来托儿所的大小房间，只是新开了一些门窗彼此加强联通。我们工作的使用反过来去适应既有布局：一间大活动室做大办公室，另一间做模型工作室，两者之间的大盥洗室改造成合伙人办公室；原来的厨房和主走廊转变为一大一小两个多功能厅，用来陈列、聚会、展览、放置运动器材等；厨房旁边有一小房间，原本可能是教师餐厅，现在是一个图书室兼会议室。就这样，430平方米的室内面积被自然划分成两个区域：固定的办公区和灵活的多功能活动区。由于是凑原来空间的用法，我们集中工作占用的面积很少，剩下的区域反而闲置出来，无论是平时行走休息，还是举行沙龙聚会，都感觉空间很大，活动很自由。[图1]

尽管有此优势，工作室的室内看着很普通，并没有特别惹眼的空间或形式。然而，在我们看来，这个工作室是宜人的，有特色的，是经年成长的，四时变化的景象替代了视觉化的固定形式。与内部空间的适应性改造相比，我们对近1000平方米的院落的整理更主动些：除了靠围墙栽种各种树木爬藤外，我们还在新的门厅南侧，利用施工垃圾堆出了一个木平台，中植香樟，与原来活动室外抬高的凉廊连成一体，后来又在凉廊外搭起了葡萄架。在此，

134

For Shanghai-based Atelier Archmixing, design practice is informed by a turn to the everyday. Since its establishment in 2009, the studio has been concentrating on familiar, typical programmes in Shanghai and its neighbouring cities, towns, and villages in the Yangtze River Delta. The majority of the projects have been small educational, commercial and community-service facilities with humble budgets, and the briefs have included partial interior or facade renovations for modest structures of a type not usually considered historically significant. Attention to everyday urbanism has proven a necessary and effective way of grasping the ever-changing essence of the region's built environment, and of developing homegrown design strategies in response.

New Year, New Office

In recent decades, Chinese cities such as Shanghai have undergone all manner of architectural change, from top-down development and renovation to informal, bottom-up construction and temporary installation. Since 2012, Atelier Archmixing has undertaken a series of urban studies in Shanghai, both independently and collaboratively, and these have contributed to the studio's belief that everyday transformations—large or small, glorious or banal—are not inconsequential to new practices, but rather a source of inspiration. In 2014, due to fail to find another suitable long-term space, the practice initiated a "new year, new office" plan, moving its workplace to a different quarter of the city each year, meanwhile observing, experiencing and analysing everyday urbanism at neighbourhood scale. To facilitate this programme, the studio was divided into three parts, based on function and frequency of use. Storage is now hidden inexpensively in the suburbs; the seasonal exhibition and lecture venue is in the downtown area, where it realizes economic independence as a flexible commercial space; and the main office is nomadic [fig. a]. Atelier Archmixing has so far transformed the functional and formal traces of five diverse spaces into suitable design studios [fig. b]. This constant seeking out, adapting, adjusting and reusing of different spaces has encouraged the architects to focus more on the interior space of both buildings and cities.[1] "New year, new office" has been not only an experiment in one practice's positioning itself within the city, but also a laboratory for cost-effective contextual design, light working and living style.

Detective Restoration

Atelier Archmixing's urban research focuses on utility and the requirements of living and how these are expressed in the built environment. They have found that changes in the everyday world encompass both adaptation to existing conditions and the application of realizable forms and readily available crafts and materials. Huangma Club Courtyard, a residential complex or settlement [fig. c], showcases what an

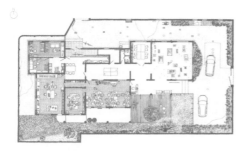

1 长顺路工作室　手绘平面
Sketch for the Changshun Rd. Office(2009-2014)

2 长顺路工作室　入口
Entrance for the Changshun Rd. Office

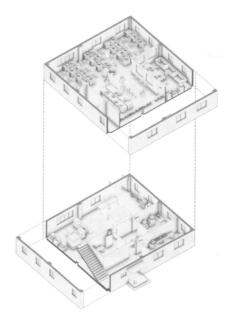

3 桂平路工作室
The Guiping Rd. Office (2014-2015)

b The Xujiahui Office (2017-2018)
徐家汇工作室

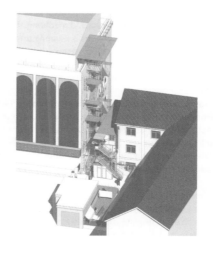

c Urban Study "Huangma Club", Tongxin Road, Shanghai,
China, 2016-2017
城市研究：同心路皇玛会所建筑夹缝加建

我们自得其乐于小院内的四季更替：春天，爬山虎悄悄铺满整个墙面与窗户，影子水墨画般地印在白色的窗帘上，蔷薇、杜鹃盛开，樟树换叶；夏秋，凌霄、桂花渐次开放，葡萄藤蔓茂密，果实累累。与此相伴的，还有一季一回的讲座沙龙。这个普通小区的庭院在很多员工和访客心里都是一个美好的场所。[图2]

在这个混杂的居住小区，我们安定地工作了5年，每天跟光顾小区门口那悄悄扩大小地盘的地摊菜市的居民同进出，天晴时可以看到住宅楼伸出老远的晾衣杆上壮观的晒衣景象。比起正规漂亮、充满设计感的写字楼来，我们更习惯这个轻松而有点随意的办公室。相安无事中，我们也成了这个社区进进出出的一分子，日常社区生活的旁观者。在这里，某种程度上，我们对于城市建筑的认知从抽象状态变得更加具体了，工作室最初确立的概念化的混合设计理念慢慢发展为对日常城市的改变、调整、有效建造等的观察和认知，我们的设计实践同时寻找着结合与检验这些认知的方式。²

安身于这些周而复始的变化当中，不知不觉让人忘了时间，设计也更不会去在意那些固定的视觉形式与空间冲击了。不过，这样的稳定状态与即将来临的变化比起来，反差巨大，令人心中充满了不安。因为业主要回收利用这一公共资产，我们的第一个工作室未获续约。因此机缘，对于自己想要的实践方式的直觉开始作用，促使我们去尝试变化，让我们不要安定下来。

未打开的包装箱／等不到的新工作室

我们需要的基本东西其实很少，但安定地积累可能会使人感到安全。这是我们在第二个工作场所，一处临时过渡空间产生的体会。

留恋于最初五年的安定，我们决定在刚接手的一个国营厂区改造项目中建造一个后续永久的办公室。在新楼建成之前，就把基地内一座数月后将拆除的闲置小厂房当作我们的临时工作地。与之前嘈杂的居民小区迥异，这个厂区基本已人走楼空，只有一栋内还有少许国企留守人员，显得空旷寂静。对于这处独栋两层的小楼，我们基本未作改造装饰，而是直接根据既有状况加以利用。合伙人的工作室安排在大空间旁一个带观察窗的房间里，搬进去后，感觉自己是车间主任，工作在热火朝天的车间氛围里。主

informal construction can achieve both spatially and technologically in a leftover urban corner. The 260-meter-long facade of Hengfengli [fig. d] had acquired in the course of its living evolution countless structural and mechanical additions. To determine the divergences between current conditions and the original construction, Atelier Archmixing developed an approach called "Detective Restoration", which applies separate diagrams to the various supplements or alterations to the former structure. When classifying these items, according to either orthodox architectural categories or new, ad-hoc groupings, all elements, architectural and non-architectural (conventionally conceived), are accorded equal weight. Each contributes independently to an authentic living purpose, without the aggregate necessarily coalescing into a unified logic. Effectiveness is the only criterion.

Spatial Redundancy

In Chinese everyday urbanism, a part or fragment typically relies on a whole system to realise a practical goal. A balcony turns into a kitchen; a staircase supports a room; a roof is home to a magnificent pigeon coop. For instance, in the research project of the "One Half House" in Shanghai, hidden in an ordinary residential area, the long linear structure is half dead, with bricks blocking the windows and doors guarding against illegal occupation after the previous residents had moved out. Due to structural, economic and social reasons, the other half, with all its surface additions, including air conditioners, laundries, and plants, is still functioning and busy with residents... Here, the unused part can be seen as an extreme example of "spatial redundancy"[II], such that the modification, accumulation, repetition, superabundance, residue, and dislocation of material spaces and cultural symbols are not assessed negatively, as "remnant" or "superfluous". Impure, inefficient and imperfect sites are not necessarily harmful; rather, they are inevitable. As in the field of information technology, where unused spaces and redundancy are harnessed for error correction and to avoid critical failure, spatial redundancy uncovers the complexity and contradiction of the urban built environment, especially in developing regions such as China, and reserves otherwise unvalued aspects of the everyday for the future city

Seen through a historical lens, "spatial redundancy" reflects the evolution of living spaces. It encourages architects to reconsider what "interior"—of both buildings and the city—means for future architecture. Interior has long been underestimated in the architectural field, as secondary and not as essential as the exterior. Nevertheless, in a well-developed and constantly changing world, as a space directly interacts with real life, its interior becomes the primary space within which architects can operate. Layer upon layer, the accumulation of the inner surfaces of diverse components results in a new architecture. In the urban context, Inner lanes

要办公区少了固定的空间分隔，设计人员参与项目交流反而更随意了。[图3]

　　考虑到几个月后就要再搬家，我们一开始就把以往工作生活的大部分物品打包入箱，存于楼下储物空间，只选了极少量的图书和文件资料放在外面。不料设计好的那个办公室迟迟未能开工，原计划暂住三四个月的地方，一拖就用了11个月。这期间，因为随时准备要搬走，我们就一直在最精简的模式下工作。有意思的是，在这将近一年的时间里，我们发现，楼下的包装箱从未打开，却丝毫不影响我们手头的工作。换言之，包装箱里大部分是以往工作积累下来，不舍得扔掉的东西，平时工作基本不用。还有一些看似必需，其实也是可有可无。抛开陈年积累，实现轻质办公，并非妄想。

　　期待已久的新办公室终于要开工了，但我们的临时小楼也被要求提前拆除，我们不得不另觅他处过渡等待。由此造成的阴差阳错，让我们发现了工作室的新可能。

意想不到的城市空间／寻找新工作室

　　寻找新的过渡工作室的过程是有启发性的。除了因为不想租而没有考察的标准写字楼外，我们考察了形形色色可能用作办公的空间场所：有厂房、多层产业园区、别墅、沿街店铺，甚至还有体育场内能够看到赛场的包厢与看台下没有直接采光的剩余空间。结果发现：在上海这样的大都市中，存在着各式各样的使用空间。并且，这些场所的供给是有时间性的，它们不停地被租用占有，又不停地被腾空出来。对于像我们这样的寻求者来说，可供选择与利用的空间仿佛处在不断的产生，又不断的消失中。这样的状况让我们感到很刺激，不禁要重新思考办公室的周期长短及其意义。

一个十年还是十个一年／我们未来的工作室

　　当我们在等待一个十年的安定办公室时，几个月的临时环境让我们反思了这种想法，并开始观察我们办公究竟需要些什么。当我们在寻找一个一年的过渡工作室时，几星期的搜索让我们发现城市在不断转手或空置出来各种有意思的地方。选择一个十年的办公空间还是十个一年的办公空间？选择一处安定还是十处逗留？选择省力还是麻烦？怀着对变化带来的丰富可能的期许，阿科米星的几个

137

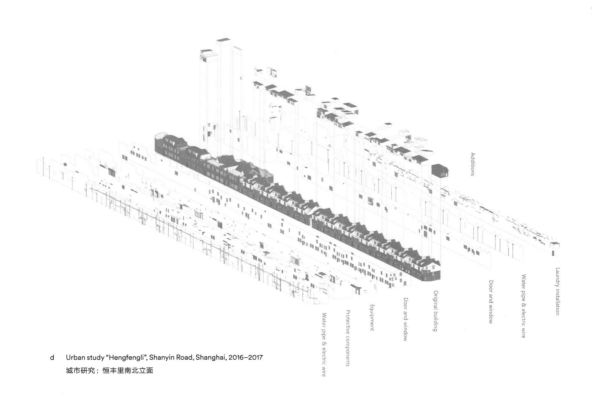

d　Urban study "Hengfengli", Shanyin Road, Shanghai, 2016–2017
城市研究：恒丰里南北立面

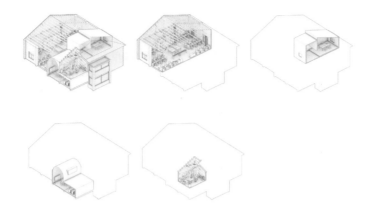

4 龙漕路工作室
The Longcao Rd. Office (2015–2016)

5 龙漕路工作室，会议室
Meeting room, the Longcao Rd. Office

6 龙漕路工作室，大空间工作区
Main workspace, the Longcao Rd. Office

合伙人一致选择了后者。

为了实施这一计划，我们要做的事有：租一处永久便宜的仓库，归类储藏我们的模型、不用的图纸、档案、书籍等；在搬到下一处工作场所之前完成办公的轻质化组织，包括设计好便于拆搬但牢靠的家具，将电脑换成一体机，改有线网络为无线，培养好团队简化的工作习惯。

阿科米星的第三个工作室，是在此想法指导下实现的第一个工作室：三周找到场地，两周"格式化"，租期一年，现状是一个由厂房改造的摄影棚。选择这个地方是因为原来的空间大体匹配我们的需要，不用做大幅度的改造，但又留有足够的余地可供适当调整。仅用12天微调空间和布线后，我们就入驻了。

这是一个残留着过往使用痕迹的城市内部空间：有着近6米层高的厂房大空间被从事婚纱摄影的上家分隔得高高低低，上上下下的，室内很多窗口有趣地贯通着，坐在办公室里，时不时就能看见、听见紧挨的城市轻轨呼啸而过。与那些中规中矩的精致办公环境相比，这样的状态虽然喧嚣，却不无聊。

调整设计基本保留了原来的空间格局，只在局部设计了新的功能区，比如会议空间，大工作区中央的多功能场地，合伙人工作的亭子间等。这些局部的改变不求风格统一，有点各自为政，以期形成不同体验的空间效果 [图4-图8]。新的布局再次影响了我们的工作方式：老板们变得高高在上，可以透过楼上控制窗瞭望楼下的大工作间和会议区，而直接交流则需要经过数次上上下下的空间转换。对于新办公空间的使用调整还在陆续进行，比如需要在冬天来临前用薄膜把大办公区分隔成更小的节能空间等。这些快速更新的内部空间虽然比较粗糙，但也很自由，可以在一年周期内不断更替改变，来实验我们的设计方法。我们很快又租下一处闲置的郊区农舍作为存储模型和其他材料的仓库，并着手设计新的家具。

与此同时，下一个工作场所也开始计划。

我们当时计划尝试十年的"搬家"计划，它对我们自己也是一种考验。因为这并非只是一种实验式的行动计划，某种程度上，这也是一种心理实验：面对持续变化的办公空间，面对不断更换的城市环境，城市人究竟有多大的承受能力？我们会最终安于这样的改变吗？

139

7　虹口工作室可见轻轨三号线
Visible Metro Line 3 at the Hongkou Office (2017-2017)

8　虹口工作室，连接合伙人工作室和公共办公区的"桥"
"Bridge" addition between the principals' office and the main workplace, Hongkou Office

9　虹口工作室，自由布置的办公区
Flexible arrangement workspace, the Hongkou Office

10　"虹口1617"展览
Hongkou 1617 exhibition

e　Aerial view, Renovation of Baoshan
　Beibeijia Olion Kindergarten
　宝山贝贝佳欧莱幼儿园，鸟瞰

f　Interior scene, Renovation of Baoshan Beibeijia Olion Kindergarten
　宝山贝贝佳欧莱幼儿园，室内场景

瞭望虹口的阁楼

阿科米星第四个工作室位于虹口区西江湾路，周围紧邻着虹口体育场，虹口公园，龙之梦商业综合体，多伦路、甜爱路等历史文化街区，大大小小各种商业餐饮丰富的日常街道与社区，这是生活环境最舒适的一个工作室。工作室的主体是一处阁楼，可以眺望周围环境。与前一个工作室相似，地铁三号线还在不远的视野内，每天充满了活力。工作室的另一部分与主体空间原来并不连通，我们开辟了一条小小的架空甬道把两个空间联系起来。这个工作室采用了随意散布、随时改变与组合的桌面布置，这个布置深受大家欢迎，感觉交流更方便，环境更轻松。在这个工作室工作的一年里，我们完成了历次城市调研中规模最大的一次，研究了周边各种类型的城市建筑的局部与片段的改变。在要离开时，我们和另外两个团队一起在再次搬空的空间里举办了一个展览——"虹口 1617"。

粉红色墙面的幼儿园

在研究了建筑局部的改变后，我们计划继续研究建筑内部的改变，于是新的工作室选址在徐家汇商圈，以便勘查这里庞大的城市地下空间和地面商业空间的内部。工作室租了一个待拆迁的幼儿园二层，紧挨着港汇广场，在徐家汇地铁站 18 号口的正上方。幼儿园室内是一连串有着粉红色墙面的教室，我们拆除了护墙板，任由斑驳的墙面暴露出来，在三个相邻教室的隔墙上打开一些洞口，使彼此能跨越连通，长长的连续日光灯斜着直直地穿过相邻的房间，一直延伸到走道上。设计师把这里的房间戏称为"包间"，但大部分人还是思念虹口聚在一起的散乱的桌面，认为那样更好些。在徐家汇的内部课题的城市研究比之前的局部城市研究困难得多，可以说是举步维艰，然而在项目的设计方面，在这期间反而做了很多跟内部有关的设计与建造，获得了很多宝贵的经验。

小白楼

小白楼是一栋厂房，整个工作室是一个无柱的大空间，这是一个新的开始。由于开始试验个人的移动办公，团队的远程云上办公，所以我们尝试把这里做得更像一个工作室的总部。总的想法是能创造更多的可以讨论或者独处的角落。因此，合伙人办公室、财务、储藏、司机休息

are commonly encountered that have been gradually built up from various architectural or structural fragments and domestic items: Gates and doors, steps, platforms, drying racks, bicycle shelters, canopies, outdoor furniture, and even mop buckets can constitute the urban interior, such that no boundary divides public life from private.

According to the systematic thinking embedded in classical and modern architecture, change is meaningful, and, if positive, progressive. By contrast, Atelier Archmixing maintains that all buildings are in a temporary state of present usage. The urban context is constituted of successive "independent" moments, and the extant spaces from other times, with their divergent origins and features, are akin to the varied life forms simultaneously coexisting on earth.

The Unrecognisable System

To challenge the established "Recognisable System" in mainstream academic thinking, which values architectural phenomena and design canons with legible features and obvious sources, Atelier Archmixing has coined a new term, "Unrecognisable System"[III] to signify architectural instances with opaque origins and hybrid qualities. The "Unrecognisable System" is a theoretical understanding/reading of the existing built environment, as well as a foundation for future design practice. It advocates taking the urban context as a neutral background, applying all kinds of concepts, forms and techniques without prejudice to meet new utilitarian requirements, using and mixing these flexibly, and liberating them from their origins and inherited meanings.

"The Unrecognisable System" describes both an attitude to design and a methodology. On the one hand, it views the current situation, whether natural or artificial, as neutral; on the other, it means never to privilege a new intervention or a contemporary idea over a common tradition. For instance, Olion Kindergarten [fig. e–f] was a commission to renovate a former community centre, used only for five years, into a day nursery in an emerging suburban area. The designer took the banal three-storey building as a neutral platform instead of a final spatial and structural order. The maximum number of classrooms with standard facility units was inserted in the conventional column-and-beam system. How, then, were its distinctive characteristics achieved? Double spaces and scales were introduced; the 2.25-metre-height suspended ceilings were shaped to form the dominant scale, creating a little world. Scattered boxes, vertical or inclined, solid or transparent, colourful or white, cut through the lower level to touch the structural ceiling 3.5 metres to 4.5 metres high. The resulting houses-in-a-house, like spatial nesting dolls, helped to achieve diversity within standard rooms. All equipment was exposed equally, as building elements. Old and new structures and scales integrate, not only inside but also outside. Colourful squares painted alternately on the exterior surfaces

室等被布置为既符合自己最小使用，又能创造相互交流的角落的形状。我们还布置了一个十分大的咖啡吧台，能够在这里聚会与互动。同时，这次，我们又再次把桌面布置回了自由散乱的模式。

城市的内在空间 / 研究与实践

在上海不断寻找、适应、调整、使用工作室的经历让我们更加关注建筑的内部空间和城市的内在空间，并开始把它纳入到我们对于建筑学的反思之中，看是否能带来新的认识和方法。我们从中得到的启发包括：区分内在与外在空间的因素重要的并非是建筑意义上的室内与室外的物质界限，而是对于这两者的价值认同、专业认识、法规认可的不同。换言之，内外的区分主要来自不同的视角。

在中微观层面，虽然设计师普遍期望建筑内外统一，但是在我们熟知的实践领域，尤其是在中国，建筑设计与室内设计如同两个世界，有着各自不同的领地。建筑师主要负责空间布局和外观，室内设计主要负责内部细分和装饰，并通常不受建筑设计规范的管理，大部分也不纳入建筑的评价体系。此外，相对于建筑改造，室内的变化要自由得多，也更司空见惯，但人们并不重视，也从未把这种被统称为装修的空间、材料、装饰等的更替与建筑学关心的价值联系起来。

在宏观层面，中国近 30 年快速城市化发展，产生的最多的是城市的内在空间、建筑的内部空间。随着经济增速的放缓，单纯扩张式的城市发展模式将受限制，尤其是在像上海这样城市化水平已经很高的大都市，在新增建设用地控制越来越严格的情况下，城市内部存量空间的改造更新成为最近的热门话题。虽然这种转变的意义在于，有利于积极转化原来大量产生而积累下来的闲置和消极的城市资产，但也可以看到，维持空间大量生产的热情和乐观思想却并未改变。后者的具体表现如：大量的旧地块改性，拆除新建增容；产业化、运动式的文创艺术等类型化空间的批量生产，等等。空间再次的大规模生产是否能带领我们发现更深入的、新的建筑学研究呢？我们表示怀疑，认为这都将掩盖城市内在空间改变利用的普遍意义，也很难触及并发现新的价值。

通过对日常城市的持续观察、研究和实践，我们体会到，城市的内在空间与建筑的内部空间由于被利用而呈现

were deliberately organized to obscure the former storey divisions. Using colour patterns to distinguish the renovated building from its surroundings was economical and effective; no change to the old architectural organization, even of the windows, was needed.

Five urban facade renovations Atelier Archmixing completed from 2012 to 2017 well illustrate the firm's belief that the fragment matters to both everyday urbanism and new design[IV]. One noteworthy example is the renovation for Longhua Elder Care Center [fig. g – fig. h], located in a dense residential area in downtown Shanghai. In this instance, a new building with only the foundation completed would be redesigned. In the previous construction drawings, the plan was poorly arranged, with all rooms leading off the corridor and no public spaces, just like in a hospital. The corridor was dark. The one balcony was isolated, and what was worse, it was largely occupied by the air-conditioner. Initially, the only parts subject to the designer's intervention were the exterior walls, balconies, and roofs. To explore these parts' potential to humanize senior residents' daily life, the architect persuaded the client to refocus the program, from surface beautification to spatial reorganization. Continuous balconies of varying sizes were built out from the exterior walls. All rooms were provided two public accesses. Some parts of the corridor were widened, and roof windows were added to improve illumination and ventilation. Glazed meeting rooms

were installed on the empty roofs, where residents could watch television, play cards, chat or just sunbathe. These new communal spaces incorporate light and inexpensive structures and materials, in ways that reflect the informal additions and modifications widespread in the everyday surroundings. Whether from the perspective of the program or the design strategy, such interventions are "soft" and not easily categorized, but they are effective and efficient in solving functional problems. Moreover, such subtle changes are exactly where a true architectural identity resides.

"The Unrecognisable System" tends to break the boundaries between inside and outside, private and public. The "LILI" house [fig. j–k] showcases Atelier Archmixing's insight into the architectural meaning of the interior, not only of the building but also of the city. This was a renovation and extension of an aged, plain workshop building in an ancient town near Shanghai. All around the structure, with its two adjoining gable roofs, are sloped-roof dwellings. The designer chose to access this single-storey house from a narrow lane beside the gable wall, rather than from the front yard. A walk along the town's canal, down its main street, through the dark entry lane and finally into the building offers an impressive experience of progressive interiorization within a traditional town environment. Since the sloping roof is another interface with the surroundings, a small bridge was built to connect skylight and slope. When walking out onto it, one is totally

11   2017—2018年，徐家汇工作室
The Xujiahui Office (2017–2018)

12   2018年至今，小白楼工作室
Little White House (2018–)

13   小白楼工作室，吧台区
View towards the office from the coffee bar, Little White House

g   South elevation, Longhua Street Elder Care Center
徐汇区龙华街道敬老院，南立面

h   North Elevation with surroundings, Longhua Street Elder Care Center
徐汇区龙华街道敬老院，社区环境里看到的北立面

14　小白楼，入口区域
Entrance, Little White House

j　Axonometric drawing, LILI
黎里，轴测分析图

k　Roof night view, LILI
黎里，夜晚屋顶景观

出了新的启示，这些不同方式的利用和不断更迭，足以使空间从旧有的教义与认知中解放出来。因为受到现代主义建筑思维的影响，空间结构应具有明确的对应性，空间与使用功能需要形成关联性，这些专业认识一直挥之不去。虽然如今，以"形式追随功能"为代表的固化使用与对应空间的观念已经慢慢让位于使用与空间模式，或价值与空间逻辑的对应，但空间存在的意义与具体特定的意图相关联，这样的想法依旧支配着专业领域的思考，也将建筑学领域的主要认知与建筑、城市存在的中性状态分离开来。我们总是在思想上顽固地试图控制城市和建筑空间，将空间的增长、进化与创新视为设计的本质，却无视建成环境的自然属性。

我们认为，换个角度看，空间的本质是中性的，它具有独立于主观意志的存在。无论既有空间带有怎样的特征，都可以被重新适应和改变。无论新创造的空间带有何种特征，都可能经历无法预测的调整与变化。城市内在空间和建筑内部空间的这种持续更替，蕴含着我们未知的建筑学价值，有待我们去发现、研究和转化。

阿科米星正在实施的"城市内的工作室"计划就是希望从自己的体验开始进行这方面的研究：我们为自己的使用寻找、改变城市的内在空间，建筑的内部空间，自己工作在其中，体验认识与工作是否有效。

本文作者系庄慎、华霞虹，最初发表于《时代建筑》2015 (5): 100–107，在此扩充了 2015—2018 年的三个工作室案例。对应的英文论文并非此文的翻译，而是由华霞虹、庄慎发表于 A&HC! 收录的英国杂志《建筑设计》(Architectural Design, 2018(6): 52–57) 上的英文论文《日常、改变与非识别系统》"Everyday, Change and Unrecognisable System"。

embraced by hills of grey tiles. Under the roof, patchy sunlight penetrates through 40 traditional-style skylights that connect the otherwise gloomy inside with the blue sky. At one corner of the hall stands a diagonal glass-box entrance. When reaching the end of the dim back alley, a passer-by will encounter this bright portal and witness the private scene.

The Architecture of Change

Following years of urban studies and design practice, Atelier Archmixing advocates an Architecture of Change, fostered by the belief that the meaning of building is to provide a temporary vessel for ever-changing life. As a dynamic process, the building incorporates a continuously evolving set of objectives, strategies, and actions; it is not its own end, as a design product or artistic creation.

Architectural change is not synonymous with progress or innovation. Design practice entails applying effective strategies and technologies to meet present demands, rather than chasing revolutionary concepts, pure forms, novel materials or elaborate constructions.

To a large extent, all architectural changes are equivalent. The system has no priority over the fragment; unity has no priority over parts; the exterior has no priority over the interior. For everyday urbanism, typical features are never monumental landmarks of permanence, but fragments of highly-compressed space and time. In a region with a large population and rapid urbanization such as China, a signature architectural performance is seldom around for long, whereas utilitarian efficiency is ever more urgent and pragmatic [v].

The Chinese paper was coauthored by Zhuang Shen and Hua Xiahong in the title "Work within City" and firstly published in Time + Architecture, 2015 (5): 100–107. Three new studios from 2015 to 2018 were added in this book. The English paper was coauthored by Hua Xiahong and Zhuang Shen in the title "Everyday, Change and the Unrecognisable System"and firstly published in Architectural Design, 2018 (6): 52–57. Wiley Press

7

走向城市建筑学的可能：
"虹口 1617 展览暨城市研究"
研讨会评述
Possibilities Towards
an Urban Architecture:
Notes on the Symposium of
"Hongkou 1617 Exhibition and
Urban Studies"

1　"三号线上"视频截图
　　Video screenshot of "Line 3"

2017年5月下旬,阿科米星建筑设计事务所、冶是建筑工作室和同济大学建筑系城市日常效率研究小组(CEED)联合在那行零度空间举办了"虹口1617"展览,内容是三个团队在2016—2017年间对上海虹口区三号线沿线和虹口足球场附近地区所作的城市空间调研成果。期间,来自北京、南京、杭州、上海四地多所大学和建筑事务所的十一位嘉宾受邀就城市研究相关话题展开研讨。

会议当天,三个团队的负责人——同济大学副教授华霞虹,冶是建筑合伙人李丹锋与周渐佳,阿科米星主持建筑师庄慎分别介绍了"Line3"[1]、"弗兰肯斯坦"[2]、"逆向还原"[3]的研究思路,及其与各自团队持续的学术兴趣和设计研究之间的关联。北京绘造社社长、《一点儿北京》作者李涵,东南大学建筑学院副教授李华,南京大学建筑与城市规划学院鲁安东教授与窦平平副教授,建筑和艺术评论人和策展人王家浩,同济大学建筑与城市规划学院的王骏阳、童明、王方戟三位教授,以及与阿科米星从2013年开始合作"上海计划"(SHP)城市再研究项目[4]的无样建筑工作室主持建筑师冯路、致正建筑工作室主持建筑师张斌和上海交通大学建筑系副教授范文兵十一位学

者,对于"虹口1617"的研究成果和存在的疑问,建筑师开展城市研究的目的、方法和意义,以及中国当代城市与建筑的现实矛盾和总体趋向展开了热烈的讨论。

建筑师开展城市研究的目的:社会批评,空间认知,还是设计实践?

城市是复杂的物质空间和社会文化载体。无论针对中国还是世界范围,城市研究的角度和成果都异常丰富。要对"虹口1617"这个由一线实践建筑师牵头的具体研究展开兼具针对性和普遍性的评价和反思,首当其冲需要对此类研究的目标和方法加以定性。探讨建筑师开展城市研究的目的,不仅是从对现实城市的认知中梳理总结新的建筑设计理论和方法的可能性,更是在快速城市化之后的中国当代城市语境中,界定建筑学存在的价值和学科的边界。

有学者主张,"城市研究应该让建筑师打破设计这种单一的介入社会的实现方式,戳破设计还有希望的幻象,只有这样才有利于对空间政治等深层机制的研究,以及对建筑环境的重构。"[5]其他学者则基本认同,在社会系统中,建筑学是宏观的政治经济关系的一部分,但相对比较

148

In late May 2017, Atelier Archmixing, YeArch Studio (YEAS), and the City Everyday Efficiency Detectors (CEED) of the Department of Architecture, Tongji University jointly organized the exhibition "Hongkou 1617" in the Nextmixing Zero-degree Space, which included urban space studies carried out by these three teams in Shanghai Hongkou district along metro line 3 and near Hongkou Football Stadium from 2016 to 2017. During this period, eleven guests from several universities and architectural firms in Beijing, Nanjing, Hangzhou, and Shanghai were invited to discuss topics related to urban research.

At the meeting, the leaders of three teams, Hua Xiahong, associate professor of Tongji University Li Danfeng and Zhou Jianjia, partners of YeArch Studio, and Principal architect Zhuang Shen, from Atelier Archmixing, separately introduced the research ideas of "Line 3"[1], "Frankenstein"[2] and "Analytic Restoration"[3], and the relationship between these studies with the continuous academic interests and design research of each team. Eleven academics including Li Han, Principal of Beijing Drawing Architecture Studio, author of *A Little Story of Beijing*; Associate Professor Li Hua from School of Architecture, Southeast University; Professor Lu Andong and Associate Professor Dou Ping Ping from School of Architecture and Urban Planning, Nanjing University; Wang Jiahao, Architecture and Art Critic and Curator; Professor Wang Junyang, Professor Tong Ming, and Professor Wang Fangji from College of Architecture and Urban Planning,

Tongji University; Feng Lu and Zhang Bin, Heads of Wuyang Architecture and Atelier Z+; and Fan Wenbing, Associate Professor of Architecture Department, Shanghai Jiaotong University, discussed enthusiastically the purpose, method, and significance of architects-led urban research, as well as the realistic conflicts and general trend of contemporary Chinese cities and buildings. Feng lu, Zhang Bin, Fan Wenbing have also been engaged in the Shanghai Project (SHP)[4] in cooperation with Atelier Archmixing since 2013.

Purpose of Architects' Urban Study: Social Criticism, Spatial Cognition or Design Practice

A city is a complex physical space and a carrier for social culture. Whether in China or around the world there are rich perspectives and achievements in urban research. In order to evaluate and reflect pertinently and universally on "Hongkou 1617", a specific research led by front-line practical architects, it is necessary to define the objectives and methods of such research. The purpose of discussing architects' urban research is not only to sort out the possibility of discovering new architectural design theories and methods through learning from the real cities, but also to define the values and the boundaries of architectural discipline in the context of contemporary Chinese cities after rapid urbanization.

Some scholars advocate that "urban research should allow architects to break through the use of design as their

末端，批评和反抗社会系统不是其强项和主旨。但建筑学"不可被替代"，因为其作为"一个空间支撑和空间配置的系统，相对中性，可以对接很多其他学科，对接各种社会需求"[6]。因此，建筑师开展城市研究的重点在于促进认知和指导实践，包括："了解当下建筑学的背景，了解建筑何以在此，应如何观看和评价等，并以此为基础探讨学科和知识的定位"[7]，"对碎片化的城市现实进行规则化和整体化的思考，并在此基础上展开专业的干预、介入和操作"[8]，"把城市空间中的原形、概念提炼出来指导设计"[9]，"通过观察使用者对自身环境的改变，在设计之初考虑更好的包容性，或将这些逻辑用作新的设计资源和策略"[10]，等等。

以建筑学专业认知和操作为导向的城市研究"不是那种宏观的、框架式的、理论化的，而是微观的、具体的、集中于建筑学本体的问题"。因此更应"去除被外在赋予的抽象的社会文化意义和所谓神性的内容，聚焦于中性的物质现象本身，不只是空间，也是建筑所承载的生活和其他功能"[12]。

"抱着建筑学专业仍可自我更新的希望，城市研究也可能成为一种突破的方向"。在城市中传统建筑学失效，比

如城市总体是很多偶然因素（而不是系统的规划）起着决定作用，在宏观的生产消费体系中，所有的建筑创新都成为一种商品美学的"边缘性差异"，建筑师精心设计和建构的作品一旦投入使用就不断经历改变，精确的性能预设本质上无用等状况，"如果无法通过实际的建造来改变，可能需要通过知识的创造去改变"[13]。"建筑学应该变为一种从认识到干预的过程。所谓的城市研究其实是让操作变为一种试验——城市作为一种实验室，通过建筑学进行操作。这是建筑学无法为其他学科所取代的独特魅力，因此未来无论在建筑教育中，还是建筑学科发展中都有很大的潜力"。

图像化再现的必要性和有效性

图像化再现是今天可见的城市研究采用的主要表达方式，"虹口1617"也不例外。根据各自研究对象的特点，三个研究小组分别选择了视频影像（"Line3"）、分解图（"弗兰肯斯坦"）、爆炸图（"逆向还原"）等方式加以呈现。CEED对Line3的研究源于对虹口足球场和虹口公园周边地区不同尺度、不同年代的自然和人造物的并置和冲突的困惑。如何呈现像三号线这样的混凝土巨构和在空中

single and only way of social intervention. It should smash the illusion that design is still hopeful; only in this way can it be conducive to the study of deep mechanisms such as spatial politics, and to the reconstruction of building environment"[5]. Other scholars generally agree that architecture is a part of the macro political and economic network in the social system, but it is relatively at the end of this system. So criticizing and resisting the social system is not their focus and purpose. But architecture is "irreplaceable" because as a "spatial support and configuration system, it is relatively neutral and can be integrated with many other social demands"[6]. Therefore, urban researches focus on promoting cognition and guiding practice, including: First, "know why the building is here, how to view and evaluate it, and on this basis exploring the discipline and knowledge"[7]. Second, "regularize and integrate fragmented urban reality, then carry professional interference, intervention, and operation"[8]. Third, "guide designing with prototype and concepts discovered in urban space"[9]. Fourth, "Consider better inclusiveness at the beginning of design by observing how the users change their environment, or use the logic of this change as new design resources and strategies"[10], etc.

The urban study aims at professional cognition and architectural operation "is not a macroscopic, framed and theoretical study. It is a microcosmic, concrete study focusing on architectural ontology."[11] Therefore, we should "remove the abstract social-cultural significance and so-called divine

content endowed externally. We should focus on the neutral physical phenomenon, including the spatial, living and other functions carried by the building."[12]

"With the hope that architecture can still renew itself, urban research may become a breakthrough". There are many incidents (rather than systematic planning) in the city. They are decisive factors led to the failure of traditional architecture in the city. All architectural innovations become "marginal differences" of commodity aesthetics in the macro production and consumption system. Though carefully designed and constructed by architects, once the building is put into use, it undergoes constant changes. Its preset performance is finally useless. "If real world construction cannot change this situation, knowledge creation may be required"[13]. "Architecture should become a process from cognition to intervention. The so-called urban research actually turns operations into experiments—cities are laboratories. These experiments are implemented by architecture. This is the unique charm that makes architecture irreplaceable by other disciplines. So in the future, great potential is expected in both architectural education and the development of architectural discipline".

Necessity and Effectiveness of Visual Representation

Visual representation is the main method of expression used in today's urban research. This method was also adopted in "Hongkou 1617". According to the characteristics of each

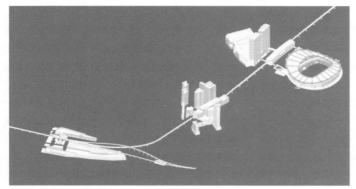

2 弗兰肯斯坦总体鸟瞰图
Aerial View of "Frankenstein"

3 逆向还原分解图
Decomposition diagram of "Analytic Restoration"

4 在周边社区，三号线的通行成为一种日常的节律，视频截图
Video screenshot of Line 3 producing a daily rhythm in neighboring communities

5 拱形构筑物下通行的公共汽车看到的场景，视频截图
Video screenshot of buses passing under the arch-shaped structure

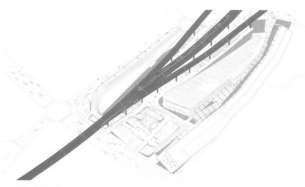

6 虬江路音像城
Qiujiang Road Audio-visual City

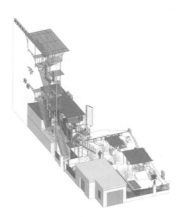

8 田林新村立面加建
Tianlin New Village facade addition

7 同心路皇玛会所夹缝加建
Addition in the crack of Huangman Clubhouse on Tongxin Road

不时呼啸而过的列车对城市空间和城市生活的影响？研究者认为，相对于单纯视觉的图纸，声像合一、时空合一的四维影像能更好地展现城市空间的复杂和变化[14][图1]。城市建造物的失控有时就像科幻小说中的人造物弗兰肯斯坦的自主觉醒，治是工作室通过圣鲁迅（虹口足球场、三号线轻轨站、虹口龙之梦）、东宝兴路站以及虬江路音像城三个案例的研究去思考都市中的拼合、对峙与碰撞。这些"城市混合体"怪异的合理性逻辑使经典学科中的种种教义统统失效，研究者选择采用无法被"清洁"的建筑图纸，既是对这样的非理性感受的传达，图示本身也是一种对城市／建筑，计划／未计划的重构实验[15][图2]。"逆向还原"是一种为显示建筑物改变而采用的记录与模拟城市建筑状态的方法，其对虹口地区九个不同类型和属性的建成物进行的研究，用不同形式的图像和图解来展示在两个时间点——考察的时刻与推测的建成之初——之间的物质改变[16][图3]。

与会学者在肯定这些图解与影像的独特性和吸引力的同时，对于城市研究采用图像化再现是否必要和有效提出了不同的见解。因为原始的素材用什么方式再现，不仅取决于研究对象本身的特征，也反映了研究的立场、视角和目的。城市研究的再现既是对复杂现实的解析，也是对其背后隐形逻辑和原型策略的提炼。

图像化再现作为城市现实的认知手段

有学者批评图像化再现会"加剧物化倾向，无法实现历史和社会诊断的意义"，其他学者[17]则认为，研究成果用图画表达，既显示图画作为建筑学不能为其他学科所取代的特殊工具，也是其专业优势。从观察三维的物质世界到从中提取并将其转化为二维图像，是对碎片化的现实的捕捉，对其中的逻辑通过思维将其整体化、系统化的过程，也支持了对（建筑）形式的认识和理解。精心选择的图解表达能够超越对城市现实的简单还原，使我们获得与以往不同的认知。

城市的物质空间是异质的，日常生活的体验混杂而丰富，尤其是像上海这样在过去一百多年间经历了翻天覆地的政治、经济和社会变迁的中国城市。三个团队对这种复杂研究对象的记录与表达体现了各自对问题的理解和认知。

"line3"的五段视频希望通过镜头实现的主观凝视来

research subject, three teams selected videos ("Line 3"), decomposed diagrams ("Frankenstein"), explosion diagrams ("Analytic Restoration") and other ways to express. CEED's study of Line 3 stems from the confusion about the juxtaposition and conflict between nature and man-made objects on different scales and from different times around Hongkou Football Stadium and Hongkou Park. How do we present the impact of concrete mega-structures of Line 3 and its whizzing trains on urban space and life? Researchers believe that the four-dimensional image of space-time and sound-visual integration can better represent the complexity and changes of urban space than simple visual drawings[14] [fig. 1]. The runaway urban construction is sometimes like the self-driven awakening of Frankenstein, the man-made character in science fiction. Based on their studies on three cases, namely St. Luxun (Hongkou Football Stadium, Station Site, Hongkou CapitaLand), Dongbaoxing Road Station and Qiujiang Road Audio-visual City, YeArch Studio thought about the integration, confrontation, and collision in the city. The bizarre but reasonable logic of these "urban mixtures" invalidates those classical disciplines. Researchers choose architectural drawings that cannot be "cleaned" to convey this irrational feeling. The illustration itself is a planned / unplanned reconstruction experiment of city/architecture[15] [fig. 2]. *Analytic Restoration* is a method of recording and simulating the state of urban buildings to demonstrate their changes. For nine buildings of

different types and attributes in Hongkou district, different forms of images and diagrams are used to show the material changes between two-time points—the point when the researches began and the estimated point when the building was established[16] [fig. 3].

While acknowledging that these illustrations and images are unique and attractive, the participants raised different views on the necessity and effectiveness of visual representation in urban research. Because how the original material is represented, not only depends on the characteristics of the object itself, but also reflects the position, perspective, and purpose of the study. The representation of urban research is not only an analysis of complex reality, but also extraction of the implicit logic and prototype strategy behind it.

Visual Representation as a Cognitive Method of Urban Reality

Some scholars criticized that visual representation would "aggravate materialization and fail to realize historical and social diagnosis", while others[17] believed that visual representation is a special tool that makes architecture irreplaceable. This is also its professional advantage. From observing the three-dimensional material world to extracting and transforming it into two-dimensional images, it captures the fragmented reality. The process of integrating its logic supports the cognition and understanding of architectural forms.

捕捉冗余、无序的普通城市和日常生活中不应该被忽视的力量。"这些相对客观的记录构成了一种可以被共享的日常记忆，看上去是主观感受，事实上是用模拟的方式去打造对城市真实性碎片的一种认识，是有立场的观察"。这些影像记录"在捕捉城市的复杂体验和时间性上面具有优势，能把平时比较容易忽视的非视觉因素，比如声音的感知和体验强化出来[图4]。其中一些拍摄视角，比如在公共汽前后车窗拍摄轻轨下拱形支撑的高架桥下的空间感受，揭示了城市基础设施通常被认为是副作用的另一面，对于未来创造城市体验是一种新的参考"[18][图5]。

三个团队的表达，"'Line3'主要是再现，'弗兰肯斯坦'不再描摹现实，而是力图重构，'逆向还原'则开始创造。冶是团队具有视觉冲击力的图解，比如对虹江路音像城的描绘[图6]，"为哪怕很熟悉这一城市空间的人也揭示出了特别的属性"。阿科米星团队把建筑在使用过程中发生的不同搭建物剥离出来制作的爆炸图，"采用一种失重的状态，把历时性的结果用共时性的方式表达了出来"[图7]。"虹口1617"、阿科米星的田林新村调研[图8]和冶是在同济新村调研中绘制的《新村的猫》[19]等图画"让

读者看到了不同的视角"，"这种复杂性的叠加，是中国城市所特有的"。

关于这些图像的价值和作用，有人主张，"具体的表象并不比抽象的概念更次要。就城市研究而言，通过图绘在表象和感官效果上做到极致，实现视觉冲击力也已达到了目的，或可留待批评家去寻找其他意义"[20]。其他人则更倾向于"这些效果强烈的图像具有表现性，但更是分析性的，是很重要的研究的中间过程"[21]。

图像化表达作为城市研究向设计实践转化的桥梁

对于阿科米星团队负责人庄慎而言，"这些研究和再现是理论假设在先的，所谓的观察分析是一个对此假设进行论证的过程，然后以这样一个循环的方式纳入到实践体系中"。作为研究向实践转化的桥梁，"图示的作用不是为了表现现实，而是为了承接观念和手法。无论拼贴，还是爆炸，图示的手法体现了对现实的一种看法。就像在设计实践中，我们会根据概念设计一些原型和模式，以便用到现实的设计中。研究中的图解同样可以看成是这样一种不是概念设计的概念，表达的可能是对现象的感知，也可

The graphic expressions carefully chosen can transcend the simple restoration of urban reality and generate perceptions different from the past.

The physical space of a city is heterogeneous and daily life is mixed and rich, especially in Shanghai, which has undergone tremendous political, economic and social changes in the past 100 years. The recording and expression of this complex subject by the three teams reflect their understanding and cognition of the problems.

The five videos of "Line 3" expect to capture the redundant, disorderly ordinary cities and the power that should not be ignored in everyday life through the camera. "These relatively objective records constitute a shared everyday memory. It appears subjective on the surface, but in fact, simulates a perception of the fragments of urban authenticity. It is an observation with a position". These videos "have the advantage of capturing the complex experiences and temporality of the city. They can reinforce the often neglected non-visual factors, such as the perception and experience of sound [fig. 4]. Some of these shooting angles, such as recording the space of the arch-supported elevated road under the light rail at the front and rear windows of the bus, reveal another side of the urban infrastructure that is often seen as generating negative effects; thus forming a new reference for creating urban experience in the future"[18] [fig. 5].

In the expression of the three teams, "Line 3" is mainly a

representation, *Frankenstein* no longer describes reality, but attempts to reconstruct, *Analytic Restoration* began to create". Illustration with visual impact by YeArch Studio, such as the description of the Qiujiang Road Audio-visual City [fig. 6], "reveals special properties even for those who are very familiar with the city's space" The explosion diagrams by Atelier Archmixing team which strip off different structures that had occurred during the use of the building "express the diachronic results in a synchronous manner and weightless state" [fig. 7]. "Hongkou 1617", "Tianlin New Village Investigation" by Atelier Archmixing [fig. 8] and "Cats in New Village"[19] and other pictures drawn by YeArch in Tongji New Village Investigation "let the readers see different perspectives", "this complex superposition is unique in Chinese cities".

As for the value and function of these images, it has been argued that "concrete representation is no less important than abstract concepts. As far as urban research is concerned, the visual impact has been achieved by drawing to the extreme in appearance and sensory effect, but critics could also look for other meanings."[20] Others preferred: "these highly effective images are expressive and even analytical. They are an important intermediate process of research."[21]

Visual Representation as a Bridge between Urban Study and Design Practice

For Zhuang Shen, head of the Atelier Archmixing team,

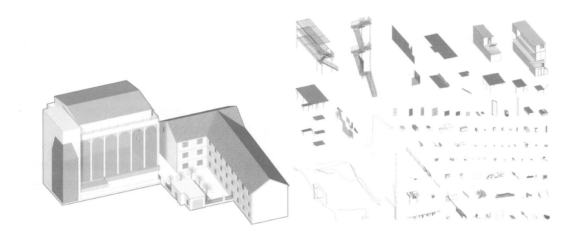

9　山阴路恒丰里，分类清单图
Classification list of Hengfengli, Shanyin Road

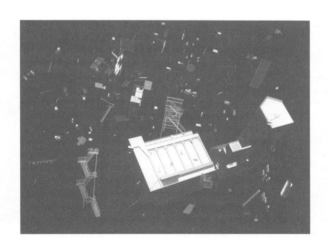

10　山阴路恒丰里，爆炸图
Explosion diagram of Hengfengli, Shanyin Road

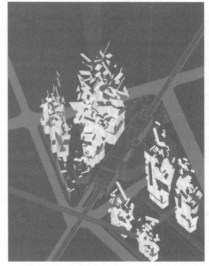

11　东宝兴路站，分解图
Decomposition diagram of Dongbaoxing Road Station

能是对设计方式和手法的理解"[22]。比如"逆向还原既是一种记录现实、模拟变化、阐述观念的方法，同时也包含了设计实践中的观念、策略和手法运用。设计这种再现方式如同设计物理实验一样，实验的目的、方法、结果之间相互影响。方法来自目的，方法也塑造结果"。总体而言，视觉再现问题与建筑设计和本体研究之间的关系是具有普遍意义的。

对分类模式和概念的批评

城市研究始于捕捉事实，却并不以积累事实为目的。整体化思维，包括对事实现象进行分类重组，基于现实规律提出具有普遍意义的概念，是从城市研究中获得新认知，最终实现理论化的基础。至于这样的概念是对研究的描述、总结，还是先从设计实践中获得理论预设，再通过事实调研加以印证，这也是"虹口1617"研究成果引发争议的地方。

新的分类模式

分类是简化事实以掌握规律的有效手段，也能体现新

的认知和理论视角。比如阿尔多·罗西主张用类型和类型学取代简单的功能分类，既体现了城市建筑的复杂属性，也使建筑形式超越了功能主义所包含的生物和物质层面的简单因果关系，将社会、文化、历史、记忆等非物质要素融合其中。《东京制造》和《上海制造》分类上的不同，也揭示了这两个从主题到图解都看似相仿的研究在目标和认识上的差异，前者偏向设计原理的研究，而后者则更是展览性的和历史梳理性的。

为了解在城市生活中，时间积累和使用需要所形成的建造事实，"逆向还原"的分解图以建造完成之初的状态与研究时刻的建筑现实为两个确定的分析点，将两者的差异，即在时间积累中增加和改变的内容剥离出来，并按照不同的类型罗列展示，成果既包括像手术解剖一样整齐的归类图解 [图9]，也有任意混杂呈现的爆炸图。[图10]

"建筑师观察使用者参与对环境的改变，各种元素、线索、片段的现象罗列，应该理清类型和体系。比如场地、结构、表皮、设备和内部这样的建筑层级，这些层级有不同的使用寿命，满足不同的要求，上一层级会影响下一层级。还有使用过程中设备的更新和室外的拓展，楼

"these studies and representations are theoretical hypotheses. The so-called observation and analysis is a process of demonstrating these hypotheses. In this way, they have been incorporated into the practice system." As a bridge between research and practice, "the illustration is not used to express reality, but to inherit ideas and techniques. Whether it is a collage or explosion, the illustration reflects a view on reality. Just like in design practice, we design prototypes and patterns according to some concepts so that we can use them in real design. The deconstructive diagrams in the study can also be seen as a concept unrelated to conceptual design. It may express either perception of phenomena or understanding of design methods and techniques."[22] For example, "Analytic Restoration is a method of recording reality, simulating changes and explaining concepts. It includes the use of concepts, strategies, and techniques in design practice. Like designing a physics experiment, in the process of designing this representation, purpose, method, and result influence each other. The method comes from purpose and shapes the results." Generally speaking, the relationship of visual representation with architectural design and ontological research is of universal significance.

Critics on Classification and Conceptualization

Urban research begins with collecting facts but does not aim at accumulating facts. Integrated thinking includes classifying and reorganizing factual phenomena and puts forward universal concepts based on realistic laws. It is the basis of gaining new cognition from urban research and ultimately realizing theorization. Whether such a concept is description and study on research, or theoretical presupposition obtained first from design practice, and then verified through factual survey, this is the debates aroused by "Hongkou 1617".

New Classification

Classification is an effective means to grasp laws by simplifying facts. It can also reflect new cognitive and theoretical perspectives. Aldo Rossi, for example, advocates replacing simple functional classifications with type and typology. This proposal reflects that urban architecture is complex. Besides, it enables architectural forms to transcend the simple causal relationship on biological and material levels contained in functionalism. It integrates immaterial aspects such as social, cultural, historical, and memory. The difference in classification between *Made in Tokyo* and *Made in Shanghai* also reveals the differences in goals and understanding between these two similar studies, either in terms of topic or illustration. The former tends to favor study on design principles, while the latter is exhibitive and historical.

To understand the construction facts formed by time accumulation and need for use in urban life, the deconstructive diagrams of Analytic Restoration takes two analysis

梯、阳台等局部的潜力。对这种适应变化的局部通过逆向还原的掌控，可以看到整体和局部之间组合关系的多样性，为下一步的建筑操作提供了参考"。

城市研究的成果可以采用物质形式（比如图像化再现）去建构生活，"但是日常生活有其自己的运行系统，这种逻辑与物质空间之间到底是什么关系在现在'虹口1617'的研究表达中尚未体现出来。究其原因有二：其一，口头介绍中，现实是动态的、变化的、有趣的，但是图像却是静态的。其二，现在物质的分类看上去很系统，比如在时间中不断增生的附加物，包括毛巾、衣服等细节，但是彼此处于相互割裂的状态，因为所呈现的并非这些事物真正发生关系的状态，所谓的并置并不清晰。之所以达不到预想的效果是因为借助了已有的分类系统，依旧是建筑空间中生活物品习惯性的分类，而庄慎、华霞虹曾经提出的'非识别系统'的意义正在于超越了既有的分类模式。这种分类可以有设计师的立场，有日常生活的立场，但只有出现另外一种分类时，才能引发真正有意思的并置"。

甚至，"按照现有分类，反而生活为商品所控制的无望局面更为突显。相较于把毛巾、牙刷等物品全部展示在图纸上的震惊，打破原有物品的边界，就可以打破既有秩序，再物化的效果会更加震惊，也利于在此基础上建构新的物质系统，包括设计"。

概念：城市研究的描述、总结，还是预设？

关于研究，图示是一个开始，一个启发，继续深化就应该"在概念层面上推演"。这是比较困难的一步，因为"可纳入建筑学话语的概念，不仅需要联系到物质和生产的层面，也要能放进更广泛的语境，与政治、文化等更为宏观抽象的事物关联起来"。[23]

冶是团队提出的关键词包括：并置、重叠和内爆。这些引用的术语对研究结果的理解是否有效？是否能成为研究的结论性概念？研究者认为，"作为建筑师开展研究，不是把这些词视为概念，而是把它们当作与设计有关的动词。在现有环境下的并置与完全新建的并置不同"[24]。[图11] 与会学者则建议"引用已有的分类和概念可能都会带来问题，应该通过研究提出新的概念"，当然，"对原有的词做新的阐释和发明新词一样可能获得新认知"[25]，但是，"通过迅速的观察提出概念和采用暗喻帮助思考可能存在风险"。

points—a point of when the researches began and the other point of when the building was established. The differences between them, i.e. the content added and changed in the accumulation of time were separated and exhibited based on different types. The results include a neat classification diagram [fig. 9] as well as a random mix-up of explosion diagrams. [fig. 10]

"Architects should clarify the types and systems when observing the changes made by participants to the environment. They also observe the list of all elements, clues, and fragments, including architectural elements such as the ground, structure, surface, equipment and the interior. These architectural levels have a different service life and satisfy different requirements; the upper level will affect the next level. There are also potentials for architectural parts like staircases, balconies in the process of equipment renewal and outdoor expansion. Controlling these change-adapted parts through Analytic Restoration can reveal the diverse combinations between the whole and the part, thus provide references for further architectural operations."

The results of urban research can be used for building life in material form (such as visual representation), "But everyday life has its own operating system. The relationship between this logic and physical space has not been concluded in "Hongkou 1617". There are two reasons: first, in an oral presentation, the reality is dynamic, changing and interesting, but the image is static. Second, the classification of substances seems to be very systematic, such as the proliferation of attachments in time, including towels, clothes and other details, but they are separated, because what is presented is not a real relationship between these things, and the so-called juxtaposition is not clear. The effect is less than expected because it is a habitual classification system of living things in architectural space. The meaning of the "Unrecognizable System" proposed by Zhuang Shen and Hua Xihong is beyond the existing classification model. The existing classification contains positions of designs and daily life, but only when there is another kind of classification, can it trigger really interesting juxtaposition".

Furthermore, "according to the existing classification, it highlights the hopeless situation that life is controlled by commodities. Compared with the shocking display of all the towels and toothbrushes on the drawings, we can destroy the existing orders by breaking the boundaries of original objects. The effect of re-materialization will be even more shocking, which is also conducive to establish a new material system, including design".

Concept: Description, Summary or Presupposition of Urban Research

With regard to research, illustration is a start and inspiration. Further research should be "deducted at the conceptual

阿科米星城市研究的基础包括近年提出的"空间冗余"概念，认为相对于贬义的多余和过剩，冗余这个在工程信息和生物科技中已经广泛使用的科学名词是个中性的术语，它可能造成破坏和浪费，也可以在系统出错和受损时成为有用的防线，避免系统崩溃。提出空间冗余的概念是要强调因为时间积累而形成的空间的重复和多余，可能具有同样的效能，一样应中性看待。基于对空间冗余的新认识，室内、局部等曾经被认为是整体的附属品的概念，也并非不能独立于整体而存在。

其他学者则认为，"空间冗余"关心的是"建筑学语境中形式系统的冗余，表面是冗余，内在其实是短缺，短缺来自于空间的不对等。所谓传统建筑学的精确化，或者是以完善的结构和性能为导向的建筑学所追求的设计和形式极致化的建筑，背后其实是冗余的资源。今天我们看到的冗余、不确定和社群的割裂是中国当下快速发展所造成的无法回避的沉重话题，与现在大城市的整治也密切相关，要改变这样的状况很难用传统的建造方式，或许要借助知识，包括概念的创造"。

当然，"城市研究—表达—设计实践并不是单向的认知—总结—应用的关系。新的认知可能在设计实践、对现实的观察和思考，以及理论假设等不同的过程中产生，新的方法也可能同时在研究和实践中进行实验"。对阿科米星而言，概念的提出总是试图兼顾对现实的认知和在设计中的运用。比如"空间冗余"既是对城市现实的描述，也是对建成环境本质属性的认识，同样，"非识别体系"既是对城市以使用为目的开展建造的特征的总结，也是对来源不同、意义不同的内容和形式根据有效性自由选择，不放弃任何可能的设计策略的概括。

日常生活：非建筑，反建筑，还是零度的建筑？

城市是日常生活的载体。在由无数人的日常生活日积月累所构成的大熔炉里，自上而下的规划和建筑产品不必，也无法再辨析设计概念和真实建造之间的差距。无论美丑，它们的价值在于被占有、使用或误用、改变，与自下而上的建造和反建造彼此纠缠，不断混合积累，形成难以描述、无法归类的城市空间和建筑现象。这些平庸甚至丑陋的建成环境承载着不一定和谐，却总是充满活力的日常生活。

level". It is difficult to do so because "as an architectural concept, it needs to be linked not only to the material and production levels, but also be placed in a broader context and associated with more macroscopic and abstract things such as politics and culture"[23].

The keywords proposed by the YeArch team are juxtaposition, overlap, and implosion. Are these quoted terms effective in understanding the research results? Can they be the conclusive concepts in the research? Researchers argue that "when research is started, the architect does not primarily regard these words as concepts. They are just verbs related to design. The juxtaposition in the existing environment is quite different from a new juxtaposition"[24] [fig. 11]. Scholars at the meeting suggested that "citing existing classifications and concepts may both cause problems. New concepts should be put forward through research". Though "we can acquire new knowledge by new explanations of the existing words or inventing words"[25], "it might be risky to define concepts with quick observations or with a metaphor".

The basis of the city research by Atelier Archmixing includes the "Spatial Redundancy" proposed in recent years. Redundancy, a scientific term widely used in engineering information and biotechnology, is considered to be a neutral term compared with such derogatory words as surplus and excess. It may cause damage and waste, or it may become useful defensive lines to avoid system crashes in case of sys-

tem failure or damage. The concept of "spatial redundancy" is put forward to emphasize that duplication and redundancy of space formed by time accumulation may have the same effect and should be treated as neutral. Based on the new understanding of "spatial redundancy", the interior, parts and other elements which were once considered as attachments to the whole, are possible to exist independently.

Other scholars believe that "spatial redundancy" is concerned with "form redundancy in architecture. Ostensibly it is redundancy, actually it is a shortage. A shortage caused by spatial asymmetry. The so-called precision of traditional architecture, or the buildings with ultimate design and form pursued by structural performance oriented architecture, is actually supported by redundant resources. Today redundancy, uncertainty, and social fragmentation are unavoidable and serious issues arising from China's rapid development. They are closely related to urban renovation. It is difficult to change this situation in traditional construction. Perhaps we shall resort to knowledge, including creating new concepts."

Obviously, "relationships between urban research, expression, and design practice are not one-way cognition, summary, and application. New perceptions may arise from different processes of design practice, observation, and reflection of reality, and theoretical assumptions. New methods may have simultaneously experimented in research and practice." For Atelier Archmixing, the concept is always

以建筑学本体的认知和方法为导向的城市研究，包括"虹口1617"、《上海计划》、《小菜场上的家》[26]、《一点儿北京》等，感兴趣的正是日常生活所依赖的这些非历史、非文化的普通建成环境的物质特征和建造规律。它们最大的吸引力并非来自专业设计的良苦用心，而是来自实用的智慧，甚至是生存的本能，是各种力量博弈和妥协的产物。

在关注日常生活使用的城市研究中，很多对象可以被归入跟自行车棚同类的只关注物质使用的"建物"，而非具有人文内涵的"建筑"，甚至连完整独立的建物都算不上。比如"逆向还原"关注的九个案例都是局部，诸如商业裙房、立面、违章搭建、设备立面等。其中"城市内巷"由不同建筑、结构、设备界面构成，宽度从0.9米至4.3米不等，短短的巷道有七次转折，完全没有统一性，却因为日常使用形成了连续的、具有私人领域感的城市公共空间。"弗兰肯斯坦"研究的虹江路音像城诞生于两条轻轨线交汇形成的城市孤岛中，与城中村、篮球场、绿地和小广场一起构成蒙太奇式画面，嘈杂与安静毗邻而居。"Line3"中，超过五层高的巨大的门式框架下爬满了藤蔓，伴随车水马龙行进时，仿佛在穿过一个又一个绿意盎然的山洞。本以为恼人的轻轨交通噪声因为熟悉而变成了周边生活社区里忠实的节律。对这些被主流建筑学排除在外的非建筑现象的研究，让设计者对城市生活有了更多不同于抽象概念的感知和理解。权宜的、粗暴的、冲突的城市"非建筑"，它们缺乏文化象征，无意展示概念，但从承载个体和群体生活的角度来看蕴含着建筑学意义。

日常生活世界被视为反建筑的领域，一方面是因为缺乏秩序和美学，大量的、重复的、或平庸或奇观，比如高速公路带的商业建筑，比如广普城市、垃圾空间，也比如国内屡屡被媒体上吸引眼球的山寨和具象建筑。另一方面，正如亨利·列斐伏尔在对日常生活的批判中揭示的那样，在整体现代生活被生产-消费系统所控制时，日常的建造，那些无序的、非正规的、不符合传统形式美学的建造活动和生活体验反而被看成逃离的缺口，是对资本和权力控制的社会的抵制，比如被占用的垂直贫民窟——委内瑞拉的大卫塔、《东京制造》讨论的"滥建筑"[27]、像野草一样顽强的"城中村"、"违章建筑"，以及玛格丽特·克劳福特提出的"日常都市主义"等。阿科米星团队

put forward in an attempt to take into account both the cognition of reality and its use in design. For example, "spatial redundancy" is not only a description of the urban reality, but also an understanding of the built environment. Similarly, "unrecognizable system" has summarized the characteristics of city constructions aiming at use. Also, it is a summary of design strategies that seek every possibility to freely choose contents and forms, which are of different origins and significance based on their effectiveness.

Everyday life: Non-architecture, Anti-architecture or Zero-degree Architecture

The city is the carrier of everyday life. With countless people's daily life, it is unnecessary and unable to analyze the gap between design concepts and real construction in top-down planning and buildings. Whether beautiful or ugly, their value lies in being occupied, used, misused or changed. These buildings are intertwined among bottom-up construction and anti-construction. They are constantly mixed and accumulated. In this process, the indescribable and unclassified urban space and architectural phenomena are created. These mediocre and even ugly built environments carry not necessarily harmonious, but always vibrant daily life.

Urban research, guided by the cognition and methodology of architectural ontology, be it "Hongkou 1617", *Shanghai Project*, *Home Above Market*[26], or *A Little Story of Beijing*, is interested in the material characteristics and construction laws of these non-historical and non-cultural ordinarily-built environments on which everyday life depends. Their greatest attraction does not come from professional design. It comes from practical wisdom, even the instinct for survival. These are results of power games and compromises.

In urban research that concern everyday use, many objects can be classified as "building" that focus only on material use, like a bicycle shed, rather than "architecture" with humanistic connotations. They are even not complete and independent buildings. For example, the nine cases in Analytic Restoration all focus on local parts: commercial podium, facade, illegal building, and equipment facade, etc. The "urban lane" is composed of different buildings, structures, equipment interfaces, ranging from 0.9-4.3 meters in width. There are seven turnings in the short lane. The public space inside is not unified. But because of daily use, it forms a continuous urban public space with private sense. The Qiujiang Road Audio-visual City studied by Frankenstein is located in the isolated area formed by the intersection of two light rail lines. It is a half noisy and half tranquil montage picture in which a village in the city, basketball court, the green space, and the small square stay together. In *Line 3*, vines are crawling beneath a gigantic portal frame more than five stories high. The traffic flows by as if passing through green caves. The familiar annoying traffic noise has become a faithful

调研的皇玛俱乐部，依托着消防楼梯，违章加建的三部分仿佛从两座原有建筑的夹缝之间"生长"出来：与洗浴中心相连的室外钢结构疏散楼梯、主体加建钢结构建筑（员工宿舍），以及两座原有建筑与垃圾房围合成的院子，用于停车和洗漱。为了方便和节省成本，建筑充分利用了两座原有建筑之间的各种空间。家具、电器、生活用品、废弃物等随着生活的累积而凌乱自由地散布在空间的每个角落，四处都是生活的痕迹。所有增建附属物都是自治的，不一定和原建筑有逻辑关系。在近期的拆违运动中，伴随着对破墙开店的封堵，这个在夹缝中恣意生长的生活空间也就消失了。与主流的建筑学中通过建造把概念变为现实的意义不同，这种非正规实践是一种"作为权利的建造"。

无论是将日常空间对象归类为非建筑还是反建筑，日常生活被视为"一种空间实践的开启维度"和"一种设计视角"，这样的城市研究感兴趣的是另一种建筑学——"普通生活与物质环境之间关系的规律"，而非创新概念与诗意建构的完美结合。"日常"被与罗兰·巴特的"零度"概念关联起来，并非日常生活未承载意义，而是因为相对于"非凡的"自上而下的规划和建筑设计作品，这些自下

而上的"平凡的"建成环境倾向于"摆脱宏大文化叙事和意识形态的纠缠"，"也不再把佩夫斯纳关于'建筑'与'建物'的区分或者艾森曼批判建筑学高定义的'内在性'和'概念性'作为自身前提"，它们是相对"低定义的"，走向了一种"更加平和和包容的建筑学议题"。

城市建筑学：建构中国当代建筑学的一种可能？

基于城市现实的建筑学研究是否可能发展成为一种"城市建筑学"[28]，从主流学科系统所忽视的日常建成环境中发现建筑学的新认知和新方法？这种将研究理论化的期望近年来在中国建筑领域颇为高涨。跟其他现代化后发地区一样，中国建筑学科从20世纪初以来一直追随欧美现代建筑的楷模，传统与现代的融合，或者说"中国的现代的建筑"是一个始终追逐而尚未完全实现的梦想。建构一种中国当代建筑学，无论是从历史传统出发（比如王澍本人的实践及其领导的中国美院建筑学院不断实验的教学探索），从当下现实出发（比如刘家琨主张的"此时此地"），从建筑本体出发（比如结构建筑学、建构理论），还是从新兴技术和科学出发（比如数字建造和性能建筑

rhythm in surrounding communities. The study on these non-architectural phenomena excluded from the mainstream architecture discipline gives designers more perception and understanding of urban life. They are different from abstract concepts. These are expedient, brutal and conflicting urban 'non-architecture'. They lack cultural symbols and have no intention to display concepts, but they carry architectural significance from the perspective of individual and group life.

The world of everyday life is regarded as an area of anti-architecture, partly because of a lack of order and aesthetics. There was a large number of shameless repetition, mediocracy or spectacle aimed at seeking profit. Like commercial buildings beside highway, generic city, junk space and popular domestic copycats and iconic buildings appear in media. However, on the other hand, as Henri Lefebvre's critique of everyday life reveals: when the modern life is controlled by the production and consumption system, construction activities and life experiences in everyday construction that are disorderly, informal and non-conforming could be taken as resistances to a society controlled by capital and power. Examples include the occupied vertical slums "The Tower of David" in Venezuela, "Da-me Architecture"[27] discussed in *Made in Tokyo*, weed-stubborn' "Village in City" and "illegal buildings", as well as "everyday urbanism" proposed by Margaret Crawford, etc. The Huangma Clubhouse is a case studied by Atelier Archmixing team. Relying on an

emergency staircase, the added three illegal parts "grows" out of the cracks between two original buildings: an outdoor steel evacuation staircase connected to the bathing center, a main additional steel building (staff dormitory), and a courtyard formed by two existing buildings and garbage house used for parking and washing. The building makes full use of the space between these two original buildings to facilitate life and save cost. Furniture, electrical appliances, daily necessities, waste, etc. scatter in every corner. There are life traces everywhere. All the additional attachments are autonomous and not necessarily logically related to the original buildings. In the recent demolition campaign, this space disappeared. Unlike mainstream architecture, which transforms concepts into reality through construction, this informal practice takes "construction as a right".

Whether everyday spatial objects are classified as non-architecture or anti-architecture, everyday life is regarded as "an open dimension of spatial practice" and "a design perspective". These urban studies are interested in another architecture—"the law of the relationship between ordinary life and the physical environment" rather than the perfect combination of creative concept and poetic construction. "Everyday" is associated with Roland Barthe's "zero degree" concept. This is not because daily life does not carry any significance, but rather because these "ordinary" building environments tend to "get rid of grand cultural narratives and

学、建筑热力学），背后都隐藏着"对学科系统和本土身份的普遍焦虑，以及主动应对的强烈诉求"[29]。"城市建筑学"无疑属于其中的现实主义立场。因为近三十年快速城市化创造了无数的建造现实，包括巨大的成就和无穷的问题，这既是"城市建筑学"可观的研究素材，也是急迫的反思对象。

在城市现实中发掘当代性与本土性

与溯源和延续传统文化艺术来建构中国建筑学的立场不同，主张从城市现实中汲取营养的建筑师和研究者，没有所谓"中国性"的宏大主题的诉求。相对于"中国建筑"的抽象概念，他们更看重此时此地的具体空间和生活经验，认为每个城市、每个区域，乃至每个建筑都有所不同。随着世界城市化水平的快速提高，城市成为兼具当代性和本土性的建成环境。同《向拉斯维加斯学习》《癫狂纽约》《洛杉矶：四个生态的建筑学》《隐形逻辑》《东京制造》《宠物建筑》《一点儿北京》《上海制造》等研究课题一样，"上海计划""虹口 1617"也聚焦于特定城市的建筑现象，并旨在从一个个具体的经验中寻找特征和规律。

城市中的日常建筑之所以不受重视是因为数量太大，形式太平庸，无法归类也难以描述。"这种典型性与通常建筑学的典型性不同，并不是通过个体建筑物体现，也不能归结为某种类型，而是通过无数不单独具有典型性的个体或片段不断发生的状态来形成的"。这种重复的典型片段，对于纽约是方格网地块中利润最大化的摩天楼，对于美国东海岸郊区战后兴建的诸如独立小别墅和商业中心这样乏善可陈，"拒绝严格定义"的"日常建筑"，对于拉斯维加斯是美国西部城市自称纪念碑的商业建筑，对于东京是高密度城市变迁下小私权产业的"宠物建筑"，对于像上海这样在过去百余年经历了政治、经济和社会巨变的中国城市来说，则是各种公私利益竞争的混杂产物。这些很难被归类和描述的"沉默的大多数"城市建筑的现状，就构成了每个具体城市（和区域）的建成环境和生活方式的当代性和地方性。

罗西在《城市建筑学》一书中将城市视为艺术品，虽然他并不否认城市总体的复杂和变化，但更强调永恒的纪念物，类型和结构的延续性对城市的决定意义，这是基于意大利城市深厚的历史积累。与之相对比，中国当下城乡

consciousness" when compared to "extraordinary" top-down planning and architectural designs. Pevsner's distinction between "architecture" and "building" or Eisenman's criticism on "internality" and "conceptuality" as architectural high definition is no longer taken as their own premises. They move towards a rather "low-definition", "more peaceful and inclusive architectural issue".

Urban Architecture: a possibility of Constructing Chinese Contemporary Architecture?

Is it possible to develop the architectural research based on urban reality to an "Urban Architecture"[28] so as to discover new concepts and methods of architecture from the daily built environment neglected by the mainstream disciplinary system? This expectation of its theorization has been quite active in Chinese architectural field in recent years. Like other late-modernized regions, Chinese architecture has been following the model of modern architecture in Europe and America since the early 20th century. It is an integration of tradition and modernity, or we could say, "modern architecture in China" is a dream that has been pursued but not yet fully fulfilled. To construct a contemporary Chinese architecture, whether starting from historical tradition (such as Wang Shu's practice and the experimental teaching exploration of China Academy of Art, School of Architecture), or from the current reality (such as the "here and now" advocated

by Liu Jiakun), or from the architectural ontology (such as structural architecture, theory related to constructivism), or from emerging technologies and sciences (such as digital fabrication, performance architecture and architectural thermodynamics), there hide a "general anxiety about disciplinary systems and indigenous identity, and there is a strong demand for proactive response"[29]. "Urban architecture" undoubtedly stands on a realistic position; because with the rapid urbanization in the past 30 years, numerous construction realities have been created, including enormous achievements and endless problems. For urban architecture, these are considerable research materials and objects requiring urgent reflection.

Discovering Modernity and Locality in Urban Reality

Different from continuing the traditional culture and art and tracking down their origins, architects and researchers who advocate drawing inspirations from urban reality have no appeal for the "Chinese character". Compared with the abstract concept of "Chinese architecture", they attach more importance to concrete space and life experience here and now. They believe that every city, every region, even every building is different. With the rapid development of urbanization in the world, cities turn to be the built environment with both contemporary and local characteristics. Similar to the research topics in *Learn from Las Vegas*, *Delirious New York: A Retroactive Manifesto for Manhattan*, *Los Angeles: The*

日常建成环境既粗野顽强，又短暂脆弱，宏观上快速同质化，微观上却相当异质。不断变化是其普遍特征，实用至上是其基本原则。建立在这样的城市现实基础上的"城市建筑学"主张永恒和整体化理论的失效，指向碎片化和不确定性的意义，反对设计作品的唯一性和权威性，主张用即时的、现场的效能取代预定的、目标的性能，主张自由的应用，而不是任何理想的、普遍性规则的引用。

从使用与应用出发的动态建筑学

"上海计划""小菜场上的家""虹口1617"等以上海普通建成环境为对象展开的城市研究，其目标是设计研究和应用。在此基础上建构的"城市建筑学"，其本质是对现代建筑设计基本原理与此时此地的城市空间和日常经验的综合运用。重点考察的使用行为与物质空间、材料技术与建造成果等之间的关系，既是城市建成环境的客观事实，也是建筑设计的核心内容。城市现实的复杂性与偶然性为其赋予活力和特征，但也使传统设计的预设目标统统失效。因此，"虹口1617"的研究主张打破专业认知中既有分类和价值的界限。分类不仅包括功能属性，也包括尺

度规模、室内/室外、整体/局部、公共/私密、正规/非正规、建筑/设备等。比如"逆向还原"的四川北路案例正面是普通的商业建筑外立面改造，背面则是依附于居住建筑表皮的壮观的设备立面。"皇玛俱乐部"是在建筑夹缝中生长的违章建筑，现已被拆除。"弗兰肯斯坦"的"圣鲁迅"案例则包括了虹口足球场、三号线轻轨站、虹口龙之梦三个大型建筑（综合体）及其之间的连接设施。价值不仅包括美丑、好坏，也包括有用/无用、合理/不合理、传统/现代等的评判。更重要的是，对既有现实的研究包含了时间的积累，甚至动态的时间本身。"line3"多个视频都是对空间不同速度和时长的动态体验，由此获得的经验不是单体建筑的功能形式分析所能揭示的。

传统建筑学把重点放在设计作品的创造与评价上，评判的是概念与成果之间的匹配度。"城市建筑学"则把重点放在建成环境的改变上，包括改变的使用原因，改变的方式和结果等。对于城市环境来说，无论是专业的设计还是后期的使用增减都被视为同样性质的改变过程。"城市建筑学"主张一种动态的建筑学。其中，积累和改变是城市建筑的常态，全面的目标设定、功能形式的匹配、完美

Architecture of Four Ecologies, Invisible Logic: Hongkong as Asian Culture of Congestion, Made in Tokyo, Pet Architecture, A Little Story of Beijing, and Made in Shanghai, our researches on "Shanghai Project" and "Hongkou 1617" also focus on architectural phenomena in specific cities. These two studies aim to seek characteristics and laws from specific experiences. The reason why everyday architecture in cities is not valued is that there are too many of them and their form is too mediocre to classify and describe. "This typicality, unlike the architectural typicality in general, is not embodied in individual building, nor can it be attributed to a certain type. It is formed by the constant occurrence of numerous non-characteristic individual structures or fragments that do not have typicality independently."[16] Such repetitive and typical sections are found in the most profitable skyscrapers in New York, in everyday mediocre architecture that "refuse to be strictly defined" such as Independent Villas and Business Centers established in American East Coast suburbs at postwar period. Also, these sections are the commercial buildings that self-proclaimed as monuments in Las Vegas, a western city of the United States. They are the "pet architecture" of the small private property industry in highly urbanized Tokyo. These sections are the mixed product of the competition between public and private interests in Shanghai, which has undergone great political, economic and social changes in the past 100 years. These "silent and major" urban buildings, which are

difficult to classify and describe, constitute the contemporary and local nature of the built environment and lifestyle of each specific city (and region).

Aldo Rossi regards the city as a piece of artifact in his book The Architecture of the City. Although he does not deny the overall complexity and change of the city, based on the profound historical accumulation of Italian cities, he emphasizes the decisive significance of eternal monuments and continuity of types and structures to a city. In contrast, the current urban and rural built environment in China is crude, tenacious, short-term and fragile. They are quickly homogenized macroscopically and quite heterogeneous microscopically. This environment is constantly changing. People are used to be practical in the process of construction. In "Urban Architecture" based on this urban reality, we advocate that the eternity and integration are invalid; the urban architecture is fragmented and uncertain. We oppose that the design works be unique and authoritative. We argue that predetermined, goal-oriented performance should be replaced by instant, on-site and live effect. Free applications are recommended rather than any quotation of ideal and universal rules.

Dynamic Architecture with the Purpose of Usage and Application

Urban studies including Shanghai Project, Home Above Market, "Hongkou 1617", which focus on commonly-built envi-

永恒的作品不再重要，对于日常城市空间而言，这些甚至没有可能，因此也没有意义。即使是重要的地标，概念的凝固也是瞬间，只是使用变化的速度相对慢一点而已。基于现代主义建筑理想的确定计划和精准目标，建筑的纯粹性和完整性，与我们身处的快速城市化背景下的高密度聚居现实格格不入。城市建筑与空间的真正生命周期是建成之后使用者与空间的斗争与融合。这不仅体现在日常百姓的自发搭建中，也体现在存量发展时期各种改造更新的专业实践中。当改变被视为一种建筑的自然生长而不是进步行动时，无论是原创设计还是一般建造才能被一视同仁为一种以实用性和有效性为目的的环境调整。在"城市建筑学"中，不同时间、不同来源、不同性质的空间和物质同时并存，因此具有同等的意义。研究的目的是从经时间积累的改变现实中发掘使用与物质空间之间的普遍性关系和原理。设计的出发点和目标则是将既有现状作为中性的基础，将设计作为基于当下的需求所做的一次调整。它是一个过程而不是终点和目标，因此会进入持续使用和调整的循环中。

日常城市的改变与调整通常只关注局部或临时的利益和效率，倾向于采用灵活有效的策略和手段，往往信手拈来，少有章法。具体如形式、材料、建造，抽象如概念、原理、方法，一概不问出处，不求系统。它所关注的并非预设性能的完成度，而是实际效能的满足，完全是一种实用主义的应用策略。这种认知和方法同样适用于新的设计，尤其是那些满足普通生活需要而非重要历史文化象征的建筑类型和城市空间的新建与改造，比如一般的居住、商业、教育、公共服务设施等。阿科米星在实践中主张的混合与"非识别体系"，即没有预设地将各种理念、技术和方法视为等价物进行选择，灵活糅杂地加以应用，不追究背后特定的意义，不追溯来源的正统与乡野，这是基于城市现实的实践策略。利用既有资源根据新的使用要求做轻微操作尤其适用于普通的改造项目，阿科米星近年来完成的多个立面改妆（比如衡山坊8号楼、宝山陈化成纪念馆移建改造、上海龙华老人院等）[图12]和内部改造项目（比如宝山贝贝佳幼儿园、悦阅书店等）都采用了这样的策略。

系统化的悖论

将城市中自发的建造经验和无序的建筑现象系统化为

162

ronment in Shanghai, are all aiming at design research and its application. "Urban Architecture" constructed on this basis, in essence is the combinative application of modern architectural design principles and present urban spatial and daily life experience. These studies mainly focuses on the relationship between usage and physical space, between material technology and construction results. This relationship is not only the reality for the urban built environment, but also the core issue for architectural design. Although the complexity and uncertainty of the urban reality can endow itself vitality and characteristics, they can also invalidate the traditional design with preset objectives. Therefore, the study of "Hongkou 1617" advocates breaking the boundaries of classification and values in professional cognition. Classification includes not only functional attributes, but also scale, indoor/outdoor, overall/partial, public/private, formal/informal, building/equipment, etc. For example, the "Analytic Restoration" in North Sichuan Road, this case includes two renovations. A renovation of the facade on the front of ordinary commercial buildings and other equipment facade attached to the surface of residential buildings on the back. "Huangma Clubhouse" is an illegal building in the cracks of buildings and has now been demolished. Frankenstein's "St. Lu Xun" case includes three large buildings (complexes) and their connecting facilities. These complexes are Hongkou Football Stadium, Line 3 Light Rail Station, Hongkou CapitaLand. Value includes not

only beauty and ugliness, good and bad, but also usefulness/uselessness, rationality/irrationality, tradition/modernity, etc. More importantly, the study on reality includes time accumulation and even dynamic time. For example, many videos in *Line 3* are dynamic experiences of space with different speeds and lengths. However, functional or formal analysis of individual buildings is unable to provide such experience.

Traditional architecture focuses on the creation and evaluation of design works, judging how well the concepts match the results. "Urban Architecture" places its priority on changes in the built environment, including reasons for change, methods for change and results after change. For the urban environment, both professional design and increase or decrease in later use are regarded as the same process of change. "Urban Architecture" advocates a dynamic architecture. Accumulation and change usually happen in this architecture. It is no longer important whether the building is designed with considerate goals, whether there is a good match in its functions and forms, or whether the work is perfect or eternal. These points are meaningless because they aren't even possible for everyday urban space. Even if it is an important landmark, its urban space is still changing at a relatively slow speed. The precise planning and objectives of modernist architectural ideals, the purity and completeness of architecture, they are all incompatible with the reality of highly-dense settlements in the context of rapid urbanization.

12　徐汇区龙华街道敬老院立面
Facade of Xuhui Longhua Elder Care Center

The real life cycle of urban architecture and space begins with users' struggle and integration with space after completion. This is not only reflected in the spontaneous construction by local people in everyday life, but also in the professional renovation in the process of development. When change is seen as a natural growth of architecture rather than a progressive action, both original design and general construction can be treated equally as an environmental adjustment for practical and effective purposes. In "Urban Architecture", space and matter of different times, sources and properties coexist, so they have the same significance. The purpose of the study is to discover the universal relationship and principle between usage and physical space in the constantly changing reality. Design starts from taking the existing situation as a neutral basis, then makes adjustment to meet current needs. It is a process, neither a destination nor a goal, so it will enter a cycle of continuous use and adjust.

Everyday changes and adjustments in cities usually only focus on local or temporary benefits and efficiency. Designers tend to adopt flexible and effective strategies and means. As a result, concrete issues such as form, material, construction, concept, principle, method, are all adopted without seeking source and system. Compared with the present performance, people pay more attention to their actual effect. It is a completely pragmatic application strategy. This cognition and approach are also applicable to new designs, especially those ordinary building types and urban spaces, such as normal residential, commercial, educational and public service facilities. Because these designs usually aim at satisfying the ordinary life rather than representing an important historical and cultural symbol. The "Unrecognizable System" advocated by Atelier Archmixing in architectural design is a practical strategy based on urban reality. It regards various ideas, techniques, and methods as equivalents for selection without assumptions. It does not explore the specific meaning behind them, nor trace back to their origin. It applies them flexibly. Slight adjustments operated with the help of existing resources according to the new requirements are especially suitable for ordinary renovations. This strategy was applied by Atelier Archmixing to many renewal projects, including facade renovation, such as Building #8 in Hengshanfang, removal renovation of Chen Huacheng's Memorial in Baoshan district, Shanghai Longhua Elder's Care Center [fig. 12], etc.; and interior renovation, such as Baoshan Beibeijia Kindergarten, Yueyue Bookstore, etc.

Systematic Paradox

Is it practical and effective to systematize the spontaneous construction experience and disorderly architectural phenomena into rational professional design theories and methods? To what extent can the new design be preset and tolerant to the uncertainty in urban life? If, no matter how

理性的专业设计理论和方法是否切实有效？新的设计在多大程度上可能预设并包容城市生活的不确定性？假如无论设计考虑得多周到，随着时间推移，项目的使用对象、性质、需求都会持续改变的话（变是绝对的），建筑师的工作是否会因此陷入虚无和无据可依的境地？

城市的建造现实是一种广义的建造，大多并非出自专业人员之手——或是出自使用者的非正规搭建，或是因为时间积累混杂而成。"这种作为生存权利的建造跟以作品为导向的专业建造存在本质差异，究竟多大程度上可能在项目实践中加以学习和运用，还是研究和创作只能处于分裂状态？"[30] 如果单纯从形式上模仿这种片段和不确定是否会过于简单？与会学者对于阿科米星在项目实践中直接混合的形式策略，比如徐汇龙华老人院等提出质疑。[31]

更进一步，"传统建筑学是一种有明确限定的小建筑学，在这样的前提下才会讨论所谓神性、崇高、感知等内容，而日常生活、城市的复杂性、人的自主性，这些都是传统建筑学以外的内容，如果建筑学要覆盖这些领域就会成为一个大建筑学。这两种建筑学本质上是矛盾的。既然以现代主义为核心的经典建筑在城市现实中常常失效，

那么，我们转换之后创造出的建筑学就一定有效并适应中国的土壤吗？建构一种当代本土的建筑学是否真的可能和必要，难道只是专业人士的一厢情愿或者为了保留饭碗、留住权力的底线吗？"这些都是与城市研究和"城市建筑学"相关但不能轻易回答和下结论的问题。

针对"虹口1617"这样一个具体的、不尽完善的城市研究课题，众多学者和建筑师之所以能展开如此热烈的讨论和持续的追问，说明中国当下建成环境与建筑学主流系统之间的矛盾冲突已构成了明显的理论焦虑和策略困境。基本的共识是：无论参考久远的经验（传统）还是遥远的经验（西方），他山之石或可攻玉，但都不能取代我们在朝夕相处的建成环境和日常生活中获取的经验。此时此地由沉默的大多数建筑构成的城市现实中隐藏着未知的规律，只有不断地从现实中学习，并在认知和实践中超越现实，才可能走向"城市建筑学"——建构一种基于中国本土城市现实的当代建筑学。

本文作者系华霞虹，论文最初发表于《建筑学报》2017 (9): 103–109。

thoughtful the design is, the target, nature, and needs of the project will continuously change over time (absolutely), will the architect loose theories or strategies to follow?

The urban building reality is constructed in a broad sense. Most of them are not designed by professionals. They can be user's informal construction or a mixture formed as time goes by. "There is a fundamental difference between a construction aimed at a right for survival and a professional construction aimed to be a great work. To what extent is it possible to learn and apply in project practice? Can research and creation only be left separated?"[30] Would it be too simple to purely imitate this fragment and uncertainty in form? Scholars at the meeting questioned the direct mixing strategy adopted by Atelier Archmixing in its projects, such as Xuhui Longhua Elder's Care Center.[31]

Furthermore, "Traditional architecture as a discipline is a small architecture with a clear definition. Only under such definition will so-called divinity, sublimity, perception be discussed. However, the complexity of daily life and city, and human autonomy are beyond mainstream architecture. If architecture intends to cover these areas, it will become a bigger architecture. These two architectures are contradictory in nature. Though classical architecture with modernism as its core often fails in urban reality, will the architecture that we created be effective and adapted to China's situation? Is it possible and necessary to create contemporary indigenous architecture? Is it just the wishful way for professionals to keep their job and power? These are questions related to urban research and "Urban Architecture" which cannot be easily answered and concluded.

Given the specific and imperfect urban research topic of "Hongkou 1617", many scholars and architects have been able to launch such heated discussions and persistent questioning. It shows that the contradiction and confliction between the current built environment and the mainstream system of architecture in China have led to obvious theoretical anxiety and strategic dilemma. All the participants agreed that though traditional and western experiences can help us, the experience we acquire in the domestic built environment and daily life is incomparable. Unknown rules are hiding in urban reality, in those silent buildings. Only by continuous learning from reality and surpassing reality in cognition and practice can we move toward "Urban Architecture"—a modern architecture based on the urban reality in China.

The paper was written by Hua Xiahong, firstly published in *Architectural Journal* 2017 (9): 103–109.

8

《火星救援》与二手宇宙
The Martian and Used Universe

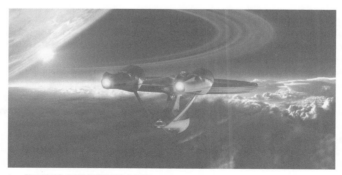

1　《星际迷航》电影里的宇宙飞船 企业号Enterprise_NCC1701
Spacecraft Enterprise_NCC1701 in the movie *Star Trek*

我们从何种角度来讨论建筑学里的"性能"[1]？

二手宇宙

在《星际迷航》[2]系列里，企业号[图1]像一个放在支架上的盘子，漂浮在黑色宇宙的背景里，形象看上去有点怪异，它的形式细节十分洁净流畅，通体一色，动力部分闪着幽蓝色的光芒。企业号的船员们同样身着统一的星际联盟的制服。没有比简约统一的技术腔更能在大众文化里象征智慧民主、性能先进、思想超越了。探索宇宙新边疆、发现生命存在意义的精神被简约优美的美学形式反映出来。

与这种崭新的、完整的形式形成对比的另外一种电影情景——二手宇宙[3]，是《星球大战》[4]里采用的道具与布景的制作方式。导演卢卡斯用一种旧宇宙[图2]的场景手法，一方面为节约制作费用，另一方面配合故事里以古老银河系作为背景的史诗故事的构想。这些场景当中混合了陌生银河星球的自然场景和各色星际生命文化。为星迷津津乐道的，自然有那想象力无限的技术装备，例如星帝国的行星毁灭者死星，帝国的行走机器人，号称全星系最

快的走私飞船千年隼，当然更有绝地武士的光剑，机器人好基友 R2D2 和 3PO。这些看上去感觉历经磨损的、外壳斑驳的飞行器、武器、机器人、器具，令人感觉仿佛到了外星的中世纪，或者是一个西部的银河系，形成了一道大众文化的未来思古大餐。

从性能角度来观察故事里的器具、设备、环境，无论是原装的《星际迷航》还是二手的《星球大战》，在观众、导演的世界里，工具或技术的性能被默认为满足需要的最高值。星际迷航的柯克船长和他的船员们每次遇到危机的时候，除了智慧勇气之外，科幻的技术每每也是帮助他们化险为夷的主要保障。技术无限可能与性能无限满足都服务于剧情的需要，可以任意选择。这些设备与武器是完美的，但它们的完美并非靠性能如何决定，决定它们的关键是符号性——工具或技术性能的形式才是被讨论与关注的。就像所有的童话故事一样，星战中黑武士的黑色铠甲面具、嘶嘶的呼吸声象征了大能原力的黑暗面，而打扮成僧侣组织长老会气质的绝地武士，使用着象征了绝地武士的精神、力量与身份标识——古老而精致的光剑，代表了原力大能的光明集合。这些都成为典型的电影工业文化制

From what angle shall we discuss the "performance" in architecture? [1]

Used Universe

In the *Star Trek* series,[2] Enterprise [fig. 1] looks like a tray on a bracket, floating in the black universe. It looks a little weird with clean and smooth form details, all in one color, and the power section glowing blue. The crew on Enterprise is also dressed in the uniform of the Star Alliance. There is no better symbol of wisdom and democracy, advanced performance and transcendent ideas in popular culture than a simple and unified technology. The spirit of exploring the new frontier of the universe and discovering the meaning of life's existence is reflected in the simple and beautiful aesthetic form.

In contrast to this brand-new and complete form, *Star War*[4] applied another style to make props and movie scenes, which was known as "Used Universe".[3] Director Lucas uses an Old Universe [fig. 2] scenario to save production costs on the one hand and to match the idea of an epic story set in an ancient galaxy on the other. These scenes are mixed with the natural scenes of the strange galactic planets and their living culture. The *Star War* fans indulge in those unimaginable technological devices, such as the Walking Robot, the Death Star of the Star Destroyer designed by Galactic Empire, the Millennium Falcon, the fastest smuggling spaceship in the galaxy, not to mention the lightsaber of the Jedi Knights, and

robots R2D2 and 3PO. These seemingly worn-out aircraft, weapons, robots, and appliances with mottled hulls make one feel like an alien medieval, or a Western Milky Way, forming a great piece of recalling the past in the future for popular culture.

With the perspective of performance, for both audiences and directors, when observing the appliance, device, and environment, whether in the original Star Trek or the used Star Wars, a tool or technology is defaulted to possess the most satisfied quality. Captain Kirk of Star Trek and his crew, in addition to their courage and wisdom, are often assisted with Sci-Fi technology to survive every crisis. Unlimited technical possibility and performance are all needed to serve the plot and can be chosen at will. These devices and weapons are perfect, but their perfection is not determined by performance, but symbolism — the form of tools or technical performance is the one that would be discussed and concerned. Like all fairy tales, the black armor masks and hissing breaths of the black samurai in Star Wars symbolize the dark side of the Almighty Power, while the Jedi Knights dressed up as the PCUSA, a monk organization, use the ancient and exquisite lightsaber, the symbol of the Jedi spirit, strength and identity as the bright set of Almighty Power. All these have become the products of the typical film industry culture.

In the first *Star Wars* movie, Luke Skywalker, dressed in coarse clothes, looked out over a barren planet with two suns; then Obi-Wan, a secluded man, told him a long, dusty history

造的产物。

　　第一部星战电影里，刚登场的天行者卢克身着粗布衣服，在空旷荒瘠的有着两个太阳的行星上眺望远方；之后隐居的欧比旺向他讲述久远尘封的历史与身世，展示绝地的精致武器光剑，这件形式颇具仪式感的武器舞动时会引发嗡嗡的空气震颤声。广阔宇宙的孤独情怀、银河系穷乡僻壤的日常生活、大能精神的技术混合在一起。在电影故事的世界里，文化在这样的背景里被烘托出来 [图3]。在那里，并非性能本身，而是工具与技术性能的精神情怀与文化是被追求的最高目标，在二手质感的衬托下，形式成为一种象征与仪式。

　　在电影这样的虚幻世界的内外，物质、情感、文化、技术都是建构故事的各种元素，同样，性能也是一个可供设定的虚幻元素。

性能与表现

　　在建筑学的学术建构里，关于性能的讨论是否同样也存在着这样根据"剧情需要"来定义的情况？

　　我们在讨论建筑学的技术与性能的时候，显然不只是

2　二手宇宙
Used Universe

and his life experience while displaying the finest weapon of the Jedi, lightsaber, which trembled when brandished. The loneliness of the vast universe, the everyday life in the backwoods of the galaxy, and the technology of the Almighty Spirit mingle. In the movie story, culture is set up in such a background [fig. 3]. There, not the performance itself, but the spiritual feelings and culture of tools and technical performance are the highest goal to be pursued, and form becomes a symbol and ritual against the backdrop of used texture.

In a fictitious world like movies, material, emotion, culture, and technology are elements that construct the story. Similarly, performance is also a fictitious element that can be set.

Performance and Presentation

In the academic construction of architecture discipline, does the discussion of performance also exist in such a way as to be defined according to the plot?

When discussing the technology and performance of architecture, it is obviously not limited to the principle and effect of architectural technology and performance itself. Like the "used universe" in movies, the study and practice of a discipline, no matter to what extent, can never avoid the question of how to formally express the characteristics and spirit of technology or performance. Performance is required to meet functional demands, it is also combined in archi-

3　《星际迷航》电影里的天行者卢克
Luke Skywalker in the movie *Star Trek*

在讨论建筑技术与性能本身的原理与功效。如同电影里的二手宇宙一样，学科的研究与实践不管程度如何，最终都回避不了在形式上如何表达技术或性能的特征与精神这个问题。性能不仅需要满足功能的需要，而且需要被结合在建筑形式里，同时呈现为一种属于建筑学的视觉语言、空间体验。就如同结构设计不仅要是安全的，而且形式要是具有安全感的；环境控制设计不仅要求实际是有效的，而且形式要有控制与交流感。越是在意学科的自主性，就会越强调建筑形式表现语言的自主性，对于性能的讨论也会更趋典型化和类型化，这进一步加剧了对作为文化表现而非具体效用的性能的追求，甚至最终不知不觉局限于此。以往从结构技术到建构方式，都受到这种趋向的影响，有时会出现结构化的建筑形式，构造化的建筑细节。建筑学的不断发展，使以往在认识上被分离在外的设备技术、环境控制等更多的层面逐步开始被重新整合并纳入到本学科系统化的思考中来。但同样值得提醒，并需要作为研究和实践来思考的问题是，我们要讨论的究竟是技术还是技术化的建筑形式，是性能还是性能化的建筑表现？抑或应该是两者之间的一种形式？

更进一步，现实世界有很多与性能使用相关的现象不被建筑学讨论所重视，不会被视作建筑学世界的一部分。最典型的莫过于对"建筑"与"建物"的刻意区分，所谓"自行车棚不是建筑"，就是把纯粹功能使用、不具有文化属性的建造物排除在学科讨论范围以外，并以此建构建筑学的边界和建筑的意义。又比如日常生活世界里那些普通的建筑使用改造就不是典型的建筑学，即便讨论，也是作为一类边缘的现象。如果在一个资源相对充沛的星球上，衣食无忧，没有像故事里面那样的担心，包括随时食物短缺，空气无法呼吸，户外气温瞬间冻死你，真空抽干你体内的水分这样的情况，建筑的存在被认为必然是一种构筑了很多文化、思想、潮流、时尚的东西，那么我们在讨论怎样的建筑的性能？是面对使用条件苛刻的真枪实弹，还是将其界定在某种特定语境内讨论？

性能符号化，性能被文化选择，成为故事化的性能、表现的性能，这样的情况使得关于性能的讨论似乎经常被局限在功能与表现之间打转，之所以会这样，很重要的一个原因是因为既有的建筑学的研究与实践语境一直处在设计与完成之间，处在预设与检验之间，是一种"预设—检

tectural form as a kind of architectural visual language and spatial experience. Just like structural design, which shall not only ensure safety, but also in a form of safety; the design of environmental control not only requires actual effectiveness, but also a sense of control and communication in the form. The more concerned about the autonomy of the discipline, the more emphasis will be placed on the autonomy of the language of architectural form expression, and the discussion of performance will become more typical and typified, which further intensifies the pursuit of performance as a cultural expression rather than specific utility, and even ultimately unconsciously confined to this. In the past, from structural technology to construction methods, all are subject to such a trend, which sometimes become a structurized architectural form, or tectonicized architectural details. With the continuous development of architecture, equipment technology and environmental control, which were separated from knowledge in the past, are gradually being re-integrated and incorporated into the systematic thinking of this subject. But it is also worth reminding and considering in research and practice, what we want to discuss is technology or technologized architectural form, performance or performance-based architectural presentation, or a form between them?

Furthermore, there are many phenomena in the real world related to performance usage that is not taken seriously in architectural discussions and considered as a part of the architectural world. Nothing is more typical than the deliberate distinction between "architecture" and "building". The so-called "bicycle shed is not an architecture" is to exclude buildings with purely functional usage without cultural attributes from the scope of academic discussion, and to construct boundaries of architecture and architectural significance. Usage and transformation of ordinary buildings in the everyday world, for example, are not typical architectures, and only discussed as a marginal phenomenon. If you're on a relatively resource-rich planet with food and clothing, and you don't have to be worried as in the next story, including food shortage, air shortage, low outdoor temperatures that freeze you instantly, and vacuum drying your body, so the existence of architecture is considered more as something that constructs cultures, thoughts, trends, and fashions. So what kind of building performance are we discussing? Is it live ammunition against harsh conditions? Or is it a discussion defined in a specific language?

The symbolization of performance, that the performance is chosen by culture and becomes storytelling and expression, makes the discussion on performance seem to be often confined to the function and expression. One reason is that the research and practice context of existing architecture is always between design and completion, between presupposition and inspection. This is a system of presupposition-inspection. If we make division based on building construction

验系统"。如果我们以建筑的建成作为划分，将之前视作设计的概念阶段，建筑使用前的阶段；将之后视作设计的使用阶段，建筑的改变阶段，那么，既有建筑学并未严肃地将关心与研究的视线投到使用与变化的阶段，即使偶尔讨论与研究，也旨在为前面的设计阶段服务。至于形式与性能的表现性，可视化的性能所讨论的，则是建筑建成之前阶段的表现。

《火星救援》

如果将性能讨论放到建筑的使用改变阶段，会有什么启发？不妨来看另一个故事。让我们先抛开现实世界里很多好的建筑案例，把情况放到比日常建筑的情况更极端的状态去讨论，以便更简单清晰地进行比较论述。

《火星救援》是由美国 20 世纪福克斯电影公司出品的科幻片 [图4]。故事讲述了阿瑞斯计划 3 进行的火星计划，赫尔墨斯号飞船载着六位宇航员登陆火星，由于一场突然的火星沙尘暴，被队友误以为丧生的马克·沃特尼与他的团队失联，孤身一人被留在火星，面临在绝地环境里的生死考验，想方设法被营救回到地球的故事。这是一个

4 《火星救援》海报
Movie poster, *The Martian*

169

with the previous stages as the conceptual stage of design and pre-use stage of building, and the coming stages as the usage stage of design and change stage of building, then existing architecture discipline does not seriously focus on the usage and change stages for research. Even if occasionally discussed and studied, it is also designed to serve the previous design stage. Those discussions on the representativeness of form and performance or visual performance concern only the representation before the building is constructed.

The Martian

What will be inspired if the performance discussion is applied to the stage of architectural usage change? Here we have another story. Let's put aside a lot of good building cases in the real world and discuss the situation in a more extreme state than the situation of everyday buildings, so that it can be discussed more simply and clearly.

The Martian is a sci-fi film produced by 20th Century Fox Film Corporation [fig. 4]. The story is about the Mars program of Ares 3. The Hermes spacecraft, carrying six astronauts, landed on Mars. Mark Watney, mistaken for death by his teammates due to a sudden Martian dust storm, lost contact with his team, and was left alone on Mars, facing the test of life and death in the Jedi environment and trying to get back to earth. It's a science-fiction feature film, and because of the hard science fiction approach, the technical part of the story

5 《火星救援》影片场景种土豆
Planting potatoes in *The Martian*

科幻剧情片，由于采用了硬科幻的方式，其中如何科学求生的故事中的技术部分讲来还是有根有据。

这是一个"被逼到死角"来讨论性能的有效性的故事。事实上，故事里的自救与救援计划总是处在走钢丝的要命境地，由于留在火星上的栖息地与设备预先都没有考虑到需要长时间地维持生命系统，而只是根据短时的科研探测使用设计，失去后备支持的宇航员只能自己利用现有的条件来设法维持生命，创造条件，直到获得救援。生命仰仗着一系列被极限改造和使用的新系统来维持，而这个系统还处于随时临界和崩溃的状态。马克总是面临稍有不慎就会大难临头的情况，救命的方法往往是刚好够，按马特的语气来说就是：要么就是压根就没有解决办法，最后死翘翘，要么就是没找到那个解，同样死翘翘。这些方法不是性能使用的最优解，而是实用目的的唯一解。比如宇航员需要坚持很长时间来等待救援，马特要解决粮食短缺问题。本来储存的食物可以维持 300 个火星日，他必须利用手上的条件与资源支撑 1400 多个火星日。他最大限度地利用栖息仓 92 平方米的用地面积来培植土豆，改装了设备，改变了原来的温度、湿度等环境，创造出适合土豆生长的环境 [图5]。这些改造都不得不以达到目标为唯一衡量标准，为了有效利用仅有的少量土壤肥力多种土豆，马特不管土壤肥力的可持续，只管计算在得救的时间内土壤能有效地被充分利用。在马特的火星上，在资源匮乏的环境里，他不断地利用手上的资源与知识进行环境制造、调整、应急。在最基本的生存关头，艺术、时尚、建筑学式的语言都靠边站了。活命的有效性是整个事件中利用资源、工具，创造生存环境最重要的性能评价标准。

笔者看来，性能一词虽然本是一个中性客观的词，但由于建筑学的习惯语境与使用范围，其语义偏重于从系统的预设目标与最终系统建立后的使用测评两者之间的匹配和比较来评判设计的有效性，它更偏重针对于系统本身。需要用另外一个词来定义《火星救援》里有关性能的描述，区别于上面的"预设—检验系统"的标准。我们姑且用"效能"这个词来描述。效能偏重于从使用或者目的角度评判有效性。区分性能与效能的语境与含义，在笔者看来就是区分静态设计与动态使用两种观察与评判的角度，以使讨论性能时范围完整。《火星救援》中一直在做斗争与争取的是一个效能问题，实际问题处理的有效性。建筑

about how to survive scientifically is well documented.

This is a story of "being pushed to the dead-end" to discuss the efficiency of performance. In fact, the self-rescue and rescue programs in the story are always on the tightrope, because the habitats and equipment left on Mars do not antic-ipate the need for long-term life support, but are designed for short-term scientific exploration, and the astronauts without backup support can only make use of what he has to maintain life, create conditions until being saved. Life is maintained by a series of new systems that have been adapted and used to the limit, and that system is still in a state of critical and near collapse at any time. Mark is always faced with a difficult situ-ation if he lost his mind just for a moment and the way to save life is often just enough, just as the man said: either there is no solution at all, and finally he dies, or the solution is not found then he dies. These methods are not the optimal solutions of performance, but the only solution of practical purpose. For example, the astronaut needs to persist for a long time to wait for rescue. Mark had to solve the food shortage. The food stored support for 300 Martian days, and he would have to support more than 1,400 Martian days with the conditions and resources at hand. He maximized the use of a 92m² habitat silo to cultivate potatoes, and created a suitable environment for potatoes to grow by refitting equipment, and changing the original temperature and humidity environment [fig. 5]. In order to effectively utilize only a small amount of soil fertility for more potatoes, Mark, regardless of the sustainability of soil fertility, calculated if the soil could be effectively utilized within the time saved, taking the achievement of purpose as the only measurement criteria. On Mark's Mars, a resource-poor environment, he constantly used his resources and knowledge to make, adjust, and respond to environmental problems. In the face of the most basic survival, languages of art, fashion, and architecture are set aside in the whole event. The efficien-cy of life is the most important performance evaluation criteria for applying resources and tools to create a living environment.

I believe, although the term "performance" is a neutral and objective word, because of the customary context and the usage in the architectural field, its semantics focuses on judging the effect of design from the matching and compar-ison between the presupposed objectives of the system and its use after establishment. In other words, it focuses more on the system itself. An alternative term is needed to define the performance descriptions in *The Martian*, which differs from the presupposition-test system standard above. Let's first describe it with the term "effect". Effect is more important than judging effectiveness from the view of use or purpose. The author believes, in order to distinguish the contexts and meanings of performance and effect, which also means distinguish static design from dynamic to complete the scope of performance discussion. What has been fighting for in *The Martian* is the effect of dealing with practical problems.

设计有时候认为使用会沿着预判的设定来进行，但实际往往不是这样的，更多的时候，这是一个不断被调整的系统，不断可能重置的系统。失效之后的建筑体系会出现一种以使用为目的不断构筑的"建筑学"，它是对预设的完整系统的摧毁，也是对既有建筑学认识观念的拓展。

在这些应急改造里，原来为既定目的定制的栖息仓、火星车、升空器等统统不适合新的用处，在改造的时候原来的设计很多成了冗余。有效的使用与改造使部分改变了，去除了冗余，但部分不得不留在那里。使用的有效性是将去除不掉的冗余计算在内的，让它得以保留，有效改造也是在既有的基础上进行的，也就是说不会去耗费资源为了新的目的进行完整的整体设计与整体改造。效能是在一种有冗余的系统里出现的，是系统冗余状态下的效能。这与在一个全新系统里的精确对应的构想是完全不同的思考方式。在最后利用 MAV 火星升空器到达计划轨道的时候，为了能达到高轨道与同伴会合，宇航员几乎拆掉了能拆掉的所有重量，乘坐了一个没有顶棚，没有操作台的筒子上了天，但即使这样，还有很多无法拆除的部分留在那里，使他们担心会影响会合。回到建筑的世界里，这样的

有效性的案例在日常的城市当中是很多的。比如城市里的一些建筑，不时会出现空置或者废弃空间与正常使用空间并存的现象 [图6]。

失效与体系

《火星救援》另一个重要提示是失效，它讲了一个系统失效之后会怎样的故事。失效后的系统可以让我们更客观地回视原来系统存在的逻辑。失效让我们考查建筑学一直以来采用的习惯思维方式是否存在问题。系统失效之后暴露出来的问题，表面上看是静态系统（事先预设功能的弹性设计、可变设计也是一种静态模式）的失效问题，然而笔者认为，更关键的问题并非指向系统的静态化，而是指向创造该系统的体系完整化的思维方式。

体系完整化的思考方式从学科上并不难理解。习惯上，建筑学科的学科逻辑是一种"概念—设计（建造）成果"的完整体系，其结果是形态与概念统一完整的设计或建筑，这样的设计或建筑有着本身完整的系统。这样的思维方式，不仅来自学科本身的建构方式，也来自现代生产体系——系统化的思想也会自上而下地塑造建筑学的学科

Architectural design sometimes assumes that the use will proceed along with the predetermined settings, but this is often not the case. More often than not, this is a system that is constantly being adjusted and being possibly replaced. After the failure of the conventional building system, an "architecture" will be constantly constructed for the purpose of usage, which destructs the presupposition of the complete system, and expands the existing recognition on existing architecture.

In these emergency retrofits, the original customized habitat silo, Mars rover, launcher, and other systems are no longer suitable for new uses. Most of the original design has become redundant. Effective usage and transformation have only partially changed and removed these redundancies, some have to be kept. Some have already been included in the usage efficiency through calculation and thus kept. The effective transformation is also carried out on the existing basis. In other words, resources will not be consumed for new purposes to complete the overall design and transformation. Therefore, effect occurs in a redundant system, which is the effect of the system redundancy. This is completely different from the way of thinking in the precise correspondence of a new system. When the MAV was finally used to reach the planned orbit, the astronaut removed almost all the weight that could be removed to get to the high orbit and rendezvous with their fellow astronauts. He rode up into the sky on a barrel with no ceiling and console. But even so, there were still many parts

that could not be removed and retained, which may affect rescue mission. Back to the world of architecture, there are many examples of such effectiveness in everyday cities. For example, some buildings in the city, from time to time, appear empty or have abandoned space coexisting with spaces normally used [fig. 6].

Failure and System

Another lesson we learned from *The Martian* is failure. It tells a story about what happens after a system fails. The failed system enables us to look back more objectively on the logic of the original system and examine whether there is a problem with the customary mode of thinking used in architecture. The problems exposed after the failure of the system appear to be related to the static system (elastic design and variable design with pre-set functions are also a static mode). However, the author believes that the more important problem is not the static of the system, but the way of thinking that creates the system integrity.

It is not difficult to understand the way of thinking about system integrity from a disciplinary perspective. Traditionally, the disciplinary logic of architecture is a complete system of "concept - design (construction) results", from which, design or architecture uniformed and complete in form, and concepts are obtained within their own complete systems. This way of thinking comes not only from the construction of the discipline itself,

6　城市调研：水电路新中新村"二分之一房"
Urban Study "Half House", Shuidian Road, Shanghai, 2016–2017

7　城市调研：皇玛俱乐部夹缝加建
Urban Study "Huangma Club", Tongxin Road, Shanghai, 2016

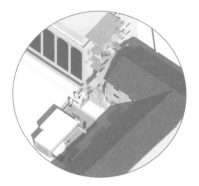

8　皇玛俱乐部楼间搭建的轴测图
Axonometric drawing of Huangma Club

9　樟吴制衣厂改造项目
Renovation of Garment Factory in Zhangwu Village

10　棉仓城市客厅改造项目
Cotton Lab Urban Lounge

思维，使之成为习惯。然而时至今日，这样的思维在建筑学研究上会越来越阻碍研究者与实践者的思路，实际是一个观念误区。这样的建筑学认为好的建筑必须是完整的；认为可以预先建构一个个建筑的系统来解决（表达）所想解决的建筑问题，这些系统是完整的，并且很重要的是能够用可视化的形式与空间来表达、表现建筑的概念。

　　然而大量的实际情况并非如此。《火星救援》中，完整的系统设计构筑出来的体系在新的情况下瞬间失效了，是应急的改变最后重新起了作用。类似的拯救与应急，从使用角度出发的建筑现象与实践在我们生活的世界里也是常态。那些建筑物被按照事先设定的功能要求设计出来，对应于预设目标的系统在投入使用后，现实的情况可能就是不断地变化与被调整，以适应不断冒出来的新的使用需求。城市里有无数这样的案例，涉及各类空间。不仅涉及单体建筑，也涉及城市空间。比如上海虹口区原皇玛俱乐部的违章居住搭建 [图7-9] 是阿科米星事务所虹口调研的一个案例，搭建者为了解决在城市里就近居住的使用需求，创造了令人惊叹的建造实例。新增构筑依附于两个建筑物之间增设的简易疏散楼梯，利用每个室内外空间与建

筑结构物件，成为能够生活使用的地方。楼梯成为居所，每个台阶与栏杆都可能成为空调、衣架、杂物的安置之地，楼下的空地围成了院子，停放非机动车，洗漱、做饭都在里面。生活分散在室内室外的各种场所。被解构的形态是一种实用的空间争取策略，在这个寸土寸金的城市里取得了一席之地。我们发现，无数类似的建筑现象反而形成了生活中的建筑的某种典型性。在这些案例里，效能与建筑的状态无关，与结构、材料、构造、设备等体系本身或既有设计的预设无关，与体系完整度无关，而和能被使用的条件与需要达到的目的有关。

　　对于这样的情况，建筑无法用习惯的体系、完整化的思维来理解与描述。发生这种情况的是习惯的建筑学思维失效的领域，却又是建筑活动效能极高的领域。类似的现象不仅是可以描述观察的日常自发现象，也同样是可以设计再现，可以用作实际解决问题的方式。比如阿科米星主持设计的樟吴制衣厂改造项目（未建）[图10] 与常州棉仓改造项目（在建）[图11]。这两个案例的实际条件与设计的目的各不相同，但由于各自的综合原因，都将原有的房屋看成是既有环境，某种像自然之物一样中性的存在物，而

but also from the modern production system. This systematic thinking has shaped the convention of architecture discipline thinking from top to bottom, making it a habit. However, today, such thinking increasingly hinders researchers and practitioners in architecture research. In fact, it is a misconception, which holds that a commendable architecture must be complete; that it is possible to pre-construct a system of buildings to solve (express) the architectural problems it intends to address; that these systems are complete, and that its concept could be expressed and represented with visual form and space.

However, this is not the case on most occasions. In *The Martian*, the system constructed on a complete system of design suddenly failed, reworked only after emergency change. Such rescue and emergency events are also common in the real world, as well as architectural phenomenon and practices that focus on usage. Buildings are designed according to pre-set functional requirements, while the system corresponding to pre-set objectives may constantly change and adjust to meet new requirements after accommodation. There are numerous such cases in the city, involving all kinds of space. It involves not only single buildings, but also urban spaces. For example, the illegal addition of former Huangma Clubhouse in Hongkou District of Shanghai [Fig. 7-9] is a case study by Atelier Archmixing. The builders have created an amazing construction example to address the demand for living nearby. The new facilities were added to the simple

evacuation staircase between two buildings. Each indoor and outdoor space and structural elements are exploited for living. Staircases become homes, each step and railing may be loaded with air-conditioners, clothes hangers or sundries, and the opening downstairs is occupied by non-motorized vehicles and become a place for washing and cooking. Life traces can be found in every corner. The decomposed form is a practical strategy for space struggle, in order to gain a place in this city where each inch of land is expensive. We find that countless similar architectural phenomena have formed some typical characteristics of everyday buildings.

In these cases, the effect has nothing to do with the state of the building, structure, material, construction, equipment and other systems or the presupposition of the existing design, or the integrity of the system, but related to the available conditions desired purposes. For such a situation, architecture cannot be understood and described in the conventional logic of systematic integrity. These situations spring in where those traditional architectural logics fail, while architectural activities remain highly effective. Similar phenomena can not only be observed and described in everyday spontaneous phenomenon, but also applied in design reproduction, or be used as a practical solution. The renovation projects of Zhangwu Garment Factory (not built) [fig. 10] and Changzhou Cotton Urban Lab [fig. 11] designed by Atelier Archmixing are examples in this regard. Although differing in actual conditions

只在室内的局部空间里创造形成解决问题的"小建筑物"，一个局部的环境。"小建筑物"内的环境与大空间的环境在设计中采用完全不同的标准策略。从这些案例可以看出，习惯上的建筑的体系完整化的思维往往是有效于被设计的建筑物的形成创立阶段，而失效于建筑使用之后或者建筑改变之时。因此，当我们讨论性能继而讨论建筑的时候，我们已不能受制于学科原有的思维范围，而应该将讨论的视野放到更大的范围内。

建筑学需要改变思维，因为要将研究与视野扩展至以前不被重视的阶段，即建筑建成之后，被使用被改变之时。建筑学需要改变思维，也因为我们设定设计策略的设计的前期条件变化也很明显，足以影响设计的认识和方法。世界的日常运行从某个角度来看，正变得越来越"轻"。一方面，建筑建构的体系越来越不稳定。或许不稳定是本来就固有的一种属性，只是一直处在主流建筑学试图一厢情愿建构的稳定的模式体系之外，被视而不见。建筑物本身具有的适应改变的弹性，建筑物设计的提前量，已不能适应现实与未来的变化节奏。另一方面，正在发生的一个重要的变化是：稳定的、"重"的东西已日益大系统化、隐形化。这就像那些看不见的巨大的电力系统、排水设施、网络系统、物流系统、生活网络一样。很多东西已经不再是传统建筑学认为的是在场的、可视的。建筑本身会成为解决功能的大系统里的一个部分，而不能再单独维持一个完整的独立系统。因此，认为单体建筑能够可视化地表现功能、维持系统的想法也开始失效，无法有效地回应出现的系统变化。需要去突破旧体系的建筑学时代，会出现跳出既有体系的策略与组织方式。新的方式必然会促成应对物质世界的新策略。在那样的情况下，物质世界的使用组织逻辑会改变。然而物质世界不可移动，因此必然会出现冗余，而且会越来越明显。这样的改变已经到来，建筑空间的未来冗余并非是由系统的败坏决定的，而是由体系的主动改变决定的。建筑学对于性能的讨论应该拓展至那样的环境下进行。

《〈火星救援〉与二手宇宙》是庄慎在《新建筑》2016 年 10 月的"工具／工艺 – 环境调控"北京研讨会上的主题演讲。本文在此基础上整理扩展而成，发表于《新建筑》2017 (5)：7–11。

and design purposes, both projects saw original houses as existing environments, some kind of neutral existence like natural things. Small buildings are designed inside the former structure to solve functional problems, achieving a partial environment. The environment in the "small building" and that of the big space adopt completely different design standards and strategies. Based on these cases, it can be seen that the architectural thinking of systematic integrity is often effective in the design stage, but invalid after the building was put into usage and began to change. Therefore, when we discuss performance and architecture, we should no longer subject to the conventional disciplinary thinking, because this should be discussed with a wider vision.

Since the pre-stage conditions for design strategies shift frequently, architecture demands different thinking. It is necessary to extend research and vision to those previously ignored stages, including the state when buildings are built, used and changed, and also those changes, which are obvious enough to affect the recognition and design methodology. From some perspectives, the everyday operation of the world becomes lighter and lighter. On one hand, the system built for architecture is less stable, which may be one of its inherent attributes long ignored by mainstream architecture discourse which insists a stable system. The designed architectural flexibility can no longer adapt to the changing rhythm of reality and the future. On the other hand, an important change that is taking place is that what is stable and "heavy" has become increasingly systematic and invisible, just like those invisible infrastructures, such as huge power systems, drainage facilities, network systems, logistics systems, and life networks, etc. Many things are no longer what the traditional architecture considers to be present and visible. The building itself will become part of the larger system of the functional solution, and no longer be able to maintain a complete, independent system alone. Therefore, the idea that a single building can visualize its functions and solve problems from the above-mentioned complicated system has begun to fail, and it is unable to respond effectively to the changes in the system. When architecture needs to break through, strategies and ways will emerge. The new way will contribute to new strategies for the physical world. In that case, organizational logic for the usage of the material world will change. However, the material world is immovable, so redundancy will definitely occur and become increasingly obvious. Such changes have come, and the future redundancy of architectural space is not determined by the failure of the system, but its active change. Discussion on performance in architecture should be expanded to such context.

"*The Martian* and Used Universe" is Zhuang Shen's keynote speech at the "Tool/Process-Environmental Regulation" Beijing Symposium in October 2016, based on which, the paper is structured and expanded, firstly published in *New Architecture*, 2017 (5): 7–11.

9

看不见的改变：
论使用端空间技术化的可能
Invisible Change:
Technologizing Space
at the User's End

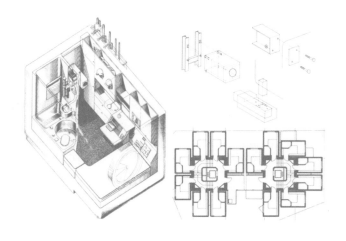

1   黑川纪章，中银舱体大楼，"舱体"单元
Kurokawa Kisho, Nakagin Capsule Tower, "Capsule" Unit

相信建筑必然会被科技发展改变的这条思维线索在建筑学里虽然时隐时显，但一直存在。

今天，建筑学内部出现越来越多的新议题，同时，建筑业再一次明显地感受到自身之外的各类技术的快速发展，感受到身处其中的这个世界，巨大的格局改变即将来临。

基于这样的预感，做出相应行动之前，有必要重新审视以往那些杰出的建筑师们应对技术变迁的思考和行动，分析他们后来行动受挫可能的原因，从这些经验中获得启示。同时，必须思索新的科技将如何改变未来的建筑。

技术乐观派的挫折

20世纪60—70年代，随着太空探索与阿波罗登月计划的成功，全世界都深信科学技术会让我们曾经分崩离析的世界再次完整地应对未来。建筑学领域早在20世纪初就为未来主义运动中所展示的技术潜力所震撼，如今更是对新技术将带来彻底的建筑革命充满信心。世界各地集中涌现出一批信奉新技术的建筑理念、团体和建筑师，比如大家所熟知的日本的新陈代谢派、英国的建筑电讯派、涉及多国建筑师和实践的高技派，等等。跟未来主义一样，他们都属于技术乐观派，相信科技和技术的作用，关注建筑发展与科技发展的紧密联系，努力要拆除建筑文化与科技文化之间的隔离。

反对技术象征主义

技术乐观派们无疑都是清醒而坚定地反对技术象征主义的，反对仅仅是因为其"……发明和创造出象征这个世界的形式"[1]，他们试图避免这个20世纪20年代的现代主义建筑大师们所犯的错误。然而，正如雷纳·班纳姆在1960年完成的著作《第一机械时代的理论和设计》一书中所述："我们可以认为第一机械时代的建筑师们是错的，但处在第二机械时代的我们，还没有超越他们的理由。"[2] 令人沮丧的是，20世纪六七十年代这些建筑团体的理念与实践最终被贴上了像"高技派"这样的标签，他们陷入自身所反对的"时代的象征"的境地。他们最终没有成为实践上一直延续的主流，其受挫的原因是很复杂的。

The thought of believing that architecture will be changed by the development of science and technology always exist, though it is not fully considered.

Today, there are more new topics emerging in the architectural field. Meanwhile, the architectural profession has apparently witnessed a rapid growth of various technologies. A huge change is coming.

Based on such vision, before taking some correspondent actions, it is necessary that we review the thoughts and actions taken by the prominent architects in the past, analyze the possible cause of their failure and learn from those experiences. And we must think deeply about how science and technology will change the future architecture.

Setback of the Technological Optimists

Back in the 1960s and 1970s, with the success of space exploration and *Apollo Plan*, the whole world started to believe that science and technology would unify again our world which had been torn apart into pieces to face the future. Early at the beginning of the 20th century, the architecture had been deeply shocked by the potential of technology presented by Futurism. Likewise, today the whole field feels great confident in a thorough revolution of architecture brought by new technologies. There had been ideas, groups and architects worshipping new technologies all over the world, such as the well-known "New Metabolism" (Japan), "Archigram" (UK), "High-Tech" composed of architects and practices in various countries. Like Futurism, they were all Technological Optimists who believed in the effect of science and technology. They kept a close eye on the link between the development of architecture and technology, and tried to break down the wall between them.

Objection of Technological Symbolism

The Technological Optimists are no doubt staunch opponents of Technological Symbolism, although what they object is only "to invent and create forms symbolizing that world"[1]. They tried to avoid the mistakes made by the modernist architects in the 1920s. However, just as Reyner Banham said in his book *Theory and Design in the First Machine Age* (1960) that "we may believe that the architects of the First Machine Age were wrong, but we in the Second Machine Age have no reason yet to be superior about them"[2]. However, it is frustrating that the ideas and practices of these architectural groups in the 1960s and 1970s were finally labeled as "High-Tech" and trapped in the idea of "Symbol of the Times" which they opposed. Eventually, they failed to be the mainstream in practice. The cause of this frustration was very complicated.

Partial Systematic Vision

The biggest problem the Technological Optimists faced in the middle of the 20th century was their limited knowledge

局部的系统视野

20 世纪中叶的技术乐观派们最大的问题是对于建构系统整体性的片面认识。

从巴克敏斯特·富勒到诺曼·福斯特，技术乐观派的共同之处是，试图重建一个大的系统。他们都认为并希望通过拥抱技术可以建立起一种可控的新的完整生态，创造系统性的最大效果。技术的视野的确为这些建筑师创造另一种新系统提供了可能。只可惜，他们重建系统的思维落脚点最终局限在建筑创造的局部体系中。对于社会整体的生产与消费系统，尤其是建筑空间对使用端的意义，他们的意识薄弱。因此，他们的理想模型注定是残缺和矛盾的。一方面，他们不再将日常生活的使用与科技、工业生产当成对立的领域来看待，比如福斯特提倡建筑即产品。但另一方面，他们仍旧是从生产端角度在思考改变，他们保留以建筑为核心构建体系的传统方式，致力于把一座建筑设计成一件理念完备、效益完美的集成产品。他们忽视了现代经济生产的价值并不局限于创造的部分或生产的部分，而应连同使用、消费、消耗一起衡量。生产和消费构成了一个循环的体系，其核心是小心翼翼地建立起周而复

始的生产—消费系统的全面平衡。令人惋惜的是，技术乐观派们的系统视野是局部的。他们为了创造更好的系统效益所做的工作与实际的社会系统是矛盾的，他们普遍想用最小的代价创造最高的建筑效益，这种思维方式与社会生产消费体系为了持续成功运转所秉持的结构性挥霍或浪费原则同样是矛盾的。

静止的系统思维

技术乐观派们第二个问题是，他们忽视了跟随经济发展和扩大生产的需要，科技具有不断更迭的本质。

也许是对所处时代的科技过于乐观，更可能是由于对于科技理念的乌托邦式的热情，他们设想的体系通常是相对静态的，以至于无法适应发展的更迭。他们常常企图在建筑范畴内建立一个与科技高度融合的体系，但没有解决建筑物与科技产品集成后更迭周期的同步问题，因为对于建筑与其他技术的集成思考过于简单化，具体的操作无法实施，导致最初构建的建筑新体系很快全面失效。最有代表性的案例是面临被拆除命运的中银舱体大厦 [图1]。1972 年在东京银座建成的这座大楼是新陈代谢派的代表作，也

about the integrity of the construction system.

From Richard Buckminster Fuller to Norman Forster, the common feature of Technological Optimists was that they tried to rebuild a large system. They hoped to establish a new complete and controllable ecology by taking advantage of technologies, and then obtain the best effect of the system. This idea did make it possible for those architects to establish a new system. Unfortunately, their idea about rebuilding a system was finally confined within an incomplete architectural creation system. They didn't have sufficient knowledge about the overall production and consumption system of the society, especially about what does space mean to users. Consequently, their ideal model was doomed to be incomplete and contradictory. They no longer treated the ordinary use as the opposite of the technological and production use, as Foster said: "buildings are products". But they still tried to change their ideas from the perspective of production, retained the traditional way of taking the building as the core of the construction system, and dedicated themselves to designing a building integrated with complete concept and perfect effect. They ignored that the value of the modern economic production is not limited in creation or production, it should be valued together with usage and consumption. Production and consumption constitute a cycle. In this cycle, it is extremely important to carefully establish comprehensive balance on cycled production and consumption system.

Sadly, the Technological Optimists' vision on system was incomplete. In fact, what they had done in order to create a better system effect contradicted the actual demands of the social system. They all tended to create the best building capability at minimal cost. Such an idea also contradicted the principles of structural waste implemented for the sustainable and successful operation of the social production and consumption system.

Static System Thinking

The second problem of the Technological Optimists was that they had ignored that technologies were to be constantly updated in order to serve the economic development and meet the requirement for expanding production.

Possibly, they were too optimistic about the technologies in their times or they had utopian enthusiasm on technologies, but the system they imagined was relatively static. It failed to adapt to the development and renovation of technology. They often tried to establish a system highly integrated with technology in architecture, but they were unable to find the solution to the synchronization of renovation cycle when the architecture and technological products are integrated. Since they oversimplified such integration, the idea was failed. As a result, their newly established architecture system collapsed. The most representative case was Nakagin Capsule Tower, a building under threat of demolition [fig. 1]. Erected in Ginza,

是黑川纪章的成名作，其模拟生物体的生长和繁衍，通过最新技术实现新旧事物的更替。无论是像胶囊一样的居住单元还是作为城市基础设施和服务内核的双塔，都集成了当时最先进的科技产品，以便实现高效的更替和改变。让人意想不到的是，那些设备和家电很快就过时了，甚至整个被系统化地迭代或淘汰了。由于"胶囊"与建筑整体设计过于集成，导致无法更换局部零件或整体改用新系统，不得不被整体废弃。这个案例是典型的因为系统集成的错误思维导致了建筑的失败。

折衷

技术乐观派们过于忠实建筑本身，建筑学的执拗使建筑中心化的思维限制了他们的思路，因此他们在充满希望地为理念寻找变现途径的过程中，一直试图维护建筑本身的整体性。这使他们不够坚决，最终他们是矛盾的、折衷的。不难理解，为什么像福斯特的香港汇丰银行，被人接受的还是其机械的、技术的美学；伦佐·皮亚诺和理查德·罗杰斯合作设计的蓬皮杜中心，一个巧置结构与设备的可变空间，却始终独一无二无法被复制。

空间技术化的认识盲区

如果把有关建筑空间的规划设计、建造完成的领域用生产体系的中性语境称为空间的生产端，那么有关建筑空间的日常使用、消费、改变的领域就是空间的使用端。为了方便论述，笔者将空间与科技技术的结合统称为"空间技术化"，并提出，迄今为止，主流建筑学领域对"空间技术化"的认知是不全面的。

比如，一直以来，技术乐观派主要围绕建筑本身的创造，包括设计和实施来构建系统理念，却忽视了空间建成后的使用现实、使用后的改变，以及再投入生产，投入消费的无限循环。被传统的技术乐观派所忽视的空间使用端，今天依旧未受到真正的重视。使用端的空间技术化的认识盲区，一方面来源于建筑学科的专业性，建筑领域之外的产业迄今尚未洞察到作为生活环境而非工业产品的建筑空间技术化的价值与意义，另一方面来源于建筑学科内部同样的认识局限。当下专业领域对空间技术化的关注仍然集中在空间的生产端，倾向于空间生产本身的技术更迭。比如：用前沿的科技系统来制定新型城市与建筑的标准，用数字科技来更新设计方式，组织建造，等等。这些

Tokyo in 1972, the Tower was a representative work of Metabolism by which Kisho Kurokawa's reputation was first made. Imitating growth and reproduction of organisms, the Tower was designed to replace old cadres with new ones by the latest technologies. In this architecture, there were capsule-like living units and twin towers which were regarded as urban infrastructure and service core. Both of them were integrated with the most advanced technological products so that the products could efficiently be renovated or changed in the future. But, quite unexpectedly, the equipment and the electronic appliances were quickly out of date and even systematically eliminated. Since the "capsule units" were excessively integrated with the Tower, it was impossible to replace the parts or the whole system. These units had to be abandoned. This is a typical failure caused by a wrong idea about systematic integration.

Compromise

Technological Optimists were too faithful to the building itself. Since their thinking was restricted by stubbornly focusing on the building, they had been trying to keep the integrality of the building in the pursuit of turning hopefully their idea into reality. Therefore, they were not resolute enough, with inner conflict and eclectic. So it is easy to understand why Foster's HSBC (Hong Kong) is widely accepted only for its mechanical and technological aesthetics, while the Centre Pompidou designed by Renzo Piano and Richard Rogers, a changeable space with particular structure and equipment, is so unique and cannot be replicated.

Blind Area of Space Technologization

If the design, construction of architectural space can be described as the production end of the space by using the terms from production field, the architectural space daily used, consumed and changed can be described as the user's end of the space. For better discussion, the integration of space and technology is defined as "Space technologization" in this paper. I believe that up till now, the mainstream architecture does not have sufficient knowledge about it.

For instance, the Technological Optimists had established systematic ideas by focusing on the creation of the building including the design and practice. They ignored the infinite cycle which consists of actual usage after completion, changes happened after usage, reproduction and reconsumption. Today, the user's end of the space ignored by traditional Technological Optimists still didn't receive any attention. The causes of blindspot of Space Technologization of the user's end include: architecture is a high professional field, the other industries have not yet realized the value and significance of space technologization as a living environment instead of an industrial product; in architecture, there was limited knowledge about space technologization. Now, the

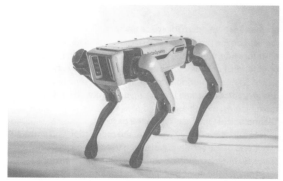

2　技术革命与空间

　　第一次工业革命，机械化革命时期"诺森伯兰人号"机车

　　第二次工业革命，电气革命时期爱迪生与碳丝白炽灯

　　第三次工业革命，信息化革命时期程序存储式计算机EDSAC

　　第四次工业革命，智能化革命时期波士顿动力公司Spot Mini机器人

Technological Revolution and Space

The First Industrial Revolution: Steam Locomotive during the mechanization revolution

The Second Industrial Revolution: Thomas Edison and his incandescent light bulb during the electrification revolution

The Third Industrial Revolution: the first stored program electronic computer EDSAC during the information revolution

The Fourth Industrial Revolution: Boston Dynamics Spot Mini Robots during the intelligent industrial revolution

认识与以往的"技术乐观派"的思维误区并无二致。

在我们看来,"空间技术化"只有将建筑空间的生产端与使用端等同看待,才可能是完整的。与执着于"生产端空间技术化"的研究者不同,我们甚至认为,以建筑和城市空间的使用为载体,发生在空间内部的"使用端空间技术化"的时代会更早来临,更快成熟。日新月异的科技作为一种关键的力量,将从外部推动空间的使用与改变。

生产系统结构性的必然

在整个社会生产系统中,建筑空间的经济和社会价值是多层面的。建筑物本身的建造和消耗是一种经济活动,满足人们的生产生活需求是一种社会经济功能,另一个迄今一直未受重视的特点是,建筑空间也是其他产业生产的各种各样成果,比如科技技术产品可能投放使用的重要载体。建筑和城市空间为社会生产的这些产品营造了最终的使用场景。尽管由于每个具体技术发展的不同步,与延用了上百年的旧建筑设备技术系统相比,今天新的设备技术、智能化科技在空间中的使用尚处于起步阶段,整体呈现碎片化的状态,基础的标准也有待建立,但这些都不足

以撼动这一事实——"使用端的空间技术化"是经济生产结构性的必然产物,建筑学应转向相应的研究与实践,且时间紧迫。

空间技术化的传导规律

建筑师是空间的专业架构者,需要主动去理解空间技术化的规律,才能够敏感地判断未来日常建筑的改变趋向。纵观历史中新技术应用与建筑空间之间的关系可以发现,技术的革命往往首先出现在生产端与使用端那些最敏感活跃的空间里,之后再逐渐传导到其他类型的日常空间中。所谓最敏感的建筑空间,包括生产端的工业空间和使用端的居住空间,这些往往是最先应用与投放最新技术体系的领域。

伴随着历次技术革命 [图2] 及相应的空间技术化,建筑空间也发生了巨大的改变。比如,18世纪第一次工业革命,也就是机械化革命时期,钢铁、玻璃、混凝土的出现使跨度更大、高度更高的空间需求成为可能。更高更大的空间变革开始出现于巨大的厂房与特殊的公共建筑中,比如水晶宫,后来才逐渐转向一般民用的公共建筑和居住建筑。

professional's concern for space technologization mainly focused on the production end of the space. They tended to pay more attention to the technological renovation of space production. For example, setting standard for new-type cities and buildings by cutting-edge technologies; renovating the design approaches and organizing construction by digital technologies, etc. This knowledge is as wrong ideas as the Technological Optimists had in the past.

In our opinion, only when are the production end and user's end of the architectural space treated equally, will space technologization be complete. Differing from those researchers who insist on "space technologization of the production end", we believe that the era for "space technologization of the user's end", which should happen inside space as it is used as a carrier of architecture and city space, will come and become mature earlier. While the ceaseless change in the science and technology, as a key power, will push the use and change of the space from outside.

Structural Necessity of the Production System

In the entire social production system, the economic and social values of architectural space vary on many levels. The construction and consumption of the building is an economic activity, its social and economic function is to satisfy people's production and life demands. Another feature of architectural space is neglected. The architectural space is the result pro-

duced by other industries. It is an important carrier at which technological products possibly aim. Building and city space are the ultimate usage scenarios for the products. Although every technology is not developed at the same speed, compared with the technological system used for a hundred years in old buildings, today's new equipment, technologies, and intelligent technologies are still taking their first step. Their use remains in a fragmented state. Basic standards are expected to be formulated. However, it is undeniable that the "space technologization of the user's end" is an inevitable outcome of the economic production structure. It is necessary and pressing that the architecture should start corresponding research and practice.

Transmission Rules of Space Technologization

Architects are professional space builders, to know better the future architectural developing trend, it is necessary for them to understand the rules of the space technologization. Based on the relationship between the application of new technologies and architectural space in the history, we conclude that the technical revolution always starts in the most sensitive and active space of both production and user's end, then influences the other everyday spatial types. The so-called most sensitive architectural space includes: the industrial space of the production end and the living space of the user's end, where the latest new technologies usually are

这些技术最初被隐藏在古典传统的立面形式之下，后来才渐渐成为内外一致的建筑语言，建立起独立的现代建筑体系。19世纪的第二次工业革命，即电气化革命时期，使用端的家庭用小型汽车的出现，推动了美国城市的郊区化，完全改变了居住与工作的城市结构。家用电器、厨房器具大量推广进入家庭，使妇女从繁重的家务劳动中解放出来，使男人可以参与家庭工作，极大地推动了社会关系和生活方式的变革。空调、洗衣机、冰箱等现代设施发明出来不久主要被应用于生产车间、社会性服务劳动场所和大型公共设施，如医院、电影院等，逐步才转为家庭民用。20世纪的第三次工业革命——信息化革命时期，世界变成了地球村，我们在物理空间之外又有了虚拟空间的维度，人们对于物理空间的认识开始改变，物质与虚拟两个空间开始交互。在此期间，空间的形式虽然没有发生革命性的变革，但是技术乐观派们正是在这一时期做出了大量意义深远的设想与实验。今天，我们正面临第四次工业革命——智能化革命。基于网络—实体系统（CPS）和物联网，伴随着人工智能的升级换代，我们生活的物质、物理空间和人的关系，人与城市、人与建筑的关系都可能再次发生根本性的

3　AGV与仓储系［北京极智嘉科技（Geek+）仓储机器人（AGV）］
　　AGV and Storage System

4　亚马逊无人店 宣传图片
　　Advertisement of Automated Shop "Amazon go"

quickly launched.

Along with the technical revolutions [fig. 2] and the corresponding space technologization, great changes have taken place in architectural field. For example, in the First Industrial Revolution in the 18th century, also known as the mechanized revolution, steel, glass, and concrete were invented; the whole society saw a boom in demand for larger and higher space. The revolution of spatial demand began to be implemented in huge plants and special public buildings like Crystal Palace. Gradually, the revolution began to spread to general civilian buildings and residential buildings. At the beginning, these technologies were concealed inside the architecture, which means behind classical and traditional facades. They were progressively applied to both inside and outside the architecture and constituted independent modern architectural system. During the Second Industrial Revolution, known as the Electrification Revolution in the 19th century, with the advent of family used cars, American cities were suburbanized. Its urban structures for living and working were totally changed. A large amount of domestic appliances and kitchen apparatus were introduced into family, women were liberated from heavy housework and men began to participate in the housework, which dramatically changed the social relationship and lifestyle. Air conditioner, washing machine and refrigerator were firstly applied in workshops, social service centers and large public facilities

like hospitals, cinemas, etc. Soon after being invented, they were applied to domestic use. The Third Industrial Revolution—Information Revolution in the 20th century turned the world into a global village, in which physical space and virtual space were both recognized. People began to change their previously view on the physical space and these two spaces even started to their interaction. Although there is no revolutionary change in the form of space, it was just the time when Technological Optimists made a lot of far-reaching ideas and carried out many significant experiments. Today, we are facing the Fourth Industrial Revolution—Intelligent Revolution. Based on cyber-physical system (CPS), Internet of Things (IoT), along with the upgrading of AI technology, there might be a fundamental change in the relationship between living materials, physical space and human beings, between human and architecture, human and city. These changes will inevitably push forward the new revolution of space design.

Invisible change

As before, similar technologization changes have taken place at the production end and user's end of the space. On the one hand, new technologies such as artificial intelligence technology have already been rapidly applied to industrial system of production end, including unmanned operations in factories and warehouses, upgrades in flexible assembly line

变化，这些改变必将推动空间设计新的革命。

看不见的改变

跟以往一样，相似的技术化改变也已经在空间的生产端和使用端同时发生了。一方面，像人工智能科技这样的新技术早已快速运用于生产端的工业体系，比如工厂、仓储的无人化运营，柔性流水线的升级等 [图3]。另一方面，在消费端，新的零售升级、无人店、智能家居、物联网的新场景已经在进行实验与应用 [图4]。

随着人工智能算法、算力的不断升级，各类智能化新技术也在蓬勃发展。科技的升级换代也会同时在生产和消费两个层面影响建筑与城市空间的设计和建造、使用与体验，促进建筑空间的更替与进化，带来更为新颖和多样的建筑体验与生活形态。另一方面，各类智能化新技术目前大多还处于碎片化、单线化的状况，有待依靠新的载体来进行整合。空间即是一个重要的载体，它会将新的科技和技术开发运用和融合在新的空间创造中。空间与科技产品这两者的相互作用，相互促进产生的新状态实际是一种更大的生产体量。

日渐隐形的大系统

今天，单个建筑的完整意义正在消解，实体建筑正在日渐成为巨大的物联网络系统的一个局部。一个重要的变化正在发生：稳定的、"重"的事物已日益大系统化、隐形化。对生活影响深远的不再是传统建筑学向来重视的在场和可视之物，而是那些常常被视而不见的巨大的电力输送架、排水设施、互联网、物流系统、物联的生活网络等。这种变化对建筑学的影响是，建筑学的职能将无法维持在原来相对独立完整的专业技术工作中，而要去尝试回应日益庞大、分解的生活大系统。换言之，单体建筑已不足以自成系统地解决问题，获得效能。显然，建筑的空间或形式的表意性象征这样的设计思维，如今也因为无法真正代表核心问题而开始失效。不过，在新的技术条件下，技术乐观派们反复尝试却未曾实现的大系统控制也将成为新的可能，一种更大的整体视野与全局思维将会出现。

成为入口的空间

空间一旦纳入网络—实体系统，就可以跟手机的作用相类比，空间会成为无数网络系统和虚拟世界的入口。空

182

[fig. 3]. On the other hand, on the consumer's end, the new retail upgrades, unmanned stores, smart homes, and the IoT are already being tested and applied [fig. 4].

With the continuous upgrading of artificial intelligence algorithms and computing power, various new intelligent technologies are also booming. The upgrading of science and technology will also affect the design and construction, the usage and experience of buildings and urban space in both production and consumption sides, promoting the replacement and evolution of architectural space, and bringing more innovative and diverse architectural experiences and lifestyles. In addition, most of the new intelligent technologies are still remain in a fragmented and single-operational state, they need to be integrated by new carriers. Space is an important carrier, which will develop and utilize new technologies, and integrate them into new areas. The interaction between space and technological products and the new state they will produce are actually larger productivity.

A Large, Increasingly Invisible System

Today, the complete meaning of a single building is fading, and physical buildings are increasingly becoming a part of the huge IoT system. There is an important change: stable and "heavy" things have become systematic and invisible. The far-reaching impact on life is no longer the present and visible things that traditional architecture has always valued.

Actually, such impact comes from the huge power transmission racks, drainage facilities, Internet, logistics systems and life network of IoT which are usually be overlooked. The impact this change has brought on architecture is that the architectural functions can't be maintained in the relatively independent and completely technical work. It is expected to solve the increasingly large and decomposed living system. In other words, single building is unable to solve problems by their own system and achieve efficiency. Obviously, the design thinking concerning ideographic symbol of architectural space or form cease to be effective. Nevertheless, with the new technologies, the large systematic control that Technical Optimists have tried repeatedly but without any achievement will become a new chance. A larger overall vision and global thinking is emerging.

Space as Entrance

Once being incorporated into the virtual-reality system, space can be compared to the mobile phones. The space will become the gateway for countless network systems and the virtual world. The deep integration of space and technology will become flexible, no longer so static and immutable. The so-called flexibility is physical. For example, instead of the long-term and certain material space, temporary building will become an architectural type in high demand; the fixed integrated system will be replaced by the variable partial

间将与技术产生深度融合，这种融合将不再是静止的，不可变的，而将成为一种柔性的集合。所谓的柔性既是物理层面的，比如临时性的建筑空间需求增多，取代长久的、确定的物质空间，可变化的局部系统取代牢固的整体系统；也是现象层面的，即使在我们实施相对稳固长久的建筑设计时，功能的组织与选择也不再只能通过实体空间的对应与组合来实现，因为虚拟空间与虚拟主体的产生，功能与实体空间、与主体的联系消散了，空间与功能之间的组织模式无法再被长久固定下来。

如果说空间与使用功能的关系，从最初的功能与新空间固定对应，到类似库哈斯在《癫狂的纽约》一书中所描述的，以及在他设计实践中所展现的，那种功能与空间不再固定，空间可以相互交换、相互组织混合的场景，这个过程还未跨越空间的物质化的话，那么在未来，建筑空间的作用在于索引，空间是通往现实世界或虚拟世界，既被实际主体使用也被虚拟主体使用的"入口"。

极具诱惑的经济体量

在网络—实体与人工智能的时代，物理空间与虚拟空间被打通，真实的、虚拟的、完整的、碎片的体验，没有一个系统是独立存在的，它们往往混合在一起，可以随时进行组合和转变。空间体验的方式也将因此改变。更进一步，在未来，如果人工智能的虚拟人具有了替代决策的能力，这意味着人的知觉和意识将被从人的整体性中分离出去，物理空间与身体的关系更将被彻底颠覆。建筑空间从可能成为一种真正的多重知觉的载体，到可能被有独立决策力的虚拟主体共用，将不再只是意味着拓展我们的知觉或者所有智能技术应用的场所，而是一种突破物理空间、人口数量限制的，成倍增长的经济体量的实体部分。因为这样，也必将诱惑经济生产体系自上而下地将这种演变最终加到建筑空间之上。

属性变化的建筑

我们可以据此来推测一下未来建筑的改变。

单体建筑会趋向无形态化。完整的建筑形态变得不再重要，因为建筑的象征性日益丧失了针对性与必要性。建筑只是大系统中一个可视的部分，本身就不完整，其形态的完整意义也就丧失了。科技创造的新体验与空间感不是

system. The so-called flexibility is also a phenomenon. Even when we design relatively stable and long-lasting buildings, the organization and selection of functions will no longer have to be realized through combining physical spaces. With the virtual space and virtual entity, it's unnecessary to keep the connection between function and physical space and bodily entity. The organizational model between space and function is no longer fixed.

When developing into what Koolhaas described in *Delirious New York* and demonstrated in his design practices, the initially fixed connection between functions and new space becomes exchangeable and mixing with each other. If in this case, the whole process still remains in the category of spatial materialization, then in the future, the architectural space will serve as an indexing access. Space will turn into a gateway of the real world or the virtual world, or an "entry" shared by both real entity and virtual entity.

Alluring Economic Volume

In the era of virtual-entity and artificial intelligence, the wall between physical space and virtual space is broken through, providing us with a real, virtual, complete, fragmented experience. No system exists independently. They are often mixed together and can be combined and transformed at any time. Thus, the way of space experience will be changed. Furthermore, in the future, if the virtual person of artificial intelligence is designed to be able to make decisions, which means the human perception and consciousness will be separated from the human integrity, then the relationship between physical space and the body will be completely subverted. Experiencing probably being a true multi-perception carrier, the building space could be designed to be shared with a virtual entity that may make decision independently. It will no longer just be a place to expand our perception or the place to which all intelligent technologies are applied. Instead, it will be an economic volume entity transcending physical space and population limit and could quickly booming. The economic production system will certainly be attracted to apply this evolved economic volume into the top-down production of architectural space.

Buildings with Changed Properties

Accordingly, we can make several predictions on the change of future buildings.

The form of a single building tends to be uncertain. Since the architectural symbolism gradually having lost its relevance, whether the architectural form is complete or not is no longer important. Being a visible part of the large system, the architecture will not be complete and the complete meaning of architectural form will also fade away. The new experience and sense of space created by science and technology are not permanent and eternal, they will vary along with the changing

固定的、永恒的，而是变化的、瞬时的，会随着需求的改变而改变，建筑的状态也不必再具有形式的倾向性，建筑可以在个性化与中性化之间不断根据需要变换状态。

单体建筑会趋向片段化，建筑的片段与局部、整体具有同等意义。空间技术化不必依附于一个完整的建筑，而是可以灵活地依附于建筑的片段与局部。"局部"的建筑、局部变化的建筑会成为常态。

单体建筑会趋向空间内部化。作为技术化的主要载体与空间基础，建筑的内部毫无疑问是未来建筑的主战场。内部很难精确定义，但建筑与城市在空间上都有内部。内部在建筑学与实际设计领域中迄今没有被充分探索过，设计研究往往也忽略内部空间自治的潜在可能。用动态的视角去看，无论是建筑还是城市的内部都充满了未知和陌生：内部其实是蔓延的，没有边界的；内部可以是冗余的，可以反复重置与组织；内部是可以自治的，既有丰富性又有复杂性……内部可以成为建筑学的新疆域。更有意思的一个视角是，内部空间可以看作是建筑的另一个维度。内部是日常生活在时间上的增殖而不是在空间上的蔓延。

结语

什么会改变未来的建筑？在扑面而来的改变来临之前，困惑会使我们关注那些看不见的改变，那些影响未来的过去，那些一直在影响建筑学，却往往被忽视之物。问题会带领我们，也许探究问题的最好方式就是做一个行动派，用身体与行动去尝试所有的可能。这同样适用于我们心底的另外一个问题，在也许是冷酷无情的未来面前，乐观的意义何在？

本文作者系庄慎，最初发表于《时代建筑》2018 (3):32–35。

social needs. Instead of having to be specifically formalized, building can be constantly customized and neutralized after demanding.

Single building tends to be fragmented. Whether for the partial or the whole building, these fragments are of equal significance. Space technology does not have to be applied to a complete building. It can be flexibly applied to fragments or parts. "Partial" buildings and buildings with partial changes will become regular.

Single building tends to be spatially internalized. As the main carrier and space foundation of technology, the interior of the building is undoubtedly the important part of the future architecture. The so-called interior is difficult to be defined precisely, but there is internal space in both buildings and cities. This interior has not been fully explored in the field of architecture and design. Besides, the potential of the internal space autonomy is often neglected by the research. From a dynamic perspective, the interior of both buildings and cities is unknown: the interior is actually spreading and with no boundaries; it can be redundant, be reset and organized repeatedly; it can be autonomous, rich and complex…It can become a new field of architecture. More interesting, it can be regarded as another dimension of architecture. It is the proliferation of daily life in time rather than the spread of space.

Conclusion

What will change the architecture in the future? Before the changes find us, we are so confused that we would like to focus on those invisible changes, those long ignored issues which kept influencing the architectural discipline and will still affect the future. Problems will be our best teacher. The best attitude for exploration is to be action-oriented and tries to seize every chance. Another question is also haunting in our mind What is the significance of optimism in front of a ruthless future?

The paper authored by Zhuang Shen was first featured in *Time + Architecture*, 2018 (3): 32–35.

10

整体的回响：
来自内部的反向思维
The Echo of the Unity:
Reverse Thinking of the Interior

1　《圆锥相交》，戈登·玛塔–克拉克，1975年
Conical Intersect , 1975, Gordon Matta–Clark

像戈登·玛塔 - 克拉克[1] 那样的艺术家，可以用洞穿、切割的方式把建筑实体的内部展现在观众面前 [图1]。而在建筑学里，内部仿佛是一个诱人的迷局。其特殊性与复杂性远远超出了从习惯的鸟瞰或通过平面与剖面展示内部的角度所能呈现的程度。稳定静态的角度难以揭示内部的确切内容和属性。正因为如此，笔者认为，从内部认知并思考建筑的方式是建筑学研究的一种新视角。[2] 从内部的角度思考建筑有什么意义？怎样揭示建筑的内部性？

这看似是与中国传统园林不一定有关系的当代建筑学问题。然而笔者在整理关于传统园林思维方式的时候，却发现了相似情况：在传统园林的认知与表达中，存在一种关于整体的内部以及整体与局部关系的成熟思维方式，它也是一种对于内部性的反向思维。因此，辨析中国传统园林世界里这种思维方式的成因与具体表现，对今天研究建筑学的内部性问题可能具有一定的参考和启发意义。

前置的观念：在"整体"中

可以这么认为：传统园林的使用与认知主体处在一个具有共识的整体世界里。这一整体世界是当时创造和理解

传统园林文化的"通识性前置设定"，正因如此，传统园林文化的呈现方式是一致的，而非各式各样或存在巨大差异的。讨论园林文化，认识整体，首先必须理解中国传统文化语境下"自然"这一概念。在中国传统的文化系统中，包括在玄学和老庄哲学里，所谓"自然"的原则是：宇宙万物不凭借外力，而是凭借自身动力而获得存在，由此产生了生机勃勃的万物，直至实现整体和谐的运转变化。因此，"自然"就是整体。换言之，中国传统文化中的"自然"并非作为主体的对立面的客观物质世界，而是一种整体的存在法则，既决定着每一个个体，包括主体和客体的运行，也决定着世界整体的状貌。这就是"此中有真意，欲辨已忘言"中的真意，也是宋明理学中的"理一分殊"中的"理"。

在今天看来，传统文化就像图册[3] [图2]影印图片上所笼罩的泛黄色调一样[4]，通过整体文化的建构，"一次性"地把宇宙万物都附上了同一种意义，一个统一的本源。换言之，人在大千世界里，在园林中，是"沉浸"其中的，或者说是在其"内部"的。根据传统的整体式思维，一方面，人（主体）是被这个内在运行的"自然"所化生的，

186

Artists like Gordon Matta-Clark[1] can show the audience the interior of buildings by penetrating and cutting [fig. 1]. In architecture, the interior seems to be a fascinating mystery. It is far more particular and complex than shown from the conventional perspective of a bird's eye view or a floor plan and section drawing. It is difficult to reveal the exact content and properties of the interior from a stable and static perspective. Therefore, I believe that the way of cognizing and thinking about architecture from the inside is a new perspective of architectural research[2]. Then what is the significance of thinking about architecture from the perspective of the interior? How to reveal the architectural interiority?

This seems to be a contemporary architectural issue not necessarily related to traditional Chinese gardens. However, when I sorted out ways of thinking about traditional gardens, I found a similar situation: in the cognition and expression of traditional gardens, there is a mature way of thinking about the interior of the whole and the relationship between the whole and parts. It is also a kind of reverse thinking about the interior. Therefore, analyzing the causes and concrete manifestations of this way of thinking in the world of traditional Chinese gardens may provide a frame of reference and some inspirations for contemporary studies of interior issues in architecture.

A Preconditioned Concept: in the "Whole"

It can be said that subjects who use and cognize traditional gardens are in a whole world of consensus. This whole world is a "general precondition" for creating and understanding the traditional garden culture. For this reason, the traditional garden culture is presented in a consistent way, rather than in various or widely different ways. To discuss garden culture and understand the whole, we must first understand the concept of "nature" in the context of traditional Chinese culture. In the traditional Chinese cultural system, including in metaphysics and Lao-Zhuang philosophy, the so-called principle of "nature" is that all things in the universe exist not by external forces, but by their own motive forces. In this way, all things are begotten, resulting in operational changes that realize a harmonious whole. Therefore, "nature" is the whole. In other words, "nature" in traditional Chinese culture is not an objective material world as opposed to subjects, but the law governing the existence of the whole, which determines not only the operation of every individual, including subjects and objects, but also the overall appearance of the world. This is the true meaning in "There is a true meaning hidden in all of this, but before I can explain it, I've forgotten the words", and also the "principle" in "one principle with different manifestations" in the Confucian school of idealist philosophy of the Song and Ming dynasties.

Traditional culture is like the yellowish hue[4] in the photocopies in picture album[3] [fig. 2]. The construction of the whole culture now seems like imposing the same meaning and a

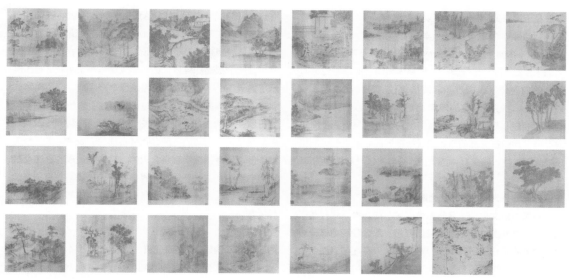

2　文徵明绘制的拙政园三十一景图
31 Illustrative Plates of the Humble Administrator's Garden

3　《听松风处》
The Place to Listen to Pine Wind

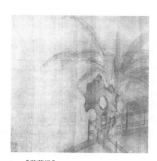

4　《芭蕉槛》
Musa Bajoo Planted by the Railing

5　《待霜亭》
The Frost Awaiting Pavilion

6　《繁香坞》
Numerous Fragrances Recess

7　《瑶圃》
Garden of Jade

8　《芙蓉隈》
Confederate Rose Bend

并被基于同样原则的万物所包围；另一方面，人就是万物之一，与草木鱼虫有着同一本质。所谓"理一分殊"就是"理"（本质）只有一个，从中产生了"万殊"（千变万化）的形式。进一步推理，这种整体和同一的思维也为万物个体的差异性表象赋予等同的地位，产生了"天人一体""天人之际"之类的观念：我即万物，万物即我。天地万物同理：我即天地，天地即是我。世界与自我被同等地看待。我们在文徵明所绘的《拙政园图咏》之一《听松风处》[图3]中可窥见其中的奥妙：松与人是一样神态的。

探索内部的行为：同自然一起造物

　　中国传统文化中"我与自然一致"的思维方式打通了人与造物之间的关系。既然我即自然，那么我同自然一般地造物就不奇怪了。其中不存在对抗，只存在与自然合拍的顺应转化。更妙的是，老天或自然创造的物与我创造的物是重叠的。所以不难回答，为什么景物在园林画中都是经过选择与经营的，是人工自然，"虽由人作，宛自天开"是理想状态。而且不同于"真实的自然"，这类"人工的自然"有一种类型化、仪式化、象征化、合折合韵的

意味。《拙政园图咏》中《芭蕉槛》[图4]所绘场景，是一个比较常见的布局，因为造园者顺应的大理念都是一致的，只是表现或修为不同。在造物的过程中，人的自主性保持在一个很高的程度。图册中《待霜亭》[图5]这幅图展示了冬天在小亭中主人全身包裹得严严实实，舒适格物的状态。有人或许生疑，既然是体悟整体，为什么不去体悟更真实严酷的自然，而要这么舒适地观看呢？个人理解，既然我是天道创造的，那么我是合理的，我的需求是合理的，舒适的身体感受就是合理的，是合乎天道的，违拗是远离自然的。主体身处的世界是不断自我建构、日益复杂的世界，而这种建构同时也是一种主体在内部探索所处世界的行为。

内部事物间的联系：有法无式

　　这种认知描述的世界表现为：一个自我驱动运转的自然化生万物，万物生动活泼，变化无常，各具秉性，但都蕴含自然。所谓"知行合一"则是从万物中认识到自然，行动的方式也遵循驱动自然万物的内在力量，也就是那个没有区别的本体、本源，但其方式可以变化无常，即"有

unified source on everything in the universe "once and for all". In other words, humans are "immersed" in or in the interior of the world and gardens. According to the traditional monolithic thinking, on the one hand, humans (subjects) are begotten by the internally operating "nature" and surrounded by all other things that are based on the same principle; on the other hand, humans are part of the universe and share the same essence as grass, trees, fish, and insects. The so-called "one principle with different manifestations" means that there is only one "principle" (essence), which produces "many manifestations" (a myriad of changes). It can be further inferred that this kind of thinking about wholeness and oneness also gives equal status to the different representations of all individual things, giving rise to such concepts as "the unity of heaven and man" and "the relationship between heaven and man": I am everything, and everything is me. Man and the universe are the same: I am the universe, and the universe is me. The world and the self are treated equally. We can get a glimpse into the mystery in "The Place to Listen to Pine Wind" [fig. 3], one of the pictures in *Landscapes of Humble Administrator's Garden* painted by Wen Zhengming: the pine trees and the man have the same facial expression and posture.

**Action of Interior Exploration:
Creating Things along with Nature**

　　The "I am in harmony with nature" way of thinking in traditional Chinese culture opens up the relationship between man and creation. Since I am nature, then it is not surprising that I create things like nature does. There is no confrontation, only a conformation and transformation in harmony with nature. Even better, things created by God or nature overlap with things created by me. Therefore, it is not difficult to answer why scenery is selected and managed in garden paintings and is artificial nature. "Artificial yet looking natural" is the ideal state. And unlike "real nature," this kind of "artificial nature" connotes categorization, ritualization, symbolization, and rhythmization. The scene depicted in "Musa basjoo Planted by the Railing" [fig. 4] in *Landscapes of the Humble Administrator's Garden* is a relatively common layout. This is because gardeners conform to the same general ideas, and they differ only in performance or attachment. In the process of creation, the autonomy of man is maintained at a high level. "The Frost-Awaiting Pavilion" [fig. 5] in the album shows a man muffled up comfortably in a small pavilion in winter. Some people may wonder, since it is the whole that is to be experienced, why not we experience the more real and harsh nature instead of watching it from such a comfortable position? My personal understanding is that since I was created by natural law, then I am reasonable, my needs are reasonable, physical comfort is reasonable and in line with the natural law, and anything to the contrary is a departure from nature. The world in which the subject lives is a world of constant self-construc-

法无式"。关于生动活泼、变化无常、有法无式，图谱本身就是个例子。图谱为什么有那么多张？就像历史上对于园林山水的反复吟咏（西湖十景、王维辋川十景、圆明园四十景图咏等），我们也许可以从另外一个角度来认识：它不仅是为了构成整个园，而且也反映一种普遍的意义，生动活泼的万物变化就是通过这种方式体现的。对于世界，对它的整体而非片段的认识是通过不断列举片段而展示的，对它的动态而非静止的把握是通过反复认识不同的情景而获得的。这同我们做城市日常调研一样，日常性是反复的碎片，这是一种非典型的典型性，非识别性的可识别体系。

感知内部的方式：反向的思维

既然整体及其局部的变化如此奇妙，那么，认知它、观察它、反映它是重要的。这既是认识"我"的过程，也是建构具体世界的过程。

那么，关键的问题来了，既然"我"身在其中，如何去认识，才能体悟整体呢？与印度寓言中盲人摸象的状况不同，盲人们并没有线索，事先不知道大象为何，而中国的古人却有。如前所述，中国传统文化中的"自然是一种统一的法则"的含义是一次性被赋予的，是一个"前置的设定"。因此，中国古人对事物有一个总体的认知，他们知道大象大致的状态，因此认知事物的行为更像在参与一次从预知到结果的推理活动，只需要能找到证明预想结果的线索与证据即可。就像《繁香坞》[图6]一图仿佛在引人发问：主人在何处？对这个过程的稔熟应用使中国古人更像是具备逆向思维的人。

如何体会整体？如何不断提示有一个我们身处其中的整体的存在？所用的方式是一种反向的思维，大部分是通过对比提示或者打破整体来显示的。具体的方法与法则包括依附、分离、阻断、断续、残缺、隔绝、断绝等，仔细辨析会发现，这些都是在内部才会采用的间接方式，这些方式本身反映了一个隐含的事实——主体在研究对象的内部。

比如《瑶圃》[图7]一图就是一个依附和分离的例子。如何显示大地的整体存在？通过草木、花朵"依附"在大地之上，显示大地有一个存在的本身。围栏把整个空间分成两块，通过内和外显示有一个整体的存在。《芙蓉

tion and increasing complexity, and such construction is also an act of exploring the world inside on the part of the subject.

The Connection Between Things Inside: Rules Without Formulas

According to this kind of cognition, the world is manifested as: a self-driven nature begets all things, all things are lively and changeable and have their own characters, but they all contain nature. The so-called "unity of knowledge and action" is to recognize nature in all things, and the way of action also follows the internal force that drives everything in nature, namely "being" and "origin" which are no different from each other, but its way is changeable, that is, "there are rules but no formulas". The album itself is an example of liveliness, changeability and "there are rules but no formulas". Why does the album, like the repeated chants about landscapes in history (Ten Views of the West Lake, Ten Views of Wang Chuan by Wang Wei, the Forty Scenes of the Yuanmingyuan, etc.) contain so many pictures? We may look at this from another angle: It not only constitutes the whole garden, but also reflects a universal meaning, and lively changes in all things are reflected in this way. For the world, the understanding of its whole rather than fragments has been demonstrated by continual enumeration of fragments, and the grasp of its dynamic rather than static is obtained by repeatedly recognizing different scenarios. It's like doing everyday urban research where the daily routine is repeated fragments. This is a kind of a typical typicality and a recognizable system of an unrecognizable nature.

Way of Perceiving the Interior: a Reverse Thinking

Since changes in the whole and its parts are so wonderful, it is important to cognize them, observe them and reflect them. This is not only a process of understanding "I", but also a process of constructing a concrete world.

So here comes the big question, "since 'I' is inside, how to understand in order to realize the whole?" Unlike the blind men in the Indian parable 'Blind Men and An Elephant' who had no clue as to what an elephant was, the ancient Chinese had the clue. As mentioned above, the meaning of "nature is a unified law" in traditional Chinese culture is given once and for all and is a "precondition". Therefore, the ancient Chinese had a general understanding of things. They had a general idea of what an "elephant" looked like, so the act of cognizing things was more like engaging in an inference exercise where the result was anticipated, and they only needed to find the clue and evidence that would prove the anticipated result. For example, the picture "Numerous Fragrances Recess" [fig. 6] seems to beg the question: Where is the master? The skillful application of this process makes the ancient Chinese look more like people capable of reverse thinking.

How to experience the whole? How to constantly remind ourselves of the existence of a whole in which we are? The

9 《小飞虹》

Little Flying Rainbow

10 《湘筠坞》

Mottled Bamboo Grove

11 《意远台》

Thoughts Floating Away Ledge

12　1989年何陋轩入口外观

The view at the entrance of Helou Shelter, 1989

13　2004年从轩内看何陋轩入口

The view to the entrance of Helou Shelter from inside, 2004

14　《梦隐楼》

Dreaming of Reclusion Tower

15　《玉泉》

Jade Spring

隈》[图8] 则显示了"阻断"的方式，古人讲流水"逝者如斯夫"，但是怎么能够感知到看似平静的水面的流动？图中显示，因为水被岸的边缘阻隔，被水中的荷花杆茎打断，人看到了波纹，看到了漩涡，所以感知到水是流动着的。《小飞虹》[图9] 可以说明断续和残缺，小飞虹在梦隐楼之前，若墅堂以北，处在连接两者的途中，横在沧浪池内。因为树丛的遮挡，这几个地方的联系仿佛被全部打断了，但是实际上人会在脑海里依据画意把它们联系起来。通过人意识中的"叙事"将片段联系起来。《湘筠坞》[图10] 中，人被包裹在竹林当中，从大千世界中分离出来，但此时，人的精神和这个世界反而因此更加直接单纯地联系在一起。《意远台》[图11] 是一个很极端的"断绝"。诗里面写，"闲登万里台，旷然心目清。木落秋更远，长江天际明。白云渡水去，日暮山纵横。"所谓"行到水穷处，坐看云起时"，当前路断绝的时候，在人的思绪中，人和宇宙或者人与自然一下子联系起来。这样的方式也可以见诸当代建筑的细节中。比如冯纪忠设计的松江方塔园中何陋轩的入口，从石板路顺着弧墙进入，入口有一个水泥铺砌的坡阶路口。何陋轩的内外标高其实差不多，而从外看

先是一段坡道，使人稍稍地往上走，到了路口的地方又走下来三级台阶 [图12, 13]。这两级台阶是一个小细节，它创造了一个停顿、一个断绝。这跟"意远台"的做法是一样的，只不过"意远台"采用一个大的断绝，让人的思绪、情怀联系到整个苍茫宇宙中，是一个大尺度。而何陋轩是小尺度，让整个人的状态和思绪进入到它所笼罩的一个小空间里。所以这是一个相对的细节，用的方法一模一样。

在这种认知方式中，整体与局部是相对的，没有固定的程式，两者的关系是千变万化的。比如虚实大小，在《梦隐楼》[图14] 中，因为有诸如功名、日月、帝京、暮山之类永恒而强大的事物，个人再大的抱负，再大的庄园，最终也不过是在小壶之中。《玉泉》[图15] 以遥远的京师玉泉命名园中景物，以心境况味相关联，虽远而近。在《听松风处》[图3] 中，从松林发出的风声（形虚）联想到流动的风的实体被松树的枝条和树叶所切割，看不见的整体为其所破，如同抽刀断水一样，感到风包裹着自我，整体又为自己所破。人与松是一样的。这是虚中带实，以虚致虚。更极端的是"于无声处听惊雷"的状况，局部并不次要，局部就是整体。这些认识都可以转化为普遍的设计方

approach used is a kind of reverse thinking, which reveals the whole mostly by comparing and hinting or breaking the whole. Specific methods and rules include attachment, separation, blocking, interruption, incompleteness, isolation, cutting off, etc. Careful analysis will reveal that these are all indirect methods that are only used internally, and these methods reflect an implicit fact - the subject is inside the object being studied.

For example, the picture "Garden of Jade" [fig. 7] is an example of attachment and separation. How to show the existence of the earth as a whole? By "attaching" grass, trees and flowers to the surface, it shows the existence of the earth. The fence divides the whole space into two parts, showing the existence of a whole through "inside" and "outside". "Confederate Rose Bend" [fig. 8] shows the method of "blocking". The ancients likened time to flowing water. But how can we perceive the flow of seemingly calm water? The picture shows that the water is blocked by the edge of the bank and broken by the lotus stems in the water, so people can perceive that the water is flowing when they see the ripple and whirlpool. "Little Flying Rainbow" [fig. 9] illustrates interruption and incompleteness. The Little Flying Rainbow is located in front of Dreaming of Reclusion Tower and to the north of Ruoshu Hall, in the middle between the two and spanning the Canglang Pond. These parts are seemingly disconnected from each other on account of being blocked out by trees, but in fact, people will connect them in their minds according to

the mood of the painting. The fragments are linked up through the "narrative" in human consciousness. A Recess in the "Mottled Bamboo Grove" [fig. 10], the person is surrounded by bamboo, separated from the world. But his spirit is thus linked to the world more directly and simply. "Thoughts Floating Away Ledge" [fig. 11] is a very extreme example of cutting off. The poem reads: "In my leisure time, I climb onto the Wanli Ledge, where my mind is refreshed by the broad and open landscape before me. Leaves are falling as autumn deepens, the horizon on the surface of the Yangtze River is clear. White clouds are crossing over the water, the sun is setting behind the mountain range." The so-called "I walk to the point where a stream ends, and sitting, watch when the clouds rise" means that when the poet finds that the road is cut off, in his mind, he is instantly connected to the universe or nature. This method can also be seen in the details of contemporary architecture. For example, at the entrance of Helou Shelter designed by Feng Jizhong in Fangta Garden in Songjiang district, Shanghai, as you walk in along the arc-shaped wall you will come to the cement-paved sloped end of the flagstone path. The floor of Helou Shelter is basically at the same level as the ground outside, but outside is a sloped section, which makes the visitor ascend a little and then descend three steps at the end of the path. [fig. 12–13] The three steps are a small detail that creates a pause and a cutoff. The same method used for "Thoughts Floating Away Ledge" is used here. But in the

16 阿那亚金山岭艺术中心
Art Center of Aranya, Jinshanling

法：显示整体、显示自己；成就他人、成就自己。

这是一种认知世界的方式，也是一种创造世界的方式，因此也可以成为一种设计的方式。在中国传统园林被广泛营造的世界里，它是一种大家所拥有的方式，如今，恐怕只能是一种个人化的方式了。但这种方式并未随着时间和旧有世界的逝去而失去其效应，今天我们依旧可以将它作为思考工具——一种与众不同的思维方式。阿科米星建筑工作室曾多次采用类似的设计方式。比如在设计一个观赏景观的山区会所建筑时，建筑师发现实地山区虽然很美，但一路到基地都是相似形态的山景，到达基地后，也没有新的不同。为了在相似的环境中创造不同的看山的方式，设计强化了一组室内实体柱体构筑物，在一个流动空间里用它们来打断外部的山景，让人们在其中走动的时候不断透过粗壮的主体看到山体，在整体的印象里把片段连缀在一起，获得新的体验 [图16]。这也是一种在整体的内部通过打破整体以获得对整体的感知的设计手法。

逝去的世界：一个参考

园林的世界是一个逝去的世界。传统文化的整体性结

case of "Thoughts Floating Away Ledge", it's a big cutoff that connects people's thoughts and feelings to the whole vast universe and the method is applied on a large scale, while in the case of Helou Shelter, the method is applied on a small scale, making the state and thoughts of the person enter the small space that envelopes him. So this is a relative detail, and the method is all the same.

In this cognitive approach, the whole and the part are relative, there is no fixed formula and the relationship between the two is ever-changing. Take the scale of imagination and reality for example, in "Dreaming of Reclusion Tower" [fig. 14], because there are such eternal and powerful things as fame, sun and moon, imperial capital and sunset over mountains, one's ambition and estate, no matter how big they are, are nothing but things in a small pot. In "Jade Spring" [fig. 15], the scene in the garden is named after Jade Spring which is in the distant imperial capital. In "The Place to Listen to Pine Wind" [fig. 3], the wind from the pine forest (of an imaginary shape) conjures up the image of the body of the wind being cut by the branches and leaves of the pine trees. The invisible air is cut as water is cut by a sword. The wind wraps around self and the whole is cut by self. The man and the pine trees serve the same purpose. It's a scene where imagination and reality are mixed and imagination arises from the invisible. "Hear thunder in the silence" is a more extreme case where parts are not of less importance as parts are the whole. These insights

can be translated into general design methods: showing the whole, showing self; making others accomplished, making self-accomplished.

The approach is a way of cognizing the world, and also a way of creating the world, so it can also be a way of design. In a world where traditional Chinese gardens were widely built, it was approach practiced by everyone. Today, it is probably only a personalized approach. But the approach has not lost its effect with the passing of time and the old world. Today we can still use it as a tool of thinking - a different way of thinking. Atelier Archmixing has adopted similar design methods on many occasions. For example, when designing a mountainous club building with a view of the surrounding landscape, the architect found that although the mountainous area was very beautiful, the scenery along the way to the site was all similar mountain scenery and there was nothing at the site. In order to create different ways of looking at the mountains in an environment of similarities, the architect highlighted a set of indoor solid column structures in the design. They are used in a flowing space to break the mountain scenery outside, so that as people move around, they constantly see the mountains through the stout columns, and link the fragments together in a whole in their minds to get a new experience [fig. 16]. This is also a design technique to gain a sense of the whole by breaking the whole inside.

构已经不存在了，碎裂了，因此园林文化本身是不可再现了。我们当下生活的世界是一个与传统园林文化完全不同的、日益分解的世界，我们习惯于在外部看待每一个碎片的形式。但园林的世界给我们提供了一个与之相反的方式：一个从内部看待世界、从内部感知整体的方式。以这样的思维来看待同处于整体中的局部或者个体，对于当代研究建筑学内部性问题具有参考价值。

本文作者系庄慎，最初发表于《时代建筑》，2018 (4): 20–23。本文主要内容根据笔者于 2018 年 4 月 14 日在上海那行空间所做的讲座《整体的回响：传统园林自身运行的理念与当代理论、实践转化努力的区分》的前半部分整理得到。该讲座是从 2017 年 11 月 3 日至 2018 年 6 月 3 日由鲁安东、童明和庄慎主讲，冯路、李兴钢、柳亦春、鲁安东、童明、王辉、王骏阳、张斌和祝晓峰等嘉宾参与讨论的关于园林的系列讲座之一。其中童明和庄慎讲座的切入点是解析文徵明所绘《拙政园图咏》。

A Lost World: A Frame of Reference

The world of gardens is a lost world. The overall structure of traditional culture no longer exists. It is broken, so the garden culture itself is irreproducible. The world we live in today is an increasingly decomposing world that is completely different from traditional garden culture, and we are used to looking at every fragment from the outside. But the world of gardens provides us with an opposite way: a way of looking at the world from the inside and perceiving the whole from the inside. The way of looking at parts or individuals in the whole with this kind of thinking provides a frame of reference for contemporary studies of interior issues in architecture.

The paper authored by Zhuang Shen was firstly published in *Time+Architecture*, 2018 (4): 20–23. The main content of this paper is based on the first half of the lecture I gave at Shanghai Naxing Space on April 14, 2018—The Echo of Unity: The Difference between the Self-referential Idea of Traditional Garden and The Contemporary Practical and Theoretical Attempt of Conversion. The lecture is one of a series of lectures about gardens delivered by Lu Andong, Tong Ming and Zhuang Shen from November 3, 2017 to June 3, 2018 and attended by Feng Lu, Li Xinggang, Liu Yichun, Lu Andong, Tong Ming, Wang Hui, Wang Junyang, Zhang Bin, Zhu Xiaofeng among other guests. Among which, both Tong Ming and Zhuang Shen started their lecture from analyzing the *Landscapes of Humble Administrator's Garden* painted by Wen Zhengming.

11

基于城市空间日常效率的普通建筑更新设计策略

Regeneration Design Strategy for Ordinary Buildings Based on the Everyday Urban Spatial Efficiency

日常城市和普通建筑的生死存亡是中国当代建成环境中一直存在的矛盾。一方面因为快速城市化，城区扩张和建筑数量急剧增长，另一方面是备受诟病的事实——建筑物的速生速死不仅造成了巨大的资源浪费，也造成日常的城市活力和多样的生活形态被粗暴地割裂。而这种日常生活的多样性，在不同的社会力量的博弈下，通常需要经过很多年才能逐渐形成。

中国城市化已经进入存量优化阶段，除历史保护区外，一般性社区改造和微更新成为未来城市深化发展的重点。比如《上海城市总体规划2017—2035》倡导有机更新、存量规划，关注社区，将15分钟生活圈视为社会治理和公共资源配置的基本单元。在《北京城市总体规划2016—2035》中，改善背街小巷公共空间面貌和城市修补被列入议程，并视为保障民生、提升宜居水平的必要措施。然而，相对于产业升级类的更新，以社区生活为目标的对普通建筑和区域更新的需求和实践缺乏多样有效的策略，尤其是政府主导的项目基本仍局限在净化和美化阶段。与之形成对比，因市场和社会的需求，普通建筑更新中自发形成了大量新的类型和富有活力的城市空间。比

如，为了降低高地价带来的投资风险，既有建筑和区域改造取代新项目开发已成为房产热点，也因此形成新的类型。开发主体也在转变：除了政府和大型房产公司，小型民营企业、私人投资者、个人业主、甚至设计师也加入了主持城乡更新的行列，如近年来如火如荼的民宿建设。因此，无论从未来规划和政策导向来看，还是从市场需求的自然规律来看，一般性城市区域和普通建筑改造更新正在成为中国当代城乡建筑实践的新趋向，也是城市发展走向社会融合和包容的过程中需要重视和解决的难题。

日常生活所具有的此时此地的真实性和活力，日常城市空间有别于自上而下规划和开发的空间的独特性及其意义，吸引了国内外不同领域研究者的关注。其中具有影响力的视角和方法包括：①政治经济学批判，将日常空间和实践视为反对资本和权力控制的突破口；[1] ②反思普通城市景观的逻辑[2]；③亚洲高密度城市空间的"隐形逻辑"和"考现学"[3]；④针对普通城市社区和街道空间的活力的研究[4]，等等。

将日常空间研究转化成建筑设计实践的经验是建筑师最关注的。犬吠工作室把考察重点放在类型叠加与周边环

196

The life and death of everyday city and ordinary buildings is an ever-existing paradox in contemporary Chinese built environment. In one aspect, it results from rapid urbanization, city expansion and vast architectural accumulation. In the other aspect, it is due to the fiercely criticized fact that the ephemeral life of Chinese buildings have caused not only a huge waste of resources, but also a violent disruption in city vigor and life style diversity, which is formed slowly with many years of competition among different social powers.

Urbanization in China has entered a stage of stock optimization. In addition to historical preservations, general community renewal and micro-renovation will become the main targets of future urban redevelopment. In *Shanghai Urban Master Plan 2017–2035*, organic renewals and stock optimization are promoted. More attention shall be directed towards community. The 15-minute life circle will become the basic unit of social governance and public resources allocation. In *Beijing Urban Master Plan 2016–2035*, public spatial improvement for the back lanes as well as urban remedy are highlighted in the livable city agenda. Nevertheless, compared with renewals in industry upgrading, regeneration practices for ordinary building and community areas enjoyed very limited strategies, especially those government-led projects, which are still restricted in clean-up and embellishment. In contrast, a large amount of new types and vigorous urban space are emerging in those ordinary building renewals driven by market and social

needs. For example, in order to lower investment risks bought by high land price, instead of new development, renovations for existing architecture and areas have become the popular topics in real estate market, thus forming a new investment type. The developer is changing as well. Other than government and large real estate developing companies, small enterprises, private investors, individual agents and even designers have been the hosts of urban and rural renewals, as you can see in the growing homestay construction in recent years. No matter considering the future plan and policy direction, or the natural law of market needs, renovation and renewal in ordinary urban areas and buildings have turned into a new trend for Chinese contemporary architectural practices in both urban and rural districts. It is also a crucial issue if we want to lead urban development to social integration and inclusion.

Everyday life, featured by its momentary realness and vigor, and everyday urban space, whose character and meaning are distinct from those of top-down plan and developed areas have drawn attention from worldwide researchers. Some of the influential perspectives and methods include: ①critique of political economy, which sees everyday space and practice as a breakthrough against capital and power control[1]; ②reflection on the logic of the ordinary cityscape[2]; ③the "invisible logic" and "modernology" in highly-dense city space in Asia[3]; ④researches on the vigor of ordinary city community and streets[4], etc..

境的关系上；张斌、冯路、范文兵等则关注室内外不同层级的共有空间与日常生活形态的对应关系；庄慎、华霞虹提出了城市"空间冗余"，即日常建筑不断改变的中性状态。但中国特色的日常城市空间的物质属性与生活效率之间的关系需要在建筑学层面做进一步系统分析。只有经过大量实例的调研，掌握建筑功能、空间和建构等规律时，才能加以应用。

存量优化城市化背景下的普通建筑更新

"普通建筑更新"主要可从以下两方面来界定：

1）既有建（构）筑物属性普通，缺乏显著的历史、社会文化、艺术美学、类型价值，主要是普通的居住、办公、小型零售商业和一般性公共功能，隶属大量标准化高速开发的重复平乏区域，或因历史积累和自发建造形成的无序混杂、片段化区域，无论是缺乏还是富有日常生活活力，它们通常被视为背景建筑。

2）更新的目的和要求普通，主要延续和改善日常使用。因为不属于以延续和发展建筑遗产生命和价值为目的的历史性标志性建筑的更新，也不致力于转变为重要的创意产业、城市地标或特殊房地产项目，此类项目中，资本和权力的驱动力相对较弱。普通建筑更新主要需要建筑设计策略而不是城市设计导则来指导，关注建筑物内外及其周边空间设施的改变和调整，跟以一般性城市公共空间为对象的城市微更新可能有交集，但重点不同。

亚洲高密度建成环境，中国特有的政治、经济、社会发展历史，过去三十年快速城市化背景使本土普通建筑更新问题具有特殊性、复杂性和不确定性。

一方面是复杂的类型和状态：不仅包括具有一般性历史文化价值的老建筑和非完整城市区域、基本不具备历史文化价值的新旧建筑和零散城市区域、不具有完整性的既有建筑局部（比如建筑屋顶、建筑立面、建筑室内等）和城市间隙、被重新开发的烂尾楼、需要临时调整使用的室内外空间，以及受城市美化运动影响的新旧既有建筑和城市空间，也包括尚在建设中，甚至尚在图纸中的各类建筑。针对不同的现状，需依据不同类型和状况针对性选择相应的设计策略。

另一方面是多样的目标和需求：无论从业主性质、工作范围、更新类型，还是从设计施工周期乃至建成后持续

What architects care most is how to turn the everyday space research into design practice experience. Relevant researches include: Atelier Bow-wow puts the emphasis on investigating the relationship between type superposition and the surrounding environment. Zhang Bin, Feng Lu, and Fan Wenbing care more about different levels indoors and outdoors common space and their coordination with the everyday lifestyle. Zhuang Shen/Hua Xiahong coined the term 'spatial redundancy' and raised the idea of a neutral urban state, calling attention to features such as constantly changing, usage adaptation and effective construction. But it needs further systematic architectural analysis to discover the relationship between the material property and living efficiency in everyday urban space in China. Only after sufficient case studies and when we master the principles of architectural functions, space and construction, can we apply them into real practice.

Ordinary Building Renewals under Stock-Optimization-Directed Urbanization

There are two aspects to "ordinary building renewals":

1) The existing building is ordinary in that they lack distinctive historic, social-cultural, artistic, aesthetic and type value. They mainly fulfill ordinary residential, office, small retailing and general public functions. These buildings belong to repetitive and monotonous areas rapidly developed under numerous standards, or orderless and fragmented areas accumulated through history and self-development. Whether they are lacking in or full of everyday vigor, they are usually seen as background architecture.

2) The aims and requirements, mainly for continuation and improvements in everyday use, are ordinary in renewal. It is different from renewals, which aim at continuing and developing the heritage and value of historical landmarks, nor does it aim to turn into important creative industry, city landmarks or special housing projects, so the driving forces of capital and power are relatively weak. In addition, ordinary building renewal mainly needs architectural design strategies instead of urban design guide. It pays attention to the change and adaptation inside and outside of buildings and their surrounding facilities and may overlap with urban micro-renewals in ordinary city public space but are different in focus.

The highly-dense built environment in Asia, the characteristic political, economic and social development history in China, the rapid urbanization in the past 30 years combined together have infused specialness, complexity and uncertainty in local ordinary architecture renewals.

On the one hand is the complex types and conditions not only include old buildings containing general historic and cultural values and incomplete urban areas; new and old buildings without historic and social values and scattered urban areas; parts of existing incomplete buildings (for example, roof, facade, interior of a building) and urban gaps, re-developed

时间来看，普通建筑更新要求有更多的不确定性和临时性。为了实现迥然不同的目的，需要灵活地提出适宜的策略，尤其要考虑有效性。

当代城市空间的日常效率

　　城市空间的日常效率主要研究中微观尺度的城市空间，从单体建筑的局部和整体，到单个街区范围的城市空间，研究它们在建成以后因为时间的不断积累而形成的各种一般性建造改变的物理结果，及其实现个体和群体日常生活目标的有效性。

　　重要的、标志性的城市空间和地标建筑具有较大的稳定性，能构成集体记忆，无论是全新设计作品还是重要的保护更新项目，都更加接近于传统建筑学中对永恒性和持久的美的追求，需要通过具有吸引力的视觉形象来获得价值认同。而日常城市则充满了变化，其发展逻辑更接近经济效能的算计。

　　城市空间的日常效率强调现象，即对建造物及其之间空间的物理属性的分析，而非意义和价值层面的解读。城市空间日常效率包含以下两个要素：

1）　日常性

空间范围：不强调系统性和完整性。

时间范围：建成以后所有的时间平等看待，日积月累持续改变。

内容范围：主要满足一般大众的日常生活，没有突出的文化象征，达不到刺激经济的目的。

形式特征：通常重复、平乏、混杂，不具有统一性。

2）　有效性

包括使用的有效性和建造的有效性，前者是目的，后者是手段。

其中使用调整的日常效率包括：内部功能改善效率、类型空间匹配效率、活动模式组合效率。讲究时效的建造效率包括与建成使用和延续时间相协调的有效的材料选择逻辑、时间效用逻辑和建构应变逻辑。

普通建筑更新设计策略

　　将城市空间的不断调整视为中性改变的立场，以设计难题和解决思路为导向，以实现良好的日常生活效率为目标的更新设计策略，主要包括以下四个层面：

198

unfinished building, interior and exterior space in need of temporary adjustments; and new and old existing buildings and urban space influenced by beautification campaign in the city; even those still under construction or on-the-paper buildings. Design strategies are needed and should be selected for different types and situations.

On the other hand is the varied objectives and needs. No matter it is from the clients' traits, job range, renewal type or design and construction cycle or even the time of duration after construction, ordinary buildings renewal encompasses more uncertainties and temporariness. To realize distinctive and different aims, we need to devise flexible and appropriate strategies and take into special consideration the efficacy.

Everyday Efficiency in Contemporary Urban Space

The study of everyday efficiency in urban space mainly examines urban space from a meso-and-micro scale, including parts and whole of a single building, all kinds of urban space in a single block, etc.. Research focuses on changes of the built environment, from the physical result of various general modification during years of usage to their effectiveness in fulfilling individual or group objectives in everyday life.

Important, iconic city spaces and landmarks tend to keep stable for they constitute collective memory. No matter as initial design or important preservation and renovation project, they would pursue permanence and lasting beauty, since in traditional architecture, appealing visual image leads to recognizable significance. While cities are full of changes, their development rely more on the logic of economic efficiency.

Everyday efficiency in urban space emphasizes the physical properties of construction sites and the spaces they form, rather than interpretation of meaning and value. Everyday efficiency in urban space includes the following two elements:

1)　Everydayness

Space range: systematic and complete space are no longer emphasized

Time range: time after construction is treated equally; changes constantly take place as time goes on

Content range: mainly to fulfill peoples' everyday living instead of building prominent cultural symbol or stimulating economic growth.

Form features: repetitive, banal, mixed, inconsistent

2)　Efficiency

This includes efficiency in use and construction. The former is the purpose and the latter is the method.

Among these, everyday efficiency in use and adaptation includes: efficiency in improvement of internal function, efficiency in coordination of type space, efficiency in combination of activity modes. Time efficiency in construction focuses on effective material selection logic, time efficiency logic and structure contingency logic coordinated with use after construction and with time extension.

1) 优化日常使用效率的功能更新设计策略

普通建筑更新最重要的出发点、动力和成效是完善优化使用效率。与之相应的功能更新策略包括：使用的具体化和拓展；使用的类型化和系统化组织；内部使用外溢后，空间形式再组织的整体考虑；在看似仅有美化意义的普通建筑表层更新中发现改进使用的契机等。

2) 重构日常体验效率的空间氛围更新设计策略

普通建筑更新经常涉及类型的改变，即使功能不变，也希望空间体验效果有本质提升。与之相应的空间氛围更新策略包括：新旧空间协调性的把握；利用既有建筑要素展开新的空间组织和氛围营造；不同类型空间氛围的协调；中性地看待历史和风格差异，按照目标灵活应用等。

3) 激发日常活动效率的生活模式更新设计策略

普通建筑更新的理想是构建具有包容性和富有活力的城市日常生活，而这正是以表面的净化和美化，或者贵族化为导向的当下中国城市更新最为缺乏的。普通建筑更新的难点是在有限的物理空间调整和改变时如何激发多样的、富有吸引力的日常活动效率。这种以内容为核心的生活模式更新策略包括：整理空间结构与生活形态的关系；

利用既有单体空间结构及其组合来重组新的功能类型的生活模式；动态看待物质空间与生活模式的对应性；探索差异并置、混合与包容的可能性等。

4) 实现日常建造效率的建构更新设计策略

相比重大公共项目，普通建筑更新更多地受到时间周期、资金投入、技术水平等各方面的限制，其材料、技术、工艺等方面的选择更需要考虑便捷性、适宜性和时间效用。相应的建构更新策略包括：根据既有建筑现状条件和目标要求，尤其是时间性要求来选择适宜的材料、结构和构造方式；打破不同材料和建造系统的界限，根据需要灵活混合与创新应用；充分考虑本土建造技术的限制并巧加组织；不可预见的过程问题变通处理等。

持续循环的现实建筑学

日常即改变是城市空间的本质属性。对以存量优化和社区营建为目的的城市更新更应坚持中性调整立场，而非单一的增长进步模式。这种基于现实的本体认知也体现了当代建筑实践从设计/建造的静态因果模式到概念/建造/使用/改变的持续循环模式发展的新趋势。

Design Strategies for Ordinary Architectural Renewal

Design strategies for ordinary architectural renewal see continuous adjustments as neutral change in urban space. They would be directed by design problems and their solutions, aiming at a suitable everyday living efficiency. There are at least four layers:

1) Function renewal strategies for optimizing everyday use efficiency

To optimize use efficiency is the most important starting point, motivation and achievement for ordinary architectural renewal. The according function renewal strategies include: specifying and extending the usage; categorizing and systemizing of usage; overall consideration of spatial reorganization after usage has exceeded internal space; discovering chances for functional improvements during ordinary building appearance renewals, which seem to have only beautifying meaning.

2) Atmosphere renewal strategies for reconstructing everyday spatial experience efficiency

Ordinary buildings renewals often involve changes in type. Even though the function keeps the same, improved spatial experience must be a major expectation. Accordingly, renewal strategies in spatial atmosphere include: creating a suitable tone for both new and old spaces; taking advantage of the existing architectural elements to form new spatial organization and atmosphere; coordinating different types of spatial atmospheres; viewing historical and stylish differences

neutrally and equally; flexibly applying principles based on their objectives and so on.

3) Life style renewal strategies for stimulating everyday activity efficiency

The ideal architectural renewal for ordinary buildings is to construct inclusive and vigorous urban everyday life. This is exactly what is lacking in those renewal programs aiming at urban purification, beautification and gentrification. The biggest challenge for ordinary building renewals lies in how it can stimulate various and appealing everyday activity efficiency through adapting and changing limited physical sources. Such life styles renewal strategy includes: organizing the relationship between spatial structure and living form; recombining life styles under new functions and types with the help of existing individual spatial structure and its composions; viewing the coordination between physical space and life styles in a dynamic process; exploring the possibilities of juxtaposition, hybridization and inclusion of differences.

4) Tectonic renewal strategies for realizing everyday construction efficiency

Compared with major public projects, ordinary architecture renewals are more constricted in time, budget, technology, and so on. Materials, techniques as well as crafts may be selected according to convenience, expediency and time efficiency. Tectonic renewal strategies include: selecting appropriate materials, structure and construction

本文作者系华霞虹，由国家自然科学基金面上项目《基于城市空间日常效率的普通建筑更新设计策略研究》（2018.1–2021.12，编号：51778419）的申请报告改写而成。该课题主持人为华霞虹，由同济大学与上海阿科米星建筑设计事务所两家单位合作研究。

200

methods based on current architectural conditions, aims and requirements, especially the time duration; breaking through the boundaries among different materials and construction systems, flexibly mixing and originally applying based on actual needs; fully considering the restrictions from local architectural techniques and skillfully organizing them; handling unpredictable problems in the process, etc..

Towards a Sustainable Architecture of Reality

Everyday change is the essence of urban space. For urban renewals aiming at stock optimization and community construction, we should insist on the position of neutral adaption instead of one-dimensional progress mode. Such ontological cognition based on reality also shows a new trend in contemporary architectural practice, moving from the static cause-and-effect mode in design/construction to a sustainable and recycling mode covering concept, construction, usage, and change circle.

The paper was written by Hua Xiahong based on the application for National Natural Science Foundation Project "Study on Design Strategies of Ordinary Building Renewal Based on the Everyday Efficiency of Urban Space" (Jan. 2018–Dec. 2021, No. 51778419). This research project is led by Hua Xiahong, cooperated by Tongji University and Atelier Archmixing.

注释与参考文献 Notes and Bibliography

阿科米星十年：寻找另一种建筑 / 建筑学
A Decade for Atelier Archmixing:
In Search of an Another Architecture

1————李东、黄居正、易娜：《思想无言——"大舍"主创建筑师访谈》，《建筑师》2006 年 8 月（总 122 期），第 55 页。

2————庄慎、华霞虹：《城市内的工作室》，《时代建筑》2015 年第 5 期，第 102 页。

3————同上。

4————王骏阳：《勒·柯布西耶 Vers une architecture 译名考》，载王骏阳：《理论·历史·评论（一）》，同济大学出版社，2017，第 58–73 页。

5————Jean-Louis Cohen, "Introduction," in *Toward an Architecture*, Le Corbusier (Los Angeles: Getty Research Institute, 2007), p.49.

6————John Summerson, "The Case for a Theory of Modern Architecture," in *Architecture Culture 1943–1968, A Documentary Anthology*, ed. Joan Ockman, Columbia Books of Architecture (New York: Rizzoli, 1993), p.229.

7————Reyner Banham, *Theory and Design in the First Machine Age* [London: Butterworth & Co (Publishers) Ltd., 1960], p.246.

8————Reyner Banham, "The New Brutalism," in *A Critic Writes: Essays by Reyner Banham*, selected by Mary Banham et al. (Berkley Los Angeles London : University of California Press, 1999), p.12.

9————Nigel Whiteley, "Banham and 'Otherness': Reyner Banham (1922–1988) and his quest for an Architecture Autre," in *Architectural History, Journal of the Society of Architectural Historians of Great Britain*, Vol. 33 (1990): 219.

10————Anthony Vidler, *Histories of the Immediate Present: Inventing Architectural Modernism* (Cambridge, MA: The MIT Press, 2008), p.134.

11————Reyner Banham, "The New Brutalism," p.12.

12————Reyner Banham, "The New Brutalism," p.14.

13————Nigel Whiteley, "Banham and 'Otherness'," p.202.

14————庄慎、华霞虹：《选择在个人和大众之间》，《建筑师》2012 年第 3 期（总 157 期），第 43 页。

15————同上，第 43–44 页。

16————同上，第 44 页。

17————同上，第 45–46 页。

18————庄慎、华霞虹：《改变即日常——阿科米星的实践综述》，《建筑师》2014 年第 2 期（总 168 期），第 131–132 页。

19————Murray Fraser, "Introduction," in *Design Research in Architecture: An Overview* (Surrey: Ashgate Publishing Limited, 2013), p.4.

20————篠原资明：《德勒兹：游牧民》，徐金凤译，河北教育出版社，2001，第 157 页。

21————庄慎、华霞虹：《非识别系统的一种高度——杰弗里·巴瓦的建筑世界》，《建筑学报》2014 年第 11 期，第 28 页。

22————Reyner Banham, *Theory and Design in the First Machine Age*, p.246.

23————庄慎、华霞虹：《看不见的改变：论使用端空间技术化的可能》，《时代建筑》2018 年第 3 期，第 34 页。

24————Anthony Vidler, *Histories of the Immediate Present*, p.134.

25————庄慎：《看不见的改变：论使用端空间技术化的可能》，第 35 页。

26————同上，第 33 页。

27————参见梁思思、张维：《基于"前策划一后评估"闭环的使用后评估研究进展综述》，《时代建筑》2019 年第 4 期，第 52–55 页。

I————Zhuang Shen and Hua Xiahong, "Work within the City" (in Chinese), in *Time + Architecture*, no.5 (2015): 102.

II————Ibid.

III————Ibid.

IV————John Summerson, "The Case for a Theory of Modern Architecture," in *Architecture Culture 1943–1968, A Documentary Anthology*, ed. Joan Ockman, Columbia Books of Architecture (New York: Rizzoli, 1993), p.229.

V————Reyner Banham, *Theory and Design in the First Machine Age* [London: Butterworth & Co (Publishers) Ltd., 1960], p.246.

VI————Ibid., p.246; 220.

VII————Nigel Whiteley, "Banham and 'Otherness': Reyner Banham (1922–1988) and his quest for an Architecture Autre," *Architectural History, Journal of the Society of Architectural Historians of Great Britain*, Vol. 33 (1990): 219.

VIII————Anthony Vidler, *Histories of the Immediate Present: Inventing Architectural Modernism* (Cambridge, MA: The MIT Press, 2008), p.134.

IX————Reyner Banham, "The New Brutalism," in *A Critic Writes: Essays by Reyner Banham*, selected by Mary Banham et al. (Berkley Los Angeles London: University of California Press, 1999), p.12.

X————Zhuang Shen and Hua Xiahong, "Standing between the Individual and the Public" (in Chinese), *The Architect*, no.3 (2012): 43.

XI————Ibid., 43–44.

XII————Ibid., 44.

XIII————Ibid., 45–46.

XIV————Zhuang Shen and Hua Xiahong, "Change is More: Atelier Archmixing's Practice" (in Chinese), *The Architect*, no.2 (2014): 131.

XV————Ibid., 132.

XVI————Murray Fraser, "Introduction," *Design Research in Architecture: An Overview* (Surrey: Ashgate Publishing Limited, 2013), p.4.

XVII————Ibid.

XVIII————Wang Jun-Yang, "A Review of the 2018 Academic Newcomer Assistance Program by the *Architectural Journal*" (in Chinese), *Architectural Journal*, no.8 (2018): 105.

XIX————Murray Fraser, "Introduction," p.7.

XX————Gilles Deleuze & Félix Guattari, *What Is Philosophy?*, trans. Hugh Tomlinson and Graham Burchell (New York: Columbia University Press, 1994), p.24.

XXI——Zhuang Shen and Hua Xiahong, "An Altitude of Unrecognizable System: The Architectural World of Geoffrey Bawa" (in Chinese), *Architectural Journal*, no.11 (2014): p.28.

XXII—— Reyner Banham, *Theory and Design in the First Machine Age*, p.246.

XXIII——Reyner Banham, "The New Brutalism," p.11.

XXIV——Reyner Banham. *The Architecture of Well-tempered Environment* (London: The Architectural Press, 1969), p.23.

XXV——Ibid., p.111.

XXVI——Zhuang Shen, "Invisible Change: Technologizing Space at the User's End" (in Chinese), *Time + Architecture*, no.3 (2018): 34.

XXVII——Ibid.

XXVIII——Anthony Vidler, *Histories of the Immediate Present*, p.134.

XXIX——Zhuang Shen, "Invisible Change: Technologizing Space at the User's End": 35.

XXX——Lu Andong, "Cotton Lab Urban Lounge: A Manifesto of Interiority" (in Chinese), *Architectural Journal*, no.7 (2018): 52–59.

XXXI——Zhuang Shen, "Invisible Change: Technologizing Space at the User's End": 33.

XXXII——Liang Sisi and Zhang Wei, "A Review of Research Progress on Post-Occupation Evalutation Based on the Close-Loop System of 'Analysis-first-Evalutaion-after'" (in Chinese), *Time + Architecture*, no.4 (2019): 52–55.

葛明 × 庄慎：城市建筑学的核心问题
GE Ming × ZHUANG Shen:
Core Issue on Urban Architecture

1——葛明：《微园记》,《建筑学报》2015 年第 12 期，第 30–37 页。
Ge Ming, "Notes on the Wei Yuan Garden" (in Chinese), *Architectural Journal*, no.12 (2015): 30–37.

2——葛明：《日常生活——空间的方法》,《新建筑》2014 年第 5 期，第 4–9 页。
Ge Ming, "Everyday Life: Design Methodology of Space"(in Chinese), *New Architecture*, no.5 (2014): 4–9.

3——葛明：《体积法 (1)——设计方法系列研究之一》,《建筑学报》2013 年第 8 期，第 7–13 页；葛明：《体积法 (2)——设计方法研究系列之一》,《建筑学报》2013 年第 9 期，第 1–7 页。
Ge Ming, "Raumplan(1): Series Study on Design Method-Part One"(in Chinese), *Architectural Journal*, no.8 (2013): 7–13; Ge Ming, "Raumplan (2): Series Study on Design Method-Part One"(in Chinese), *Architectural Journal*, no.9 (2013): 1–7.

选择在个人与大众之间
Standing Between the Individual and the Public

1——弗兰克·盖里设计的古根海姆博物馆使日益没落的西班牙工业城市毕尔巴鄂一跃成为举世瞩目的旅游胜地，创造了大量就业机会，促进了经济和城市的复兴。这种通过形象工程的建设实现城市复兴的现象被称为"毕尔巴鄂效应"，作为经营城市的成功典范得到全世界的关注和效仿。
The Guggenheim Museum designed by Frank Gehry catapulted the declining Spanish industrial city of Bilbao into the status of a world-renowned tourist destination, creating many job opportunities and promoting economic and urban revitalization. The phenomenon of revitalizing a city through the construction of image projects is known as the "Bilbao Effect", which as a successful example of city management has captured attention

and been emulated worldwide.

2——如科幻电影《我，机器人》中具有自主意识的 NS-5 型机器人 Sonny。电影改编自美国作家艾萨克·阿西莫夫出版于 1950 年的科幻小说短篇集。阿西莫夫提出了著名的机器人技术的四大定律。第零条定律：机器人不可以伤害人类，也不允许机器人在人类遇到危害时毫无反应；第一条定律：机器人不允许伤害一个人，或者在那个人遇到危害时毫无反应，除非这会违背第零条机器人技术定律；第二条定律：机器人必须遵从人的命令，除非这会违背第零条定律或者第一条定律；第三条定律：机器人必须保护它自己的存在，只要这种保护不违背第零条、第一条、第二条定律。
Such as the self-aware NS-5 robot Sonny in sci-fi movie "I, Robot". The film was adapted from a collection of science fiction short stories by American writer Isaac Asimov which was published in 1950. Asimov introduced the famous "Four Laws of Robotics". Zeroth Law: A robot may not injure humanity, or, by inaction, allow humanity to come to harm. First Law: A robot may not injure a human being or, through inaction, allow a human being to come to harm. Second Law: A robot must obey the orders given it by human beings except where such orders would conflict with the First Law. Third Law: A robot must protect its own existence as long as such protection does not conflict with the First or Second Law.

3——庄慎：《中国庭院的生命精神》，硕士学位论文，上海：同济大学建筑与城市规划学院，1997。
Zhuang Shen, "The Life Spirit of Chinese Courtyards" (Master diss., Shanghai: CAUP of Tongji University, 1997).

4——宗白华：《宗白华全集（第一～第四卷）》，安徽教育出版社，1994。
Zong Baihua, *Complete Works of Zong Baihua*, Volumes 1–4 (in Chinese) (Hefei: Anhui Education Press, 1994).

5——阿卡汗建筑奖，1977 年由伊斯兰什叶·伊斯玛仪勒教派第 49 代世袭精神领袖阿卡汗殿下创立，奖项涉及所有的当代建筑、社会住宅、社区改造、历史建筑和街区的保护与更新以及景观设计，目的是加强对伊斯兰社会建筑的理解和实践。阿卡汗建筑奖的官方网址是 www.akdn.org/index.html。
The Aga Khan Award for Architecture was established in 1977 by the Aga Khan, the 49th hereditary Imam of the Shia Ismaili Muslims. The award covers the renovation of all contemporary buildings, social housing and communities, the conservation and renewal of historical buildings and blocks, and landscape design with the aim of enhancing the understanding and practice of architecture in Islamic societies. The official website of the Aga Khan Award is www.akdn.org/index.html.

6——同济大学建筑与城市规划学院，编：《建筑弦柱：冯纪忠论稿》，上海科学技术出版社，2003。
College of Architecture and Urban Planning, Tongji University ed., *Pillars of Architecture: Manuscript by Feng Jizhong* (in Chinese) (Shanghai: Shanghai Science and Technology Press, 2003).

7——关于"离"的美学解释详见《宗白华全集》中的《中国美学思想专题研究笔记》一文。
For an aesthetic explanation of "Separation", see the article "Notes on A Special Study of Chinese Aesthetic Thoughts" in *Complete Works of Zong Baihua*

8——[法]让·波德里亚：《象征交换与死亡》，车槿山译，译林出版社，2006。
Jean Baudrilltard, *Symbolic Exchange and Death* (in Chinese), trans. Che Jinshan (Nanjing: The Yilin Press, 2006).

9———出自马克思·恩格斯的《共产党宣言》"……一切固定的僵化的关系以及与之相适应的素被尊崇的观念和见解都被消除了，一切新形成的关系等不到固定下来就陈旧了。一切等级的和坚固的东西都烟消云散了，一切神圣的东西都被亵渎了。人们终于不得不直面……他们生活的真实状况和他们的相互关系。"

Excerpted from *The Communist Manifesto* by Marx and Engels "... All fixed, fast-frozen relations, with their train of ancient and venerable prejudices and opinions, are swept away, all new-formed ones become antiquated before they can ossify. All that is solid melts into air, all that is holy is profaned, and man is at last compelled to face ... his real conditions of life, and his relations with his kind."

10———[法] 尚·布希亚:《物体系》，林志明译，上海人民出版社，2001，第 163 页。

Jean Baudrillard, *The System of Objects* (in Chinese), trans. Lin Zhiming (Shanghai: Shanghai People's Publishing House, 2001), p163.

非识别体系的一种高度：杰弗里·巴瓦的建筑世界
An Altitude of Unrecognizable System: The Architectural World of Geoffrey Bawa

1———斯里兰卡，旧称锡兰，是一个南亚岛国，南部为热带雨林气候，北部为热带草原气候。在公元前 5 世纪印度僧伽罗人迁入，公元前 2 世纪，南印度泰米尔人迁入，从此两个种族冲突不断。1521 年为葡萄牙船队占领，1656 年为荷兰占领，1796 年则是英国，1802 年成为英国殖民地，直到 1948 年宣布独立，1972 年，斯里兰卡共和国成立，1978 年，斯里兰卡民主社会主义共和国成立，2009 年 5 月 18 日，政府军击毙猛虎组织最高领袖，终于宣布内战结束。

Sri Lanka (formerly Ceylon) is an island nation in South Asia. It has a tropical rainforest climate in the south and a savannah climate in the north. The Sinhalese arrived in the 5th century B.C. from India; Tamils arrived in the 2nd century B.C. from South India. Since then, the two ethnic groups have been fighting each other. It was occupied by a Portuguese fleet in 1521, by the Netherlands in 1656 and by Great Britain in 1796, became a British colony in 1802 and declared independence in 1948. The Republic of Sri Lanka was established in 1972; the Democratic Socialist Republic of Sri Lanka was established in 1978. On May 18, 2009, government forces killed the leader of the LTTE, bringing the civil war to an end.

2———巴瓦的祖父为摩尔人后裔，祖母为法国人后裔，父亲本杰明是当时锡兰著名的大律师，母亲贝莎则是荷兰裔德国雇佣军的后裔，外祖父和舅舅均为橡胶园主。巴瓦的哥哥比维斯曾是军人（侍奉英国军官）和橡胶园主，后来通过营建自己的庄园成为著名的园艺师，同时也是画家和作家。

Bawa's paternal grandfather was of Moorish descent, his paternal grandmother was of French descent. His father Benjamin Bawa was a famous barrister in Ceylon at that time, his mother Bertha Bawa was a descendant of a Dutch German mercenary, and both his maternal grandfather and maternal uncle were rubber plantation owners. Bawa's older brother Bevis Bawa was a soldier (serving British officers) and a rubber plantation owner, and later became a famous gardener by building his own estate. He was also a painter and writer.

3———http://www.geoffreybawa.com/work/

4———大卫·罗布森是《巴瓦作品全集》等书的作者，也是巴瓦最主要的研究者和巴瓦基金会的主要负责人。

David Robson is the author of *Geoffrey Bawa: The Complete Works*, among other books. He is also the lead researcher for Bawa and the person principally in charge of the Geoffry Bawa Trust.

[1]———Charles Correa, Kenneth Frampton, David Robson. *Modernity and Community: Architecture in the Islamic World*[M]. Thames & Hudson, 2001.

[2]———Michael Keniger. *Bawa: Recent Projects 1987–95*[M]. Brisbane: Queensland Chapter of the RAIA, 1996.

[3]———David Robson. *Geoffrey Bawa: The Complete Works*[M]. Thames & Hudson, 2002: 17.

[4]———David Robson. "The Genius of the Place: The Building and Landscape of Geoffery Bawa"[M]// Charles Correa, Kenneth Frampton, David Robson. *Modernity and Community: Architecture in the Islamic World*. Thames & Hudson, 2001: 17–48.

[5]———David Robson, Dominic Sansoni. *Bawa: The Sri Lanka Gardens*[M]. Thames & Hudson, 2008.

[6]———A+U 中文版编辑部. 专辑：杰弗里·巴瓦——斯里兰卡之光. A+U 中文版 039, 2011 (6).

[7]———David Robson. *Beyond Bawa: Modern Masterworks of Monsoom Asia*[M]. Thames & Hudson, 2007.

[8]———Jimmy Lim. Interview with Geoffrey Bawa[J]. Majalah Arkitek. 1990 (1–2). www.geoffreybawa.com

[9]———有方. 旅行手册《变化即永恒：巴瓦的启示》第 1 期，2014.

日常·改变·非识别体系
Everyday, Change and the Unrecognizable System

1———庄慎、华霞虹:《选择在个人与大众之间》,《建筑师》2012 年第 3 期，第 43–51 页。

2———庄慎、华霞虹:《改变即日常：阿科米星的实践综述》,《建筑师》2014 年第 2 期，第 131–137 页。

3———该作品系阿科米星建筑设计事务所与亘建筑事务所合作设计。

4———庄慎、华霞虹:《非识别体系的一种高度——杰弗里·巴瓦的建筑世界》,《建筑学报》2014 年第 12 期，第 27–35 页。

I———Atelier Archmixing has moved offices five times in the past eight years (2009–17). After working stably for five years in the first workplace located in an old residence in the city centre, the practice failed to find another suitable long-term workplace for stable rent. The partners then initiated a plan of ten-year "moving", namely moving the workplace once a year and adjusting its spatial organisation. The workplace was then divided into three parts, a fixed and cheap storage space in the countryside, a multi-functional space in the city centre, and a flexible office space that changed each year. This plan is not only a laboratorial action, but also a kind of mental experiment. Faced with an office space and city environment of constant change, will we finally become used to this instability? The experience of constantly seeking, adapting, adjusting and using the workplace in Shanghai makes Atelier Archmixing pay more attention to the internal architectural and urban space. See: Zhuang Shen and Hua Xiahong, "Work within the City" (in Chinese), *Time + Architecture*, no.5 (2015): 100–107.

II———Zhuang Shen and Hua Xiahong, "Spatial Redundancy" (in Chineses), *Time + Architecture*, no.5 (2015): 108–119.

III———Zhuang Shen and Zhou Jianjia, Li Danfeng, "An Alternative to Open a City: A Work Session on Urban Research towards

Contemporary Shanghai" (in Chinese), *Time + Architecture*, no.5 (2015): 114–129.

IV———Hua Xiahong and Zhuang Shen, "On Facade Renovation" (in Chinese), *Time + Architecture*, no.4 (2016): 24–32.

V———Zhuang Shen and Hua Xiahong, "Everyday, Change, Unrecognizable System" (in Chinese), *New Architecture*, no.6 (2014): 16–19.

VI———Hua Xiahong, "Quotation and the Construction of Chinese Architectural Identity," *Perspecta 49: The Yale Architectural Journal* (2016), pp.201–212.

VII———Ibid., p. 209.

空间冗余
Spatial Redundancy

1———如数据库系统中，数据冗余是指一个字段在多个表里重复出现，可能导致数据异常和损坏。

For example, in databases, data redundancy refers to a repetitively present field, which may lead to data anomalies and corruption.

2———计算机中的数据多重备份、工程中的超静定结构、多路电源配置等都是这样专门设计的防范性措施。

Multiple backup of data in computer, statically indeterminate structure in the project, multi-channel power configuration, etc. are especially designed as preventive measures.

3———Jerold S. Kayden, "the New York City Department of City Planning, the Municipal Art Society of New York," *Privately Owned Public Space: The New York City Experience* (John Wiley & Sons, 2000), p. 7–19.

4———Denise Scott Brown, "Learning from Pop," *Casabella* (Dec. 1971): 359–360.

5———Rem Koolhaas, "'Life in the Metropolis' or 'The Culture of Congestion'," *Architectural Design* (Aug. 1977). 转引自 K.Micheal Hays ed., *Architecture Theory since 1968*, (Cambridge: The MIT Press. 2000), pp. 320–330.

6———Rem Koolhaas, "Junkspace," *October* (Spring 2002): 175–190.

7———庄慎、华霞虹：《日常·改变·非识别体系》，《新建筑》2014 年第 6 期，第 16–19 页。
Zhuang Shen and Hua Xiahong, "Everyday, Change and the Unrecognizable System" (in Chinese), *New Architecture*, no.6 (2014): 16–19.

城市内的工作室
Work Within the City

1———庄慎、任皓：《选择在个人与大众之间——阿科米星设计事务所办公楼》，《城市·环境·设计》第 55 期，第 238–241 页。

2———王方戟、庄慎《关于建筑形式的对话—一个围绕阿科米星建筑事务所最新实践的讨论》，《建筑师》2014 年第 2 期，第 120–131 页。

I———Zhuang Shen and Hua Xiahong, "Work Within the City" (in Chinese), *Time + Architecture*, no.5 (2015): 100–107.

II———Zhuang Shen and Hua Xiahong, "Spatial Redundancy" (in Chinese), *Time + Architecture*, no.5 (2015): 108–111.

III———Zhuang Shen and Hua Xiahong, "Everyday Change, Unrecognizable System" (in Chinese), *New Architecture*, no.6 (2014): 16–19.

IV———Hua Xiahong and Zhuang Shen, "On Facade Renovation" (in Chinese), *Time + Architecture*, no.4 (2016): 24–28.

V———This paper was funded by the NSFC(National Natural Science Foundation of China) programme "Study on Design Strategies of Ordinary Building Renewal Based on the Everyday Efficiency of Urban Space"(No. 51778419).

走向城市建筑学的可能：“虹口 1617 展览暨城市研究”研讨会评述
Possibilities Towards an Urban Architecture: Notes on the Symposium of "Hongkou 1617 Exhibition and Urban Studies"

1———CEED 负责的“Line 3”采用五种方式和视角来采集资料，以期从不同侧面展现 3 号线介入城市空间和城市生活的复杂面貌。①延时摄像。在西江湾路原阿科米星工作室办公室窗外架设延时相机，定点连续拍摄 16 天。②轻轨上。将两个手机固定在车厢相对两侧的位置同时拍摄，从赤峰路到宝山路。早晨晴，自北向南，下午阴雨，自南向北。③公交车上。在 942 路大巴士前后车窗同时定点拍摄，从上农新村到中兴路宝兴路。④步行。沿三号线西侧自北向南步行 1 小时，手机持续拍摄。⑤社区。从三号线周边多个社区可以看到轨道的地方由内向外定点拍摄，每段拍摄持续 3~10 分钟。

In CEED's "Line 3", five ways and perspectives are used to collect data. They expected to reveal from different aspects the complexity of Line 3's involvement in urban space and urban life. ①Time-lapse Camera. A time-lapse camera was set up outside the office window in former Atelier Archmixing Studio on West Jiangwan Road for continuous shooting at a fixed point. (16 consecutive days) ②On light rail. Shooting simultaneously with two mobile phones fixed on symmetric points in the compartment, from Chifeng road to Baoshan Road. Sunny day in the morning, travel from north to south and rainy in the afternoon, travel from south to north. ③On the bus. Shooting at the front and rear windows simultaneously on Bus No. 942 from Shangnong New Village to Zhongxing Road Baoxing Road. ④Walking. One hours' walk from north to south along the west side of Line 3 for continuous shooting with mobile phone. ⑤Community. From several neighborhoods around Line 3 where the light rail can be seen, shooting in fixed places, 3 to 10 minutes each video.

2———玛丽·雪莱笔下的《弗兰肯斯坦》讲述的是科学家试图通过肢体的缝合、用看似严谨的方法创造人造物，伴随着人造物自主的觉醒，二者的关系终于从主宰变成失控，由附属走向反噬。冶是团队借用这个名字，通过圣鲁迅（虹口足球场、三号线轻轨站、虹口龙之梦）、东宝兴路站以及虬江路音像城三个案例去思考都市中的拼合、对峙与碰撞。

In Mary Shelley's *Frankenstein*, scientists attempt to create a creature by stitching their limbs and using seemingly rigorous methods. With the autonomous awakening of the creature, the relationship between the two has finally changed from domination to out of control, from attachment to counterattack. YeArch team borrowed the name to think about the combination, confrontation and collision in the city through three cases: St. Luxun (Hongkou Football Stadium, Station, Hongkou CapitaLand), Dongbaoxing Road Station and Qiujiang Road Audio-visual City.

3———“逆向还原”是一种为显示建筑物改变而采用的记录与模拟城市建筑状态的方法，记录的对象是城市中的普通建筑物，具体方法是描述对比建筑物的两个记录点：一个是可记录的当前考察时建筑的即时状态，另一个是可推测描述的建筑物开始建立时的状态。这样的方法既不是考现，也不是考古。它更像一次有意思的侦探历程，需要透过业已改变的现在，来寻找甚至猜测最初的样子。阿科米星团队开展此研究的目的是探讨城市中不断改变的建筑带来的建筑学新认知和新方法。

"Analytic Restoration" is a method of recording and simulating the state of urban buildings in order to show their changes. The target of the recording is ordinary buildings in the city. The specific method is to describe and compare buildings at two points in time: one is the immediate state of the buildings when the current investigation is recorded; the other is the state of a building which can be speculatively described when the construction started. Such a method is neither examination of reality nor archaeology. It's more like an interesting detective journey, looking for and even guessing what it was like through the changes. The aim of this study, conducted by the Atelier Archmixing team, is to explore new architectural insights and approaches brought about by changing buildings in cities.

4——"上海（城市再研究）计划"是从 2013 年开始，无样建筑工作室主持建筑师冯路、致正建筑工作室主持建筑师张斌、上海交通大学建筑系副教授范文兵和阿科米星建筑工作室庄慎合作在上海开展的城市调研项目，已完成的项目包括：田林新村、浦东 13 号线站点城市公共空间研究、青浦航运新村研究及社区服务中心改造等。
Shanghai (Urban Re-studies) Project (SHP, Shanghai Project) is a joint urban research project in Shanghai initiated in 2013 by Feng Lu and Zhang Bin, the Head from Wuyang Architecture Studio and Atelier Z+, respectively, Fan Wenbing, Associate Professor of Architecture Department, Shanghai Jiaotong University, and Zhuang Shen from Atelier Archmixing Studio. The completed projects include: Tianlin New Village, Pudong Line 13 Station Urban Public Space Research, Qingpu Shipping New Village Research and Community Service Center Renovation, etc.

5——王家浩发言。
Speech by Wang Jiahao.

6——鲁安东发言。
Speech by Lu Andong.

7——李华发言。
Speech by Li Hua.

8——童明发言。
Speech by Tong Ming.

9——范文兵发言。
Speech by Fan Wenbing.

10——窦平平发言。
Speech by Dou Pingping.

11——王骏阳发言。
Speech by Wang Jun-Yang.

12——王方戟发言
Speech by Wang Fangji.

13——张斌发言。
Speech by Zhang Bin.

14——华霞虹，微信公众号"ceedTJ"，虹口 1617/Line3 。
Hua Xiahong. WeChat official Account "ceedTJ", Hongkou 1617/Line 3.

15——周渐佳，微信公众号"冶是建筑 YeAS"，弗兰肯斯坦。
Zhou Jianjia, WeChat official Account "YeAS", Frankenstein.

16——庄慎，微信公众号"阿科米星"，逆向还原。Zhuang Shen. WeChat official Account" Archmixing"，Analytic Restoration.

17——包括王骏阳、童明、李华和冯路。

Including Wang Jun-Yang, Tong Ming, Li Hua and Feng Lu

18——为了跨过内环高架，三号线轻轨从宝山路到赤峰路之间架高超过五层，且采用比轨道宽的门式框架，中间为机动车道。行道树在框架间沿着轨道两侧向上生长，混凝土柱上爬满了藤蔓，中间还安装了大型霓虹灯，伴随车水马龙行进时，仿佛在穿过一个又一个绿意盎然的山洞。这种体验跟抽象地认为混凝土巨构基础设施给城市带来的都是粗暴非人的体验相反。
In order to cross the inner ring elevated road, Line 3 is elevated to a height of more than five stories from Baoshan Road to Chifeng Road, and adopts a portal frame wider than the track, with a motor lane in the middle. There are trees on both sides of the track, vines on concrete columns, and large neon lights installed in the middle, when you go underneath, it feels like passing through one green cave after another. This experience is contrary to the abstract assumption that the infrastructure of concrete mega-structures gives cities a rough and inhuman experience.

19——从猫狗的视角来观察同济新村的空间的图绘。
Drawings illustrating space in Tongji University New Village from the angle of dogs and cats.

20——李涵发言。
Speech by Li Han.

21——包括王骏阳、鲁安东。
Including Wang Jun-Yang and Lu Andong.

22——庄慎发言。
Speech by Zhuang Shen.

23——比如李涵认为，常见的研究逻辑是从观察现实出发，总结规律，提炼原型，但是并置等概念似乎是已知的，不需要通过研究和建模才得到结论，也不需要研究就可以在设计中使用。
For example, Li Han believes that the common logic can be found by observing reality, summarizing rules, and discovering the prototype. But juxtaposition seems to be known already. It can be used in design directly without research or modeling.

24——李丹锋发言。
Speech by Li Danfeng.

25——冯路发言。
Speech by Feng Lu.

26——"小菜场上的家"是同济大学建筑与城市规划学院教学实验班三年级设计课题——"菜场及住宅综合体设计"。课题尝试用长周期来进行结构、功能及城市关系要求上更为综合和复杂的课题，基地通常选择在上海的普通社区。相关教学研究成果包括：王方戟、张斌、水雁飞《小菜场上的家》，同济大学出版社，2014；王方戟、张斌、水雁飞《小菜场上的家 2》，同济大学出版社，2015。
" Home Above Market" is a design project for the Grade 3 of the teaching experimental class in the College of Architecture and Urban Planning, Tongji University - "Market and Residential Complex Design". The project attempts to use a long period of time to carry out a more comprehensive and complex subject with structural, functional and urban relations requirements. The base is usually located in ordinary community in Shanghai. Relevant teaching and research results include: Wang Fangji, Zhang Bin and Shui Yanfei, *Home Above Market* (Shanghai: Tongji University Press, 2014); Wang Fangji, Zhang Bin and Shui Yanfei, *Home Above Market (2).* (Shanghai: Tongji University Press, 2015).

27——缺乏协调感和美观，以耿直态度面对环境的日常建筑和基础设施。

Lack of harmony and beauty, facing the environment's everyday buildings and infrastructure in the environment with a straight attitude.

28———王骏阳、鲁安东、窦平平发言。
Speech by Wang Jun-Yang, Lu Andong and Dou Pingping.

29———张斌、华霞虹发言。
Speech by Zhang Bin and Hua Xiahong.

30———张斌坦言，因为研究证明了传统建筑学的全面失效，而工作却跳不开正统建筑学的框架，自己的城市研究和设计工作基本是分裂的，城市研究方面的工作，感觉有一点像自我交流。
Zhang Bin admitted that though the study proved the overall failure of traditional architecture, his work couldn't step forward without it. His urban studies and architectural designs are basically split. His studies are more like self-communication.

31———王骏阳、张斌、冯路发言。
Speech by Wang Jun-Yang, Zhang Bin and Feng Lu

[1]———冯路，张斌，庄慎，范文兵．重新向城市学习——"上海计划"对谈 [J]．时代建筑 2017 (2)：42-46．

[2]———[法]尚·布希亚．物体系 [M]．林志明译，上海：上海人民出版社，2001：163．

[3]———冶是建筑工作室．工作室中的同济新村 1.0[J]．时代建筑，2017(2)：56-67．

[4]———贝岛桃代，黑田润三，塚本由晴．东京制造 [M]．林建华译．台北：田园城市出版社，2007．

[5]———李翔宁，李丹锋，江嘉玮．上海制造 [M]．上海：同济大学出版社，2014．

[6]———庄慎，华霞虹．空间冗余与非识别体系 [J]．建筑师，2016 (6)：21-26．

[7]———庄慎，华霞虹．空间冗余 [J]．时代建筑，2015(5)：108-111．

[8]———张斌，张雅楠，孙嘉秋，徐杨．从"溢出"到"共生"——田林新村共有空间调研 [J]．时代建筑，2017(2)：47-55．

[9]———Chase J, Crawford M, Kaliski J. Everyday Urbanism (Expanded Edition)[M]. The Monacelli Press, 2008.

[10]———朱渊，朱剑飞．日常生活：一种空间实践的开启维度——2016 年"日常生活：现代化背景下的空间设计与空间实践"国际会议评述 [J]．建筑师 2016 (6)：6-10．

[11]———朱渊，朱剑飞．日常生活：作为一种设计视角的关注——日常生活国际会议评述 [J]．建筑学报 2016(10)：19-22．

[12]———王骏阳．日常——建筑学的一个零度（下）[J]．建筑学报，2016 (11)：16-21．

[13]———汪原．零度化与日常都市主义策略 [J]．新建筑，2009 (6)：26-29．

[14]———张卫平．隐形逻辑：香港，亚洲式拥挤文化的典型 [M]．南京：东南大学出版社，2009．

[15]———Yoshiharu Tsukamoto Laboratory, Tokyo Institute of Technology and Atelier Bow-Wow. Pet Architecture Guide Book[M]. Japan: Word Photo Press, 2002.

[16]———Harris St, Berke D. Architecture of the Everyday[M]. New York: Princeton Architectural Press, 1997: 1-8, 222-226.

[17]———Aldo Rossi. The Architecture of the City[M]. The MIT Press, 1984.

《火星救援》与二手宇宙
The Martian and Used Universe

1———建筑学里，功能空间组织、结构体系、构造方式、设备系统选择、环境调控控制、材料选用、建造工具，都会涉及性能评价。从性能角度，可以有效地评价一幢建筑、一个体系、一个观念。这也是讨论性能的意义。

In architecture, performance evaluation is involved in functional spatial organization, structural system, structural mode, equipment system selection, environmental regulation and control, material selection, and construction tools. From the angle of performance, it can effectively evaluate a building, a system and an idea. This is also the significance of discussing performance.

2———《星际迷航》是由美国派拉蒙影视制作的科幻影视系列，由 6 部电视剧、1 部动画片、13 部电影组成。该系列最初由编剧吉恩·罗登贝瑞于 20 世纪 60 年代提出，经过近 50 年的不断发展而逐步完善，成为全世界最著名的科幻影视系列之一。
Star Trek is a science fiction series produced by Paramount Pictures, Inc. It consists of six TV series, one animated film and 13 movies. Originally proposed by screenwriter Gene Roddenberry in the 1960s, the series has evolved over the past 50 years and become one of the most famous science fiction movies and TV series in the world.

3———"二手宇宙"是卢卡斯提出的美学主张，他认为大到宇宙船，小到激光枪，都应该像用过很久一样，有点脏，有点土，随处可见磨损、掉漆、油渍和锈迹。
The "Used Universe" is Lucas's aesthetic proposition that he believes all props from the cosmic ship to laser guns should be seemed as if they were used for a long time, with some bit dirty, wear and tear, paint damage, oil stains and rust.

4———《星球大战》系列电影是由卢卡斯电影公司出品的科幻电影。卢卡斯电影公司首先于 1977 年推出了《星球大战》，之后又分别在 1980 年和 1983 年推出了《星球大战 2》和《星球大战 3》。之后又推出了星球大战前传三部曲，前传 1、2、3 分别于 1999 年、2002 年和 2005 年上映。
Star Wars is a series of sci-fi movies produced by Lucas film Ltd., which first launched Star Wars in 1977, then Star Wars 2 and Star Wars 3 in 1980 and 1983, respectively. Star Wars Prequel Trilogy 1, 2 and 3 were released in 1999, 2002 and 2005 respectively.

看不见的改变：论使用端空间技术化的可能
Invisible Change: Technologizing Space at the User's End

1———系各罗皮乌斯谈包豪斯及其和这个机械时代中的世界的关系时的用语。[美]雷纳·班纳姆：《第一机械时代的理论和设计》，袁熙旸、顾华明译，江苏美术出版社，2009，第 409 页。
Walter Gropius used these sentences to explain the relationship between BAUHAUS and the world in machine age. Reyner Banham, Theory and Design in the First Machine Age, trans. Yuan Xiyang and Gu Huaming (Nanjing: Jiangsu Fine Arts Publishing House, 2009), p409.

2———同上：第 419-420 页。
Ibid., pp. 419-420.

[1]———雷纳·班纳姆．第一机械时代的理论和设计 [M]．袁熙旸、顾华明译．南京：江苏美术出版社，2009：409，420．

[2]———罗杰斯，等．小小地球上的城市 [M]．仲德崑，译．北京：中国建筑工业出版社，2004：16-28．

[3]———尼尔·波斯曼．技术垄断：文化向技术投降 [M]．何道宽，译．北京：北京大学出版社，2007：11-32．

[4]———Ed. Ian Lambot. Norman Foster：Team 4 and Foster Associates, Building and Projects：1964-1973[M]. The Watermark Press, 1991.

[5]———Keller Easterling. Extrastatecraft: The Power of Infrastructure Space[M]. London & New York: Verso, 2014: 10-23.

[6]————华霞虹．消融与转变：消费文化中的建筑 [D]．上海：同济大学建筑与城市规划学院，2007: 90–96．

整体的回响：来自内部的反向思维
The Echo of the Unity: Reverse Thinking of the Interior

1————美国艺术家 (1943—1978)。
American artist (1943–1978).

2————阿科米星建筑事务所 2017—2018 城市研究的课题——"建筑的内部"。
Atelier Archmixing's topic of urban research from 2017 to 2018—"the interior of buildings".

3————《拙政园图咏》，1533 年文徵明绘制的拙政园三十一处景图。原作迄今不见消息。目前，仅三十一开的《拙政园图咏》尚有影印本行世。
Landscapes of the Humble Administrator's Garden consists of 31 scenes painted by Wen Zhengming for the Humble Administrator's Garden in 1533. The original work has been missing. At present, there is only a photocopied version of the 31-page Landscapes of the Humble Administrator's Garden.

4————该次讲座采用的说明例子是《拙政园图咏》，本文的图片均出于此。
All the illustrative example used in the lecture is Landscapes of the Humble Administrator's Garden, from which all the pictures used in this paper come. According to research, the original album is colored. The photocopied version published by Zhonghua Book Company in Shanghai during the period of the Republic of China was black and white due to technical limitations at that time.

[1]————庄慎．中国庭院的生命精神 [D]．上海：同济大学建筑与城市规划学院，1997.
[2]————董寿琪．苏州园林山水画选 [M]．上海：上海三联书店，2007.
[3]————宗白华．宗白华全集 [M]．合肥：安徽出版社，1994.
[4]————王毅．园林与中国文化 [M]．上海：上海人民出版社，1990.
[5]————庄慎，华霞虹．选择在个人与大众之间 [J]．建筑师，2012 (3): 43–51.
[6]————童明．作为异托邦的江南园林 [J]．建筑学报，2017 (2): 98–105.
[7]————鲁安东．隐匿的转变：对 20 世纪留园变迁的空间分析 [J]．建筑学报，2016 (1): 17–23.
[8]————冯纪忠．人与自然：从比较园林史看建筑发展趋势 [J]．建筑学报，1990 (5): 25–30.
[9]————童寯．江南园林志 [M]．北京：中国建筑工业出版社，1984.

基于城市空间日常效率的普通建筑更新设计策略
Regeneration Design Strategy for Ordinary Buildings Based on the Everyday Urban Spatial Efficiency

1————如 Henri Lefebvre、Michael De Certeau、Margaret Crawford、朱剑飞、汪原、杨宇振等人的研究。
Such as researches by Henri Lefebvre、Michael De Certeau、Margaret Crawford、Zhu Jianfei, Wang Yuan, Yang Yuzhen etc.

2————如库哈斯的广普城市和垃圾空间，Steven Harris/ Deborah Berke 的日常建筑，N.J. Habraken 普通的形式、场所和文化结构。美国学者对洛杉矶、拉斯维加斯的学习（班纳姆、文丘里等）。
Such as researches on Generic City and Junkspace by Rem Koolhaas, on Everyday Architecture by Steven Harris and Deborah Berke, on ordinary form, sites and cultural structures by N.J. Habraken. Studies on Los Angelos and Las Vegas by American researchers such as Banham, Robert Venturi and Dennis Scott Brown, etc..are also relevant.

3————如库哈斯指导的珠三角城市研究，缪朴提出亚洲城市的公共空间问题，张卫平探讨香港城市隐形逻辑。今和次郎的《考现学入门》和藤森照信等的《路上观察学》引发近年中日学者打破审美贵贱限制关注缺乏协调感和美观的日常建筑的热潮，如贝岛桃代、黑田润三、塚本由晴《东京制造》的"滥建筑"、受该书启发创作的《上海制造》（李翔宁、李丹锋、江嘉玮）、《一点儿北京》（李涵、胡妍）等。
Such as the Pearl River Delta urban research by Rem Koolhaas, public space problems of Asian cities pointed out by Miu Pu; the invisible logic of Hong Kong explored by Zhang Weiping. Introduction to Modernology by Iwa Jiro and Road Observation by Terunobu Fujimori have in recent years broken the aesthetic restrictions and brought attention to the lack of coordination and beauty of everyday buildings; as can be seen in the "Da-me architecture" in Made in Tokyo by Momoyo Kaijima, Junzo Kuroda, and Yoshiharu Tsukamoto; Made in Shanghai which was inspired by the former book by Li Xiangning, Li Danfeng and Jiang Jiawei, A taste of Beijing series by LI Han and Hu yan.

4————如清华大学朱文一教授指导和发表的夜市、行乞等弱势空间系列研究，张雪伟探讨的日常生活空间等。
Such as in the series researches directed and published by Prof. Zhu Wenyi from Tsinghua University on long negaleted public spaces such as night markets and begging space; everyday living space discussed by Dr. Zhang Xuewei from Tongji University.

图片来源 Image Credits

阿科米星十年：寻找另一种建筑 / 建筑学
A Decade for Atelier Archmixing: In Search of an Another Architecture

1———— https://www.archdaily.com/211054/xiayu-kindergarten-shang-hai-atelier-deshaus (16:33 1/19, 2020)

2———— 张嗣烨摄影
Photo by Zhang Siye

3———— https://www.gooood.cn/office-fact-13-deshaus.htm (16:35 1/19, 2020)

4———— 王骏阳摄影
Photo by Wang Jun-Yang

5———— https://www.amazon.co.uk/Vers-une-Architecture-Corbusier-Saugnier/dp/B0014K965A (16:35 1/16, 2020)

6———— http://cultureandcommunication.org/deadmedia/index.php/Dymaxion_House (16:28 1/16, 2020)

7———— https://dwz.cn/keAD0Vy3 (16:20 1/19, 2020)

8———— http://drawingcities-zscapes.blogspot.com/2011/12/plug-in-city-by-archigram.html (16:00 1/16, 2020)

9———— https://www.jessyeb.com/blog-news/tag/New+Brutalism (16:08 1/16, 2020)

10———— http://arquitextosblog.blogspot.com/2016/07/gold-en-lane-housing-1952-londres-alison.html (16:11 1/16, 2020)

11———— https://www.architecture.com/image-library/features/this-is-tomorrow.html (15:42 1/16, 2020)

12———— https://www.amazon.com/Made-Tokyo-Guide-Junzo-Kuroda/dp/4306044211 (16:40 1/19, 2020)

13———— https://www.pinterest.com/pin/391461392600165805/?lp=true%20(18:20%201/23,%20 2020)

14———— https://rudygodinez.tumblr.com/post/66808366578/james-sterling-and-james-gowan-with-michael-wilford-and (16:37 1/16, 2020)

15———— https://www.flickr.com/photos/ihynz/32545901084 (10:37 1/17, 2020)

葛明 × 庄慎：城市建筑学的核心问题
GE Ming X ZHUANG Shen: Core Issue on Urban Architecture

3———— 张嗣烨摄影
Photo by Zhang Siye

4–1, 5———— 唐煜摄影
Photo by Tang Yu

6———— 庄慎摄影
Photo by Zhuang Shen

9———— 唐煜摄影
Photo by Tang Yu

鲁安东 × 庄慎：设计如何适应未来变化
LU Andong × ZHUANG Shen: How can Design Adapt to Future Change

1———— 吴清山摄影
Photo by Wu Qingshan

2———— 苏圣亮摄影
Photo by Su Shengliang

5,6,8———— 唐煜摄影
Photo by Tang Yu

9, 11———— 吴清山摄影
Photo by Wu Qingshan

12———— 唐煜摄影
Photo by Tang Yu

14–16———— 唐煜摄影
Photo by Tang Yu

18———— 陈平楠摄影
Photo by Chen Pingnan

选择在个人与大众之间
Standing Between the Individual and the Public

1———— http://movie.mtime.com/14859/posters_and_images/306522/ (10:35 1/16, 2020)

2———— 董寿琪著，衣学领主编. 苏州园林山水画选. 上海：上海三联书店，2007：75、49.
Dong Shouqi. *Selected Landscape Paintings of Gardens in Suzhou* (in Chinese). ed. Yi Xueling, Shanghai: Shanghai Sanlian Bookstore, 2007: 75, 49.

6———— *EL croqui*s: 1987–1998 OMA/Rem Koolhaas

7———— 董寿琪著，衣学领主编. 苏州园林山水画选. 上海：上海三联书店，2007：75、49.
Dong Shouqi. Selected Landscape Paintings of Gardens in Suzhou (in Chinese). ed. Yi Xueling, Shanghai: Shanghai Sanlian Bookstore, 2007: 75, 49.

8, 17–2———— 庄慎摄影
Photo by Zhuang Shen

17–3———— 张嗣烨摄影
Photo by Zhang Siye

18–2———— 唐煜摄影
Photo by Tang Yu

19———— 苏圣亮摄影
Photo by Su Shengliang

非识别体系的一种高度——杰弗里·巴瓦的建筑世界
An Altitude of Unrecognizable System: The Architectural World of Geoffrey Bawa

1–5———David Robson, *Geoffrey Bawa: the Complete Works*. Thames & Hudson, 2002.

6,7———胡康榆（有方）摄影
Photo by Hu Kangyu (POSITION)

8———章勇摄影
Photo by Zhang Yong

9,10———庄慎摄影
Photo by Zhuang Shen

11———David Robson, Dominic Sansoni. *Bawa: The Sri Lanka Gardens*. Thames & Hudson, 2008.

12———原源（有方）摄影
Photo by Yuan Yuan (POSITION)

13,14———庄慎摄影
Photo by Zhuang Shen

15———章勇摄影
Photo by Zhang Yong

16———David Robson, Geoffrey Bawa: the Complete Works, Thames & Hudson, 2002.

日常·改变·非识别体系
Everyday, Change and the Unrecognizable System

1———亘建筑工作室提供，孔锐摄影

2–4,6———唐煜摄影

a———Photo by Tang Yu

e, f———provided and drawn by YeArch Studio

g,o,r———Photo by Tang Yu

城市内的工作室
Work Within the City

2,5,6———唐煜摄影

7———陈平楠摄影

8–10———唐煜摄影

11–14———陈平楠摄影

e, f———Photo by Wu Qingshan

g,h,j———Photo by Tang Yu

走向城市建筑学的可能——"虹口1617展览暨城市研究"研讨会评述
Possibilities Towards an Urban Architecture: Notes on the Symposium of "Hongkou 1617 Exhibition and Urban Studies"

1———CEED 提供，视频制作：罗西若、房玥
Provided by CEED, Video Produced by Luo Xiruo and Fang Yue

2———冶是建筑工作室提供，绘图：冶是建筑工作室
Provided and Drawn by YeArch Studio

3———阿科米星提供，绘图：鲁昊霏、陈平楠、董智伟
Provided by Atelier Archmixing and Drawn by Lu Haofei, Chen Pingnan and Dong Zhiwei

4———CEED 提供，视频制作：邓希帆、房玥、顾金怡、姜鸿博、罗西若
Provided by CEED and video Produced by Deng Xifan, Fang Yue, Gu Jinyi, Jiang Hongbo and Luo Xiruo)

5———CEED 提供，视频制作：邓希帆、顾金怡
Provided by CEED and Video Produced by Deng Xifan and Gu Jinyi

6———冶是建筑工作室提供，绘图：冶是建筑工作室、陈嘉禾、徐濛
Provided by YeArch Studio and Drawn by YeArch Studio, Chen Jiahe and Xu Meng

7———阿科米星提供，绘图：陈梓威
Provided by Atelier Archmixing and Drawn by Chen Ziwei

8———阿科米星提供，绘图：李聪
Provided by Atelier Archmixing and Drawn by Li Cong

9,10———阿科米星提供，绘图：蒋珊珊
Provided by Atelier Archmixing and Drawn by Jiang Shanshan

11———冶是建筑工作室提供，绘图：冶是建筑工作室、陶曼丽
Provided by YeArch Studio and Drawn by YeArch Studio and Tao Manli

12———阿科米星提供，摄影：唐煜
Provided by Atelier Archmixing and Photo by Tang Yu

《火星救援》与二手宇宙
The Martian and Used Universe

1———http://www.carlofilippofollis.name/appunti-di-navigazione-dia rio-di-bordo/

2———《新周刊》第 166 期
From *New Weekly*, No. 166

3———https://airows.com/culture/this-modernized-trailer-for-star-wars-a-new-hope-is-incredible

4———https://movie.douban.com/photos/photo/2271641254/

5———https://movie.douban.com/photos/photo/2263538828/

6———陈平楠摄影
Photo by Chen Pingnan

7———陈梓威摄影
Photo by Chen Ziwei

看不见的改变：论使用端空间技术化的可能
Invisible Change: Technologizing Space at the User's End

1———https://architecturetokyo.wordpress. com/2016/09/14/1972-nagakin-capsule-tower-kisho-kuroka-wa/ (21:10 1.19, 2020)

2–1———http://blog.sina.com.cn/s/blog_616a97150102v5z9.html

2–2———https://dwz.cn/zEhwn1XX

2–3———http://amuseum.cdstm.cn/AMuseum/xinxiguan/htm/skzljisuanji. htm

2–4———https://www.bostondynamics.com

3———http://www.geekplus.com.cn/news/view?id=41)

4———Amazon Go Video

整体的回响：来自内部的反向思维
The Echo of the Unity: Reverse Thinking of the Interior

1———https://publicdelivery.org/matta-clark-conical-intersect/

2–11———董寿琪著，衣学领主编. 苏州园林山水画选. 上海：上海三联书店，2007
Dong Shouqi. *Selected Landscape Paintings of Gardens in*

Suzhou (in Chinese). ed. Yi Xueling, Shanghai: Shanghai Sanlian
Bookstore, 2007.

12———龙永龄摄影
Photo by Long Yongling

13———庄慎摄影
Photo by Zhuang Shen

14–15———董寿琪著，衣学领主编 . 苏州园林山水画选 . 上海：上海三联书店，
2007
Dong Shouqi. *Selected Landscape Paintings of Gardens in
Suzhou* (in Chinese). ed. Yi Xueling, Shanghai: Shanghai Sanlian
Bookstore, 2007.

附录
Appendix

事务所简介 About Archmixing

阿科米星建筑设计事务所成立于 2009 年 7 月，由庄慎、任皓创建，唐煜、朱捷加入合伙，华霞虹担任学术顾问。

"阿科米星"是"Archmixing"的谐音，意为"混合建筑"，源于成立之初，我们认为："设计需要消除从专业领域到社会价值的各种狭隘的界限，不放弃去尝试各种可能性。"我们的设计无论内容还是范围都不拘一格：从城市设计到小型建筑，从专业建造到民间建造，我们的工作兴趣和实践策略丰富而灵活。

在国内实践二十余年，阿科米星的主持建筑师们秉持知行合一的精神，均拥有丰富的专业实践与研究经验。我们越来越认识到，快速城市化和全面市场化是我们实践的语境，纷繁复杂的中国城市（城乡）现状是我们设计的出发点，也是自己身处其间，无法忽视的日常环境。在这样的实践环境中试图发现一些建筑学的新经验，一直是我们工作的动力。这其中，越来越吸引我们的正是那看上去问题无穷，却又生机勃勃，仿佛蕴藏着巨大力量的日常城市与建筑。

在这样的实践研究里，我们将视野更多地投放到建筑的使用端，发觉了"改变"这个既有建筑学的盲点。我们越来越明确地认识到，"什么改变了既有的城市与建筑""什么会改变未来的建筑"这两个问题会有效地引导我们的设计研究与实践。

Atelier Archmixing was founded by Zhuang Shen and Ren Hao in July 2009. Joined partners are Tang Yu and Zhu Jie. Hua Xiahong serves as an academic advisor.

The studio's Chinese name A Ke Mi Xing echoes the pronunciation of "Archmixing", which means Mixing Architecture, a critical position as well as a strategy we hold from the very beginning. We think it necessary to move beyond our narrow area of expertise to a wider range of unlimited boundaries by seeking every opportunity and employing strategies with no prior notions. The projects we have completed feature in various scales and functions, covering the range from urban design to artistic installation, from professional manufacture to informal locale craftsmanship. We boast in extensive design interests as well as flexible practicing strategies.

Through more than two decades' practices, Atelier Archmixing's principal architects have accumulated plenty of practicing and researching experiences. We see China's rapid urbanization and extensive commercialization as our design context, China's controversial urban and rural status quo, which is also the everyday environment we live in and impossible to ignore, as our departure point. Is it possible to draw new strength for architectural discipline from these circumstances? We especially see opportunities in everyday urban life and built environment, which is problematic but also energetic and vibrant.

Under such a context, we focus more on the user's end of architecture and discover one blind spot in the mainstream Architecture, Change. The following two concerns, "what changes the existing cities and buildings" and "what will change the future architecture" will effectively guide our design research and practice.

阿科米星合伙人庄慎（中）、任皓（左2）、唐煜（右1）、朱捷（右2），以及学术顾问华霞虹（左1）

Atelier Archmixing's partners: Zhuang Shen (middle), Ren Hao (left 2), Tang Yu (right 1), Zhu Jie (right 2), and academic advisor Hua Xiahong (left 1)

获奖

2020——IFI 卓越设计奖购物空间类银奖 ["一条"线下店（莘庄店）]

2019——Archdaily 2019 年度最佳改造建筑大奖（棉仓城市客厅）

2019——AIA 上海卓越设计奖室内设计奖（棉仓城市客厅）

2018——WA 中国建筑奖之 WA 设计实验奖优胜奖（棉仓城市客厅）

2018——《ELLE DECORATION 家居廊》最佳年度商用零售空间奖（棉仓城市客厅）

2018——DFA 亚洲最具影响力设计奖银奖（棉仓城市客厅）

2018——入围"Dezeen Awards 2018"零售类室内设计前 5 名（悦阅书店）

2017——上海市建筑学会第七届建筑创作奖之公共建筑优秀奖（张江集电港剑腾三期）

2016——自然建造·第四届中国建筑传媒奖青年探索奖（庄慎）

2016——上海建筑学会首届科技进步奖三等奖（衡山坊 890 弄 8 号楼外立面）

2015——上海市建筑学会第六届建筑创作奖之佳作奖（衡山坊 890 弄 8 号楼外立面）

2015——第六届最佳设计酒店大奖"最佳新酒店"（富春俱舍）

2012——中国建筑传媒奖居住建筑特别奖提名（黎里黎里）

2012——WA 中国建筑佳作奖（上海文化信息产业园 B4/B5 地块）

2010——英国皇家特许建造学会"施工管理杰出成就奖"（嘉定新城规划展示馆）

214

Major Awards

2020——The silver medal of Commerce Award of IFI. (Offline Retail Space of Yitiao. TV -Xinzhuang Store)

2019——The 2nd place Refurbishment in Architecture Award 2019, hosted by Archdaily (Cotton Lab Urban Lounge)

2019—— Interior Architecture Honor Award of AIA Shanghai | Beijing Design (Cotton Lab Urban Lounge)

2018——The 1st prize of Design Experiment Award, issued by *World Architecture* China. (Cotton Lab Urban Lounge)

2018——Best Commercial Retail Space Award, issued by *ELLE DECORATION*. (Cotton Lab Urban Lounge)

2018——The silver medal of DFA Design of Asia Awards. (Cotton Lab Urban Lounge)

2017——The 7th Architectural Creation Award for Excellent Public Building from ASSC. (ZhangJiang IC Harbour Phase III China Fortune Wisdom Mark)

2016——The Young Explorer Award of 4th China Architecture Media Award (Zhuang Shen)

2016——The 3rd prize in the Technological Progress Award of ASSC. (Facade Renovation of Building 8, Lane 890, Hengshan Road)

2015——Architectural Creation Award of ASSC. (Facade Renovation of Building 8, Lane 890, Hengshan Road)

2015——Best New Hotel of the Year of the 6th Best Design Hotel. (Fuchun Kosa)

2012——Residential Special Award Nominee, China Architecture Media Award. (LILI)

2012——Best Chinese Architecture Award, issued by *World Architecture* China. (B4/B5 Blocks of Shanghai Culture & Information Industrial Park)

2010——Outstanding Achievement in Construction Management Award, issued by CIOB. (Jiading New City Exhibition Hall)

阿科米星论文目录 Archmixing Publications List 2009–2019

阿科米星论著
Publications by Archmixing

1———庄慎. 上海嘉定新城规划展示馆 [J]. 时代建筑, 2009 (6): 138–145.
Zhuang Shen. Urban Planning Exhibition Hall of Jiading New Town, Shanghai [J]. *Time + Architecture*, 2009 (6): 138–145.

2———华霞虹. 当代中国的消费梦想和建筑狂欢 [J]. 时代建筑, 2010 (1): 124–128.
Hua Xiahong. Consumption Dreams and Architectural Carnival in China [J]. *Time + Architecture*, 2010 (1): 124–128.

3———华霞虹. "悬挂的庭院"——上海文化信息产业园 B4/B5 地块的设计策略 [J]. 时代建筑, 2011 (3): 106–113.
Hua Xiahong. Hanging Courtyard—The Design Strategy for Blocks B4/B5 of Shanghai Culture & Communication Industry District [J]. *Time + Architecture*, 2011 (3): 106–113.

4———庄慎, 任皓. 个人与大众之间: 阿科米星建筑设计事务所办公楼 [J]. 城市环境设计, 2011 (4): 238–241.
Zhuang Shen, Ren Hao. Between Individual and Public: The Workplace of Atelier Archmixing [J]. *Urban Environment Design*, 2011 (4): 238–241.

5———庄慎, 华霞虹. 嘉定秋霞圃西侧地块五轮设计方案 [J]. 时代建筑, 2012 (1): 48–51.
Zhuang Shen, Hua Xiahong. 5 Proposals for the Block West to Qiuxia Garden, Jiading District [J]. *Time + Architecture*, 2012 (1): 48–51.

6———唐煜. 上海嘉定新城紫气东来景观配套建筑设计概况 [J]. 时代建筑, 2012 (1): 58–61.
Tang Yu. Supplemental Buildings for Jiading New Town Ziqidonglai Park, Shanghai [J]. *Time + Architecture*, 2012 (1): 58–61.

7———华霞虹, 庄慎. 加建 [J]. 新建筑, 2012 (2): 66–71.
Hua Xiahong, Zhuang Shen. Addition [J]. *New architecture*, 2012 (2): 66–71.

8———庄慎, 华霞虹. 选择在个人与大众之间 [J]. 建筑师, 2012 (6): 43–51.
Zhuang Shen, Hua Xiahong. Standing Between the Individual and Public [J]. *The Architect*, 2012 (6): 43–51.

9———王方戟, 庄慎. 关于黎里"黎里"及陆巷"双栖斋"的对话 [J]. 时代建筑, 2012 (6): 77–81.
Wang Fangji, Zhuang Shen. A Conversation on LILI in LILI and Twin Trees Pavilion in Luxiang [J]. *Time + Architecture*, 2012 (6): 77–81.

10———庄慎, 任皓. 上海文化信息产业园 B4/B5 地块 [J]. 城市环境设计, 2012 (6): 56–61.
Zhuang Shen, Ren Hao. B4/B5 Block of Culture and Information Industrial Park, Shanghai [J]. *Urban Environment Design*, 2012 (6): 56–61.

11———庄慎, 任皓. 客厅 [J]. 城市环境设计, 2012 (6): 196–197.
Zhuang Shen, Ren Hao. Living Room [J]. *Urban Environment Design*, 2012 (6): 196–197.

12———田丹妮. 双栖斋与黎里的建造 [J]. 城市环境设计, 2012 (10): 228.
Tian Danni. The Construction of Twin Trees Pavilion and LILI [J]. *Urban Environment Design*, 2012 (10): 228.

13———庄慎, 任皓, 唐煜, 等. 双栖斋 [J]. 城市环境设计, 2012 (10): 229.
Zhuang Shen, Ren Hao, Tang Yu, et al. Twin Trees Pavilion [J]. *Urban Environment Design*, 2012 (10): 229.

14———庄慎, 任皓, 唐煜, 等. 黎里 [J]. 城市环境设计, 2012 (10): 230–231.
Zhuang Shen,, Ren Hao, Tang Yu, et al. LILI[J]. *Urban Environment Design*, 2012 (10): 230–231.

15———赵磊, 董功, 庄慎. 松紧之间: 赵磊、董功、庄慎三人谈 [J]. 时代建筑, 2013 (4): 40–43.
Zhao Lei, Dong Gong, Zhuang Shen. Between Relaxation and Strictness: A Conversation among ZHAO Lei, DONG Gong and ZHUANG Shen [J]. *Time + Architecture*, 2013 (4): 40–43.

16———庄慎. 混合设计——一种城市实践的立场与策略 [J]. 城市环境设计, 2013 (3+4): 104–105.
Zhuang Shen. Mixing Design: An Urban-oriented Practical Strategy [J]. *Urban Environment Design*, 2013 (3+4): 104–105.

17———庄慎, 华霞虹. 改变即日常: 阿科米星的实践综述 [J]. 建筑师, 2014 (2): 131–137.
Zhuang Shen, Hua Xiahong. Change is More: Atelier Archmixing's Practice [J]. *The Architect*, 2014 (2): 131–137.

18———王方戟, 庄慎. 关于建筑形式的对话——一个围绕阿科米星建筑事务所最新实践的讨论 [J]. 建筑师, 2014 (2): 120–131.
Wang Fangji, Zhuang Shen. A Dialogue on Architectural Form: Reviewing Atelier Archmixing's Latest Designs [J]. *The Architect*, 2014 (2): 120–131.

19———唐煜. 搭棚记——阿科米星的莫干山蚕种场改造 [J]. 城市环境设计, 2014 (4): 190–195.
Tang Yu. Build a Shed—Renovation of Moganshan Silkworm Egg Production Farm by Archmixing [J]. *Urban Environment Design*, 2014 (4): 190–195.

20———庄慎, 王侃. 上海衡山路 890 号 8 号楼立面改造 [J]. 时代建筑, 2014 (4): 128–131.
Zhuang Shen, Wang Kan. Facade Renovation for Building 8, 890 Hengshan Road, Shanghai [J]. *Time + Architecture*, 2014 (4): 128–131.

21———华霞虹, 庄慎. 上海嘉定新城双丁路幼儿园设计 [J]. 建筑学报, 2014 (1): 66–73.
Hua Xiahong, Zhuang Shen. Shuangding Road Kindergarten, Jiading New City [J]. *Architectural Journal*, 2014 (1): 66–73.

22———庄慎, 华霞虹. 非识别体系的一种高度: 杰弗里·巴瓦的建筑世界 [J]. 建筑学报, 2014 (11): 27–35.
Zhuang Shen, Hua Xiahong. An Altitude of Unrecognizable System: The Architectural World of Geoffrey Bawa [J]. *Architectural Journal*, 2014 (11): 27–35.

23———庄慎, 华霞虹. 日常·改变·非识别体系 [J]. 新建筑, 2014 (06): 16–19.
Zhuang Shen, Hua Xiahong. Everyday, Change, and the

Unrecognizable System [J]. *New architecture*, 2014 (06): 16–19.

24———庄慎．莫干山庾村蚕种场 [J]．世界建筑，2015 (2)：84–87+132．
Zhuang Shen. Mogan Mountain Silkworm Hatchery, Huzhou, Zhejiang, China, 2013[J]. *World Architectureure*, 2015 (2): 84–87+132.

25———庄慎，徐好好．对话庄慎：改变与反思 [J]．新建筑，2015 (3)：24–29．
Zhuang Shen, Xu Haohao. Dialogue with Architect Zhuang Shen: Changes and Reflections [J]. *New architecture*, 2015 (3): 24–29.

26———鲁安东，庄慎．被栖居的实验室——庄慎谈杰弗里·巴瓦工作室 [J]．世界建筑，2015 (4)：43–45．
Lu Andong, Zhuang Shen. A Dwelled Laboratory: Conversation with ZHUANG Shen on Geoffery Bawa's Workspaces [J]. *World Architectureure*, 2015 (4): 43–45.

27———张斌，冯路，庄慎，等．从认识到表达 [J]．时代建筑，2015 (5)：82–87．
Zhang Bin, Feng Lu, Zhuang Shen, et al. From Awareness to Expression [J]. *Time + Architecture*, 2015 (5): 82–87.

28———庄慎，华霞虹．城市内的工作室 [J]．时代建筑，2015 (5)：100–107．
Zhuang Shen, Hua Xiahong. Work within the City [J]. *Time + Architecture*, 2015 (5): 100–107.

29———庄慎，华霞虹．空间冗余 [J]．时代建筑，2015 (5)：108–111．
Zhuang Shen, Hua Xiahong. Spatial Redundancy [J]. *Time + Architecture*, 2015 (5): 108–111.

30———庄慎，周渐佳，李丹锋．打开城市的另一种方式：关于上海当代城市研究的一次工作对谈 [J]．时代建筑，2015 (5)：112–116．
Zhuang Shen, Zhou Jianjia, Li Danfeng. An Alternative to Open a City: A Work Session on Urban Research towards Contemporary Shanghai [J]. *Time + Architecture*, 2015 (5): 112–116.

31———庄慎．象征与虚无 [J]．城市环境设计，2015 (5)：179．
Zhuang Shen. Symbolicalness and Immateriality [J]. *Urban Environment Design*, 2015 (5): 179.

32———庄慎，华霞虹．平常的开始，平常的结果——宝山陈化成纪念馆移建改造 [J]．建筑学报，2015 (12)：48–53．
Zhuang Shen, Hua Xiahong. From the Ordinary to the Ordinary: Replacement and Renovation of Baoshan Chen Huacheng Memorial [J]. *Architectural Journal*, 2015 (12): 48–53.

33———庄慎，华霞虹．应用：作为行动和认知 [J]．新建筑，2016 (2)：10–16．
Zhuang Shen, Hua Xiahong. Application as Action and Cognition [J]. *New Architecture*, 2016 (2): 10–16.

34———庄慎，唐煜，王骁彬．体现上海性格的可变肌肤——衡山坊890弄8号楼外立面改造 [J]．设计家，2016 (2)：52–54．
Zhuang Shen, Tang Yu, Wang Xiaobin. Architectural Facade Renovation, Building 8, Hengshanfang [J]. *Designer & Designing*, 2016 (2): 52–54.

35———庄慎，任皓，唐煜，等．把工作室搬来搬去好不好 [J]．设计家，2016 (3)：124–125．
Zhuang Shen, Ren Hao, Tang Yu, et al. Is It OK that the Office Move too Often [J]. *Designer & Designing*, 2016 (3): 124–125.

36———华霞虹，庄慎．改妆记 [J]．时代建筑，2016 (4)：24–28．
Hua Xiahong, Zhuang Shen. On Facade Renovation [J]. *Time + Architecture*, 2016 (4): 24–28.

37———刘宇扬，庄慎．张江华鑫慧天地 [J]．时代建筑，2016 (4)：68–73．
Liu Yuyang, Zhuang Shen. Huaxin Wisdom Mark, Zhangjiang [J]. *Time + Architecture*, 2016 (4): 68–73.

38———庄慎．YoungBird 室内空间改造．世界建筑，2016 (4)：98–103．
Zhuang Shen. YoungBird Interior Renovation [J]. *World Architecture*, 2016 (4): 98–103.

39———庄慎．陈化成纪念馆移建改造 [J]．世界建筑，2016 (5)：114–115．
Zhuang Shen. Removal Renovation of Chen Huacheng Memorial Hall, Shanghai, China, 2015 [J]. *World Architecture*, 2016 (5): 114–115.

40———阿科米星．衡山坊 8 号楼立面改造．建筑与都市（日文版），2016 (3)：152–155．
Atelier Archmixing. Facade Renovation for Building No. 8 Hengshanfang [J]. *A+U* (Architecture and Urbanism), 2016 (3): 152–155.

41———庄慎，华霞虹．空间冗余与非识别体系 [J]．建筑师，2016 (6)：21–26．
Zhuang Shen, Hua Xiahong. Spatial Redundancy and Unrecognizable System [J]. *The Architect*, 2016 (6): 21–26.

42———庄慎．大进深户型与交错的互跃户型 [J]．时代建筑，2016 (6)：60–65．
Zhuang Shen. Deep-depth Unit and Cross-compound Unit [J]. *Time + Architecture*, 2016 (6): 60–65.

43———庄慎，华霞虹．向日常世界学习 [J]．建筑研究季刊（英文版），2017，21 (3)：222–233
Zhuang Shen, Hua Xiahong. Learning from the Everyday World [J]. *Architectural Research Quarterly*, 2017, 21 (3): 222–233.

44———庄慎．火星救援与二手宇宙 [J]．时代建筑，2017 (5)：7–11．
Zhuang Shen. Rescuing from the Mars and Used Universe [J]. *Time + Architecture*, 2017 (5): 7–11.

45———华霞虹．走向城市建筑学的可能——"虹口1617展览暨城市研究"研讨会评述 [J]．建筑学报，2017 (9)：103–109．
Hua Xiahong. Possibilities towards an Urban Architecture: Notes on the Seminar of 'Hongkou 1617 Exhibition and Urban Study' [J]. *Architectural Journal*, 2017 (9): 103–109.

46———庄慎．黎里黎里，江苏，中国 [J]．世界建筑，2017 (9)：98–99+129．
Zhuang Shen. LILI, Jiangsu, China, 2012 [J]. *World Architecture*, 2017 (9): 98–99+129.

47———朱捷，庄慎．敦煌莫高窟窟门的一次公益设计和改造实验 [J]．世界建筑，2017 (12)：22–25．
Zhu Jie, Zhuang Shen. A Volunteer Design and Renovation Experiment for the Gate of Mogao Grottoes in Dunhuang [J]. *World Architecture*, 2017 (12): 22–25.

48———庄慎，华霞虹．逆向还原：城市"空间冗余"的日常逻辑——对话庄慎与华霞虹．城市中国，2017 (10)：48–59．
Zhuang Shen, Hua Xiahong. Reverse Restoration: Daily Logic of Urban Space Evolution/ Interview with ZHUANG Shen and HUA Xiahong [J]. *Urban Wisdom Advancing with China*, 2017 (10): 48–59.

49———华霞虹．一扇门打开两个书店 [J]．时代建筑，2018 (1)：128–133．
Hua Xianghong. One Door Opens to Two Bookstores [J]. *Time + Architecture*, 2018 (1): 128–133.

50———庄慎．看不见的改变：论使用端空间技术化的可能 [J]．时代建筑，2018 (3)：32–35．
Zhuang Shen. Invisible Change: Technologizing Space at the User's End [J]. *Time + Architecture*, 2018 (3): 32–35.

51———庄慎．整体的回响：来自内部的反向思维 [J]．时代建筑，2018 (4)：20–23．

Zhuang Shen. The Echo of the Unity: Reverse Thinking from the Interior [J]. *Time + Architecture*, 2018 (4): 20–23.

52———庄慎，王迪，邓健. 建筑结构设备一体化的"屋中屋" [J]. 时代建筑，2018 (4)：96–103.
Zhuang Shen, Wang Di, Deng Jian. House within House, the Integration of Architecture, Structure and Equipment [J]. *Time + Architecture*, 2018 (4): 96–103.

53———庄慎，唐煜，华霞虹. 柔性倍增——基于人工智能、移动机器人、智能立库的未来居住空间概念研究 [J]. 华中建筑，2018 (3)：61–66.
Zhuang Shen, Tang Yu, Hua Xiahong. Flexible Multiplication: Spatial Concept on Future Living Integrating Technology of AI, VAG and Intellectual Elevator-shaft Garage [J]. *Huazhong Architecture*, 2018 (3): 61–66.

54———华霞虹，庄慎. 日常·改变·非识别体系 [J]. 建筑设计（英文版），2018 (6)：52–57.
Hua Xiahong, Zhuang Shen. Everyday, Change and the Unrecognisable System [J]. *Architectural Design*, 2018 (6): 52–57.

55———庄慎，华霞虹. 棉仓城市客厅 [J]. 建筑学报，2018 (7)：42–51.
Zhuang Shen, Hua Xiahong. Cotton Lab Lounge [J]. *Architectural Journal* 2018 (7):42–51

56———陈平楠，庄慎. 常州棉仓城市客厅 [J]. 城市建筑，2018 (10)：78–83.
Chen Pingnan, Zhuang Shen. Changzhou Cotton Urban Lounge, China [J]. *Urbanism and Architecture*, 2018 (10): 78–83.

57———庄慎，任皓，唐煜，等. 常州棉仓城市客厅 [J]. 世界建筑，2019 (1)：53–57.
Zhuang Shen, Ren Hao, Tang Yu, et al. Changzhou Cotton Lab Urban Lounge, Jiangsu, China, 2018 [J]. *World Architecture*, 2019 (1): 53–57.

58———庄慎. 阿科米星工作室 [J]. 建筑中国（英文版），2019 夏：116–219.
Zhuang Shen. Atelier Archmixing [J]. *Architecture China*, 2019 (summer): 116–129.

刊载阿科米星作品与思想的论著
Publications on Archmixing

59———彼得·罗，夏怡. 时代降临：当代中国建筑师第三浪潮的涌现 [J]. 亚洲建筑（英文版），2013 (1)：8–13.
Peter Rowe, Har Ye Kan. Coming of Age: The Emergence of 'Third Stream' Architects in Comtemporary China [J]. *Asia Architecture*, 2013 (1): 8–13.

60———上海文化信息产业园 B4/B5 地块 [M]// 支文军，戴春，徐洁. 中国当代建筑 (2008–2012). 上海：同济大学出版社，2013：130–139.
B4/B5 Blocks of Culture and Information Industrial Park, Shanghai[M]// Zhi Wenjun, Dai Chun, Xu Jie. *The contemporary Chinese Architecture* (2008–2012). Shanghai: Tongji University Press, 2013: 130–139.

61———庄清湄，等. 庄慎：建筑师应该是理想主义者 [J]. 外滩画报，第 550 期：44–45.
Zhuang Qingmei, etc.. Zhuang Shen: The Architect Should Be An Idealist [ ]. *THE BUND Magazine*, No.550: 44–45.

62———黄正骊，庄慎. 混合建筑学 [J]. 城市中国，第 60 期：100–107.
Huang Zhengli.. A Mixed Architecture: Interview with ZHUANG Shen [J]. *Urban Wisdom Advancing with China*, Vol.60: 100–107.

63———庄慎：走向内心愈深，走向世界愈广 [J]. Pro. Design，2014 (2)：84–99.

Zhuang Shen: Walk Deeper in Heart, Walk Wider in World [J]. *Pro Design*, 2014 (2): 84–99.

64———庄慎：改变的日常，建筑学的另一种可能 [J]. 生活，2014 (12)：64–67.
Jiang Yinmu. ZHUANG Shen, Change is More: Another Possibility for Architecture' Focuses on Atelier Archmixing's Design Philosophy [J]. *Life Magazine*, 2014 (12): 64–67.

65———《建筑七人对谈集》编委会. 建筑七人对谈集 [M]. 上海：同济大学出版社，2015.
Book Editorial Board. *Dialogues between Seven Architects*[M]. Shanghai: Tongji University Press, 2015.

66———刘匪思，庄慎：建筑师需要有严肃的思考精神 [J]. 室内设计师，2015 (4)：102–109.
Liu Feisi. ZHUANG Shen: Architect Needs Critical Thinking [J]. *Interior Designer*, 2015 (4): 102–109.

67———短暂的建筑——庄慎访谈录. 室内设计与装修，2015 (11): 108.
An Interview with ZHUANG Shen [J]. *Interior Design and Construction*, 2015 (11): 108.

68———同济大学建筑与城市规划学院. 同济八骏：中生代的建筑实践 [M] 上海：同济大学出版社，2017.
College of Architecture and Urban Planning, Tongji University. *Architectural Practice of Middle-Aged Generation from Tongji* [M] Shanghai: Tongji University Press, 2017.

69———鲁安东. 棉仓城市客厅：一个内部性的宣言 [J]. 建筑学报，2018 (7)：52–55.
Lu Andong. Cotton Lab Lounge: A Manifesto of Interiority [J]. *Architectural Journal*, 2018 (7): 52–55.

70———王方戟，王梓童. 图纸引导体验——上海宝山贝贝佳欧莱幼儿园设计 [J]. 建筑学报，2018 (11)：90–94.
Wang Fangji, Wang Zitong. Perceptions Guided by Drawings: A Case Study of Baoshan Beibeijia Olion Kindergarten [J]. *Architectural Journal*, 2018 (11): 90–94.

阿科米星微信公众号文章
Archmixing Wechat

71———庄慎. 用扩展与对称的方式设计一个小茶室 [EB/OL]. (2016–01–14)[2019–09–09].
Zhuang Shen. Applying Expansion and Symmetrical Strategy to Design a Small Teahouse[EB/OL]. (2016–01–14)[2019–09–09].
https://mp.weixin.qq.com/s/xe1bLDeHeR9_0c5fGCbVwQ.

72———庄慎. 大眼睛与长鼻子 [EB/OL]. (2016–01–18)[2019–09–09].
Zhuang Shen. Big Eye and Long Nose[EB/OL]. (2016–01–18)[2019–09–09].
https://mp.weixin.qq.com/s/sqL90TdoHlRRHq3GfwBd7QA.

73———庄慎. "带着鲑鱼去旅行" [EB/OL]. (2016–06–08)[2019–09–09].
Zhuang Shen. "Il secondo Diario Minimo"[EB/OL]. (2016–06–08)[2019–09–09].
https://mp.weixin.qq.com/s/wmhvsG_OSLAdoh-u_-izlA.

74———庄慎. 两种调整 [EB/OL]. (2016–07–21)[2019–09–09].
Zhuang Shen. Two Adjustments[EB/OL]. (2016–07–21)[2019–09–09].
https://mp.weixin.qq.com/s/oAvq_QUzlo2-NA0qDT6_bQ.

75———庄慎. 做户型与抠平面 [EB/OL]. (2016–08–22)[2019–09–09].
Zhuang Shen. Crafting Plan and Apartment Unit[EB/OL]. (2016–08–22)[2019–09–09].
https://mp.weixin.qq.com/s/5rRagwhFHpqtGaeM4Tt17g.

76———庄慎．把工作室搬来搬去好不好 [EB/OL]．（2016-11-03)[2019-09-09]．

Zhuang Shen. Is It OK to Move Office too Often[EB/OL]. (2016-11-03)[2019-09-09].

https://mp.weixin.qq.com/s/BMIDAIFDIINRCHW9FV37DA.

77———庄慎．局部 [EB/OL]．（2017-04-18)[2019-09-09]．

Zhuang Shen. Parts[EB/OL]. (2017-04-18)[2019-09-09].

https://mp.weixin.qq.com/s/NNr9MMNJNg2G8Uy6AePDeQ.

78———庄慎．内部 [EB/OL]．（2017-05-02)[2019-09-09]．

Zhuang Shen. Interior[EB/OL]. (2017-05-02)[2019-09-09].

https://mp.weixin.qq.com/s/eHtdyylOpssSkCh0dgbsAA.

79———庄慎．有关冗余的笔记 1 : poché[EB/OL]．（2017-05-18)[2019-09-09]．

Zhuang Shen. Note on Redundancy 1: poché[EB/OL]. (2017-05-18)[2019-09-09].

https://mp.weixin.qq.com/s/5YiAkN5iCVrx-wdxt6Z CaA.

80———庄慎．有关冗余的笔记 2:老白的实验室 [EB/OL]．（2017-07-31)[2019-09-09]．

Zhuang Shen. Note on Redundancy 2: Water White's Laboratory [EB/OL]. (2017-07-31)[2019-09-09].

https://mp.weixin.qq.com/s/exgBZZI4jMpQIj2PiHPELQ.

81———游诗雨．志达书店改造记录 [EB/OL]．[2018-05-10)[2019-09-09]．

You Shiyu. Renovation Record on Zhida Bookstore[EB/OL]. (2018-05-10)[2019-09-09].

https://mp.weixin.qq.com/s/Mx7loNFRpSK5NieLz6RzFg.

82———张灏宸．"舞台建筑"两则 [EB/OL]．（2018-03-21)[2019-09-09]．

Zhang Haochen. Two Articles on "Stage Architecture"[EB/OL]. (2018-03-21)[2019-09-09].

https://mp.weixin.qq.com/s/vkbe0NS5uVrXswvEiWmnoA.

83———张灏宸．欧莱幼儿园改造记 [EB/OL]．（2018-11-29)[2019-09-09]．

Zhang Haochen. Renovation Record on Olion Kindergarten[EB/OL]. (2018-11-29)[2019-09-09].

https://mp.weixin.qq.com/s/cdOr49m5mqeHwTBCNxedEg.

84———庄慎，张灏宸．实用是一种专业常识——阿科米星的两个幼儿园设计 [EB/OL]．（2019-01-10)

Zhuang Shen, Zhang Haochen. Be Practical is a Professional Knowledge: Two Kindergarten Designs by Atelier Archmixing[EB/OL]. (2019-01-10)

https://mp.weixin.qq.com/s?__biz=MzA3NjUxNTQxOQ==&mid=2703430828&idx=1&sn=fe882135f3778996fcba73d432f36e94&chksm=bbb7a5988cc02c8ee52aba6bf8ae869469f787bed8d0141653e28d071f22788e9942df5eec89&token=454719635&lang=zh_CN#rd

阿科米星作品目录 Archmixing Project List 2009-2019

1 昆明文明街串联庭院设计

类型：旧城更新

地点：云南 昆明

时间：2006

规模：189 000 ㎡

状态：方案设计

合作设计：大舍建筑设计事务所 *

Promenade Courtyards, Renewal of Kunming Wenming Street

Type: Old City Renewal

Location: Kunming, Yunnan Province

Date: 2006

Size: 189,000 ㎡

Status: Schematic Design

Collaborator: Atelier Deshaus*

2 嘉定新城规划展示馆

类型：办公、展示

地点：上海 嘉定

时间：2007-2009

规模：6 700 ㎡

状态：建成

合作设计：大舍建筑设计事务所 *

Urban Planning Exhibition Hall of Jiading New Town

Type: Office & Exhibition

Location: Jiading District, Shanghai

Date: 2007-2009

Size: 6,700 ㎡

Status: Completed

Collaborator: Atelier Deshaus*

3 上海文化信息产业园一期 B4/B5 地块

类型：办公

地点：上海 嘉定

时间：2008-2010

规模：24 900 ㎡

状态：建成

合作设计：大舍建筑设计事务所 *

B4/B5 Blocks of Shanghai Culture & Information Industrial Park, Phase I

Type: Office

Location: Jiading District, Shanghai

Date: 2008-2010

Size: 24,900 ㎡

Status: Completed

Collaborator: Atelier Deshaus*

4 嘉定博物馆新馆

类型：文化

地点：上海 嘉定

时间：2008-2011

规模：9 600 ㎡

状态：建成

合作设计：大舍建筑设计事务所 *

Jiading New Mesuem

Type: Cultural

Location: Jiading District, Shanghai

Date: 2008-2011

Size: 9,600 ㎡

Status: Completed

Collaborator: Atelier Deshaus *

5 一院一世界

类型：商业

地点：四川 成都

时间：2010-2012

规模：3 400 ㎡

状态：建成

A Court, A World

Type: Commercial

Location: Chengdu, Sichuan Province

Date: 2010-2012

Size: 3,400 ㎡

Status: Completed

6 嘉定新城双丁路公立幼儿园

类型：教育

地点：上海 嘉定

时间：2010–2013

规模：6 100 ㎡

状态：建成

Shuangding Road Public Kindergarten

Type: Educational

Location: Jiading District, Shanghai

Date: 2010–2013

Size: 6,100 ㎡

Status: Completed

7 诸暨剧院

类型：文化

地点：浙江 诸暨

时间：2011–2017

规模：32 000 ㎡

状态：建成

合作设计：同济大学建筑设计研究院（集团）有限公司

Zhuji New Theatre

Type: Cultural

Location: Zhuji, Zhejiang Province

Date: 2011–2017

Size: 32,000 ㎡

Status: Completed

Collaborator: TJAD Group

8 SVA 综合办公楼

类型：建筑改造

地点：上海 徐汇

时间：2011–2014

规模：8 539 ㎡

状态：建成

SVA Office Complex

Type: Building Renovation

Location: Xuhui District, Shanghai

Date: 2011–2014

Size: 8,539 ㎡

Status: Completed

9 诸暨规划展示馆和科技馆

类型：文化

地点：浙江 诸暨

时间：2011–2016

规模：46 000 ㎡

状态：建成

合作设计：同济大学建筑设计研究院（集团）有限公司

Zhuji Urban Planning Exhibition Center & Science and Technology Museum

Type: Cultural

Location: Zhuji, Zhejiang Province

Date: 2011–2016

Size: 46,000 ㎡

Status: Completed

Collaborator: TJAD Group

10 黎里

类型：建筑改造

地点：江苏 黎里

时间：2011–2012

规模：200 ㎡

状态：建成

LILI

Type: Building Renovation

Location: LILI, Jiangsu Province

Date: 2011–2012

Size: 200 ㎡

Status: Completed

11 富春俱舍 书院

类型：文化

地点：浙江 杭州

时间：2011–2013

规模：300 ㎡

状态：建成

Fuchun Kosa, Academy

Type: Cultural

Location: Hangzhcu, Zhejiang Province

Date: 2011–2013

Size: 300 ㎡

Status: Completed

12 富春俱舍 走马楼
类型：建筑改造
地点：浙江 杭州
时间：2011–2014
规模：464 ㎡
状态：建成

Fuchun Kosa Zoumalou
Type: Renovation
Location: Hangzhou, Zhejiang Province
Date: 2011–2014
Size: 464 ㎡
Status: Completed

13 昆山文化艺术中心景观配套建筑
类型：服务配套
地点：江苏 昆山
时间：2011–2013
规模：1 261 ㎡
状态：建成

Kunshan Culture and Art Center Landscape Supporting Buildings
Type: Service Support
Location: Kunshan, Jiangsu Province
Date: 2011–2013
Size: 1,261 ㎡
Status: Completed

14 中国福利会嘉定新城幼儿园新建工程
类型：教育
地点：上海 嘉定
时间：2011–2015
规模：13 073 ㎡
状态：建成

CWI Kindergarten in Jiading New City
Type: Educational
Location: Jiading District, Shanghai
Date: 2011–2015
Size: 13,073 ㎡
Status: Completed

15 张江集电港三期 华鑫慧天地
类型：办公
地点：上海 浦东
时间：2011–2016
规模：128 760 ㎡
状态：建成
合作设计：刘宇扬建筑事务所

ZhangJiang IC Harbor Phase III China Fortune Wisdom Mark
Type: Office
Location: Pudong District, Shanghai
Date: 2011–2016
Size: 128,760 ㎡
Status: Completed
Collaborator: Atelier Liu Yuyang Architects

16 张江集电港一期 华鑫智天地
类型：办公
地点：上海 浦东
时间：2012–2017
规模：54 700 ㎡
状态：建成
合作设计：刘宇扬建筑事务所

ZhangJiang IC Harbor Phase I China Fortune Smart Mark
Type: Office
Location: Pudong District, Shanghai
Date: 2012–2017
Size: 54,700 ㎡
Status: Completed
Collaborator: Atelier Liu Yuyang Architects

17 双栖斋
类型：建筑改造
地点：江苏 苏州
时间：2012
规模：56 ㎡
状态：建成

Twin Trees Pavilion
Type: Building Renovation
Location: Suzhou, Jiangsu Province
Date: 2012
Size: 56 ㎡
Status: Completed

18 嘉定区国际汽车城核心区 05B-01 地块   05B-01 Block Middle School,
    初级中学新建工程（安亭中学）   Jiading International Automobile City
    类型：教育   Type: Educational
    地点：上海，嘉定   Location: Jiading District, Shanghai
    时间：2012–2017   Date: 2012–2017
    规模：15 000 ㎡   Size: 15,000 ㎡
    状态：建成   Status: Completed

19 上下居——芦墟运河边上的院子   The Ladder House – Courtyard by the Luxu Canal
    类型：建筑改造   Type: Building Renovation
    地点：江苏 芦墟   Location: Luxu, Jiangsu Province
    时间：2012   Date: 2012
    规模：50 ㎡   Size: 50 ㎡
    状态：建成   Status: Completed

20 衡山路 890 弄（衡山和集）8 号楼   Facade Renovation for No.8 Building,
    外立面改造   Lane 890 Hengshan Road
    类型：立面改造   Type: Facade Renovation
    地点：上海 徐汇   Location: Xuhui District, Shanghai
    时间：2012–2014   Date: 2012–2014
    规模：230 ㎡   Size: 230 ㎡
    状态：建成   Status: Completed

222

21 斜土社区活动中心立面改造   Facade Renovation for Xietu Community Center
    类型：立面改造   Type: Facade Renovation
    地点：上海 徐汇   Location: Xuhui District, Shanghai
    时间：2013–2014   Date: 2013–2014
    规模：6 750 ㎡   Size: 6,750 ㎡
    状态：建成   Status: Completed

22 宝山区奇石陈列馆   Stone Gallery in Baoshan District
    类型：文化   Type: Cultural
    地点：上海 宝山   Location: Baoshan District, Shanghai
    时间：2012–2016   Date: 2012–2016
    规模：3 600 ㎡   Size: 3,600 ㎡
    状态：施工中   Status: Under Construction

23 安龙森林公园东部码头小镇商业建筑   Commercial Building at East Dock Town
                                        in AnLong Forest Park
    类型：商业   Type: Commercial
    地点：浙江 杭州   Location: Hangzhou, Zhejiang Province
    时间：2013   Date: 2013
    规模：2 900 ㎡   Size: 2,900 ㎡
    状态：方案设计   Status: Schematic Design

24 莫干山庾村文化市集蚕种场改造
类型：建筑改造
地点：浙江 湖州
时间：2012–2013
规模：3 000 ㎡
状态：建成

Silkworm Hatchery Renovation, Yucun Culture Market, Mogan Mountain
Type: Building Renovation
Location: Huzhou, Zhejiang Province
Date: 2012–2013
Size: 3,000 ㎡
Status: Completed

25 徐汇区龙华街道敬老院立面改造
类型：立面改造
地点：上海 徐汇
时间：2013–2018
规模：10 500 ㎡
状态：建成

Facade Renovation for Longhua Street Elder Care Center
Type: Facade Renovation
Location: Xuhui District, Shanghai
Date: 2013–2018
Size: 10,500 ㎡
Status: Completed

26 宝山陈化成纪念馆移建改造
类型：建筑改造
地点：上海 宝山
时间：2014–2015
规模：198 ㎡
状态：建成

Removal Renovation of Chen Huacheng Memorial
Type: Building Renovation
Location: Baoshan District, Shanghai
Date: 2014–2015
Size: 198 ㎡
Status: Completed

27 舟山东门车站及周边改造项目一期工程
类型：交通、商业
地点：浙江 舟山
时间：2013–2018
规模：70 329 ㎡
状态：建成

Renovation of Zhoushan East Gate Station and Surroundings, Phase I
Type: Transportation & Commercial
Location: Zhoushan, Zhejiang Province
Date: 2013–2018
Size: 70,329 ㎡
Status: Completed

28 陕西南路复兴中路沿街立面改造
类型：立面改造
地点：上海 徐汇
时间：2013
规模：3 800 ㎡
状态：方案设计

Facade Renovation at the intersection of Shaanxi S. Rd and Fuxing M. Rd
Type: Facade Renovation
Location: Xuhui District, Shanghai
Date: 2013
Size: 3,800 ㎡
Status: Schematic design

29 南京下关区永宁街地块
类型：商业、办公、住宅
地点：江苏 南京
时间：2013
规模：370 000 ㎡
状态：方案设计

Yongning Street Plot, Xiaguan District, Nanjing
Type: Commercial & Office & Residence
Location: Jiangsu, Nangjing Province
Date: 2013
Size: 370,000 ㎡
Status: Schematic Design

30 敦煌莫高窟窟门优化设计
类型：产品设计
地点：甘肃 敦煌
时间：2013–2017
状态：建成

Design and Renovation for the Gate of Mogao Grottoes in Dunhuang
Type: Product Design
Location: Dunhuang, Gansu Province
Date: 2013–2017
Status: Completed

31 沪宁高速公路昆山高新区互通项目
类型：交通
地点：江苏 昆山
时间：2014–2018
规模：4 200 ㎡
状态：建成

Shanghai-Nanjing Expressway Toll Station in Kunshan New & Hi-tech Industrial Development Zone
Type: Transportation
Location: Kunshan, Jiangsu Province
Date: 2014–2018
Size: 4,200 ㎡
Status: Completed

32 前滩休闲公园 4,5 号建筑
类型：服务配套
地点：上海 浦东
时间：2014
规模：900 ㎡
状态：方案设计

No.4 & No.5 Buildings in Qiantan Park
Type: Service Support
Location: Pudong District, Shanghai
Date: 2014
Size: 900 ㎡
Status: Schematic Design

33 港城广场
类型：酒店、办公、展览、住宅
地点：上海 浦东
时间：2014–
规模：554 000 ㎡
状态：施工中
合作设计：致正建筑工作室

Harbour City Plaza
Type: Hotel & Office & Exhibition & Residence
Location: Pudong District, Shanghai
Date: 2014–
Size: 554,000 ㎡
Status: Under Construction
Collaborator: Atelier Z+

34 港城广场 展示中心
类型：展示、接待
地点：上海 浦东
时间：2015
规模：700 ㎡
状态：建成

Exhibition Center of Harbour City Plaza
Type: Exhibition & Reception
Location: Pudong District, Shanghai
Date: 2015
Size: 700 ㎡
Status: Completed

35 彰吴村制衣厂改造
类型：建筑改造
地点：浙江 湖州
时间：2014
规模：2 900 ㎡
状态：方案设计

Renovation of Garment Factory in Zhangwu Village
Type: Building Renovation
Location: Huzhou, Zhejiang Provinvce
Date: 2014
Size: 2,900 ㎡
Status: Schematic Design

36 桦墅乡村工作室
类型：建筑改造
地点：江苏 南京
时间：2014–2015
规模：252 ㎡
状态：建成

Huashu Rural Studio
Type: Building Renovation
Location: Nanjing, Jiiangsu Provinvce
Date: 2014–2015
Size: 252 ㎡
Status: Completed

37 YoungBird 室内空间改造
类型：室内改造
地点：上海 杨浦
时间：2015
规模：236 ㎡
状态：建成

Interior Renovation of YoungBird Office
Type: Interior Renovation
Location: Yangpu District, Shanghai
Date: 2015
Size: 236 ㎡
Status: Completed

38 上海嘉北郊野公园北游客中心
类型：服务配套
地点：上海 嘉定
时间：2015–2017
规模：1598 ㎡
状态：建成

North Visitor Center of Shanghai Jiabei Country Park
Type: Service Support
Location: Jiading District, Shanghai
Date: 2015–2017
Size: 1,598 ㎡
Status: Completed

39 爱运动的小伙伴
类型：艺术装置
地点：上海 徐汇
时间：2015–2016
状态：建成

Sports Lovers
Type: Art Installation
Location: Xuhui District, Shanghai
Date: 2015–2016
Status: Completed

40 新天地临时读书空间
类型：临时装置
地点：上海 黄埔
时间：2016
规模：143 ㎡
状态：建成

Temporary Reading Pavilion in Xintiandi
Type: Temporary Installation
Location: Huangpu District, Shanghai
Date: 2016
Size: 143 ㎡
Status: Completed

41 田林路 192 号装饰工程
类型：室内、立面改造
地点：上海 徐汇
时间：2016–2017
规模：2 895 ㎡
状态：建成

Renovation of No.192 on Tianlin Road
Type: Interior & Facade Renovation
Location: Xuhui District, Shanghai
Date: 2016–2017
Size: 2,895 ㎡
Status: Completed

42 三岔港森林公园单体建筑

类型：服务配套

地点：上海 浦东

时间：2016

规模：1 150 ㎡

状态：方案设计

Entrance Building of Sanchagang Forest Park

Type: Service Support

Location: Pudong District, Shanghai

Date: 2016

Size: 1,150 ㎡

Status: Schematic dDesign

43 徐汇养老基地项目

类型：医疗养老

地点：上海 徐汇

时间：2016

规模：43 500 ㎡

状态：初步设计

Xuhui Elder Care Center

Type: Healthcare

Location: Xuhui District, Shanghai

Date: 2016

Size: 43,500 ㎡

Status: Development Design

44 成都麓湖生态城 D6D7 地块小学幼儿园

类型：教育

地点：四川 成都

时间：2016

规模：31 500 ㎡

状态：方案设计

合作设计：致正建筑工作室

Primary School & Kindergarten on Plots D6D7 in Chengdu Luhu Ecological City

Type: Educational

Location: Chengdu, Sichuan Province

Date: 2016

Size: 31,500 ㎡

Status: Schematic Design

Collaborator: Atelier Z+

45 申威达厂房改造

类型：建筑改造

地点：上海 徐汇

时间：2016–2019

规模：11 721 ㎡

状态：建成

Renovation of No.2 Building of Shen Wei Da Workshop Space

Type: Building Renovation

Location: Xuhui District, Shanghai

Date: 2016–2019

Size: 11,721 ㎡

Status: Completed

46 东岸云桥：三林北港桥及三林塘港桥

类型：基础设施

地点：上海 浦东

时间：2016–2017

状态：建成

合作设计：冶是建筑工作室

East Bund Footbridge: North Sanlin Bridge and Sanlintang Bridge

Type: Infrastructure

Location: Pudong District, Shanghai

Date: 2016–2017

Status: Completed

Collaborator : YeArch Studio

47 悦阅书店

类型：室内改造

地点：上海 杨浦

时间：2016–2017

规模：94 ㎡

状态：建成

Yueyue Bookstore

Type: Interior Renovation

Location: Yangpu District, Shanghai

Date: 2016–2017

Size: 94 ㎡

Status: Completed

48 成都麓湖水镇民宿岛-酒店 B
类型：酒店
地点：四川 成都
时间：2016
规模：3 377 ㎡
状态：初步设计

Homestay Island Hotel B, Luhu, Chengdu
Type: Hotel
Location: Chengdu, Sichuan Province
Date: 2016
Size: 3,377 ㎡
Status: Development design

49 成都麓湖水镇民宿岛-酒店 F
类型：酒店
地点：四川 成都
时间：2016
规模：3 050 ㎡
状态：初步设计

Homestay Island Hotel F, Luhu, Chengdu
Type: Hotel
Location: Chengdu, Sichuan Province
Date: 2016
Size: 3,050 ㎡
Status: Development Design

50 舟山青龙山公园入口改造
类型：文化
地点：浙江 舟山
时间：2016-2019
规模：1 080 ㎡
状态：建成

Qinglongshan Park Entrance Renovation
Type: Cultural
Location: Zhoushan, Zhejiang Province
Date: 2016-2019
Size: 1,080 ㎡
Status: Completed

51 棉仓城市客厅
类型：建筑改造
地点：江苏 常州
时间：2017-2018
规模：6 300 ㎡
状态：建成

Cotton Lab Urban Lounge
Type: Building Renovation
Location: Changzhou, Jiangsu Province
Date: 2017-2018
Size: 6,300 ㎡
Status: Completed

52 宝山贝贝佳欧莱幼儿园
类型：建筑改造
地点：上海 宝山
时间：2017
规模：5 400 ㎡
状态：建成

Renovation of Baoshan Beibeijia Olion Kindergarten
Type: Building Renovation
Location: Baoshan District, Shanghai
Date: 2017
Size: 5,400 ㎡
Status: Completed

53 上海南汇新城中法学院
类型：教育
地点：上海 浦东
时间：2017-
规模：29 000 ㎡
状态：施工中

Sino-French Institute, Nanhui City
Type: Educational
Location: Pudong District, Shanghai
Date: 2017-
Size: 29,000 ㎡
Status: Under Construction

54 永嘉路口袋广场
类型：城市更新
地点：上海 徐汇
时间：2017–2019
规模：767 ㎡
状态：建成

Pocket Plaza, Yongjia Road
Type: Urban Renewal
Location: Baoshan District, Shanghai
Date: 2017–2019
Size: 767 ㎡
Status: Completed

55 上海棋院实验小学
类型：教育
地点：上海 静安
时间：2017–
规模：20 095 ㎡
状态：施工中

Shanghai Chess Experimental Primary School
Type: Educational
Location: Jing'an District, Shanghai
Date: 2017–
Size: 20,095 ㎡
Status: Under Construction

56 徐汇区南部职业学校
类型：教育
地点：上海 徐汇
时间：2017–
规模：92 387 ㎡
状态：初步设计

Vocational School in the South of Xuhui District
Type: Educational
Location: Xuhui District, Shanghai
Date: 2017–
Size: 92,387 ㎡
Status: Development design

57 复兴西路街道邻里汇
类型：公共建筑
地点：上海 徐汇
时间：2017
规模：341 ㎡
状态：方案设计

Community Centre on W. Fuxing Road
Type: Public Building
Location: Xuhui District, Shanghai
Date: 2017
Size: 341 ㎡
Status: Schematic Design

58 徐汇三江路售楼处改造
类型：建筑改造
地点：上海 徐汇
时间：2017
规模：1 120 ㎡
状态：方案设计

Renovation of Sales Office in Sanjiang Road
Type: Building Renovation
Location: Xuhui District, Shanghai
Date: 2017
Size: 1,120 ㎡
Status: Schematic Design

59 智慧欧莱托育园
类型：建筑改造
地点：上海 宝山
时间：2017–2018
规模：1 467 ㎡
状态：建成

Wisdom Olion Nursery
Type: Building Renovation
Location: Baoshan District, Shanghai
Date: 2017–2018
Size: 1,467 ㎡
Status: Completed

60 "一条"线下店（莘庄店）

类型：室内改造

地点：上海 闵行

时间：2018

规模：685 ㎡

状态：建成

合作设计：蘑菇云设计工作室

Offline Retail Space of Yitiao. TV (Xinzhuang Store)

Type: Interior Renovation

Location: Minhang District, Shanghai

Date: 2018

Size: 685m²

Status: Completed

Collaborator: Supercloud

61 阿那亚金山岭艺术中心

类型：商业

地点：河北 承德

时间：2018–

规模：875 ㎡

状态：施工中

Art Center of Aranya, Jinshanling

Type: Commerical

Location: Chengde, Hebei Province

Date: 2018–

Size: 875 ㎡

Status: Under Construction

62 普陀白沙岛沙头交通码头改扩建

类型：交通

地点：浙江 舟山

时间：2018–

规模：285 ㎡

状态：施工中

Renovation of Shatou Wharf, Baisha Island, Putuo

Type: Transportation

Location: Zhoushan, Zhejiang Province

Date: 2018–

Size: 285 ㎡

Status: Under Construction

63 石龙路临时公寓

类型：住宅

地点：上海 徐汇

时间：2018–

规模：17 000 ㎡

状态：施工中

Temporary Apartments in Shilong Road

Type: Residence

Location: Xuhui District, Shanghai

Date: 2018–

Size: 17,000 ㎡

Status: Under Construction

64 宝山绿心幼儿园

类型：教育

地点：上海 宝山

时间：2018–

规模：6 923 ㎡

状态：施工中

Greenheart Kindergarten in Baoshan District

Type: Educational

Location: Baoshan District, Shanghai

Date: 2018–

Size: 6,923 ㎡

Status: Under Construction

65 昆山实验小学西侧地下车库改扩建

类型：教育、基础设施

地点：江苏 昆山

时间：2018–

规模：36 600 ㎡

状态：施工图设计

**Expansion and Renovation of
Kunshan Experimental Primary School**

Type: Educational & Infrastructure

Location: Kunshan, Jiangsu Province

Date: 2018–

Size: 36,600 ㎡

Status: Construction Design

66 昆山高新区阳科园学校

类型：教育

地点：江苏 昆山

时间：2017–

规模：77 188 ㎡

状态：初步设计

Yangkeyuan School in Kunshan New & Hi-tech Industrial Development Zone

Type: Educational

Location: Kunshan, Jiangsu Province

Date: 2017–

Size: 77,188 ㎡

Status: Development Design

67 虹桥好望角商业广场

类型：立面改造

地点：上海 青浦

时间：2019–

规模：12 359 ㎡

状态：施工中

Hongqiao Cape Commercial Plaza

Type: Facade Renovation

Location: Qingpu District, Shanghai

Date: 2019–

Size: 12,359 ㎡

Status: Under Construction

68 贝尔厂房改造

类型：立面改造

地点：上海 静安

时间：2019–

规模：15 188 ㎡

状态：施工中

Renovation of Bell Factory

Type: Facade Renovation

Location: Jing'an District, Shanghai

Date: 2019–

Size: 15,188 ㎡

Status: Under Construction

230

69 天等路项目装饰工程

类型：建筑改造

地点：上海 徐汇

时间：2019–

规模：11 252 ㎡

状态：施工中

Tiandeng Road Decoration Project

Type: Building Renovation

Location: Xuhui District, Shanghai

Date: 2019–

Size: 11,252 ㎡

Status: Under Construction

* 庄慎主创

* Created by Zhuang Shen

后记

阿科米星建筑工作室成立十年了，能同时出版一本作品集和一本理论文集，我们格外欣喜。因为阿科米星从创建以来，建筑设计与建筑学思考始终是并行且相互支撑的。而从第一个工作室选择在长顺路的普通居民小区内开始，我们已自然而然地把自己的工作和生活融入上海这座城市的日常生活中。2013年起系统开展的城市研究，2015年正式实施的"一年一个工作室"计划和2019年试水的"移动办公模式"，都是我们对如何成为真正的"城市建筑师"的一些拓展。

阿科米星理论写作的切入点是"今天的建筑／建筑师／建筑学还能干什么"，知行合一是阿科米星建筑／建筑学思考的原则，也是其动力。阿科米星的工程实践类型非常广杂，其中碰到最多的是城市中各种普通建筑、空间或局部的改造。正是这些正规设计单位难以触及的边缘性项目触发了我们对快速城市化之后中国建筑／建筑学的持续反思，提出了"空间冗余""建筑中性""非识别体系"等既包含对现实的认知，又包含设计策略的新概念，并把"改变"，包括"什么改变了既有的建筑，什么会改变未来的建筑"作为我们思考和实践的中心。

阿科米星的建筑思考有赖于强大的团队支持。庄慎、任皓、唐煜、朱捷四位合伙人与学术顾问华霞虹组成的核心团队同心同力，勤奋执著。要在各种普通的工程项目中发掘原创设计的可能性，不仅需要新的专业认知，更需要强大的执行力。要在高强度设计实践的同时，平行开展城市研究、理论写作，以及各种各样的自我实验，包括实施"搬家"计划、成立"那行"空间、开展"未来建筑"研究，等等，更是费心费力的考验。然而，阿科米星的团队在这十年里就这样神奇而快乐地成长着，前后共有80余名员工为之不懈努力，享受着各种折腾。

我们首先要感谢中国科学院院士郑时龄教授为我们撰写了非常肯定和鼓励的序言。在他指导的庄慎的硕士论文《中国庭院的生命精神》（1997）和华霞虹的博士论文《消融与转变：消费文化中的建筑》（2007）中，蕴藏着阿科米星设计研究和理论反思的萌芽。正是从融合中国传统文化思维和消费文化逻辑这两种看似迥异的思想观念开始，阿科米星的建筑实践和学术写作不断反思既有建筑学的不足，致力于消除从专业领域到社会价值的各种界限，尝试从日常世界中寻找建筑学的新认知和新方法。

非常感激南京大学王骏阳教授为我们的理论文集撰写了如此褒扬和充满启发的综述，极为严谨地不断改进中英文文稿。在从现代到当代世界范围内建筑学探索的整体语境中，在中国当下建筑／建筑学发展的宏观背景下，我们明白自己对"另一种建筑／建筑学"的探寻和实践才刚刚进入正轨。

非常感激同济大学李翔宁教授站在建筑学科和中国当代城市与社会发展现实的双重高度上，为我们的作品集《阿科米星2009—2019》撰写了既切中要害又细致入微的评述。时空高度压缩的本土日常城市环境中充满了未知与变革的力量，轻装上阵，不断前行，我们总能有所发现，有所突破。

没有中国当代建筑师／建筑学者对专业与学科的普遍反思，阿科米星的理论写作也是无源之水。阿科米星的建筑思考很大程度上得益于与众多同行的共同研究和学术交流。为了十周年的出版，东南大学葛明教授、南京大学鲁安东教授、中国建筑设计研究院集团总建筑师李兴钢、同济大学王方戟教授和致正工作室主持建筑师张斌受邀与庄慎开展了对谈。这四篇对谈不仅是对阿科米星设计实践和理论思考真挚而深入的发掘，也是对当代中国建筑／建筑学，尤其是本体价值、设计研究和设计方法的全面探索。本文集载入的文章部分直接受益于期刊约稿和相关学术论坛的启发。为此我们还要特别感谢东南大学的李华教授、李海清教授、史永高教授、英国纽卡斯尔大学的朱剑飞教授、《建筑学报》执行主编黄居正老师和《时代建筑》杂志副主编彭怒教授。

最后，如果没有同济大学出版社"光明城"品牌负责人秦蕾的组织和晁艳的精心编辑，没有阿科米星媒体主管陈平楠，多位设计师和实习生协助整理资料、绘制图纸，以及梯工作室雅致的版面和装帧设计，本书也会失色许多。

庄慎　华霞虹

2020 年 1 月 15 日

Postscript

We are extremely excited about publishing a theoretical anthology together with a design monograph when Atelier Archmixing celebrates the ten-year anniversary. The studio was born with parallel design practice and architectural thinking. When we set the first workplace inside an ordinary residential compound, we have naturally immersed our work and life in the everydayness of Shanghai. To test how to be a true "urban architect", we initiated systematic urban research in 2013, launched the "New Year New office" plan in 2015 and kicked-off a "Mobile Office Mode" in 2019.

Atelier Archmixing starts the theoretical writing from this question, what architecture/architect/Architecture can accomplish today? Its principle and driving force are integrating these contemplations with architectural design. Among various projects, we frequently deal with renovations for ordinary buildings, urban spaces and fragments. It is exactly these marginal projects most design companies never encounter inspired us examining Chinese contemporary built environment after rapid urbanization. Based on our understanding of the urban reality, we have coined new terms such as "spatial redundancy", "architectural neutrality" and "unrecognizable system", in which new design strategies may emerge. Now our architectural reflection and practice focus on "change", mainly "what changed the existed building" and "what will change the future building"?

Atelier Archmixing's architectural thinking is supported by a strong team. Four partners, Zhuang Shen, Ren Hao, Tang Yu, Zhu Jie and the academic advisor, Hua Xiahong form the core, working together with the same ideal and passion. To apply original strategy in ordinary projects, we are anxious for new architectural cognition, and also rely on powerful execution. Because in addition to heavy design burdens, we are also challenged by parallel urban research, theoretical writing and all kinds of self-experiments, such as moving office every year, running a multiple activity space, the Nextmixing and exploring the future architecture. For the passing ten years, the magic team of Atelier Archmixing keeps various practices, all together more than 80 employees have involved in these radical experiments.

The most grateful acknowledgment must send to Prof. Zheng Shiling, a member of Chinese Academy of Sciences, for his extremely positive and encouraging preface. The design research and theoretical reflection by Atelier Archmixing can trace back to Zhuang Shen's master thesis, *The Life Spirit of Chinese Courtyards* (1997) and Hua Xiahong's doctoral dissertation, *Melting and Transforming, Architecture in Consumer Culture* (2007), both under Prof. Zheng's academic guidance. Through mixing the two seemingly contradicted topics, the spirit of Chinese traditional culture and the logic of consumer culture, Atelier Archmixing paved the road for transcending the mainstream architectural field, trying to break the boundaries between different areas and values, and discover new architectural cognition and methodology from the everyday urban world.

We are indebted to Prof. Wang Jun-yang from School of Architecture and Urban Planning, Nanjing University, for his commending and inspiring critic to our theoretical thinking and his rigorous crafting for both Chinese and English manuscripts. When entering the international context of architectural reflection from modern times to present, and the grand scenario of Chinese contemporary architecture development, our searching for an Another Architecture is just on the track.

We also wish to express our sincere appreciation to Prof. Li Xiangning from College of Architecture and Urban Planning, Tongji University, for his comprehensive and accurate critic on our architectural practice, standing on a theoretical height both for the evolution of architectural discipline and the development of Chinese contemporary urban and social reality. With the power of unknown and change hidden in the local everyday urban context of high time-space compression, when keep proceeding with light pack, we can always reach discovery and break-through.

Atelier Archmixing's theoretical writing is cultivated in the vast field of Chinese

233

contemporary architectural reflection and nurtured by those cooperation researches and academic discussions with many colleagues. For these two publications, Prof. Ge Ming from Southeast University, Prof. Lu Andong from Nanjing University, the chief architect Li Xinggang from China Architecture Design and Research Group, Prof. Wang Fangji from Tongji University and Zhang Bin, the principal architect from Atelier Z+ were invited to communicate with Zhuang Shen. Four dialogues between these architects and scholars not only evaluated sincerely and deeply Atelier Archmixing's practices and theories, but also explored those major topics for Chinese contemporary architecture, especially about the ontological values, design research and design methodology. Some articles compiled in this anthology are also benefited from academic forums and publication invitations from journals. Special thanks should go to Prof. Li Hua, Prof. Li Haiqing and Prof. Shi Yonggao from Southeast University, Prof. Zhu Jianfei from Newcastle University, Mr. Huang Juzheng, the executive editor-in-chief from *Architectural Journal* and Prof. Peng Nu, the deputy editor-in-chief from *Time+Architecture*.

Without the publication plan by Qin Lei and careful editing by Chao Yan from Tongji University Press, without the fundamental works by Chen Pingnan, the media chief and many designers and interns from Atelier Archmixing, without Telos Studo's elegant layout design, the book will also lose colors.

Zhuang Shen, Hua Xiahong
Jan. 15, 2020

234

图书在版编目（CIP）数据

改变：阿科米星的建筑思考 / 庄慎，华霞虹著 . --
上海：同济大学出版社，2020.5
　ISBN 978-7-5608-8949-8

　Ⅰ.①改… Ⅱ.①庄…②华… Ⅲ.①建筑学 - 文集
Ⅳ.① TU-53

　中国版本图书馆 CIP 数据核字 (2019) 第 288883 号

"国家自然科学基金"（51778419）资助项目

改变

阿科米星的建筑思考

庄慎 华霞虹 著

出 版 人：	华春荣
阿科米星团队：	庄慎、华霞虹、任皓、唐煜、朱捷、陈平楠、刘霞
英文初译：	李蒙洲、赵灿、张文华
英文审校：	王骏阳（综述）、华霞虹
平面设计：	周安迪、邱江月（梯工作室）
责任编辑：	晁艳、李争
责任校对：	徐春莲

版　　次：	2020 年 5 月第 1 版
印　　次：	2020 年 5 月第 1 次印刷
印　　刷：	上海安枫印务有限公司
开　　本：	889mm × 1194mm　1/16
印　　张：	15.5
字　　数：	496 000
书　　号：	ISBN 978-7-5608-8949-8
定　　价：	98.00 元

Change is More

Architectural Thinking by Atelier Archmixing

by　Zhuang Shen　　Hua Xiahong

ISBN 978-7-5608-8949-8

Publisher:	Hua Chunrong
Archmixing Team:	Zhuang Shen, Hua Xiahong, Ren Hao, Tang Yu, Zhu Jie, Chen Pingnan, Liu Xia
Translation:	Li Mengzhou, Zhao Can, Zhang Wenhua
English Proofread:	Wang Jun-Yang (Review), Hua Xiahong
Graphic Designers:	Andy Zhou, Qiu Jiangyue (Telos Studio)
Editors:	Chao Yan, Li Zheng
Proofreader:	Xu Chunlian

出版发行：	同济大学出版社
地　　址：	上海市杨浦区四平路 1239 号
邮政编码：	200092
网　　址：	http://www.tongjipress.com.cn
经　　销：	全国各地新华书店

Published in May 2020, by Tongji University Press,
1239, Siping Road, Shanghai, China, 200092.
www.tongjipress.com.cn

光 明 城

LUMINOCITY

luminocity.cn

"光明城"是同济大学出
版社城市、建筑、设计专
业出版品牌，由群岛工作
室负责策划及出版，致力
以更新的出版理念、更敏
锐的视角、更积极的态
度，回应今天中国城市、
建筑与设计领域的问题。